Urban Dynamics

URBAN DYNAMICS

Jay W. Forrester

The M.I.T. Press

Massachusetts Institute of Technology
Cambridge, Massachusetts, and London, England

To My Father
M. M. F.

Foreword

Much has been written of the crisis of the cities, the greatest domestic crisis to challenge America in a century. The National League of Cities and the United States Conference of Mayors in July 1968 issued a joint statement on the urban situation, which said in part:

The crisis of the City is in reality a *national* domestic crisis. It affects every segment of our society: urban jobless require welfare paid for by Federal dollars nationally collected, inadequate urban schools cast upon the nation another generation of people unprepared to make their own way, urban traffic congestion adds millions of dollars to the cost of items on neighborhood store shelves around the country. The crisis of the cities belongs to the nation.

The nation cannot dissolve the urban dilemma by ignoring it or by suppressing its manifestations. The nation must face it, as it has faced crises in the past, by: acknowledging its basic causes; recognizing the nation's will and ability to resolve them; accepting that objective as its obligation to current and future generations; and reordering national priorities to assure the commitment of the kind and magnitude of resources required.

In this important and provocative book, Professor Forrester asks whether the measures we have adopted to alleviate urban problems have not in fact intensified them. If he is right in contending that some solutions in the past have been less successful than their proponents anticipated—and in a few cases even counter-productive in the long run—we must re-examine the problems of our cities, abandon a number of old approaches, and adopt or invent new modes of attack.

Whether Professor Forrester's conclusions are right will be a matter of considerable and spirited debate. He offers them as tentative proposals and invites challenge, comment, or amendment. The very debate this book will provoke—no matter what the outcome—will constitute an important and helpful event in the battle to save our cities.

The plight of urban America is so grave and complex that it clearly defies simple remedies. Professor Forrester makes the point that long experience with simple systems has shaped our intuitive short-term responses and that, however well motivated, they may be ineffective or even detrimental when applied to such a complex system as an urban area.

His book presents a new analysis of our urban dilemma based on the methods of "industrial dynamics" as applied to a simulation-computer model, or "system," of an urban area. Using a digital computer to simulate the behavior of the system, Professor Forrester attempts to isolate the dynamic characteristics of the system and to show how the behavior of the actual system might be modified.

JOHN F. COLLINS
Former Mayor of Boston, 1960–1967
Past President of National League of Cities
Former Executive Committee Member of
United States Conference of Mayors

Massachusetts Institute of Technology
Cambridge, Massachusetts
November 1968

Preface

The problems of our aging urban areas are examined here by using recently developed methods for understanding complex social systems. The plight of our older cities is today the social problem of greatest domestic visibility and public concern. In this book the nature of the urban problem, its causes, and possible corrections are examined in terms of interactions between components of the urban system.

This book emerged when my work in "industrial dynamics" converged with the efforts of Professor John F. Collins to focus attention of the academic community on the troubles of our cities. This examination of the urban system began in discussions with Professor Collins, who had taken the next office as a visiting professor at M.I.T. after leaving his position as mayor of Boston. His enthusiasm and his desire to continue to analyze and improve urban processes led to a joint endeavor to structure and model the dynamics of urban decay and revival.

Expecting the most valuable source of information to be, not documents, but people with practical experience in urban affairs, I suggested that Professor Collins organize informal discussions with such men. He invited Daniel J. Finn, Joseph S. Slavet, and others to attend a series of lengthy meetings with us and a changing group of M.I.T. students.

I approached these discussions knowing the conceptual nature of the structure being sought, but not the specific details of the structure or the institutional components of behavior to be fitted into it. The others brought the knowledge of the pressures, motivations, relationships, reactions, and historical incidents needed to shape the theory and structure of the specific social system. Discussions between the others, focused by me at the desired degree of aggregation to maintain balance between detail and generality, gradually revealed a system structure that related system components to system behavior. When a system theory takes shape as a simulation model, its behavior precipitates more discussion and brings out additional supporting and contradictory information that helps refine the theory. The results of this process of discussion, crystallization, and re-examination are presented here.

The history of this effort explains why there are no references to the urban literature in this book. Several reviewers of the manuscript criticized the absence of ties to the literature on the assumption that such ties must exist but had not been revealed. Actually the book comes from a different body of knowledge, from the insights of those who know the urban scene firsthand, from my own reading in the public and business press, and from the literature on the dynamics of social systems for which references are given. There are indeed relevant studies on urban behavior and urban dynamics, but to identify these is a large and separate task.

This study has depended heavily on having a time-shared computer facility available. Without the immediate accessibility provided by a personal computer terminal in my study at home, with day, evening, and week-end service, this exploration of urban dynamics would probably not have been undertaken. About four thousand pages have been processed through the computer terminal to establish the model, the computer runs, the definitions, and the organization of printed information. Part of the background studies of social systems were facilitated by time-shared computer service made available by Project MAC at M.I.T. Computer time for the publication of this book has been supported by the Ford Foundation through the Urban Systems Laboratory at M.I.T.

Alexander L. Pugh III has been especially helpful in expediting this work with his skill and patience in accelerating the schedule of the DYNAMO II compiler to handle this large simulation model. His willingness, even at night and on week ends, to solve programing difficulties has substantially shortened the time required for this investigation.

The encouragement of Gordon S. Brown and Charles L. Miller gave impetus for the additional effort needed to convert into a book what started as an informal series of discussions aimed at mutual enlightenment. Particularly helpful have been the criticisms of the first draft of the manuscript by O. E. Dial, Albert G. H. Dietz, Ithiel de Sola Pool, and Allen E. Pritchard, Jr. I am also grateful for the comments of Billy E. Goetz, Jack I. Hope, Edward J. Logue, Edward B. Roberts, Richard L. Schmalensee, and Paul N. Ylvisaker.

In developing the model and in preparing the manuscript and organizing related seminars and lectures, I have benefited from the enthusiastic assistance of Bruce A. Enders, Randall J. Hekman, and Phillip P. Weidner, all students at M.I.T. The willingness of Miss Isabella S. Evans to retype the manuscript many times, under time pressure and often beyond normal office hours, has sustained the schedule of the book.

JAY W. FORRESTER

Massachusetts Institute of Technology
Cambridge, Massachusetts
November 1968

Contents

1 Orientation

This book is about the growth processes of urban areas. An urban area is a system of interacting industries, housing, and people. Under favorable conditions the interplay between the parts of a new area cause it to develop. But as the area develops and its land area fills, the processes of aging cause stagnation. As the urban area moves from the growth phase to the equilibrium phase, the population mix and the economic activity change. Unless there is continuing renewal, the filling of the land converts the area from one marked by innovation and growth to one characterized by aging housing and declining industry.

If renewal is to succeed and a healthy economic mix is to continue, the natural processes of stagnation must not run their normal course. But the interactions between economic and social activity are so complex that intuition alone can not devise policies that prevent decay.

This book examines the life cycle of an urban area using the methods of industrial dynamics that have been developed at the M.I.T. Alfred P. Sloan School of Management since 1956.* The term "industrial dynamics" has become too restrictive because the methods are applicable in many fields other than industrial management. The concepts of structure and dynamic behavior apply to all systems that change through time. Such dynamic systems include the processes of engineering systems, biology, social systems, psychology, ecology, and all those where positive- and negative-feedback processes manifest themselves in growth and regulatory action.

From the standpoint of industrial dynamics, systems are seen as feedback processes having a specific and orderly structure. From the structure of the particular system arises its dynamic behavior. The industrial-dynamics approach to a social system organizes the growth and goal-seeking processes of the system into a computer model. A digital computer is then used to simulate the behavior of the system. The computer simulation reveals the dynamic characteristics of the system that was described in the structure-formulating stage. By changing the guiding policies within the system, one can see how the behavior of the actual system might be modified.

*See Reference 1.

1

In this book a particular simulation model of an urban area is examined. Such a model is a theory of urban structure and internal relationships. The model is a selection, from numerous alternatives, of factors that are believed pertinent to questions about urban growth, aging, and revival.

The growth model starts with a nearly empty land area and generates the life cycle of development leading to full land occupancy and equilibrium. A variation on the model is started with the equilibrium conditions that are reached at the end of the growth life cycle. This equilibrium model is used to explore how various changes in policy would cause the condition of the urban area to be altered over the following fifty years.

Various common urban-management programs are examined. This model of an urban system suggests that many past and present urban programs may actually worsen the conditions they are intended to improve. Promising alternative programs, addressed to the underlying *causes* of urban decay rather than to *symptoms,* suggest different approaches.

The theory (model) of urban behavior presented in this book has so far been subjected to the scrutiny of only a few people who are professionally competent in the urban field. Interest and enthusiasm have been great enough to suggest that the results should at this time be more widely available than through informal seminars. Only with wider comment and criticism can the methods, the assumptions, and the results be adequately evaluated.

Although this book is presented as a method of analysis rather than as policy recommendations, it is probably unavoidable that many will take these results and act on them without further examination of the underlying assumptions. Doing so is unjustified unless the pertinence of the model itself is first evaluated against the requirements of the particular situation. The approach presented in this book is suggested as a method that can be used for evaluating urban policies once the proposed dynamic model or a modification of it has been accepted as adequate.

1.1 Preview

The next six chapters contain the results from the simulation model and their implications for urban programs. The detailed description of the computer model itself is deferred to Appendix A on the assumption that most readers will want to see the uses to which the model can be put before devoting time to understanding the detailed internal structure.

Chapter 2 outlines the principles of structure found in any system and interprets how they apply to an urban area. The resulting model describes construction and population movement within a specific area. The area could be the political boundary of a city but usually will differ. The area treated here would be only a part of our larger cities. The appropriate area is small enough so that cultural, economic, and educational interchange is possible between its component populations. It could be a suburban area or the core area of a city but probably not an area containing both.

The urban area is represented as a social system set in an environment with which it communicates. People in three categories—managerial-professional, labor, and underemployed—can move into and out of the area. The flow to and from the area depends on the relative attractiveness of the area compared to its surrounding environment. Conditions in the surrounding environment are taken as a reference (which can be changing) and the attractiveness of the area rises and falls with respect to that moving reference. The attractiveness of the area, compared to its environment, depends on the conditions and activities within it. The environment is taken as a limitless source. It can supply people as long as the area is more attractive. It can absorb people who leave when the area is less attractive. These three concepts of specific land area, relative attractiveness, and the limitless environment are important in understanding this model of urban processes. (They are explained more fully in later sections.)

In Chapter 3 the life cycle of an urban area is generated by the simulation model and shows how growth gives way to maturity and then stagnation. The area is a complex, self-regulating system that creates internal pressures to modify economic activity and shift the uses of land, structures, and people. These changes are dominated by the construction, aging, and demolition of industry and housing combined with concurrent population movements.

As a preview of Chapter 3, Figure 1-1 is a 250-year life cycle of an urban area generated by the computer in accordance with the urban theory described in the model. The figure shows the area starting with almost empty land and developing over a period of 100 years. By that time the land area has become filled, new construction decreases, and the urban system stagnates into a high level of underemployed housing and declining industry. The economic mix becomes unfavorable with too high a ratio of underemployed to skilled labor. Too high a proportion of the housing is in the underemployed-housing class, and too high a proportion of industry is in the declining-industry category.

These changes, as the area emerges from growth and enters the stagnation phase, occur as a result of the aging of structures and the consequent change of activity occurring in them. In the growth phase industry has a high intensity and employment per unit of industrial land area is high. At the same time housing is constructed for those engaged in the expanding industry, the residential population is economically successful, and the population density is low per unit of residential land area. The type of construction determines and freezes the ratio of industrial to housing area. Then, as the structures age, the industrial vitality declines, new industries start elsewhere, and employment per unit of industrial land declines. But the opposite happens to population as housing ages. Rental costs decline and the kind of occupancy shifts to those people whose economic circumstances force more crowded population density per unit of residential land. In short, starting from a balance between industry and people at the end of the growth phase, employment declines while population rises until an equilibrium is reached in which the economic condition of the area falls far enough to limit further growth in population.

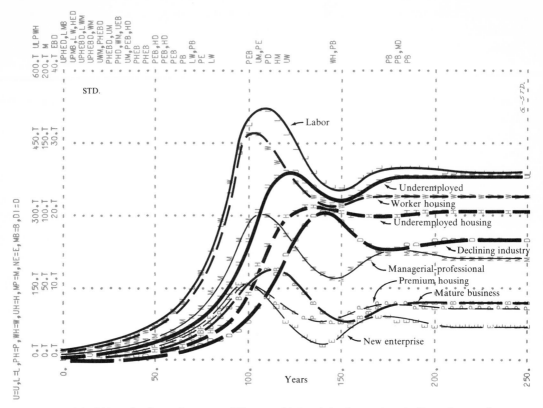

Figure 1-1   Life cycle of an urban area—250 years of internal development, maturity, and stagnation.

Chapter 4 examines urban-revitalization programs of four common kinds, none of which yield substantial improvement. Some of the programs make conditions of the area worse (as in Figure 1-2). Here the urban area starts in equilibrium with the same stagnation conditions that existed at the 250th year in Figure 1-1. At time = 0 in Figure 1-2 a low-cost-housing program has been started. Low-cost housing is constructed each year for about 2.5% of the underemployed population. The result is a further unfavorable shift in the condition of the area.

In Figure 1-2 housing for the underemployed rises 45%, most of the change occurring in the first 30 years. Because of the added attractiveness of the area created by the housing, the underemployed population rises 10% in the first 10 years but then falls back as the decrease of industry reduces the number of available jobs, diminishing the attractiveness of the area. The labor population (skilled labor) falls 30%, as does worker housing for labor. The additional low-cost-housing construction slightly reduces the available land area and alters the population mix. This pressure on available land, along with a 16% rise in tax rate (not shown in the figure), makes the area less attractive for business and leads to a decline of 49% in new enterprise and 45% in mature business. This surprisingly large change results from shifts in the multiplicity of delicate balances that often exist in a social system in equilibrium. Here a regenerative process has caused the labor population to fall, which makes the area less attractive to industry; hence there are fewer jobs, which further discourages labor. Because available jobs have decreased while the number of underemployed remains almost constant, the underemployed/job ratio (not shown until Chapter 4) has risen 30% by the end of 50 years. A program can have subtle ramifications when it disturbs the equilibrium within an urban system. Although the underemployed/housing ratio (not shown) fell from an initial satisfactory value of .8 to a final value of .5 (representing a very low population density for that economic class) there was an associated increase in the ratio of underemployed to available jobs.

The unfavorable change in employment opportunities accompanying an improvement in housing (as in Figure 1-2) is not accidental. As will be seen throughout this book, the urban area tends toward an attractiveness equilibrium with its surroundings. The area has a certain composite attractiveness to each class of person. (At the lower end of the economic scale this might better be referred to as unattractiveness.) A mixture of many components (for example, housing, jobs, public services, legal restrictions, prejudice, racial and ethnic

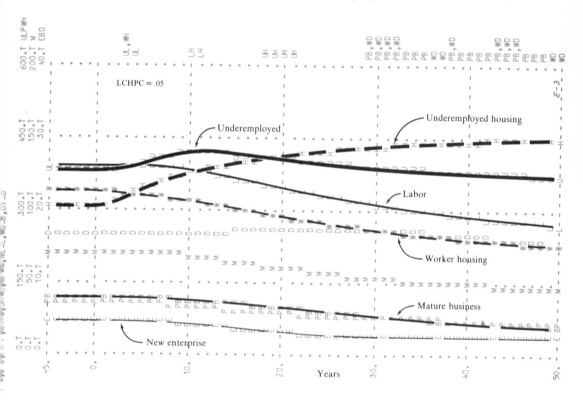

Figure 1-2 Changes in an urban area resulting from low-cost-housing construction for 2.5% of the underemployed each year.

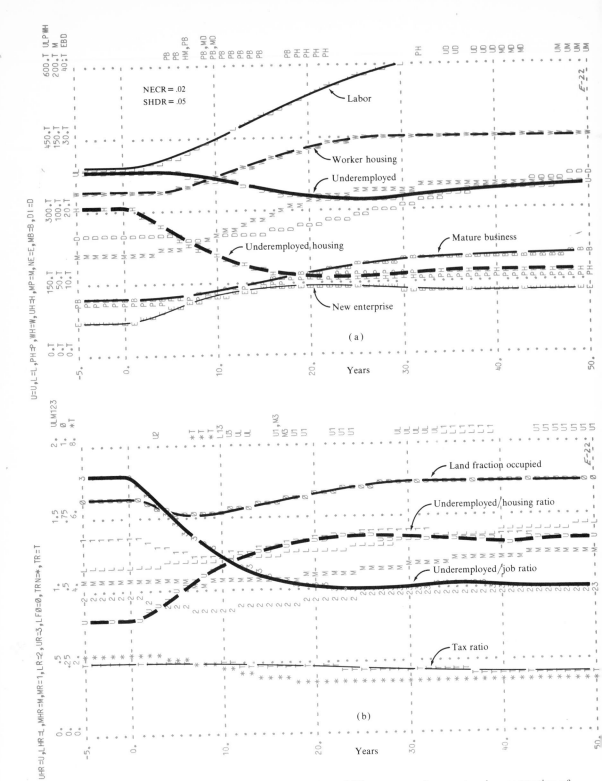

Figure 1-3 Changes caused by slum-housing demolition of 5% per year and new-enterprise construction of about 2% per year started at time = 0. In 1-3*a* note the rise in labor, mature business, and new enterprise; the decrease in underemployed housing; and the upward economic movement of underemployed into the labor class. In 1-3*b* see the decrease in the underemployed/underemployed-jobs ratio. The underemployed/underemployed-housing ratio necessarily rises to more crowded conditions as the job ratio improves.

groupings, and traditions) forms the attractiveness image of an area. Because of freedom to migrate (tempered by all the forces contributing to attractiveness), attractiveness to any class of person tends to become the same for all regions. If not, population flow continues until attractiveness equilibrium is reached.

However, a specific composite attractiveness can result from many different mixtures of attractiveness components. As one component rises, another can fall. The urban area may have no choice in the composite value of attractiveness because of the equalizing effect of population movement, yet it may have a wide choice in the trade-offs between components of that attractiveness. In Figure 1-2 the area, through its natural processes, raises unemployment to compensate for improved housing.

Chapter 5 examines a series of policies for reversing urban decline. These policies are directed, not at a frontal and expensive assault on the symptoms of trouble, but instead at the causes. An example is Figure 1-3 where, at time = 0, two program changes have been made which continue through the following 50 years.* One program is the demolition of 5% per year of underemployed housing (slum housing). The other program is the generation of between 1% and 2% per year of new enterprise.

Figure 1-3a shows a decrease of 44% in underemployed housing. The population in the underemployed category falls 8%. Skilled labor climbs 62%, while worker housing for that population class rises 33%. Mature business and new enterprise both increase 75%. The economic balance of the area has shifted substantially in the direction of more activity and a much more favorable ratio of skilled labor to underemployed. This shift from underemployed to labor population is accomplished by a higher upward economic mobility for the underemployed that accompanies the industrial revival. At the same time a corresponding shift from underemployed to worker housing delays an increase in the underemployed immigration rate so that economic rebalancing is not defeated.

Figure 1-3b shows other variables in the urban system during the same time interval as Figure 1-3a. The underemployed/job ratio has improved from 1.8 to 1.0 by increasing employment opportunities to balance with the underemployed population. The underemployed/housing ratio has risen from .8 to 1.3, or 63%, indicating a housing shortage. Tax assessments have fallen 19%.

Because of the demolition of slum housing and its replacement by industry, the new policies in Figure 1-3 might appear at first glance to favor the upper-income groups at the expense of the underemployed. But the number of underemployed living in a city is not a measure of the city's social value; quite the contrary. The city should not concentrate the less successful economic classes into decaying areas that lack economic opportunity. If we think of the city as a socioeconomic converter, one measure of its effectiveness is the upward economic mobility from the underemployed to the labor class. In Figure 1-3 the net flow of people from underemployed to labor (not shown) has increased 114%. After reaching a better

*Figure 1-3 combines the conditions of Figures 5-6 and 5-10.

economic balance, the area is more effective in upgrading skills and earning ability.

Although the policies of slum demolition and new-enterprise construction in Figure 1-3 have reduced the underemployed population, this has not been done by driving underemployed from the city (more detailed information in Chapter 5 and Appendix B). At all times after the inauguration of the new policies, the underemployed-arrival rate into the city is higher and the departure rate is lower than before the policy changes. The reduction in underemployed population results from greater movement of underemployed into the labor class. At the same time underemployed-housing conditions have shifted to limit the inward population flow so that it does not rise faster than the revitalized area can absorb. Because the populations are constant in equilibrium, the greater intake of under-employed must be balanced by a higher outflow of trained labor and managers, representing greater economic contribution from the revived area to the surround-ing environment.

Figure 1-3 shows the converse of the behavior shown in Figure 1-2. Because of the reduced availability of underemployed housing, immigration does not rise excessively and the ratio of underemployed to jobs has an opportunity to improve. In both situations the city comes into an attractiveness equilibrium with its environment, but in the second situation this equilibrium is produced by a lower housing attractiveness (less availability but probably higher quality) coupled with much-improved job opportunities.

In the stagnant city there is crowding and empty housing at the same time. The ratio of people to housing may be low, but for economic reasons many of the dwelling units are unoccupied. Scarce jobs and low income force people to share space and rental costs. To start the renewal process illustrated here, slum demolition begins to make room for industrial sites to provide employment. Employment begins the upgrading of skill and income to shift population to the labor status and into the new worker housing for which they create a demand. Continuing demolition of slum housing keeps the underemployed influx from rising faster than the increase in employment opportunities.

Chapter 6 comments on simulation and the modeling of social systems.

Chapter 7 illustrates how model studies can be interpreted in terms of urban policies and programs. The city emerges as a social system that creates its own problems. If the internal city system remains structured to generate blight, external help will probably fail. If the internal system is changed in the proper way, little outside help will be needed. Recovery through changed internal incentives seems more promising than recovery by direct-action government programs. But to generate this recovery, trends in tax laws and land-use zoning will need to be reversed.

In complex systems long-term improvement often inherently conflicts with short-term advantage. The greatest uncertainty for the city is whether or not education and urban leadership can succeed in shifting stress to the long-term actions necessary for internal revitalization and away from efforts for quick results that eventually make conditions worse. Political pressure from the outside to help the city emphasize long-term, self-sustaining recovery may be far more important than financial assistance.

1.2 Background

This study of urban dynamics was undertaken principally because of discoveries made in modeling the growth process of corporations. It has become clear that complex systems are counterintuitive. That is, they give indications that suggest corrective action which will often be ineffective or even adverse in its results. Very often one finds that the policies that have been adopted for correcting a difficulty are actually intensifying it rather than producing a solution.

Choosing an ineffective or detrimental policy for coping with a complex system is not a matter of random chance. The intuitive processes will select the wrong solution much more often than not. A complex system—a class to which a corporation, a city, an economy, or a government belong—behaves in many ways quite the opposite of the simple systems from which we have gained our experience.

Most of our intuitive responses have been developed in the context of what are technically called first-order, negative-feedback loops. Such a simple loop is goal-seeking and has only one important state variable. For example, warming one's hands beside a stove can be approximated as a first-order, negative-feedback loop in which the purpose of the process is to obtain warmth without burning one's hands. The principal state variable of the loop is the distance from the stove. If one is too close he burns his hands, if too far away he receives little heat. The intuitive lesson is that cause and effect are closely related in time and space. Temperature depends on the distance from the stove. Too much or too little heat is clearly related to the position of the hands. The relation of cause and effect is immediate and clear. Similarly, the simple feedback loops that govern walking, driving a car, or picking things up all train us to find cause and effect occurring at approximately the same moment and location.

But in complex systems cause and effect are often not closely related in either time or space. The structure of a complex system is not a simple feedback loop where one system state dominates the behavior. The complex system has a multiplicity of interacting feedback loops. Its internal rates of flow are controlled by nonlinear relationships. The complex system is of high order, meaning that there are many system states (or levels). It usually contains positive-feedback loops describing growth processes as well as negative, goal-seeking loops. In the complex system the cause of a difficulty may lie far back in time from the symptoms, or in a completely different and remote part of the system. In fact, causes are usually found, not in prior events, but in the structure and policies of the system.

To make matters still worse, the complex system is even more deceptive than merely hiding causes. In the complex system, when we look for a cause near in time and space to a symptom, we usually find what appears to be a plausible cause. But it is usually not the cause. The complex system presents apparent causes that are in fact coincident symptoms. The high degree of time correlation between variables in complex systems can lead us to make cause-and-effect associations between variables that are simply moving together as part of the total dynamic behavior of the system. Conditioned by our training in simple systems, we apply the same intuition to complex systems and are led into error. As a result we treat symptoms, not causes. The outcome lies between ineffective and detrimental.

This failure of intuition has often been found in the corporate setting by the process of building a simulation model of the policy structure of the organization.* Often it is possible to show that those policies and practices of which the organization is most aware are by themselves sufficient to create the difficulties that plague the organization. In fact, often the very things being done to correct the difficulty make it worse. If the attempted solution intensifies the problem, wrongly attributed to another source, the organization likely will redouble its "corrective" action, producing more difficulty and pressure for still more remedial action. A destructive spiral becomes established.

The likelihood that these same counterintuitive processes might be at work in a system as complex as a city provided the major incentive for undertaking this study.

The pervasive sense of failure and frustration among men concerned with management of urban affairs points to the likelihood that the inherent behavior of complex systems defies the intuitively "obvious" solutions of the past. Among political leaders, managers of redevelopment activity, and political scientists interviewed in connection with this study, there was the overwhelming opinion that the problems of the urban area remain severe in spite of the variety of programs that have been tried over the last three decades.

Contributing to the selection of ineffective programs is the nature of the conflict between short-term and long-term considerations in complex systems. Very often the actions that seem easiest and most promising in the immediate future can produce even greater problems at a later time. Humanitarian impulses coupled with short-term political pressures lead to programs whose benefits, if any, evaporate quickly, leaving behind a system that is unimproved or in worse condition. Job-training programs, low-cost-housing programs, and even financial aid, when used alone without improvements in the economic climate of a city, can fall into this category of short-term promise followed by detrimental long-term change.

Another purpose of this study is to focus attention on the entire life cycle of an urban area. A few of those interested in urban areas have shown a tendency to turn away from the old, decaying inner city and to concentrate on new cities as a solution to the urban problem. But a new city becomes old. If the normal processes of stagnation and decay are allowed to continue in young cities that

*Reference 2, where suppression of growth in a product caused by the capital-investment policy can easily be attributed to assumed shortcomings in the sales department.

are still in good health, they too will falter. Furthermore, the processes of stagnation and decay that one sees in today's urban areas will, unless preventive measures are taken, overwhelm the present healthy suburban areas. Urban difficulties are not a matter of location so much as a phase in the normal life cycle of occupied land.

For all these reasons it seems urgent that we begin to understand the growth and aging process of a city. This book is intended as a contribution to that understanding. It is preliminary. It suggests a method of attack. It is not presented as a set of final answers to guide urban policy-making. Before implementing the kinds of policy changes that are explored in this book, there should be much more examination of the theory of urban growth herein proposed.

2 Structure of an Urban Area

2.1 General Structure of Systems

Before discussing the specific structure chosen here to represent an urban area, the general nature of structure as found in all dynamic systems will be summarized.* To model the dynamic behavior of a system, four hierarchies of structure should be recognized:

Closed boundary around the system
   Feedback loops as the basic structural elements within the boundary
      Level (state) variables representing accumulations within the feedback loops
      Rate (flow) variables representing activity within the feedback loops
         Goal
         Observed condition   as components of
         Detection of discrepancy   a rate variable
         Action based on discrepancy

Closed-System Boundary. To develop a complete concept of a system, the boundary must be established within which the system interactions take place that give the system its characteristic behavior. Figure 2-1 symbolizes the closed-boundary concept. The boundary is chosen to include those interacting components necessary to generate the modes of behavior of interest. If a particular difficulty in a system is being investigated, the system described within the boundary should be capable of generating that difficulty. The closed-boundary concept implies that the system behavior of interest is not imposed from the outside but created within the boundary.

The closed boundary does not mean that the system is unaffected by outside occurrences. But it does say that those outside occurrences can be viewed as random happenings that impinge on the system and do not themselves give the system its intrinsic growth and stability characteristics.

*For additional discussion of the general theory of structure, see References 4 and 6.

12

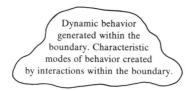

Figure 2-1   Closed boundary defining a dynamic system.

To build a computer simulation model of a system, one must first estimate what components are interacting to produce the behavior being investigated. The choice selects those components which lie within the dynamic boundary for the particular study and excludes all other potential components as being irrelevant to the study and therefore outside the dynamic boundary.

Feedback-Loop Structure. The dynamic behavior of systems is generated within feedback loops. Feedback loops are the fundamental building blocks of systems. Figure 2-2 shows the simplest possible feedback-loop structure. A feedback loop is composed of two kinds of variables, called here rate and level variables. These two kinds of variables are necessary and sufficient. The simplest possible feedback loop must contain one of each. A feedback loop is a structure within which a decision point—the rate equation—controls a flow or action stream. The action is accumulated (integrated) to generate a system level. Information about the level is the basis on which the flow rate is controlled.

The distinction between rates and levels—often with other terminology—is recognized in many fields. In economics flows and stocks are often used to mean the same as rates and levels mean here. In accounting the two kinds of variables are sharply distinguished. The balance sheet of a corporation lists the values of level variables. The profit-and-loss statement represents rates of flow and corresponds to the rate variables (except for a small technicality arising because

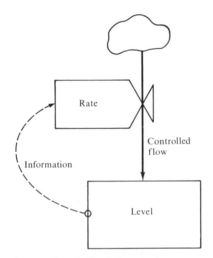

Figure 2-2   Simplest possible feedback loop having one rate and one level.

profit-and-loss variables are averaged over a time period rather than being instantaneous values). In psychology Lewin* describes psychological field theory in such terms that it is clear his "life space" is a set of level variables subject to being changed by various rates. In engineering the "state-variable" approach to engineering systems refers to the same concept here called levels.

In a feedback loop the level variables are accumulations or integrations. A bank balance, the number of people in a city, the number of new enterprises, or the amount of slum housing are all level variables. Each results from accumulating or integrating the inward and outward flows. The rates of flow cause the levels to change. The levels provide the information inputs to the rate equations which control the flows. Levels are changed only by rates of flow. The rate variables depend only on information about the levels. No rate can directly affect any other rate and no level directly affects any other level. One level can affect another only through an intervening rate. Any path through the structure of a system will encounter alternating levels and rates, never two variables of the same type in succession.

The rate equations are the statements of system policy. They determine how the available information is converted to an action stream. Within each rate equation there is explicitly or implicitly a goal toward or away from which that decision point in the system is striving. There is also a process whereby the observed condition of a system is detected. It is the observed condition, not the true condition, that determines action. Very often in systems the perceived condition of the system is distorted and lags with respect to the true condition. A rate equation states the discrepancy between the goal and the observed condition. And finally, the rate equation states the action that will result from the discrepancy.

Using these concepts of structure, we now proceed to represent an urban area.

2.2   Structure of the Urban Model

When first modeling a social system it is usually best to model the general class of system rather than a specific system. Here, this means a model to represent the central processes common to all urban areas rather than to represent those of a specific area. The general model will be simpler and more basic because it omits the peripheral considerations that may be special to a particular place. It focuses on those system components that are always to be found interacting in urban growth and stagnation. The model should include only those processes necessary to the creation and correction of urban decay.

Boundary of the Urban System. The first step in modeling the urban interactions is to choose a system boundary that defines the concepts that interact to produce the behavior of interest. Interest here is in the broad sweep of how an area evolves. The model should show how an area develops from empty land and eventually

---

*Reference 3.

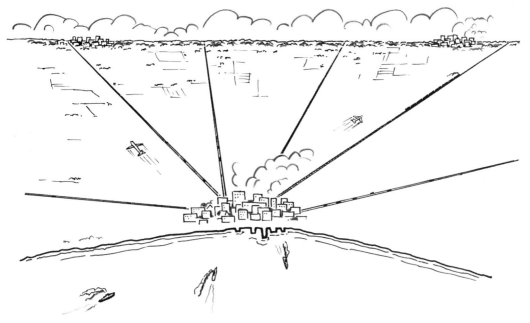

Figure 2-3 The urban area in its limitless environment.

fills that land with decaying housing and declining industry to produce economic stagnation. For an urban area in its stagnation phase, we are interested in the policy changes that can produce revival and a return to economic health.

Urban growth and stagnation do not appear to require changes in the world environment as a cause. The urban problem is not limited to any single country, society, or historical era. The behavior of a city is much more directly dependent on its own economic merit and its changing internal mix of industry, housing, and population. Most urban areas seem to evolve through a similar pattern. It can be assumed that any one area is small enough in the world setting not to affect the outside environment. For our purposes the urban area can therefore be taken as a living system that communicates with an environment it does not substantially influence.

Figure 2-3 suggests an urban area in a limitless environment. The area communicates with the environment but does not alter it. People from the outside come into the area and leave it without affecting the outside.

The specific system boundary is most easily defined in terms of the interacting components that are to be included within the system. Figure 2-4 shows the principal level variables and rate variables chosen as the central framework of an urban system. The nine rectangles represent the system levels. They are accumulations generated by the net rates which flow in and out of each level. The 22 principal rates are shown by the valve symbols controlling the flow streams. Not shown is the network of information connections from the levels to the rates.

In Figure 2-4 are three subsystems: business, housing, and population. These

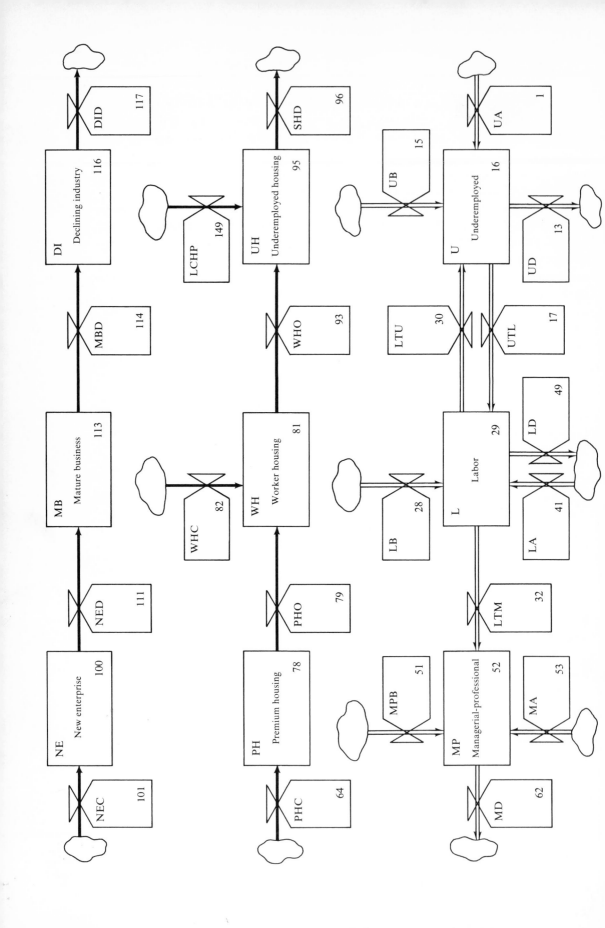

three subsystems are chosen because they appear to be the dynamic framework of urban structure. The changes in housing, population, and industry are the central processes involved in growth and stagnation. They are more fundamental than city government, social culture, or fiscal policy. Observation of the city suggests that the important changes involve shifting populations as housing structures age and industry falls behind the outside economy.

The aging of a city is here conceived as an internal process, like the aging of a person. Aging is not a series of changes generated and imposed primarily by the outside environment, although changes from the outside might hasten or retard the process. In Figure 2-4 the levels (rectangles) and rates (valves), along with the information connections from levels to rates (not shown), represent the system components within the dynamic boundary. The "cloud" symbols are the sources or destinations of flows going from or to the outside environment. The flows from or to the outside are controlled only by conditions within the system.

The Environment as a Point of Reference. If flows from and to the outside are controlled only by the levels within the system boundary, the outside environment is implicitly taken as a reference. If conditions in the urban area are more favorable than those outside, people and industry will move in, and of course the reverse is true.

There is no need to assume that the reference environment is fixed and unchanging. Of course it does change over a period of several hundred years in the life of a city. We do assume that the "normal" condition of a city changes along with the outside reference. Our attention is focused on how the particular city differs from the normal as it evolves.

This concept of the closed boundary within which lie the components that create the behavior of interest is apparently hard to explain. The closed boundary and the limitless environment are two sides of the same coin. Certain components interact to create the kinds of responses being studied. These, by definition, lie within the boundary. Anything that is not essential to creating the behavior of interest is, by that lack of essentiality, on the outside in the unspecified environment.

Elements outside the boundary are related to those inside very differently than the inside elements are related to one another. The cause-and-effect relationships between environment and system are unidirectional, whereas the internal elements are structured into feedback loops that cause the internal elements to interact. The environment can affect the system, but the system does not significantly affect the environment. In terms of loop structure, there are no loops essential to this study that run from the system to the environment and back to the system.

Let us illustrate these comments about system versus environment. Critics of the concept of an urban area as a closed dynamic system might argue that mechanization of agriculture in rural areas has accelerated migration to American cities. Or, in some countries, famine in rural areas has increased migration to the city. These comments are of course true. But these influences are not the primary causes of aging and stagnation in cities. If slum areas can be generated without such external changes, then internal interactions must be more essential.

The open-loop test of independence between system and environment can be stated as follows: Mechanization of agriculture in the environment can increase pressure on a city, but does the development of a city slum affect the mechanization of agriculture in any direct way? Probably not. Similarly, weather may affect migration, but migration does not affect weather. This break in reverse causality dynamically separates the environment from the urban system discussed in this book.

The closed dynamic boundary does not mean that the urban area is isolated. People come and go. Commerce exists. But it does mean that cause-and-effect loops do not reach outside the boundary and return. For example, migration to the area has its effect by filling and thereby altering the area, not by emptying the outside world.

These assumptions will be satisfactory as long as a city does not dominate the social system within which it lies. The assumption of a city existing in a limitless environment might need revision for analysis of a large city in a small country with strong barriers against immigation.

All other urban areas, even those that are part of the same city, are part of the outside environment. The area being modeled communicates with the surrounding countryside and other urban areas in the environmental setting.

So the urban area is represented as a living, self-controlling system that regulates its own flows of people to and from the outside environment. This approach does not assume that either the area or the outside world is static. It assumes that the technology, the living standards, and the nature of economic activity in the area change to keep pace with the outside. The changing outside environment is not pertinent to this book.* We are here concerned only with how the urban area performs relative to that outside. If the area is more attractive to a particular class of person, inward migration of that class occurs. If the area is less attractive, outward migration occurs.

Relative Attractiveness. Using the environment as a reference point means that conditions within the urban model are being generated relative to the environment. The model shows how the area becomes more or less attractive than the surrounding country and other cities and thereby causes the movement of industry and population to and from the area. Only *differences* in attractiveness between the area and environment are significant. The model does not, and need not, deal with changing technology and a rising national standard of living. We are interested in urban improvement relative to the absolute reference set by the outside environment.

---

*Appendix B shows how the choice between alternative policies is independent of outside environmental changes. The better policy remains better as the outside changes, even though the absolute desirability of the city does change with external conditions.

The Internal System. The top subsystem in Figure 2-4 contains three levels and four rates representing business activity. At the upper left new-enterprise units are created. An enterprise unit is here taken as a standard land and building area. Principally as a function of time and aging, the new enterprise shifts to the category of mature business. After the further passage of years mature business ages into the category of declining industry and still later is demolished and disappears. The flow from one category of business activity to the next depends not only on time but on the condition of the entire urban system.

The middle subsystem in Figure 2-4, containing three levels and six rates, represents the construction, aging, and demolition of housing. Premium housing, associated with the managerial-professional population, is constructed on the left. After an aging time and depending on the need for premium housing, the premium housing declines into the worker-housing category. In addition worker housing is constructed directly without passing through the premium-housing category. Worker housing ages and declines into the underemployed-housing category. The rate of obsolescence from worker housing to underemployed housing again depends on time and on the demand for worker housing. If a low-cost-housing program exists, it creates underemployed housing directly. The underemployed housing disappears through the slum-housing-demolition rate, which depends on the age of the underemployed housing and on the occupancy ratio.

The lower subsystem in Figure 2-4, with three levels and twelve rates, represents the population. Three categories of people are shown—managerial-professional, labor, and underemployed. The labor is skilled labor fully participating in the urban economy. Underemployed workers include, in addition to the unemployed and unemployable, people in unskilled jobs, those in marginal economic activity, and those not seeking employment who might work in a period of intense economic activity. People can enter each category from the outside environment and leave to the outside. Each category has an internal birth rate. There is also an upward economic mobility from the underemployed to the labor class and from the labor class to the managerial-professional group. In addition there is a downward economic mobility from labor to underemployed. The flow rates depend on the population mix, available housing, and jobs provided by industry.

In the system a direct correspondence exists between the three housing categories and the three population categories. This defines what is meant by the housing categories. The managerial-professional group live only in premium housing; the labor group, in worker housing; and the underemployed, in underemployed housing. This relates the housing to its cost and to the economic classifications of the population.

However, there is no direct correspondence between the business units and the population. Each category of business employs each population category. A new-enterprise unit of business employs more people than a mature-business unit; the latter employs more than a declining-industry unit. Furthermore, the personnel mix changes with a higher ratio of managers to skilled labor in the new-enterprise category and with the managers proportionately declining as the new-enterprise unit ages into mature business and further decays into the declining-industry category. The table below defines a productive unit in terms of the employment mix under normal economic circumstances.* For example, a new-enterprise unit under normal conditions is defined as employing 4 managers, 20 labor men, and 10 underemployed workers. The important characteristics assumed for a business unit are the declining employment and the shifting personnel mix as the business unit ages.

	Managerial-Professional	*Labor*	*Underemployed*
New Enterprise	NEM = 4	NEL = 20	10
Mature Business	MBM = 2	MBL = 15	7.5
Declining Industry	DIM = 1	DIL = 10	5

A corresponding shift in population density defines the principal distinction between categories of housing units as a unit ages and passes through the three categories of housing, as shown in the table below:

Premium-Housing Population Density (PHPD) = 3 persons/housing unit
Worker-Housing Population Density (WHPD) = 6 persons/housing unit
Underemployed-Housing Population Density (UHPD) = 12 persons/housing unit

These housing densities represent the normal if housing and population are in economic balance. The actual densities of people per housing unit may run higher or lower depending on the population and available housing.

Figure 2-4 shows the principal system levels and the related rates of flow, but it does not show the connections from the system levels to the rates. Each rate of flow is determined at any given moment by the values of several system levels. The network of connections from the level variables to the rates would be too complex and confusing to superimpose in its entirety on Figure 2-4, but in the next section one information network, that connecting the system levels to the underemployed-arrival rate, will be examined as a typical illustration of how all system rates are related to levels. (The detailed development of the computer model representing the dynamics of an urban area is given in Appendix A.)

2.3   Example of a Flow Rate

Connections between system levels and one rate are shown in Figure 2-5. Here the nine principal system levels, carried over from the preceding figure, appear in the background. The dash lines carry the system levels through various intermediate concepts shown in the circles to generate the attractiveness-for-migration

---

*As will be seen later, the jobs open to the underemployed depend on the ratio of skilled labor to labor jobs. If labor is in short supply, the underemployed fill a proportionately larger fraction of the jobs. If labor is in oversupply, labor tends to fill the jobs that would otherwise be available to the underemployed. In the table above the letter groups are the symbols used in the model equations in Appendixes A, C, D, and E.

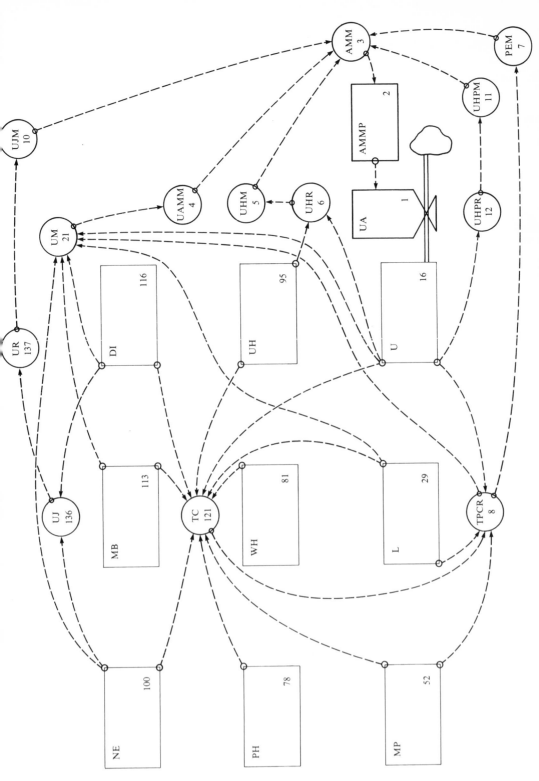

Figure 2-5 A typical set of influences controlling a flow rate. Shows how the system levels determine the underemployed-arrival rate UA. (Letter groups are the symbols in the equations and numbers identify the system equations, as in Appendix A.)

multiplier AMM. The present actual urban attractiveness is not perceived immediately by those in distant places who might migrate to the area. A perception-time delay is shown in the rectangle marked "2," for Equation 2, which generates the attractiveness-for-migration multiplier perceived AMMP. The latter in turn modulates the flow of underemployed population into the area.

In Figure 2-5 the attractiveness-for-migration multiplier AMM is based on five influences. These are the underemployed-arrivals-mobility multiplier UAMM, the underemployed/housing multiplier UHM, the public-expenditure multiplier PEM, the underemployed/job multiplier UJM, and the underemployed-housing-program multiplier UHPM. These five variables combine to influence the underemployed arrivals UA entering the area. Figure 2-6 summarizes these five influences on the underemployed-arrival rate. Upward economic mobility expressed by UAMM makes the area more attractive. Available housing as generated by

Graphic Symbol	Name of Multiplier	Situation Evaluated by Multiplier	Response to Evaluation
UAMM UAMMT 4	UNDEREMPLOYED-ARRIVALS-MOBILITY MULTIPLIER	How readily are the underemployed moving into the skilled-labor class?	The larger the percentage that moves from the underemployed to the labor class per year, the more attractive is the city to outsiders.
UHM UHMT 5	UNDEREMPLOYED/ HOUSING MULTIPLIER	Are there underemployed-housing vacancies in the city?	The more underemployed-housing vacancies in the city, the greater the attractiveness of the city.
PEM PEMT 7	PUBLIC-EXPENDITURE MULTIPLIER	How much tax money is being spent per capita in the city?	The more spent per capita, the greater is the public service offered by the city and the greater its attractiveness to outsiders.
UJM UJMT 10	UNDEREMPLOYED/ JOB MULTIPLIER	How many jobs are available for underemployed people?	The more jobs available, the more attractive is the city to outsiders.
UHPM UHPMT 11	UNDEREMPLOYED-HOUSING-PROGRAM MULTIPLIER	Is there a construction program for low-cost housing in operation?	The more houses constructed per year in the program, the greater the attractiveness of the city.

Figure 2-6 Influences on underemployed-arrival rate.

UHM attracts underemployed to the area. Public expenditure PEM for schools, services, and welfare makes the area attractive. The measure of available jobs UJM is a strong influence on attracting those looking for economic opportunity. And a low-cost-housing program as manifested in UHPM is favorable to the underemployed and produces attractiveness beyond and in addition to housing availability.

Although a full discussion of the model equations will be left until Appendix A, details of the first several equations will be discussed here as examples of how the model represents urban interactions.

Figure 2-7 shows the detailed relationships between some of the concepts that appeared in Figure 2-5. It also illustrates how the influences that were outlined in Figure 2-6 are combined to generate the flow of underemployed arrivals into the area.

In this model all rates of flow are stated in terms of a "normal" set of conditions. This normal rate of flow is then modified by a multiplier that represents the deviation of the actual urban-area conditions from the normal.

As given in the following equation, the normal value of the underemployed-arrival rate is expressed as a fraction of the population already in the area. Here the population is taken as the sum of the underemployed plus the labor groups. The multiplier UAN with a value of .05 states the concept that under normal conditions the underemployed-inflow rate will be 5% per year of the under-employed plus labor populations.

$$UA.KL=(U.K+L.K)(UAN)(AMMP.K) \qquad\qquad 1,R$$

$$UAN=.05 \qquad\qquad 1.1,C$$

UA	—	UNDEREMPLØYED ARRIVALS (MEN/YEAR)
U	—	UNDEREMPLØYED (MEN)
L	—	LABØR (MEN)
UAN	—	UNDEREMPLØYED ARRIVALS NØRMAL (FRACTIØN/ YEAR)
AMMP	—	ATTRACTIVENESS-FØR-MIGRATIØN MULTIPLIER PERCEIVED (DIMENSIØNLESS)

The last term in Equation 1 is the attractiveness multiplier as perceived AMMP. The perceived multiplier is a delayed value of the actual multiplier. The actual multiplier AMM is the true present state of the system. The attractiveness multi-plier as perceived modifies what would otherwise be the normal migration into the area. When the attractiveness of the area is normal, the multiplier has a value of 1; its actual value can range from zero to several.

The following equation introduces the perception-time lag between the true present attractiveness-for-migration multiplier AMM and the perceived value AMMP (this is a first-order exponential delay*):

*See Reference 1, Chapter 9.

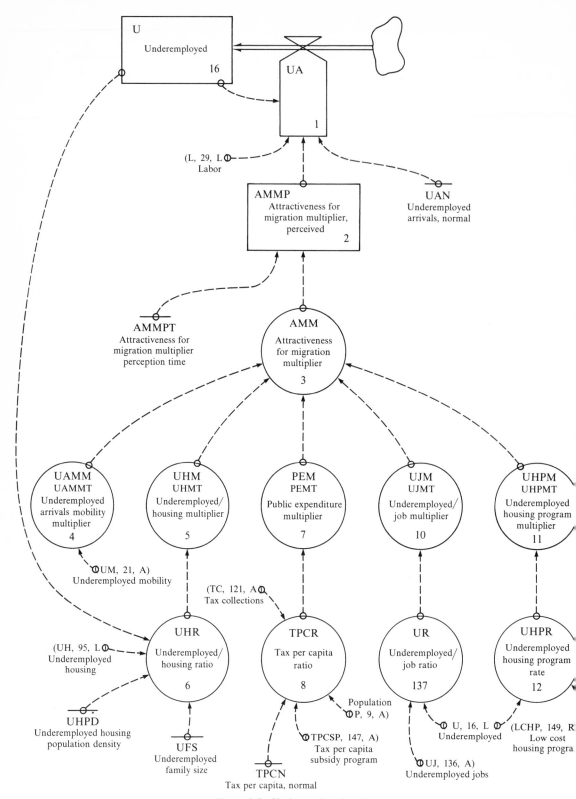

Figure 2-7 Underemployed-arrival rate.

AMMP.K =AMMP.J+(DT/AMMPT) (AMM.J −AMMP.J)   2,L

AMMP=1   2.1,N

AMMPT=20   2.2,C

        AMMP   − ATTRACTIVENESS−FØR−MIGRATIØN MULTIPLIER
                 PERCEIVED (DIMENSIØNLESS)
        AMMPT − ATTRACTIVENESS−FØR−MIGRATIØN−MULTIPLIER
                 PERCEPTIØN TIME (YEARS)
        AMM   − ATTRACTIVENESS−FØR−MIGRATIØN MULTIPLIER
                 (DIMENSIØNLESS)

In the preceding equation the perception delay has been taken as 20 years. This means that a 20-year time lag occurs between the true condition of the area and the perception of that condition by remote members of the underemployed population. This is about one generation and seems to be approximately the time required to become aware of changing conditions in our social institutions. Of course this time delay is a function of communications and would have been longer a hundred years ago than it is today with television and with more rapid transportation. However, the perception-time delays are not very important in this study because they do not have any influence on the equilibrium conditions but only influence the duration of transients as the area changes from one stage to another. Because the numerous other time constants in the system are equal or longer in duration, the perception-time delays will have only secondary influence even on the transient changes.

All the processes within the urban area are conceived here as having certain normal values associated with the size of the area. These norms are then modulated over a wide range by the internal condition of the area. The equation below describes this modulating variable for the underemployed arrivals. The attractiveness-for-migration multiplier AMM is the input to the perception delay in Equation 2 which after the delay directly affects the underemployed-arrival rate through term AMMP in Equation 1. The following equation combines six terms into a product that represents the attractiveness of the area to the underemployed population. The terms combined are those that were summarized in Figure 2-6. They are the underemployed-mobility multiplier, the underemployed/housing multiplier, the public-expenditure multiplier, the underemployed/job multiplier, and the underemployed-housing-program multiplier. In addition a term AMF called the attractiveness-for-migration factor has been added. This factor does not represent any actual urban process but is a coefficient that can be changed as a part of model experimentation to test the sensitivity of the system to modifications in the attractiveness-for-migration multiplier AMM.

In Equation 3 the components of attractiveness are combined by multiplication rather than by addition. Multiplication produces two intended effects. First, the changes in the multipliers are mutually enhancing. Were all multipliers to increase slightly, the effect would be greater than the sum of the separate influences. Second, it is possible to have one multiplier sufficiently powerful when it becomes

$$AMM.K = (UAMM.K)(UHM.K)(PEM.K)(UJM.K)(UHPM.K)(AMF) \qquad 3,A$$

$$AMF = 1 \qquad 3.1,C$$

    AMM   — ATTRACTIVENESS-FØR-MIGRATIØN MULTIPLIER
                (DIMENSIØNLESS)
    UAMM — UNDEREMPLØYED-ARRIVALS-MOBILITY MULTIPLIER
                (DIMENSIØNLESS)
    UHM   — UNDEREMPLØYED/HØUSING MULTIPLIER
                (DIMENSIØNLESS)
    PEM   — PUBLIC-EXPENDITURE MULTIPLIER
                (DIMENSIØNLESS)
    UJM   — UNDEREMPLØYED/JØB MULTIPLIER
                (DIMENSIØNLESS)
    UHPM — UNDEREMPLØYED-HØUSING-PRØGRAM MULTIPLIER
                (DIMENSIØNLESS)
    AMF   — ATTRACTIVENESS-FØR-MIGRATIØN FACTØR
                (DIMENSIØNLESS)

0 to dominate the entire group. Such domination is particularly important if one multiplier could become strong enough to shut off the inflow of people. For example, a great enough excess of people over available housing or jobs might suppress inward migration. If any one of the multipliers becomes 0, the entire product in Equation 3 becomes 0.

Each of the five multiplier inputs to Equation 3 is represented in the model by a nonlinear table function that permits any choice of interdependence between two variables. Equation 4 illustrates how these table functions are introduced. The underemployed-arrivals-mobility multiplier UAMM is stated in terms of underemployed mobility UM. Underemployed mobility UM is generated elsewhere in the system. It gives the fraction per year of the underemployed that move into the labor category. Equation 4 describes a table function that is illustrated in Figure 2-8.

$$UAMM.K = TABLE(UAMMT, UM.K, 0, .15, .025) \qquad 4,A$$

$$UAMMT = .3/.7/1/1.2/1.3/1.4/1.5 \qquad 4.1,T$$

    UAMM — UNDEREMPLØYED-ARRIVALS-MOBILITY MULTIPLIER
                (DIMENSIØNLESS)
    UAMMT — UNDEREMPLØYED-ARRIVALS-MØBILITY-MULTIPLIER
                TABLE
    UM   — UNDEREMPLØYED MØBILITY (FRACTIØN/YEAR)

Equation 4 is not the normal algebraic equation. The word "TABLE," because it appears without either parentheses or the multiply sign "$*$," is recognized as an operating function. Here the function is a table look-up in a table known as UAMMT, the input of which is the variable UM. The range of UM is from 0 to .15 in steps of .025. Equation 4.1 gives the table itself with the values of the equally spaced points (as shown in Figure 2-8). The table-function operation enters with the value of UM, does linear interpolation, and determines UAMM.

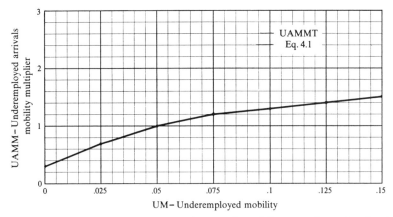

Figure 2-8 Influence of underemployed upward economic mobility on underemployed-arrival rate.

Figure 2-8 shows that a normal upward mobility of 5% per year from the underemployed into the labor category is taken as the value that will give a multiplier value of 1 for UAMM. Should there be no escape from the underemployed group, as represented by a 0 value of UM, the mobility multiplier would fall only to .3. In other words, the complete absence of upward mobility would not give the city a sufficiently unfavorable image to prevent inward migration. At the right-hand extreme of Figure 2-8 upward mobility would cause a rise in the underemployed-arrival rate but with a decreasing slope, indicating the belief that increasing mobility above normal is less influential in increasing arrivals than is decreasing mobility influential in suppressing the rate (an argument could easily be made in favor of curvature in the upward direction).

Figure 2-9 shows the relation in the urban model between housing and underemployed migration into the area. The underemployed/housing ratio is the ratio of the underemployed population to the population that could normally occupy the underemployed-housing units. As the ratio decreases, there are fewer people

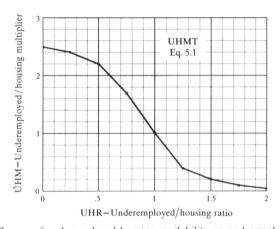

Figure 2-9 Influence of underemployed-housing availability on underemployed-arrival rate.

in relation to available housing. As the ratio increases, it indicates a higher degree of crowding. An underemployed/housing ratio of 1 produces the neutral multiplier value of 1. When there are fewer people in relation to available housing, the ratio is lower and the multiplier rises, indicating that available housing makes the area more attractive. The figure shows a fairly steep dependence of attractiveness on housing in the normal region. However, for low values of the ratio as excess housing becomes available, more housing produces little additional effect as shown by the flattening of the curve. At the right-hand extreme, where congestion rises to twice normal for this economic category of person, the unavailability of housing becomes a strong depressant on inward mobility. The shape and positioning of such a curve suggests statements about the society being described. Furthermore, the definition of underemployed housing will vary greatly depending on the country and its economic circumstances. South America and India would have a curve of similar shape but perhaps of quite different numerical values and slopes to describe the influence of housing on migration toward a city. Some persons allege that there is little interdependence between underemployed migration and housing. However, as we will see in later chapters, an old city normally tends to have an excess of underemployed housing and a deficiency of jobs. Even though there is a strong housing relationship at some parts of the curve shown in Figure 2-9, its effect may be obscured if the city system operates near the upper horizontal section of the curve where housing exerts little influence. However, for studies of new urban-management policies, one must establish a hypothesis about the entire shape of such a curve because new policies may well entail internal readjustments and a system that operates in portions of the interdependency relationships that have not historically been experienced. Figure 2-9 says that a maximum availability of underemployed housing can raise the inward-migration rate by a factor of 2.5. When the overcrowding is 2 times normal crowding, the inward migration is driven down to .05 of normal.

The per capita tax expenditure* in the area is taken as one measure of attractiveness. Figure 2-10 shows the relationship in the model. The tax per capita ratio is the ratio of taxes per capita in the area to the tax per capita in the outside environment from which people come. A ratio of 1 produces a multiplier of 1, indicating that if the tax per capita in the area is the same as in the outside environment there is no incentive from this source to move into the area. The expenditure of taxes is here used as an indication of public services, schools, welfare, and other public-supported activities. The curve states that inward migration would fall to .2 of the value it would otherwise have if expenditures declined to zero. At the other extreme an expenditure rate of 3 times normal would make the city 4 times as attractive as the outside environment. One could argue that the curves should drop more steeply and reach zero before the tax per capita

---

*Tax revenue and public expenditure are here taken as equal except for certain simulation runs where a subsidy from the outside is given to the city.

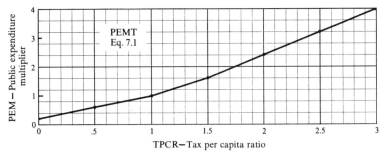

Figure 2-10 Influence of tax expenditures per capita on underemployed-arrival rate.

ratio reaches zero, but as we will see later such small variations in the functional relationships will make negligible difference in the results.

An important factor in determining migration into an urban area appears to be availability of economic opportunity as indicated by jobs. Assertions by people in the underemployed category support this view, as do social scientists. The model results in later chapters suggest that unfavorable conditions in the job multiplier have usually carried the major burden of limiting migration into cities. Fig. 2-11 shows the relation used here between available jobs and inward migration. The underemployed/job ratio UR is the ratio of underemployed to available jobs. The underemployed/job multiplier UJM gives the influence on migration. For a man/job ratio of 1, the multiplier is taken as neutral with a value of 1. As more jobs become available, the UR ratio falls and the multiplier rises but eventually levels off in the left-hand section when jobs are in excess and still more jobs would have no effect on the attractiveness of the area. In the right-hand section of the curve, inward migration falls off to a very low value as the excess of men increases. In examining such a curve one must remember that in the real-life situation there is a great deal of flexibility in defining what constitutes a job as well as what constitutes an underemployed person. The long sloping

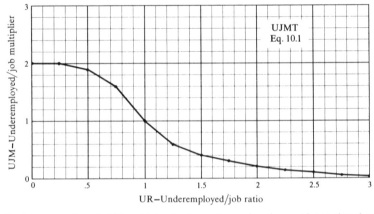

Figure 2-11 Influence of availability of jobs for the underemployed on underemployed-arrival rate.

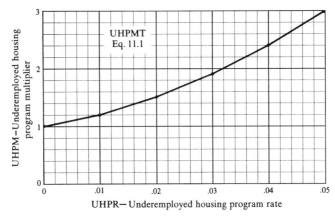

Figure 2-12   Influence of underemployed-housing program on underemployed-arrival rate.

section from a UR ratio of .5 to 1.5 indicates a region in which marginal workers and marginal jobs appear in response to economic pressures. One would not expect such a curve to show extreme steepness in the region of UR = 1 because of the broad distribution in desire to work and the broad distribution in how insistently employers will attempt to fill potential job openings.

The remaining influence on inward migration of the underemployed in this model is generated by a low-cost-housing program. Figure 2-12 shows the assumed effect. The normal condition is taken as no low-cost-housing construction. As housing rises to a rate of 5% per year of the underemployed population, the attractiveness of the city is assumed to rise by a factor of 3. The influence of a housing program is in addition to the availability of housing as given in Figure 2-9. The relationship in Figure 2-12 results from the demonstrated interest and activity of the city in behalf of the underemployed as well as the higher quality of housing that results.

This section has discussed, as a typical example, the relationships influencing the underemployed-arrival rate into the city. The preceding graphic relationships showing influences on underemployed arrivals are all part of the rate equation for UA. The auxiliary equations (indicated by an A after the equation number) are subdivisions of the rate equation they affect. As such, their presence is compatible with the statement made in Section 2.1 that a model consists of only rate equations and level equations.

2.4   Example of a Level

The level variables describe the state of a system. A level is the accumulation resulting from the flows in and out of the level. Mathematically the levels are integrations. Figure 2-4 illustrates by rectangles the nine principal system levels used here to represent a city.

The following equation for the underemployed workers in the city is a level equation:

$$U.K = U.J + (DT)(UA.JK + UB.JK + LTU.JK - UD.JK - UTL.JK) \qquad 16, L$$

$$U = 1200 \qquad 16.1, N$$

U	-	UNDEREMPLØYED (MEN)
UA	-	UNDEREMPLØYED ARRIVALS (MEN/YEAR)
UB	-	UNDEREMPLØYED BIRTHS (MEN/YEAR)
LTU	-	LABØR TØ UNDEREMPLØYED (MEN/YEAR)
UD	-	UNDEREMPLØYED DEPARTURES (MEN/YEAR)
UTL	-	UNDEREMPLØYED TØ LABØR (MEN/YEAR)

The level equation above is a simple bookkeeping statement that says the underemployed at the present time K is equal to the underemployed at the previous time of computation J plus the change that occurred in the interval DT between successive computations. During the interval from time J to time K the underemployed-arrival rate is given as UA, the underemployed birth rate as UB, the labor-to-underemployed flow as LTU, the underemployed departures as UD, and the underemployed-to-labor flow as UTL. These are the five flow rates affecting the level of underemployed. An initial value must be given to each level equation; here 1,200 underemployed is given as the initial condition of the area.

All level equations are of the same form. A new value is computed by taking the old value and adding the change during the preceding time interval. This is the process of integration or accumulation. It is the process by which systems change through time.

2.5 Summary of Flow Rates

This section identifies the major influences affecting each rate of flow. Such a summary of the system structure should be sufficient background for reading the remaining chapters. (The exact details of the structure and relationships used to represent an urban area are given in Appendix A.)

Figure 2-4 showed the 22 flow rates that affect the 9 principal system levels. One of these flow rates, the underemployed arrivals UA, has been discussed in detail in Section 2.3. The other 21 flow rates and the factors affecting them are summarized here.

The underemployed U in the area are increased by the underemployed arrivals UA, the underemployed birth rate UB, and the labor-to-underemployed downward mobility LTU. The underemployed are reduced by the underemployed-to-labor upward mobility UTL and the underemployed departures UD. All of these rates are illustrated in Figure 2-4.

Underemployed Birth Rate UB. This is the net difference of births minus deaths and is taken as .015 of the underemployed population per year.

Labor to Underemployed LTU. The downward mobility or economic dropout from labor to underemployed in the model depends on the ratio of labor to available labor jobs. A dropout rate of 3% per year exists when labor and labor jobs are in balance. The rate drops slowly when labor is insufficient for available jobs and rises rapidly as labor exceeds jobs.

Underemployed to Labor UTL. This is the upward economic mobility representing the flow of the underemployed into the labor category. When conditions are normal, it is 10% per year. However, it is modified by a number of influences. It depends on the fraction of underemployed working, rising as the fraction increases. It depends on the ratio of labor to labor jobs; a shortage of labor makes the upward mobility larger, while an excess of labor makes it smaller. Upward mobility also depends on the ratio of the labor population to the underemployed population, with the upward mobility being greater when the underemployed are small in number compared to the labor group. This means that a small number of underemployed mixed with and having good access to a more successful economic group can make the transition more easily than a large number of underemployed in an area where there is little opportunity for contact with those they might emulate. Upward mobility also depends on the tax per capita ratio, which suggests that better schooling and social services can increase the upward economic flow.

Underemployed Departures UD. The normal underemployed-departure rate is assumed to be 2% of the underemployed population. The departure rate is affected inversely to the arrival rate; that is conditions that increase the arrival rate reduce the departure rate and vice versa.

The labor level L, in addition to the UTL and LTU rates already described, is affected by the labor birth rate LB, the labor-arrival rate LA, the labor-to-manager rate LTM, and the labor departures LD.

Labor Birth Rate LB. This is the net of birth rate minus death rate and is taken as .01 per year of the labor population.

Labor Arrivals LA. Arrivals of skilled labor are influenced by factors similar to those affecting arrivals of underemployed workers. Normal arrival rate is .03 per year of the labor group. Arrival rate increases as the labor/job ratio decreases, indicating the availability of excess jobs. The labor-arrival rate depends on the ratio of the labor population to the underemployed population, with the labor-arrival rate falling as the labor population decreases in comparison to the under-employed population. This indicates that an unfavorable social climate will depress the inward movement of skilled labor. Labor arrival depends on the tax ratio, being reduced somewhat as taxes rise. Labor arrival depends on the ratio of labor population to worker housing, with a housing shortage reducing the tendency to move into the area.

Labor Departures LD. Labor departures are given a normal value of 2% per year with a multiplier that is inverse to the arrival multiplier. Factors that encourage arrival will reduce departure and vice versa.

Labor to Manager LTM. The upward economic mobility from labor to the managerial-professional class is taken as normally .02 per year of the labor group and depends on three influences. The flow LTM increases if there is a shortage of managers for managerial jobs. The flow increases if the managerial population is above 10% of the labor population and decreases when the manager/labor ratio is lower. This is based on the assumption that the availability of a substantial managerial group to act as an example and to be accessible to the labor population increases opportunities for transition into the managerial-professional class. An increase in taxes per capita, implying better educational opportunities, increases the flow from labor to management.

The managerial-professional population MP is increased by the labor-to-manager flow LTM already described, the managerial-professional birth rate MPB, and the manager arrivals MA. The managerial-professional level is decreased by managerial departures MD. No downward mobility from the managerial class to the labor class has been included because it is probably too small to be significant.

Managerial-Professional Birth Rate MPB. The birth rate minus death rate is taken as .0075 of the managerial-professional population per year.

Manager Arrivals MA. Arrivals into the managerial-professional class follow the same pattern as for the labor class. A shortage of managers compared to available managerial jobs increases the arrival rate. A higher ratio of managers to total population implies a more favorable social climate and increases the arrival-rate multiplier. Increasing taxes depresses the arrival rate. Housing affects the manager-arrival rate, encouraging arrivals when it is adequate and discouraging arrivals as housing congestion increases.

Manager Departures MD. A manager-departure rate of 2% per year of the managerial-professional population is considered normal. This is modulated by a multiplier that is generated as the inverse of the arrival multiplier. Conditions favoring managerial arrival decrease managerial departure. Conversely, an environment discouraging arrival hastens departure.

Premium housing PH is the housing associated with the managerial-professional population. It is increased by premium-housing construction PHC and is decreased by premium-housing obsolescence PHO. Premium housing declines in value and condition to become worker housing.

Premium-Housing Construction PHC. Normal premium-housing construction is considered to be 3% per year of existing premium housing. This normal growth rate is then modified by a multiplier representing a combination of six influences. The ratio of managers to premium housing indicates whether or not there is a housing shortage, with a greater shortage causing an increase in the premium-housing-construction rate. All of the housing- and business-construction rates in the model are influenced by land multipliers having shapes similar to Figure 2-13.

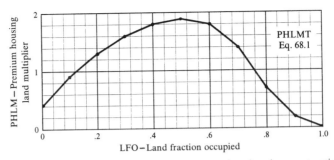

Figure 2-13 Influence of land occupancy on premium-housing construction.

When zero land is occupied, the area has not yet developed economically and the incentive for building is low. As activity in the area increases, all components of a city begin to develop and to enhance each other. Figure 2-13 asserts that the maximum influence from land occupancy occurs when the land is about 50% filled. As the land area approaches full occupancy, the more attractive and useful sections have already been built up and the economic incentive for additional construction declines. When the land is fully occupied, additional construction is physically impossible. New building can take place only as demolition makes empty land available. A third influence on premium-housing construction is the ratio of the managerial-professional class to the total population. An increase in the ratio implies a community attractive to the managerial group and encourages premium-housing construction. The tax rate affects premium-housing construction, with high taxes having an adverse influence on construction. Premium-housing construction is affected by two multipliers that indicate the degree of enthusiasm for new building. The enterprise multiplier increases premium-housing construction if the recent history of new-enterprise construction has been high. Similarly, the history of premium-housing construction itself produces a speculative incentive, with recent construction encouraging more construction.

Premium-Housing Obsolescence PHO. A normal life of about 30 years for premium housing is assumed. This means that normally .03 of premium housing per year ages into worker housing. But this normal obsolescence rate is influenced by pressures for premium housing. If premium housing is in great demand, the obsolescence rate would decline, implying a longer average life for premium housing. If premium housing is in excess supply, the obsolescence rate will be greater than normal.

Worker housing WH (as shown in Figure 2-4) is increased both by premium-housing obsolescence PHO and by worker-housing construction WHC. It is depleted by worker-housing obsolescence WHO.

Worker-Housing Construction WHC. Worker housing is built directly in addition to becoming available through the obsolescence of premium housing. The worker-housing-construction rate depends on six factors representing the same concepts as in premium-housing construction. These are the adequacy of housing, a land multiplier, the ratio of labor to underemployed as a measure of community desirability, the tax ratio, the recent trend in new-enterprise construction, and the recent trend in worker-housing construction.

Worker-Housing Obsolescence WHO. The normal average life of worker housing has been taken as 50 years, representing 2% per year transfer of worker housing into the underemployed-housing category. This normal obsolescence rate is then modified upward or downward depending on the demand for worker housing.

The underemployed housing UH is increased by worker-housing obsolescence WHO and any low-cost-housing program LCHP. It is decreased by slum-housing demolition SHD.

Low-Cost-Housing Program LCHP. This flow rate is not a normal city process. It is an externally generated program which can be activated in the model to observe the response of the urban system to the construction of housing directly for the underemployed.

Slum-Housing Demolition SHD. A 50-year life has been assumed as normal in the underemployed-housing category, implying a normal demolition rate of 2% per year. This rate is modified to increase as the occupancy ratio of the housing decreases. The multiplier also increases as the fraction of total land occupied increases. This implies that if construction in the area continues once the land reaches almost full occupancy, demolition must be taking place.

New enterprise NE is increased by new-enterprise construction NEC and reduced by new-enterprise decline NED into mature business.

New-Enterprise Construction NEC. New enterprise is assumed to be constructed under normal circumstances at a rate equal to separate fractions of each of the three business categories. This normal rate is then influenced by a multiplier that combines five influences on new-enterprise construction. The ratio of managers to managerial jobs influences new construction; the greater the supply of managers, the greater the tendency to construct new business. The land fraction occupied influences new-enterprise construction (as shown in Figure 2-13). The availability of labor encourages new construction. A high tax rate reduces construction. A speculative factor increases construction over the normal amount if there has been a recent history of high construction.

New-Enterprise Decline NED. A new enterprise is assumed to have an average life of about 12 years before becoming a mature business. The decline rate is taken as .08 of the new enterprise each year, with a multiplier that falls as the demand for new enterprise increases and vice versa. This implies that aging is less rapid in a period of high economic demand than in one of economic stagnation.

The model assumes that mature business MB is simply the older, stabilized condition reached in time by new enterprise. In turn, time is the principal determinant in the aging rate of mature business MBD into declining industry DI.

Mature-Business Decline MBD. A normal life of 20 years is used in the model for mature business. The decline rate of 5% per year is modified by the new-enterprise multiplier in such a way that mature business declines more slowly in periods of economic activity and a high demand for business.

Declining industry DI is business activity that has passed its prime. Ailing economically, it employs fewer people per productive unit than more healthy business units. In time declining industry disappears by demolition DID.

Declining-Industry Demolition DID. A 30-year life is assumed as normal for the declining-industry phase of a business unit. The average age shortens in periods of economic demand and rises in periods of economic stagnation. As with slum-housing demolition, the demolition rate of declining industry depends on the land fraction occupied in such a way that the demolition rate increases as new construction forces land occupancy to nearly 100%.

Taxes influence a number of activities within the urban model. An assessed value is ascribed to each class of business and housing, and a total assessed value is computed. "Taxes needed" are computed on the basis of population, with the assumption that public expenditures are greater per person in the underemployed category than in the labor category and greater in the labor category than in the managerial-professional class. Political power is included as the ratio of labor to underemployed. As the percentage of the population in the underemployed category rises, tax assessments increase, because the underemployed group has the political power as well as the need for tax expenditure, although it pays little tax.

2.6   Parameters in the Simulation Model

Any reasonably consistent set of coefficients could be used as the basis for this model representing urban growth and stagnation. Most of the values chosen are not critical in determining the behavior of the system.* However, the time plots and computed results are perhaps more easily understood in terms of the actual figures taken in the model. The following have been used:

MAJOR PARAMETERS

Land area (AREA)   = 100,000 acres
Land per house (LPH)   = .1 acre
Land per productive unit (LPP) = .2 acre

---

*Appendix B discusses sensitivity of parameters.

HOUSING DENSITIES

Premium-housing population density   (PHPD) = 3 persons/housing unit
Worker-housing population density   (WHPD) = 6 persons/housing unit
Underemployed-housing population density (UHPD) = 12 persons/housing unit

FAMILY SIZES

Managerial-professional family size (MPFS) = 5 people
Labor family size   (LFS) = 6 people
Underemployed family size   (UFS) = 8 people

PERSONNEL NEEDED IN BUSINESS UNITS

	Managerial-Professional	Labor	Under-employed
New Enterprise	NEM = 4	NEL = 20	10
Mature Business	NBM = 2	MBL = 15	7.5
Declining Industry	DIM = 1	DIL = 10	5

TAXES LEVIED

Premium-housing assessed value   (PHAV) = $30 thousand/housing unit
Worker-housing assessed value   (WHAV) = $15 thousand/housing unit
Underemployed-housing assessed value (UHAV) = $ 5 thousand/housing unit

New-enterprise assessed value   (NEAV) = $500 thousand/productive unit
Mature-business assessed value   (MBAV) = $300 thousand/productive unit
Declining-industry assessed value (DIAV) = $100 thousand/productive unit

TAXES NEEDED

Tax per management person   (TMP) = $150/year
Tax per labor person   (TLP) = $200/year
Tax per underemployed person (TUP) = $300/year
Tax assessment normal   (TAN) = $50/year/thousand dollars

At the start of a simulation computation initial values must be specified for all level variables in the system. These state the starting conditions of the system. The nine principal levels shown in Figure 2-4 have values given below. The system also contains certain perceived values and average growth rates that are level variables and have initial values specified in Appendix A. Generally, the initial values are not important except in determining behavior in the very early part of the simulation run. Any initial imbalance between the selected initial values is worked out within the system as new values are computed for the level variables. For most systems the ultimate equilibrium values are independent of the starting point.

New enterprise	(NE) =	200 productive units
Mature business	(MB) =	1,000 productive units
Declining industry	(DI) =	100 productive units
Premium housing	(PH) =	5,000 housing units
Worker housing	(WH) =	21,000 housing units
Underemployed housing	(UH) =	1,100 housing units
Managerial-Professional	(MP) =	3,900 men
Labor	(L) =	14,000 men
Underemployed	(U) =	1,200 men

3 Growth and Stagnation

This chapter discusses the dynamics of the urban life cycle as created by the simulation model outlined in Chapter 2. Chapters 4 and 5 will start with an urban area already in the stagnant condition and explore the effects of various changes in urban-management policies. But here, first, the broad sweep of urban growth and maturity are investigated to show how an area begins to decline.

The stages of an urban life cycle within a period of 250 years occur starting with empty land, growing to full land occupancy, maturing through a rapid realignment of internal urban balance, and emerging into an equilibrium characterized by stagnation with its unemployment, faltering industry, and increased taxes.

The serious reader who wishes to understand Chapters 3, 4, and 5 thoroughly should read them twice—first in the order in which they appear and again after reading Appendix A, which contains the full details of the model representing the urban area.

The warning given earlier should be repeated here. The results in these three chapters depend in various ways on the concepts of urban interaction that are built into the simulation model. It is possible that substantial changes in structure might affect the conclusions implied by these computed results. Before accepting the implications as a basis for action, the reader should satisfy himself that the structure adequately represents the urban system and the particular problems with which he is dealing. However (as shown in Appendix B), the system is not highly sensitive to the values chosen for system parameters. Changes as great as factors of 2, 3, or 5 can be made in many of the parameters with only slight effect on the equilibrium conditions of the urban system. Even where the parameters do affect the equilibrium condition of the system, changes in those parameters usually do not affect the direction of policy modifications that lead to improvement.

A specific land area becomes a city because its physical characteristics encourage construction and concentration of business and housing. These economic characteristics causing an urban area to develop are represented in the simulation model by the "normal" coefficients in the flow rates, by the psychological and mobility multipliers which connect the internal structure of the urban system, and by the land multipliers which relate available land to construction of business and housing.

Figure 3-1 shows the changing urban conditions during growth and aging. At the start, when time = 0, the land area is 3% occupied and a normal balance exists between the various activities. In the first stage of its life cycle, the area described in this model develops for 100 years. Between 100 and 200 years there is a period of maturing and internal readjustment. After 200 years there is continuing equilibrium.

READING THE COMPUTER PLOTS AND PRINTED VALUES

Plotted Curves

The curves (as in Figures 3-1*a*, *b*, and *c*) are computer plots showing the behavior of the system variables as generated through time by the simulation model. The horizontal axis is a time scale in years. At the left margin is a line giving the plotting symbols. For example, in Figure 3-1*a*, U = U means that the number of underemployed U is plotted on the graph with the symbol U, WH = W means that worker housing WH is plotted on the graph with the symbol W. The vertical scales at the left of the plot are marked at the top end with the plotting symbols to which they apply. For example, the first scale running from 0 to 600,000 is the scale for the variables plotted with the symbols U, L, P, W, and H. The letter T following the numerical-scale value means thousands. Along the top of the graph the letter groups indicate where curves overlap. For example, in Figure 3-1*a* at time 145, the letters WH, PB mean that the curves for W and H cross and the first symbol W is the one plotted. The curves for P and B cross too and are represented by the first symbol P.

Printed Tabulation

Printed values (as in Figures 3-1*d* and 3-1*e*) give numerical values for the same variables that are plotted and for selected variables not plotted. The printed values appear in blocks. The left column indicates the time associated with the values. The letter groupings at the head of the table give the symbol identifications of the variables in the same grouping pattern as for the numerical values. The fifth column gives line numbers as an aid to matching a letter group in the heading with its numerical value in the table. The variables to the left of the line number column are all measured in thousands. The variables to the right are all measured in units.

In Appendix C is an alphabetical list of definitions with units of measure for each of the symbol groups. In Appendix D is an alphabetical list of variables and constants giving the equation numbers where they are defined. The equation numbers refer to the model equations in Appendix E and the equation descriptions in Appendix A.

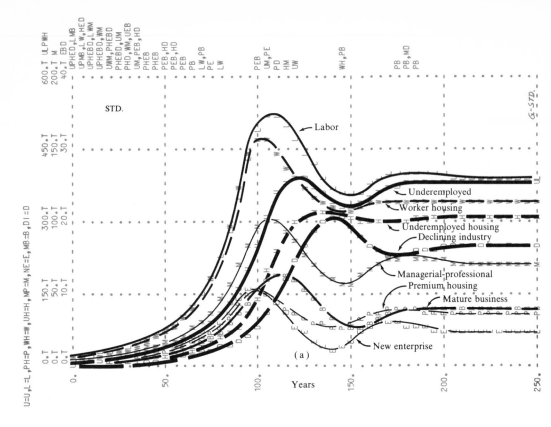

(a)

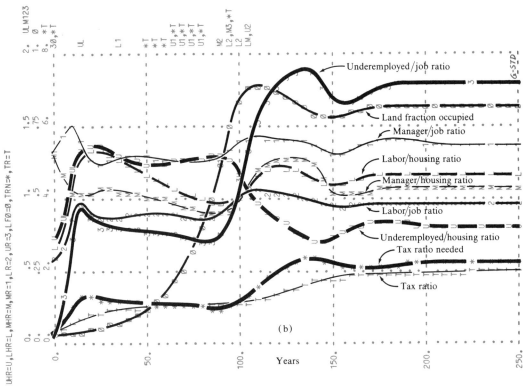

(b)

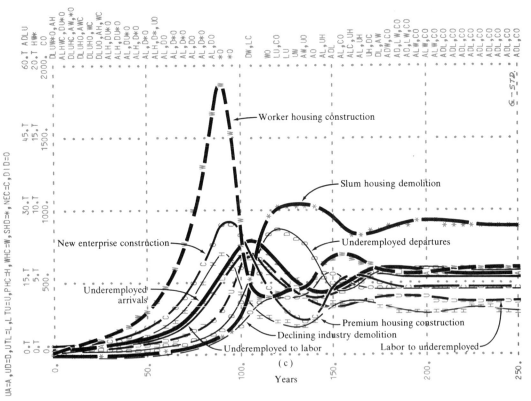

Figure 3-1 Urban development, maturity, and stagnation. Figure 3-1a shows the major levels, Figure 3-1b the important ratios, and Figure 3-1c selected flow rates.

Figure 3-1a plots the nine major system levels: the three categories of personnel, the three economic groups of housing, and the three ages of industry. The first 100 years is a period of internal development and growth in population. A social system contains numerous positive-feedback loops which can generate exponential growth behavior. One of these can be seen in Equation 1 in Section 2.3. The underemployed arrivals UA flow into and increase the number of underemployed U. But the number of underemployed U is one of the variables attracting the arrivals UA. In other words, the arrival rate increases the underemployed, which increases the arrival rate by increasing the size, visibility, activity, and communication channels of the city. This inherent feedback process is present in the arrival rates of other population classes and in the construction rates for housing and industry.

But the positive-feedback loops do not forever remain positive feedback in character. Continued exponential growth is impossible. Size itself changes the conditions of the system and suppresses the positive-feedback behavior. As the particular land area becomes full, the construction land multipliers decline toward zero and suppress new construction. As the economic and housing conditions of

TIME	AV	MB	U		AMM	LAJM	LSM	MSM	SHLM	UMM
	DI	MBD	UA	2	AMMP	LAM	LUM	NEGR	TCM	UMMP
	DID	MD	UD	3	BDM	LAMP	LUR	PEM	TPCR	UR
	DIDP	MP	UH	4	DIDM	LATM	MAHM	PHAM	TR	WHAM
	L	NE	UJ	5	DIEM	LAUM	MAJM	PHEM	TRN	WHEM
	LA	NEC	UJP	6	DILM	LCR	MAM	PHGM	UAMM	WHGM
	LCHP	NECP	UTL	7	EDM	LDM	MAMP	PHGR	UDM	WHGR
	LD	P	UTLN	8	EGM	LEM	MAPM	PHLM	UEM	WHLM
	LDC	PH	UTP	9	ELJM	LFØ	MATM	PHM	UFW	WHM
	LDI	PHC	UW	10	ELM	LHR	MDM	PHØM	UHM	WHØM
	LJ	PHCP	WH	11	EM	LLF	MHR	PHPM	UHPR	WHTM
	LTM	PHØ	WHC	12	EMM	LMM	MLM	PHTM	UHR	WHUM
	LTU	SHD	WHCP	13	ETM	LMMP	MLR	SHAM	UJM	
	MA	SHDP	WHØ	14	LAHM	LR	MR	SHDM	UM	

	thousands				units					
0.	881.	1.000	1.20	1	2.891	2.146	1.789	.386	1.000	2.040
	.100	.032	.760	2	1.000	3.532	1.400	.030	.800	1.000
	.005	.227	.009	3	.650	1.000	11.667	.753	.691	.070
	.000	3.90	1.10	4	1.802	1.117	.700	3.320	.444	.233
	14.00	.200	17.03	5	1.802	1.300	.324	1.240	.411	1.060
	.420	.051	.00	6	1.000	.585	.364	1.240	1.100	1.240
	.000	.000	.107	7	.650	.296	1.000	.030	.368	.030
	.083	113.1	-.092	8	1.240	.815	1.300	.548	.815	.548
	3.12	5.00	.000	9	1.000	.030	1.234	4.066	.893	.244
	20.00	.356	1.07	10	1.045	.667	2.911	.298	1.745	2.006
	23.12	.000	21.00	11	2.386	.014	1.300	1.300	.000	1.117
	.280	.045	.090	12	1.514	.409	1.300	1.117	.727	1.300
	.199	.034	.000	13	1.217	1.000	.279	1.545	2.000	G STD
	.117	.000	.842	14	1.133	.606	1.345	1.545	.063	
50.	3447.	1.772	38.09	1	.618	1.348	1.217	.457	1.000	1.096
	1.121	.074	3.204	2	.557	1.143	1.004	.023	.996	1.050
	.045	.663	1.289	3	.831	1.088	2.018	.862	.828	.781
	.000	15.56	20.46	4	1.338	.997	.991	1.069	1.013	1.487
	76.86	1.859	48.74	5	1.338	1.004	.371	1.185	1.129	1.046
	2.510	.185	.00	6	1.000	.813	.477	1.188	1.118	1.211
	.000	.000	3.286	7	.831	.903	.480	.024	1.692	.026
	1.389	843.6	1.264	8	1.185	.897	1.300	.989	.897	.989
	11.27	25.71	.000	9	.733	.122	.997	1.931	.822	1.867
	74.96	1.211	31.30	10	1.184	1.152	2.129	.526	.421	.730
	86.23	.000	66.70	11	1.478	.026	1.009	1.300	.000	.997
	.786	.406	3.037	12	1.443	.533	1.300	.997	1.241	1.004
	1.971	.330	.000	13	.996	.511	.202	.807	1.525	G STD
	.224	.000	.974	14	.848	.891	1.286	.807	.065	
100.	21790.	10.522	251.53	1	.464	.900	.950	.335	1.129	.840
	5.659	.519	22.514	2	.608	.857	.983	.017	1.011	1.067
	.197	5.582	11.133	3	.987	1.223	1.944	.865	.831	1.118
	.000	97.29	143.31	4	1.158	.992	.987	1.107	1.036	1.096
	489.09	10.857	225.05	5	1.026	.989	.290	1.137	1.173	1.034
	17.941	.841	.00	6	1.129	.917	.369	1.147	1.116	1.173
	.000	.000	20.525	7	.987	1.222	.465	.018	2.213	.022
	11.956	5433.2	3.474	8	1.137	.899	1.300	.539	.899	.539
	38.02	160.01	.000	9	.970	.832	.992	1.004	.765	.704
	431.57	4.419	192.35	10	.603	1.030	2.869	.997	.592	1.304
	469.60	.000	474.80	11	1.031	.036	1.013	1.300	.000	.992
	5.260	4.785	9.187	12	1.565	.391	1.298	.992	1.170	.989
	17.514	2.795	.000	13	.990	.538	.199	.864	.812	G STD
	1.357	.000	12.380	14	.970	1.041	1.387	.975	.065	

(d)

Figure 3-1 (cont.)

thousands				units					
150. 14453.	5.375	334.20	1	.488	1.142	1.089	.426	1.000	.784
19.268	.270	13.614	2	.394	.730	.720	.015	1.274	.708
.576	3.222	13.825	3	1.005	.660	1.065	1.001	1.001	1.703
.000	57.98	306.99	4	.997	.877	.953	1.375	1.766	1.334
356.05	3.545	196.21	5	.997	.813	.351	1.116	2.244	1.029
7.052	.515	.00	6	1.000	.864	.381	1.036	.874	.975
.000	.000	13.932	7	1.005	1.454	.305	.004	2.068	-.003
10.354	5099.8	3.610	8	1.116	1.001	1.300	.853	1.001	.853
28.36	92.31	.000	9	.942	.778	.877	1.547	.589	.814
344.22	3.702	196.85	10	.766	1.104	2.778	.686	1.748	1.178
372.58	.000	322.43	11	.993	.028	1.047	1.300	.000	.877
2.976	1.900	6.806	12	1.474	.522	1.226	.877	.726	.813
10.049	9.508	.000	13	.836	.418	.163	1.548	.319	G
.530	.000	7.596	14	.896	.956	1.312	1.548	.039	STD
250. 16351.	7.804	377.23	1	.449	1.087	1.055	.344	1.060	.802
16.473	.464	17.273	2	.449	.624	.712	.000	1.283	.802
.464	4.845	17.415	3	1.190	.626	1.041	1.136	1.113	1.809
.000	71.22	309.85	4	.940	.856	.932	1.546	1.951	1.543
392.86	4.884	208.56	5	.886	.808	.296	1.000	2.245	1.000
7.381	.463	.00	6	1.060	.878	.307	1.000	.935	1.000
.000	.000	16.857	7	1.190	1.678	.308	.000	2.308	-.000
13.186	5731.1	5.500	8	1.000	1.068	1.300	.624	1.068	.624
24.43	111.11	.000	9	.934	.815	.856	1.075	.557	.666
379.46	3.146	210.26	10	.655	1.170	3.402	.948	1.527	1.351
403.89	.000	335.84	11	.768	.029	1.068	1.300	.000	.856
3.647	3.161	5.897	12	1.556	.464	1.263	.856	.812	.808
11.357	9.048	.000	13	.808	.464	.181	1.377	.276	G
.658	.000	9.072	14	.830	.973	1.380	1.460	.045	STD

(e)

Figure 3-1 (cont.)

the system change, the arrival rates of people into the area are reduced and the departure rates increased until the numbers of people stabilize.

In Figure 3-1a the growth period ends at 100 years. New enterprise and premium housing have reached a peak, and the managerial-professional population, worker housing, and labor are nearly at a maximum. Figure 3-1c shows several important flow rates. By year 100 the worker-housing-construction boom has ended. The premium-housing-construction rate has declined substantially from its peak. At year 100 the urban area is at the end of its first construction phase. As shown in Figure 3-1b, land area has been almost fully utilized. (Remember that the model system is dealing with a fixed land area. The area is best thought of as a section of one of our older cities, not as the entire area within the political boundary.)

But immediately after year 100 the area begins to age. Its land is filled. New construction is suppressed by lack of land within the fixed and fully occupied area. New enterprise settles into mature business and deteriorates into declining industry. Premium housing and worker housing, which had reached a peak at 100 years, are aging, and as they decline in condition they feed the rising level of underemployed housing, which peaks at about 130 years.

The minimum in many of the curves in Figure 3-1a, occurring at about 150

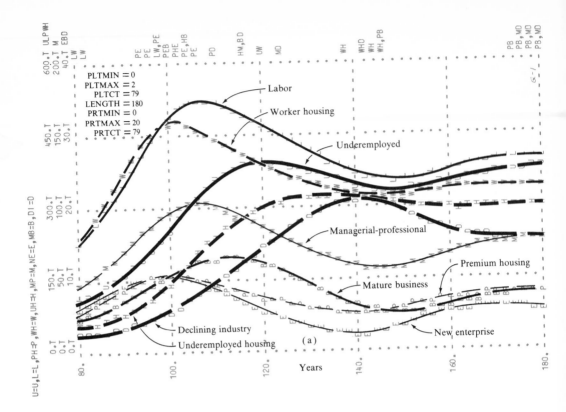

PLTMIN = 0
PLTMAX = 2
PLTCT = 79
LENGTH = 180
PRTMIN = 0
PRTMAX = 20
PRTCT = 79

Labor

Worker housing

Underemployed

Managerial-professional

Premium housing

Mature business

Declining industry

Underemployed housing

New enterprise

(a)

Years

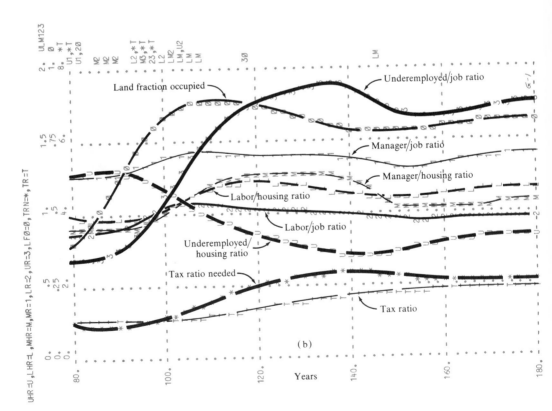

Land fraction occupied

Underemployed/job ratio

Manager/job ratio

Manager/housing ratio

Labor/housing ratio

Labor/job ratio

Underemployed/
housing ratio

Tax ratio needed

Tax ratio

(b)

Years

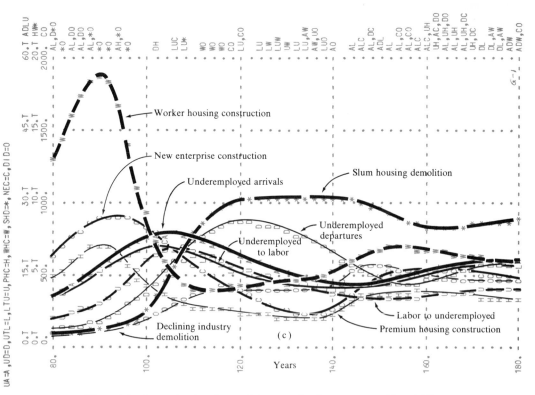

Figure 3-2 Stagnation in urban activity occurring between years 80 and 180.

years, is partly caused by the growth multipliers in the model that represent speculative and historical influences. The rapid growth prior to year 100 caused some overshoot in the amount of construction. The depression and despondency occurring between years 100 and 140 suppressed building below the normal equilibrium values. By year 200 a stable and continuing equilibrium has been established.

This model contains no random influences, so equilibrium becomes a continuing set of static values. In an actual system economic cycles external to the area, various technological innovations, and world events would cause a continuing state of fluctuation around these equilibrium values.

Figure 3-2 shows a section of the same urban behavior as Figure 3-1 but on an expanded time scale for the period from year 80 to year 180. In Figure 3-2*a* are a succession of peaks occurring as the land area fills, growth falters, and the city settles into equilibrium. The growth phase is terminated by the filling of the land area, as seen in Figure 3-2*b* where the land fraction occupied rises from .4 in year 80 to .8 in year 100. In Figure 3-2*a* the peak in new enterprise occurs just before year 100. Time causes a shift of new enterprise into the mature-business category, which peaks at year 112. The aging and deterioration of mature business causes an increase in declining industry, which peaks at year 140.

A similar succession of peaks appears in the population mix of the area but

TIME	AV	MB	U		AMM	LAJM	LSM	MSM	SHLM	UMM
	DI	MBD	UA	2	AMMP	LAM	LUM	NEGR	TCM	UMMP
	DID	MD	UD	3	BDM	LAMP	LUR	PEM	TPCR	UR
	DIDP	MP	UH	4	DIDM	LATM	MAHM	PHAM	TR	WHAM
	L	NE	UJ	5	DIEM	LAUM	MAJM	PHEM	TRN	WHEM
	LA	NEC	UJP	6	DILM	LCR	MAM	PHGM	UAMM	WHGM
	LCHP	NECP	UTL	7	EDM	LDM	MAMP	PHGR	UDM	WHGR
	LD	P	UTLN	8	EGM	LEM	MAPM	PHLM	UEM	WHLM
	LDC	PH	UTP	9	ELJM	LFØ	MATM	PHM	UFW	WHM
	LDI	PHC	UW	10	ELM	LHR	MDM	PHØM	UHM	WHØM
	LJ	PHCP	WH	11	EM	LLF	MHR	PHPM	UHPR	WHTM
	LTM	PHØ	WHC	12	EMM	LMM	MLM	PHTM	UHR	WHUM
	LTU	SHD	WHCP	13	ETM	LMMP	MLR	SHAM	UJM	
	MA	SHDP	WHØ	14	LAHM	LR	MR	SHDM	UM	

	thousands				units					
80.	10923.	4.735	106.59	1	.684	1.399	1.249	.492	1.000	1.238
	2.412	.179	10.735	2	.640	1.427	1.029	.030	.971	1.191
	.108	1.747	3.296	3	.755	1.292	2.145	.951	.939	.710
	.000	45.36	55.61	4	1.490	.989	1.037	.702	1.054	.979
	228.63	6.052	150.10	5	1.490	1.029	.394	1.242	1.003	1.061
	8.860	.645	.00	6	1.000	.800	.526	1.245	1.156	1.251
	.000	.000	10.526	7	.755	.744	.511	.031	1.546	.031
	3.401	2451.3	4.594	8	1.242	.963	1.300	1.792	.963	1.792
	44.99	83.38	.000	9	.707	.396	.989	2.500	.829	2.367
	216.18	5.005	88.36	10	1.448	.992	1.925	.436	.378	.652
	261.16	.000	230.38	11	1.764	.025	.907	1.300	.000	.989
	2.655	1.091	13.091	12	1.408	.614	1.297	.989	1.278	1.029
	5.720	.865	.000	13	.985	.581	.198	.778	1.648	ʚ~
	.695	.000	3.004	14	1.003	.875	1.257	.778	.070	
100.	21790.	10.522	251.53	1	.464	.900	.950	.335	1.129	.840
	5.659	.519	22.514	2	.608	.857	.983	.017	1.011	1.067
	.197	5.582	11.133	3	.987	1.223	1.944	.865	.831	1.118
	.000	97.29	143.31	4	1.158	.992	.987	1.107	1.036	1.096
	489.09	10.857	225.05	5	1.026	.989	.290	1.137	1.173	1.034
	17.941	.841	.00	6	1.129	.917	.369	1.147	1.116	1.173
	.000	.000	20.525	7	.987	1.222	.465	.018	2.213	.022
	11.956	5433.2	3.474	8	1.137	.899	1.300	.539	.899	.539
	38.02	160.01	.000	9	.970	.832	.992	1.004	.765	.704
	431.57	4.419	192.35	10	.603	1.030	2.869	.997	.592	1.304
	469.60	.000	474.80	11	1.031	.036	1.013	1.300	.000	.992
	5.260	4.785	9.187	12	1.565	.391	1.298	.992	1.170	.989
	17.514	2.795	.000	13	.990	.538	.199	.864	.812	ʚ~
	1.357	.000	12.380	14	.970	1.041	1.387	.975	.065	
120.	18611.	12.150	390.01	1	.318	.920	.960	.326	1.329	.636
	14.454	.889	19.119	2	.443	.566	.764	-.042	1.215	.713
	.416	6.668	25.720	3	1.464	.774	1.213	.823	.779	1.764
	.000	85.37	301.09	4	.959	.937	.744	3.038	1.336	1.708
	472.95	5.614	221.13	5	.722	.843	.284	.666	2.047	.875
	10.989	.384	.00	6	1.329	.913	.258	.870	.950	.935
	.000	.000	15.867	7	1.464	1.820	.295	-.016	3.297	-.008
	17.220	6384.6	-.607	8	.666	.867	1.300	.369	.867	.369
	18.54	113.28	.000	9	1.089	.866	.937	.793	.571	.408
	439.07	2.462	222.66	10	.502	1.221	3.905	1.334	1.382	1.717
	457.61	.000	387.29	11	.525	.035	1.256	1.300	.000	.937
	3.702	4.532	4.328	12	1.574	.357	1.261	.937	.864	.843
	16.408	10.186	.000	13	.917	.391	.181	1.273	.295	ʚ~
	.755	.000	13.297	14	.779	1.034	1.395	1.692	.046	

(d)

Figure 3-2 (cont.)

thousands				units					
140. 14070.	6.463	343.17	1	.363	.995	.997	.350	1.000	.675
20.971	.490	13.235	2	.372	.627	.722	-.064	1.270	.662
.434	4.464	20.006	3	1.515	.638	1.074	.917	.896	1.870
.000	58.88	324.47	4	.690	.889	.773	2.816	1.672	1.415
368.66	2.234	183.49	5	.690	.815	.300	.489	2.366	.808
7.059	.255	.00	6	1.000	.901	.268	.853	.879	.933
.000	.000	12.235	7	1.515	1.672	.260	-.018	2.915	-.008
12.328	5251.8	.807	8	.489	.938	1.300	.769	.938	.769
16.49	79.98	.000	9	1.024	.790	.889	1.043	.539	.594
351.33	2.254	184.95	10	.730	1.130	3.790	.970	1.790	1.450
367.82	.000	326.38	11	.482	.030	1.227	1.300	.000	.889
2.793	2.327	5.240	12	1.550	.401	1.219	.889	.705	.815
11.178	10.317	.000	13	.852	.379	.160	1.590	.252	$\varsigma\sim$
.459	.000	9.465	14	.870	1.002	1.375	1.590	.040	
160. 15931.	6.140	349.17	1	.512	1.149	1.093	.398	1.000	.824
16.728	.320	16.004	2	.441	.716	.724	.024	1.268	.776
.489	3.905	13.713	3	1.043	.696	1.079	1.082	1.068	1.673
.000	67.16	295.20	4	.974	.872	.967	1.263	1.807	1.399
376.79	5.328	208.65	5	.974	.816	.332	1.190	2.135	1.048
7.867	.545	.00	6	1.000	.863	.364	1.086	.899	1.011
.000	.000	16.205	7	1.043	1.482	.354	.011	1.964	.001
11.166	5389.9	5.519	8	1.190	1.041	1.300	.735	1.041	.735
29.28	108.36	.000	9	.889	.795	.872	1.361	.598	.775
365.93	3.817	208.79	10	.715	1.125	2.908	.778	1.592	1.220
395.21	.000	335.02	11	.942	.028	1.033	1.300	.000	.872
3.590	2.529	6.721	12	1.502	.521	1.256	.872	.789	.816
10.602	8.401	.000	13	.830	.476	.178	1.423	.331	$\varsigma\sim$
.714	.000	8.175	14	.875	.953	1.335	1.423	.042	
180. 16972.	8.156	376.62	1	.440	1.071	1.044	.333	1.094	.791
15.633	.487	17.883	2	.458	.624	.722	.001	1.270	.799
.453	5.148	17.785	3	1.193	.664	1.074	1.096	1.080	1.773
.000	75.04	302.88	4	.967	.867	.935	1.520	1.851	1.559
404.64	5.514	212.38	5	.884	.815	.288	1.005	2.164	1.001
8.060	.482	.00	6	1.094	.882	.304	1.021	.935	1.007
.000	.000	17.102	7	1.193	1.678	.322	.003	2.361	.001
13.582	5816.0	5.363	8	1.005	1.048	1.300	.583	1.048	.583
24.83	117.43	.000	9	.937	.823	.867	1.024	.568	.647
388.95	3.184	213.92	10	.630	1.175	3.430	.983	1.479	1.376
413.78	.000	344.49	11	.765	.029	1.065	1.300	.000	.867
3.784	3.461	5.903	12	1.567	.443	1.271	.867	.829	.815
11.782	8.891	.000	13	.823	.468	.185	1.342	.291	$\varsigma\sim$
.726	.000	9.478	14	.825	.978	1.390	1.468	.045	

(e)

Figure 3-2 (cont.)

for different reasons. In Figure 3-2*a* the labor and managerial categories peak at year 105. They have ceased to increase because the business units which provide jobs have already peaked. However, at year 100 there are still ample lower-skill jobs available for the underemployed, underemployed housing is still rising, and the area appears to be attractive. There is a delay in perception by the underemployed of urban attractiveness, so the inward flow continues, with a peak in the underemployed category occurring at year 120.

Housing follows a similar pattern. Premium housing and worker housing reach peaks at year 100. But the aging and decay of worker housing into underemployed housing delays the peak in underemployed housing until year 130.

The underemployed/job ratio UR in Figure 3-2*b* rises rapidly between years 90 and 130. In the time interval from year 100 to year 120 the underemployed jobs UJ have declined from 225,000 to 221,000, while the number of underemployed has risen from 251,000 to 390,000. It is in this time interval that the economic pressure on the underemployed group becomes sufficiently high to reduce the inflow of underemployed to the city and stabilize the population. During this interval from 100 to 120 years, Figure 3-2*b* shows a reversal of the roles of housing and jobs for the underemployed. Jobs, as shown by the rising underemployed/job ratio, are becoming less available. At the same time, housing, as shown by the falling underemployed/housing ratio, is becoming more available. The increase in housing is generated by the deterioration of the older parts of the city into a housing category no longer acceptable to the managerial and labor classes. At the same time construction of new industry has slowed or declined, and there has been a rise in the labor/job ratio LR. As jobs for skilled labor become less available, jobs requiring less skill are taken by more skilled labor, leaving even fewer jobs for the underemployed. Shifting conditions within the urban area are summarized in Figure 3-3, giving the attractiveness-for-migration multiplier AMM and its components at year 80 and at year 140. In the last column the values for the year 140 are given as a fraction of the values at year 80. The attractiveness multiplier AMM is the product of the four components also given in the table. The multiplier AMM declines to about half during the time interval. Upward economic mobility from the underemployed into the labor class as given by UAMM has become somewhat less favorable. On the other hand, the underemployed/housing multiplier UHM has risen by a factor of 4.7. The urban area has shifted from a shortage to an excess of housing for the underemployed. Because the capacity of the area is limited in absorbing the underemployed, some of the multipliers must fall to low enough values to generate the low attractiveness required to stabilize the population. The underemployed/job multiplier UJM carries the main burden of reducing attractiveness. The value of UJM at year 140 is only .15 of its value at year 80. In other words, the underemployed flood into the area until their falling economic circumstances act as a brake on further inward migration.

	At Year 80	At Year 140	140/80
AMM, Attractiveness-for-migration multiplier	.68	.36	.53
Components of AMM:			
UAMM, Underemployed-arrivals-mobility multiplier	1.16	.88	.76
UHM, Underemployed/housing multiplier	.38	1.79	4.7
PEM, Public-expenditure multiplier	.95	.92	.97
UJM, Underemployed/job multiplier	1.65	.25	.15

Figure 3-3   Changes in multipliers that influence underemployed arrivals.

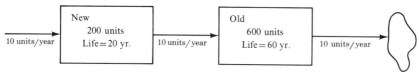

Figure 3-4 Number of units in each age category is proportional to average life.

Figure 3-3 shows the urban processes that limit inward migration and establish a population equilibrium. During the initial growth phase the area is attractive and can accept additional population. But if carried far enough, the influx of people overcrowds the area, reduces the attractiveness, reduces the population inflow, and increases the outflow until population growth stops. By this process population rises and falls to maintain the attractiveness of the area in balance with that of the surrounding environment.

The change in economic circumstances that occurs while growth is giving way to stagnation is caused by the changing proportions of people, housing, and industry. During the growth stage new construction outruns the aging process so that the decaying part of a city is little noticed in relation to the ever rising new construction. But as the land area becomes filled, new construction can take place only as the old is demolished. An equilibrium is established in which the demolition rates and construction rates must be the same.

In the equilibrium state the proportions of old and new depend on the average lifetime in each age category (as in Figure 3-4). Suppose houses are built at the rate of ten units per year to enter the new category. If the average life in the new category is 20 years, the total number of new units will, in equilibrium, be the product of the construction rate and the average life. Similarly, if the system is in equilibrium, the number of units per year passing from the new category to the old category must be the same as the construction rate. Note that the number leaving the category is the number in the category divided by the life. If the units in the old category remain an average of 60 years, the number of old units will be the average life multiplied by the flow rate, or 600 units. Because the system is in equilibrium, the discard rate from the old category must also be the flow rate of 10 units per year, which is 600 old units divided by 60 years. As shown in the figure, the number of units in each category is proportional to the average time the unit stays in the category.

In a city, if business units and housing stand in a declining condition for more years than they serve at high economic effectiveness, the old will dominate the landscape. Because the condition of buildings tends to determine the economic status of the occupants, an excess of old buildings causes a high proportion of marginal business and unskilled and unemployed people.

In Figure 3-1*a* the commercial activity is eventually dominated by the declining-industry category. The cause is found in the average lifetime of a business unit in each of the three categories. In equilibrium at 250 years, the system of

Figure 3-1*a* is operating with an average life of 10.5 years* in the new-enterprise category, 17 years in the mature-business category, and 36 years in the declining-industry category. In equilibrium the numbers of units will be in the same proportion. If the less effective declining category persists for a greater number of years than was its life in the productive category, the declining units usurp the land area.

In a similar way worker housing at the 250th year in Figure 3-1*a* is showing an average life of 37 years, while underemployed housing has an average life of 35 years. This accounts for their nearly equal proportions in the equilibrium condition. The numbers of units being proportional to the lifetime in each category assumes, of course, that the same flow occurs through each category. Were there a direct construction of underemployed housing, as in a low-cost-housing program, this would increase the underemployed housing beyond that indicated by average lifetime.

Figures 3-1 and 3-2 may not be of great concern to one interested in solving the problems of an urban area that is already fully developed. The years over which the area developed are history. Today's problems extend from the present into the future. In later chapters model runs dealing with changes in urban programs will start from the equilibrium conditions finally reached in Figure 3-1.

But the dynamics of the entire life cycle in this chapter are important in clarifying the process of urban stagnation. Furthermore, the life cycle behavior permits one of the many tests of model validity we can use to establish confidence in the model. If the model operates satisfactorily, beginning with a nearly empty land area, growing, and stabilizing in a sequence of events characteristic of a real-life area, it has passed one of many available tests.

---

*Equation 111 in Appendix A gives the transfer rate from the new-enterprise category into mature business. The fraction per year transferred is NEDN, having a value of .08, multiplied by the enterprise-decline multiplier EDM. The value of the latter is given in Figure 3-1*e* as 1.19. The product of these two is .095, which is the reciprocal of the average life, giving a life of 10.5 years. Likewise, MBDN multiplied by BDM as in Equation 114 indicates a 17-year life for mature-business units. The reciprocal of DIDN times DIDM as in Equation 117 yields a 36-year life in the declining-industry category.

4 Failures in Urban Programs

The preceding chapter has shown the normal processes of aging that change the proportions of housing, industry, and people toward an economically unhealthy combination. The consequences appear as slum areas, high tax rates, flight of industry to the suburbs, and mounting welfare rolls.

During the past three decades many different urban-management programs have been inaugurated in an effort to ameliorate these conditions. Creation of jobs, job training, financial aid to the cities, and low-cost-housing construction all have been undertaken in an effort to improve the situation of the underemployed. Most of these programs appear to have failed; in fact, conditions in the cities seem to have worsened. As conditions became more critical, greater emphasis was placed on corrective action, but even so the situation continued to deteriorate. Is it possible that these programs are neutral in effect or even detrimental?

The model of urban behavior has been equipped to simulate various classical urban-management programs (see Equations 140 through 150 in Appendix A). With these a job program for the underemployed can be introduced, underemployed training can be provided, tax expenditures for welfare and education can be subsidized, and a low-cost-housing program can generate housing directly for the underemployed category of the population.

To explore these urban-management programs, the computer runs will start from the equilibrium conditions existing at the end of Figure 3-1. The conditions at year 250 in that figure are the ones used for the time interval from -5 to 0 years in the following simulation runs.* The new management programs are introduced at time $= 0$ and their effects over the following 50 years are plotted.

4.1 Job Program

Figure 4-1 shows the effect of introducing at time $= 0$ an underemployed-job program. At time $= 0$, jobs for 10% of the total underemployed population are

*The initial conditions for the simulation runs that start in equilibrium are given in Appendix A, Section A. 14.

51

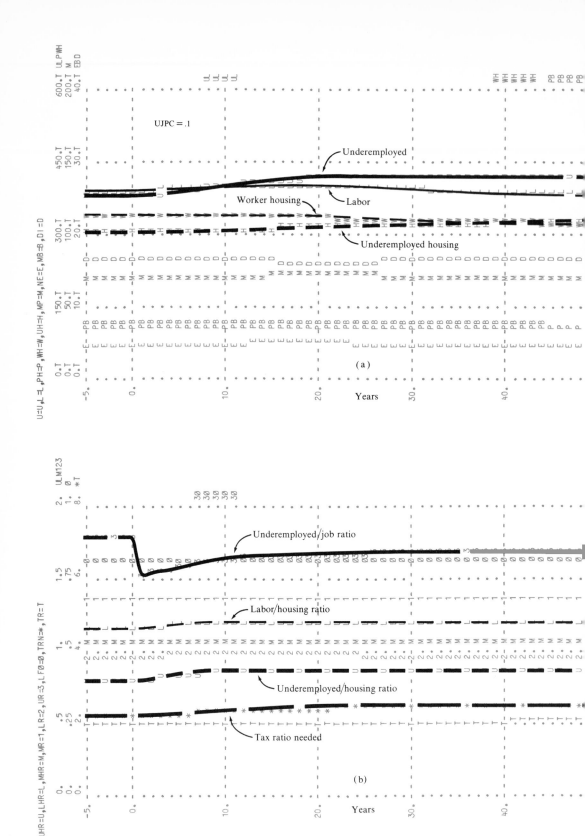

(a)

(b)

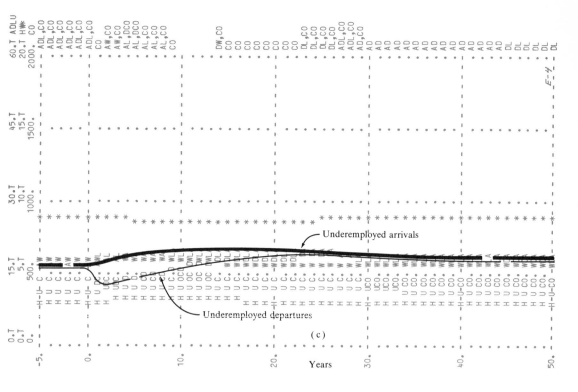

Figure 4-1   Jobs created for 10% of the underemployed.

suddenly created. This is done, not by changing the commercial and industrial conditions in the area, but by some artificial process such as transporting people to jobs elsewhere or creating public-service types of work. In the model jobs created by the underemployed-job program UJP are added directly to the underemployed jobs UJ that otherwise exist within the system (see Equation 136 in Appendix A). The effect is to decrease the underemployed/job ratio UR and to increase the underemployed/job multiplier UJM (Equation 10), which is one of the attractiveness multipliers influencing underemployed migration into the city.

At first glance Figure 4-1 shows little change resulting from the underemployed-job program, but more careful examination discloses several unfavorable changes in the composition of the urban area. In Figure 4-1a the total number of underemployed has increased. Underemployed housing has increased while worker housing has decreased. In Figure 4-1b the sudden improvement (decrease) in the underemployed/job ratio resulting at time = 0 from newly available jobs is largely dissipated over the next 20 years, even though the job program for 10% of the underemployed is continued throughout the entire 50-year period. The underemployed/housing ratio and the labor/housing ratio both become slightly higher, indicating more crowding. Figure 4-1c shows an increase over the first 10 years in the underemployed-arrival rate and a decrease in the underemployed-departure rate. The excess of arrivals over departures persists until conditions

TIME										
	AV	MB	U	1	AMM	LAJM	LSM	MSM	SHLM	UMM
	DI	MBD	UA	2	AMMP	LAM	LUM	NEGR	TCM	UMMP
	DID	MD	UD	3	BDM	LAMP	LUR	PEM	TPCR	UR
	DIDP	MP	UH	4	DIDM	LATM	MAHM	PHAM	TR	WHAM
	L	NE	UJ	5	DIEM	LAUM	MAJM	PHEM	TRN	WHEM
	LA	NEC	WP	6	DILM	LCR	MAM	PHGM	UAMM	WHGM
	LCHP	NECP	UTL	7	EDM	LDM	MAMP	PHGR	UDM	WHGR
	LD	P	UTLN	8	EGM	LEM	MAPM	PHLM	UEM	WHLM
	LDC	PH	UTP	9	ELJM	LFØ	MATM	PHM	UFW	WHM
	LDI	PHC	UW	10	ELM	LHR	MDM	PHØM	UHM	WHØM
	LJ	PHCP	WH	11	EM	LLF	MHR	PHPM	UHPR	WHTM
	LTM	PHØ	WHC	12	EMM	LMM	MLM	PHTM	UHR	WHUM
	LTU	SHD	WHCP	13	ETM	LMMP	MLR	SHAM	WM	
	MA	SHDP	WHØ	14	LAHM	LR	MR	SHDM	UM	

- - - - - - - -

	thousands				units					
-5.	16336.	7.806	377.31	1	.452	1.087	1.054	.344	1.060	.805
	16.474	.465	17.283	2	.449	.623	.712	.000	1.284	.802
	.464	4.849	17.275	3	1.190	.625	1.040	1.145	1.121	1.811
	.000	71.13	310.08	4	.939	.854	.931	1.549	1.966	1.542
	392.55	4.866	208.35	5	.886	.808	.296	1.000	2.248	1.000
	7.360	.462	.00	6	1.060	.878	.306	1.000	.936	1.000
	.000	.000	16.847	7	1.190	1.681	.307	.000	2.289	.000
	13.201	5729.4	5.497	8	1.000	1.073	1.300	.625	1.073	.625
	24.38	110.94	.000	9	.935	.815	.854	1.075	.557	.665
	379.15	3.142	210.06	10	.655	1.170	3.408	.948	1.529	1.352
	403.53	.000	335.65	11	.768	.029	1.069	1.300	.000	.854
	3.643	3.155	5.885	12	1.556	.466	1.262	.854	.811	.808
	11.349	9.054	.000	13	.805	.464	.181	1.378	.276	
	.655	.000	9.075	14	.830	.973	1.380	1.460	.045	

- - - - - - - -

	thousands				units					
10.	16425.	7.815	402.46	1	.496	1.026	1.016	.348	1.076	.747
	16.415	.459	19.700	2	.490	.567	.699	.002	1.301	.780
	.475	4.849	16.250	3	1.173	.605	.999	1.101	1.084	1.643
	.000	71.41	311.80	4	.964	.853	.928	1.576	1.977	1.607
	402.01	4.961	244.88	5	.896	.800	.299	1.012	2.379	1.003
	7.300	.484	40.25	6	1.076	.893	.308	1.001	.946	1.004
	.000	.000	19.065	7	1.173	1.817	.307	.000	2.019	.000
	14.611	5988.8	7.171	8	1.012	1.051	1.300	.604	1.051	.604
	24.73	111.03	.000	9	.969	.819	.853	1.070	.607	.667
	380.59	3.183	244.27	10	.643	1.190	3.395	.952	1.391	1.350
	405.31	.000	337.91	11	.786	.030	1.072	1.300	.000	.853
	3.715	3.170	6.041	12	1.552	.460	1.255	.853	.861	.800
	11.929	8.585	.000	13	.804	.462	.178	1.279	.343	↳↗
	.657	.000	9.124	14	.810	.992	1.376	1.377	.045	

- - - - - - - -

	thousands				units					
50.	15882.	7.556	416.79	1	.466	1.073	1.046	.345	1.053	.737
	16.653	.459	18.714	2	.467	.563	.661	-.003	1.347	.736
	.459	4.755	18.311	3	1.214	.563	.922	1.132	1.110	1.709
	.000	68.78	325.58	4	.918	.841	.928	1.577	2.091	1.605
	384.44	4.529	243.82	5	.872	.769	.297	.978	2.566	.992
	6.492	.436	41.68	6	1.053	.882	.301	.990	.924	.992
	.000	.000	18.014	7	1.214	1.828	.300	-.001	2.197	-.001
	14.054	5984.8	6.827	8	.978	1.066	1.300	.633	1.066	.633
	23.00	106.92	.000	9	.948	.813	.841	1.057	.587	.653
	370.46	2.988	244.73	10	.660	1.189	3.457	.960	1.410	1.368
	393.46	.000	323.34	11	.743	.029	1.072	1.300	.000	.841
	3.532	3.080	5.587	12	1.555	.463	1.258	.841	.853	.777
	11.180	8.868	.000	13	.781	.459	.179	1.293	.316	↳↗
	.619	.000	8.846	14	.811	.977	1.379	1.362	.044	

- - - - - - - -

(d)

Figure 4-1 (cont.)

in the area become sufficiently more unfavorable to counterbalance the attractiveness of the underemployed-job program.

Figure 4-2 summarizes the principal changes. The underemployed have risen 10%. Jobs, including those created by the job program, have risen 17%. The underemployed/job ratio has improved by declining 5.5%. Even so, the excess of underemployed beyond the underemployed jobs (U − UJ) has increased 2%. Underemployed housing has increased while worker housing has decreased. The number in the labor category has decreased and the ratio of labor to underemployed has fallen by 12%. Both underemployed housing and labor housing are more crowded. The taxes needed have risen 14% because of the increase in underemployed workers and the decrease in taxable property, as reflected in the 8% decrease in new enterprise and the 3% decrease in mature business. Although declining industry and underemployed housing have increased somewhat, they do not represent much contribution to tax revenue.

Although the changes created are relatively small, they are nearly all in an unfavorable direction. They occur primarily because the slightly improved underemployed/job ratio UR has attracted more underemployed people. This has put more pressure on underemployed housing and has reduced the slum-housing-

	Variable	Symbol	Time (years)		Change (%)
			−5	50	
a.	Underemployed-job program	UJP	0	41,700	—
b.	Underemployed jobs	UJ	208,400	243,800	+17.
c.	U-UJ		168,900	173,000	+2.
d.	UJ-UJP		208,400	202,100	−3.
e.	Underemployed mobility	UM	.045	.044	−2.
f.	L/U		1.04	.92	−12.
1.	New enterprise	NE	4,900	4,500	−8.
2.	Mature business	MB	7,800	7,600	−3.
3.	Declining industry	DI	16,500	16,700	+1.
4.	Premium housing	PH	110,900	106,900	−4.
5.	Worker housing	WH	335,600	323,300	−4.
6.	Underemployed housing	UH	310,100	325,600	+5.
7.	Managerial-professional	MP	71,100	68,800	−3.
8.	Labor	L	392,600	384,400	−2.
9.	Underemployed	U	377,300	416,800	+10.
10.	Manager/housing ratio	MHR	1.07	1.07	0
11.	Labor/housing ratio	LHR	1.17	1.19	+2.
12.	Underemployed/housing ratio	UHR	.81	.85	+5.
13.	Manager/job ratio	MR	1.38	1.38	0
14.	Labor/job ratio	LR	.97	.98	+1.
15.	Underemployed/job ratio	UR	1.81	1.71	−6.
16.	Tax ratio needed	TRN	2.25	2.57	+14.
17.	Underemployed to labor net	UTLN	5,500	6,830	+24.

Figure 4-2 Changes caused by an underemployed-job program (UJPC = .1).

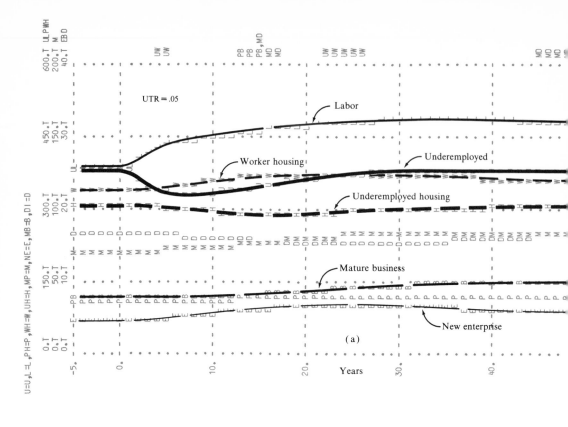

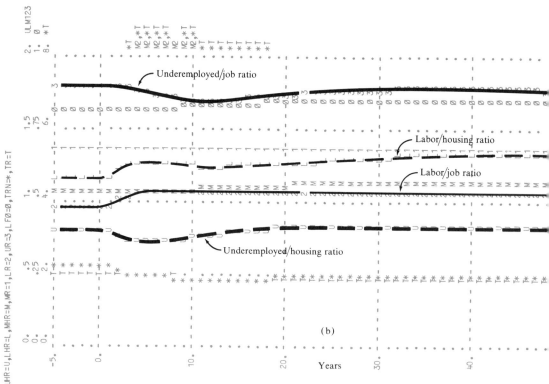

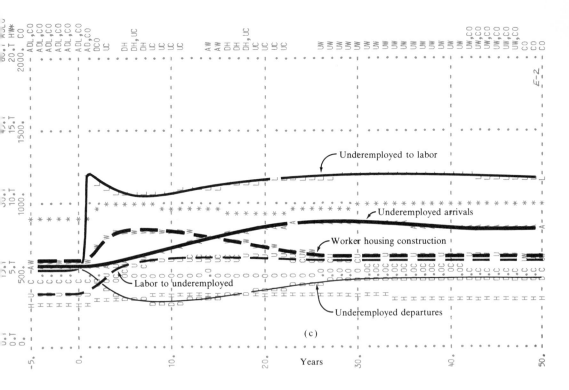

Figure 4-3 An underemployed-training program that moves 5% of the underemployed per year into the labor category.

abandoned multiplier SHAM, thereby increasing the average life of underemployed housing. A larger number of underemployed increase the tax requirements, which slightly discourages the construction of new enterprise.

4.2 Training Program

Another possible remedy for urban decay is a training program to upgrade the skills of the underemployed. Figure 4-3 shows the effect of an underemployed-training program that transforms 5% per year of the underemployed into the labor category. This transformation is done in the model system by an outside influence that simply takes people from the underemployed category and puts them into the labor category. The feasibility and mechanics of doing this are not part of the model. Nor are the costs of doing so levied against the tax system in the model. Conditions are therefore taken as highly idealized: the educational process works, and it costs nothing. Even under these favorable circumstances the improvement is far from dramatic. Figure 4-3*a* shows that the number of underemployed declines for ten years and then rises again to about its original value. Men in the labor category increase. Housing remains nearly constant, and there are some increases in new enterprise and mature business.

TIME	AV	MB	U		AMM	LAJM	LSM	MSM	SHLM	UMM
	DI	MBD	UA	2	AMMP	LAM	LUM	NEGR	TCM	UMMP
	DI D	MD	UD	3	BDM	LAMP	LUR	PEM	TPCR	UR
	DI DP	MP	UH	4	DI DM	LATM	MAHM	PHAM	TR	WHAM
	L	NE	UJ	5	DIEM	LAUM	MAJM	PHEM	TRN	WHEM
	LA	NEC	UJP	6	DI LM	LCR	MAM	PHGM	UAMM	WHGM
	LCHP	NECP	UTL	7	EDM	LDM	MAMP	PHGR	UDM	WHGR
	LD	P	UTLN	8	EGM	LEM	MAPM	PHLM	UEM	WHLM
	LDC	PH	UTP	9	ELJM	LFØ	MATM	PHM	UFW	WHM
	LDI	PHC	UW	10	ELM	LHR	MDM	PHØM	UHM	WHØM
	LJ	PHCP	WH	11	EM	LLF	MHR	PHPM	UHPR	WHTM
	LTM	PHØ	WHC	12	EMM	LMM	MLM	PHTM	UHR	WHUM
	LTU	SHD	WHCP	13	ETM	LMMP	MLR	SHAM	UJM	
	MA	SHDP	WHØ	14	LAHM	LR	MR	SHDM	UM	

	thousands				units					
-5.	16336.	7.806	377.31	1	.452	1.087	1.054	.344	1.060	.805
	16.474	.465	17.283	2	.449	.623	.712	.000	1.284	.802
	.464	4.849	17.275	3	1.190	.625	1.040	1.145	1.121	1.811
	.000	71.13	310.08	4	.939	.854	.931	1.549	1.966	1.542
	392.55	4.866	208.35	5	.886	.808	.296	1.000	2.248	1.000
	7.360	.462	.00	6	1.060	.878	.306	1.000	.936	1.000
	.000	.000	16.847	7	1.190	1.681	.307	.000	2.289	.000
	13.201	5729.4	5.497	8	1.000	1.073	1.300	.625	1.073	.625
	24.38	110.94	.000	9	.935	.815	.854	1.075	.557	.665
	379.15	3.142	210.06	10	.655	1.170	3.408	.948	1.529	1.352
	403.53	.000	335.65	11	.768	.029	1.069	1.300	.000	.854
	3.643	3.155	5.885	12	1.556	.466	1.262	.854	.811	.808
	11.349	9.054	.000	13	.805	.464	.181	1.378	.276	
	.655	.000	9.075	14	.830	.973	1.380	1.460	.045	
10.	17027.	7.930	334.85	1	.758	.835	.918	.366	1.108	.799
	16.076	.423	20.690	2	.528	.466	.802	.010	1.164	.796
	.513	4.869	9.372	3	1.067	.557	1.341	1.171	1.142	1.711
	.000	73.72	295.66	4	1.064	.858	.917	1.665	1.926	1.803
	449.07	5.550	195.70	5	.960	.868	.311	1.078	1.910	1.019
	7.504	.606	.00	6	1.108	.927	.318	1.014	1.216	1.037
	.000	.000	32.375	7	1.067	2.198	.307	.002	1.399	.005
	19.745	5741.8	14.482	8	1.078	1.085	1.300	.564	1.085	.564
	29.51	113.44	16.742	9	1.098	.827	.858	1.147	.587	.802
	390.72	3.619	196.45	10	.619	1.251	3.302	.901	1.686	1.190
	420.23	.000	358.89	11	.912	.040	1.083	1.300	.000	.858
	4.172	3.068	8.011	12	1.534	.488	1.228	.858	.755	.868
	17.786	9.766	.000	13	.811	.465	.164	1.490	.316	42
	.680	.000	8.544	14	.749	1.069	1.362	1.651	.079	
50.	18043.	9.744	382.05	1	.566	.859	.930	.350	1.217	.743
	16.675	.589	24.732	2	.572	.423	.779	-.005	1.195	.748
	.532	5.836	13.897	3	1.209	.437	1.263	1.052	1.044	1.782
	.000	81.83	306.87	4	1.064	.868	.856	2.150	1.839	2.003
	482.36	5.837	214.43	5	.875	.853	.300	.962	2.063	.986
	6.322	.543	.00	6	1.217	.923	.290	.992	1.269	.994
	.000	.000	35.257	7	1.209	2.476	.291	-.001	1.819	-.001
	23.885	6359.8	16.831	8	.962	1.026	1.300	.439	1.026	.439
	25.95	119.25	19.103	9	1.119	.852	.868	1.017	.565	.638
	429.66	3.360	216.04	10	.544	1.334	3.566	.988	1.476	1.388
	455.61	.000	361.48	11	.748	.038	1.144	1.300	.000	.868
	4.369	3.534	6.391	12	1.550	.445	1.239	.868	.830	.853
	18.436	10.007	.000	13	.825	.453	.170	1.340	.287	42
	.713	.000	10.035	14	.666	1.059	1.375	1.631	.092	

(d)

Figure 4-3 (cont.)

Figure 4-3*b* shows an underemployed/job ratio that improves slightly for the first three years and then returns to about the same ratio of underemployed to available jobs. The labor/job ratio increases, indicating a greater excess of labor over available jobs than at the beginning.

Figure 4-3*c* shows the major consequence of the training program. As people move from the underemployed group into the labor group, the population, housing, and job pressures in the underemployed sector tend to be reduced. This, along with the greater upward economic mobility represented by the training program, makes the area more attractive and the underemployed-arrival rate has increased. Conversely, the underemployed-departure rate has decreased, with a substantially larger net inward flow resulting. The underemployed-to-labor upward mobility rate is much increased by the training program. But, because an excess labor group is being created by the training program and jobs for them have not been influenced except by the secondary reactions of the system, the outflow from the labor category must increase. Because of higher labor unemployment, the dropout rate of labor to underemployed has increased, partly compensating for the training program. In addition there has been a substantial increase in the outflow of labor from the area, which is not shown in Figure 4-3*c* but which is indicated in the tabulation of Figure 4-4.

In the tabulation of changes occurring because of the underemployed-training program (created by UTR = .05 in Equation 140.1 of Appendix A), we see that the upward mobility UTL has increased by 110%. But at the same time the counterflow LTU has increased 63%. Underemployed arrivals have risen 43% while underemployed departures have fallen 20%. The total number of underemployed has risen slightly, by 1%, while at the same time underemployed housing has fallen by a like amount. Worker housing has risen 8% while the labor living in that housing has risen 23%. Because of the excess labor in the area, the labor-arrival rate has fallen 15% and the labor-departure rate has risen 81%.

The training program has created a flow through the area with a much increased underemployed-arrival rate and a much increased labor-departure rate. People come to the area because of the training program and leave when they find there is no use for the skills they have acquired. As a service to society, the program might be considered successful. But as a service to the city, its value is far less clear. The area is more crowded, the land fraction occupied has risen slightly, housing conditions are more crowded, the total of underemployed has risen very slightly, and the ratio of labor to jobs is higher, indicating a higher degree of unemployment.

Figure 4-5 gives an over-all view of the population levels and flow rates resulting from the training program. The upper figure in each pair is for the original condition of the area and the lower figure is after the new equilibrium has been established with the 5% per year underemployed-training program. A change in one part of the system causes a realignment and rebalancing throughout the system. After the rebalancing the normal flow rates and levels have all changed,

Variable	Symbol	Time (years)		Change (%)
		−5	50	
a. Underemployed-training program	UTP	0	19,100	—
b. Underemployed to labor	UTL	16,800	35,300	+110.
c. Labor to underemployed	LTU	11,300	18,400	+63.
d. Underemployed arrivals	UA	17,300	24,700	+43.
e. Underemployed departures	UD	17,300	13,900	−20.
f. Labor arrivals	LA	7,400	6,300	−15.
g. Labor departures	LD	13,200	23,900	+81.
h. L/U		1.04	1.26	+21.
1. New enterprise	NE	4,900	5,800	+18.
2. Mature business	MB	7,800	9,700	+24.
3. Declining industry	DI	16,500	16,700	+1.
4. Premium housing	PH	110,900	119,200	+7.
5. Worker housing	WH	335,600	361,500	+8.
6. Underemployed housing	UH	310,100	306,900	−1.
7. Managerial-professional	MP	71,100	81,800	+15.
8. Labor	L	392,600	482,400	+23.
9. Underemployed	U	377,300	382,000	+1.
10. Manager/housing ratio	MHR	1.07	1.14	+7.
11. Labor/housing ratio	LHR	1.17	1.33	+14.
12. Underemployed/housing ratio	UHR	.81	.83	+2.
13. Manager/job ratio	MR	1.38	1.38	0
14. Labor/job ratio	LR	.97	1.06	+9.
15. Underemployed/job ratio	UR	1.81	1.78	−2.
16. Tax ratio needed	TRN	2.25	2.06	−8.
17. Underemployed to labor net	UTLN	5,500	16,800	+205.

Figure 4-4   Changes caused by a training program that moves 5% per year from underemployed to labor (UTR = .05).

and the consequences may be far different from those expected when the original change was introduced.

The principal advantages accruing from the training program are the net increase in upward mobility UTLN, the social-service function created by the outflow of labor, and the increase in new enterprise and mature business. The underemployed-training program is converting 19,100 underemployed per year to labor, as a consequence of which the increase in UTLN is only 11,300. The discrepancy between the output of the training program and the net upward increase in flow from underemployed to labor is accounted for by the increased dropout rate LTU from labor to underemployed and a reduction in the normal upward mobility that would have occurred in the absence of a training program. Conditions have become somewhat more unfavorable for normal escape from the underemployed group and the natural processes have declined as the training program picks up the task.

The training program is moving 19,100 people per year, but the net increase in upward mobility is 11,300. The number of people that would normally move

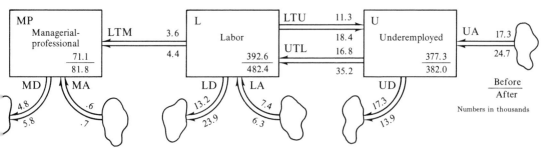

Figure 4-5 Flows and levels of men before and after starting a 5% per year training program to move under-employed to labor.

upward by internal processes has decreased by 7,800 per year. This failure to achieve the full effect of the training program illustrates a general characteristic of complex systems. An action program changes the system balance, causing the system to relax its internal pressures. As the outside effort picks up the burden, more and more is left to the outside effort.

The numerical values from these computer runs, of course, do not indicate exactly what would happen in any particular city. They do, however, indicate the ways in which a complex, interconnected social system can react. If we have reasonable confidence in the relationships assumed in the model, we can expect that the model will indicate the direction of reactions that would occur in response to changes in urban policies.

4.3 Financial Aid

A third type of program often proposed for alleviating the difficulties of the city would bring financial aid to the city from state or national government. The effect of an external tax subsidy on the model area is shown in Figure 4-6. In the model system the tax subsidy* has three direct effects. It increases the tax per capita ratio TPCR which, implying additional welfare and public services, increases the public-expenditure multiplier PEM, which is one of the coefficients influencing the inward and outward migration of the underemployed. The tax per capita ratio also influences the underemployed educational multiplier UEM and the labor educational multiplier LEM to increase the upward economic mobility from underemployed to labor and from labor to the managerial-professional category. The money for the tax subsidy is assumed to come from outside the city, to be in addition to previous expenditures, and not to affect directly the local tax assessments.

In Figure 4-6*a* the only significant changes resulting from the tax subsidy are slight increases in underemployed people and underemployed housing. In Figure 4-6*b* the most obvious change is an increase in unemployment in the underemployed category as shown by the increased underemployed/job ratio UR.

---

*The subsidy is generated in the model by setting TPCS = 100 in Equation 147.1 in Appendix A. The effect is introduced by way of Equation 147 into Equation 8 where it influences Equations 7, 27, and 40.

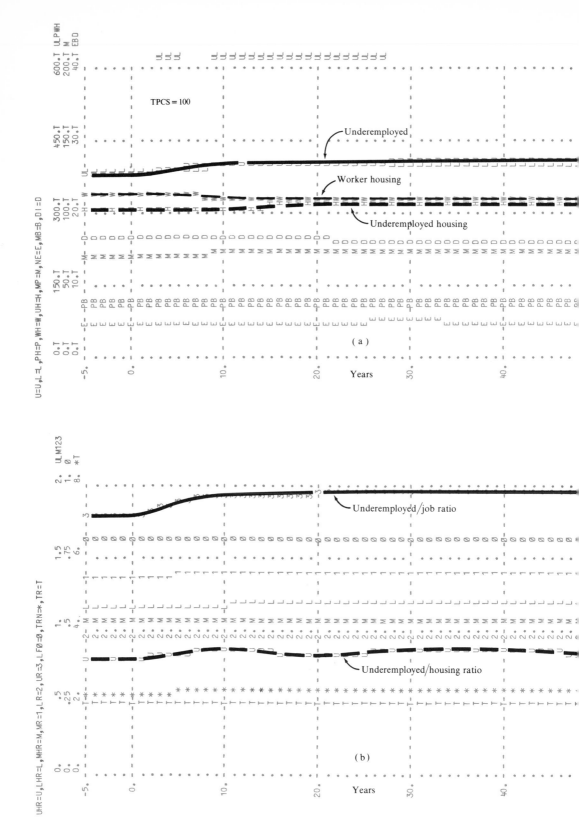

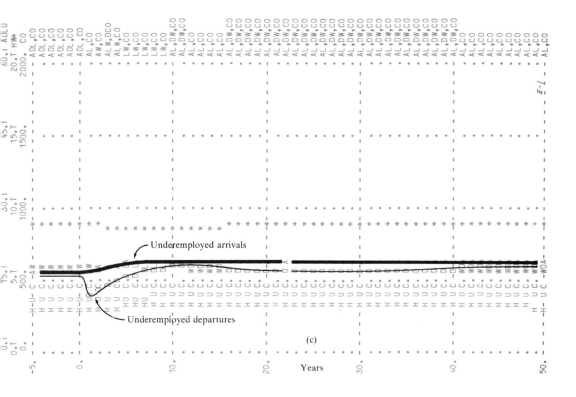

Figure 4-6 Tax subsidy of $100 per capita per year.

In Figure 4-6c the underemployed-arrival rate UA increases, while the under-employed-departure rate UD first decreases and then returns approximately to its initial value.

Figure 4-7 summarizes some of the more significant changes taken from the tabulation in Figure 4-6d. The flow from underemployed to labor UTL has risen 15%. The counterflow from labor to underemployed has risen too, but by a lesser amount. The underemployed-arrival rate has gone up 10% and the total number of underemployed has risen 8%.

The increased attractiveness of the area created by the tax subsidy has not resulted in appreciable changes in the amount of business activity and available jobs so that the underemployed/job ratio UR has risen 9%, indicating a corresponding increase in underemployed workers beyond available work opportunities.

One of the more unexpected changes in Figure 4-7 is the 8% increase in the tax ratio needed TRN from internal sources within the city. This is caused by the increased tax demands generated by the greater number of underemployed under circumstances that have produced no appreciable change in the assessed value of property within the city.

The changes discussed above suggest that financial support from the outside may do nothing to improve fundamental conditions within the city and may even

TIME	AV	MB	U		AMM	LAJM	LSM	MSM	SHLM	UMM
	DI	MBD	UA	2	AMMP	LAM	LUM	NEGR	TCM	UMMP
	DID	MD	UD	3	BDM	LAMP	LUR	PEM	TPCR	UR
	DIDP	MP	UH	4	DIDM	LATM	MAHM	PHAM	TR	WHAM
	L	NE	UJ	5	DIEM	LAUM	MAJM	PHEM	TRN	WHEM
	LA	NEC	UJP	6	DILM	LCR	MAM	PHGM	UAMM	WHGM
	LCHP	NECP	UTL	7	EDM	LDM	MAMP	PHGR	UDM	WHGR
	LD	P	UTLN	8	EGM	LEM	MAPM	PHLM	UEM	WHLM
	LDC	PH	UTP	9	ELJM	LFØ	MATM	PHM	UFW	WHM
	LDI	PHC	UW	10	ELM	LHR	MDM	PHØM	UHM	WHØM
	LJ	PHCP	WH	11	EM	LLF	MHR	PHPM	UHPR	WHTM
	LTM	PHØ	WHC	12	EMM	LMM	MLM	PHTM	UHR	WHUM
	LTU	SHD	WHCP	13	ETM	LMMP	MLR	SHAM	UJM	
	MA	SHDP	WHØ	14	LAHM	LR	MR	SHDM	UM	

	thousands				units					
-5.	16336.	7.806	377.31	1	.452	1.087	1.054	.344	1.060	.805
	16.474	.465	17.283	2	.449	.623	.712	.000	1.284	.802
	.464	4.849	17.275	3	1.190	.625	1.040	1.145	1.121	1.811
	.000	71.13	310.08	4	.939	.854	.931	1.549	1.966	1.542
	392.55	4.866	208.35	5	.886	.808	.296	1.000	2.248	1.000
	7.360	.462	.00	6	1.060	.878	.306	1.000	.936	1.000
	.000	.000	16.847	7	1.190	1.681	.307	.000	2.289	.000
	13.201	5729.4	5.497	8	1.000	1.073	1.300	.625	1.073	.625
	24.38	110.94	.000	9	.935	.815	.854	1.075	.557	.665
	379.15	3.142	210.06	10	.655	1.170	3.408	.948	1.529	1.352
	403.53	.000	335.65	11	.768	.029	1.069	1.300	.000	.854
	3.643	3.155	5.885	12	1.556	.466	1.262	.854	.811	.808
	11.349	9.054	.000	13	.805	.464	.181	1.378	.276	
	.655	.000	9.075	14	.830	.973	1.380	1.460	.045	
10.	16347.	7.795	400.45	1	.467	1.063	1.039	.328	1.070	.934
	16.459	.462	18.942	2	.476	.589	.694	.000	1.307	.893
	.470	5.095	17.587	3	1.185	.616	.988	1.589	1.491	1.939
	.000	71.85	313.31	4	.951	.852	.924	1.605	1.981	1.584
	395.64	4.875	206.50	5	.889	.795	.285	1.002	2.383	1.000
	7.312	.469	.00	6	1.070	.884	.292	1.002	.926	.998
	.000	.000	18.537	7	1.185	1.763	.302	.000	2.196	-.000
	13.948	5936.7	6.918	8	1.002	1.294	1.300	.613	1.294	.613
	24.51	111.33	.000	9	.944	.817	.852	1.094	.518	.658
	379.02	3.231	207.53	10	.648	1.182	3.546	.935	1.414	1.362
	403.53	.000	334.58	11	.773	.029	1.076	1.300	.000	.852
	3.997	3.124	5.838	12	1.572	.536	1.263	.852	.852	.796
	11.560	8.688	.000	13	.803	.505	.182	1.296	.224	ω ⁓
	.652	.000	9.114	14	.818	.980	1.394	1.386	.044	
50.	16380.	7.915	406.97	1	.473	1.058	1.036	.314	1.082	.931
	16.346	.474	19.058	2	.474	.565	.687	-.001	1.315	.931
	.468	5.334	17.543	3	1.198	.571	.975	1.624	1.515	1.971
	.000	72.69	319.47	4	.954	.846	.921	1.634	2.042	1.641
	396.78	4.894	206.49	5	.881	.790	.276	.992	2.420	.997
	6.796	.463	.00	6	1.082	.885	.280	.998	.968	.998
	.000	.000	19.270	7	1.198	1.821	.281	-.000	2.155	-.000
	14.450	5999.9	7.657	8	.992	1.306	1.300	.597	1.306	.597
	24.08	112.26	.000	9	.957	.821	.846	1.061	.509	.653
	380.06	3.164	207.03	10	.638	1.200	3.669	.957	1.422	1.368
	404.14	.000	330.58	11	.760	.029	1.079	1.300	.000	.846
	4.134	3.224	5.735	12	1.586	.520	1.266	.846	.849	.792
	11.615	9.002	.000	13	.792	.521	.183	1.301	.212	ω ⁓
	.613	.000	9.045	14	.800	.982	1.405	1.409	.047	

(d)

Figure 4-6 (cont.)

| Variable | Symbol | Time (years) | | Change (%) |
		−5	50	
a. Tax per capita subsidy	TPCS	0	100	—
b. Underemployed to labor	UTL	16,800	19,300	+15.
c. Labor to underemployed	LTU	11,300	11,600	+3.
d. Underemployed arrivals	UA	17,300	19,100	+10.
e. Underemployed departures	UD	17,300	17,500	+1.
f. Labor arrivals	LA	7,400	6,800	−8.
g. Labor departures	LD	13,200	14,400	+9.
h. L/U		1.04	.98	−6.
1. New enterprise	NE	4,900	4,900	0
2. Mature business	MB	7,800	7,900	+1.
3. Declining industry	DI	16,500	16,300	−1.
4. Premium housing	PH	110,900	112,300	+1.
5. Worker housing	WH	335,600	330,600	−1.
6. Underemployed housing	UH	310,100	319,500	+3.
7. Managerial-professional	MP	71,100	72,700	+2.
8. Labor	L	392,600	396,800	+1.
9. Underemployed	U	377,300	407,000	+8.
10. Manager/housing ratio	MHR	1.07	1.08	+1.
11. Labor/housing ratio	LHR	1.17	1.20	+3.
12. Underemployed/housing ratio	UHR	.81	.85	+5.
13. Manager/job ratio	MR	1.38	1.41	+2.
14. Labor/job ratio	LR	.97	.98	+1.
15. Underemployed/job ratio	UR	1.81	1.97	+9.
16. Tax ratio needed	TRN	2.25	2.42	+8.
17. Underemployed to labor net	UTLN	5,500	7,700	+40.

Figure 4-7 Changes caused by a tax subsidy of $100 per capita per year (TPCS = 100.).

worsen conditions in the long run by causing an unfavorable shift in the proportions of population, housing, and business. In particular, in Figure 4-7 underemployed population rises, the ratio of labor to underemployed falls, and the internal tax demands rise.

4.4 Low-Cost-Housing Construction

As a fourth type of urban-management program, the effect of low-cost-housing construction will now be examined. Low-cost housing here means housing constructed for the underemployed and not available to any other segment of the population. In the basic computer model the only housing available to the underemployed is the aging and declining housing that is dropping out of the worker-housing category. The low-cost-housing program considered here is not financed out of city tax revenues. It is a gift to the city from the outside, although its construction makes jobs for the labor and underemployed in the city. As will be shown in the following computer runs, a low-cost-housing program is much more detrimental to the long-run conditions of the urban area than the job program, training program, or tax subsidy previously examined.

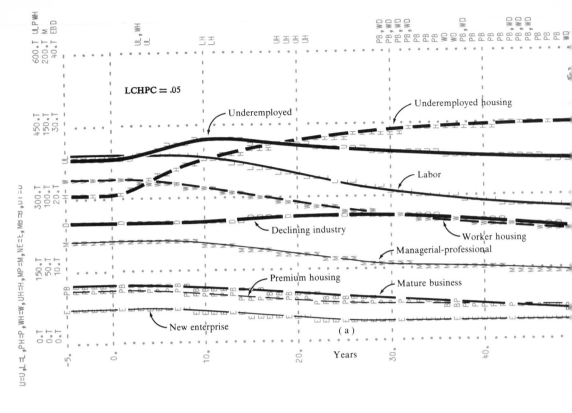

LCHPC = .05

Underemployed

Underemployed housing

Labor

Declining industry

Worker housing

Managerial-professional

Premium housing

Mature business

New enterprise

(a)

Years

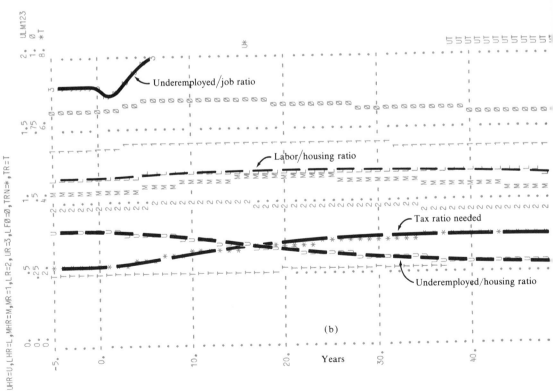

Underemployed/job ratio

Labor/housing ratio

Tax ratio needed

Underemployed/housing ratio

(b)

Years

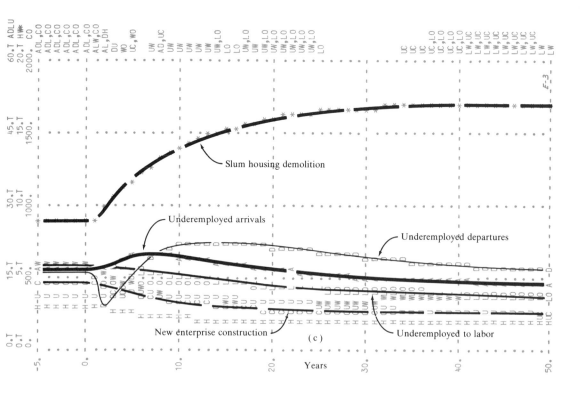

Figure 4-8 Construction of low-cost housing each year for about 2.5% of the underemployed.

The low-cost-housing program is established with the intent to build housing for 5% of the underemployed each year. However (as will be seen in Equations 149 and 150 of Appendix A), the intended construction is influenced by the land multiplier, which reduces construction as the land area becomes full, and by available labor. As a consequence the actual low-cost-housing construction LCHP provides for only 2.7% of the underemployed in the first year, 1.9% in the tenth year, and stabilizes at 3% in the fiftieth year. Annual low-cost-housing construction provides on the average for about 2.5% of the underemployed each year. If housing were coming only from the low-cost-housing program, this would mean a replacement of the housing units each 40 years.

Figure 4-8*a* shows the effect of introducing such a low-cost-housing program at year 0. The housing available for the underemployed begins to rise immediately. Because of the increased housing, more underemployed are attracted to the city and the underemployed population rises for the first 10 years. But the low-cost-housing program exerts continuous pressure on the available unfilled land, making the area less favorable for other types of construction. As a consequence worker housing, premium housing, new enterprise, and mature business all gradually decline. As the business units decline in number, the available jobs decrease, thereby bringing economic pressure on all categories of the population and causing them to decrease.

TIME	AV	MB	U		AMM	LAJM	LSM	MSM	SHLM	UMM
	DI	MBD	UA	2	AMMP	LAM	LUM	NEGR	TCM	UMMP
	DID	MD	UD	3	BDM	LAMP	LUR	PEM	TPCR	UR
	DIDP	MP	UH	4	DIDM	LATM	MAHM	PHAM	TR	WHAM
	L	NE	UJ	5	DIEM	LAUM	MAJM	PHEM	TRN	WHEM
	LA	NEC	UJP	6	DILM	LCR	MAM	PHGM	UAMM	WHGM
	LCHP	NECP	UTL	7	EDM	LDM	MAMP	PHGR	UDM	WHGR
	LD	P	UTLN	8	EGM	LEM	MAPM	PHLM	UEM	WHLM
	LDC	PH	UTP	9	ELJM	LFØ	MATM	PHM	UFW	WHM
	LDI	PHC	UW	10	ELM	LHR	MDM	PHØM	UHM	WHØM
	LJ	PHCP	WH	11	EM	LLF	MHR	PHPM	UHPR	WHTM
	LTM	PHØ	WHC	12	EMM	LMM	MLM	PHTM	UHR	WHUM
	LTU	SHD	WHCP	13	ETM	LMMP	MLR	SHAM	UJM	
	MA	SHDP	WHØ	14	LAHM	LR	MR	SHDM	UM	

	thousands				units					
-5.	16336.	7.806	377.31	1	.452	1.087	1.054	.344	1.060	.805
	16.474	.465	17.283	2	.449	.623	.712	.000	1.284	.802
	.464	4.849	17.275	3	1.190	.625	1.040	1.145	1.121	1.811
	.000	71.13	310.08	4	.939	.854	.931	1.549	1.966	1.542
	392.55	4.866	208.35	5	.886	.808	.296	1.000	2.248	1.000
	7.360	.462	.00	6	1.060	.878	.306	1.000	.936	1.000
	.000	.000	16.847	7	1.190	1.681	.307	.000	2.289	.000
	13.201	5729.4	5.497	8	1.000	1.073	1.300	.625	1.073	.625
	24.38	110.94	.000	9	.935	.815	.854	1.075	.557	.665
	379.15	3.142	210.06	10	.655	1.170	3.408	.948	1.529	1.352
	403.53	.000	335.65	11	.768	.029	1.069	1.300	.000	.854
	3.643	3.155	5.885	12	1.556	.466	1.262	.854	.811	.808
	11.349	9.054	.000	13	.805	.464	.181	1.378	.276	
	.655	.000	9.075	14	.830	.973	1.380	1.460	.045	
10.	15684.	7.576	417.16	1	.406	1.029	1.018	.306	1.223	.689
	16.754	.523	19.468	2	.487	.538	.658	-.014	1.350	.767
	.475	5.291	21.648	3	1.380	.605	.916	1.057	1.047	2.141
	.000	68.24	376.67	4	.944	.851	.869	2.046	1.993	1.636
	382.07	4.108	194.86	5	.772	.766	.271	.890	2.602	.959
	6.936	.340	.00	6	1.223	.893	.260	.938	.875	.967
	8.112	.000	15.226	7	1.380	1.893	.291	-.008	2.595	-.004
	14.468	5970.8	4.062	8	.890	1.028	1.300	.436	1.028	.436
	22.21	100.58	.000	9	.959	.853	.851	.823	.476	.436
	363.34	2.217	198.59	10	.541	1.199	3.877	1.280	1.723	1.679
	385.55	.000	318.75	11	.590	.030	1.131	1.300	.019	.851
	3.414	3.863	3.720	12	1.594	.396	1.257	.851	.738	.775
	11.324	14.036	.000	13	.801	.447	.179	1.523	.172	km
	.596	.000	10.701	14	.801	.991	1.412	1.863	.040	
50.	12017.	4.307	372.64	1	.458	1.219	1.137	.350	1.000	.692
	15.481	.275	14.288	2	.443	.569	.566	-.001	1.461	.685
	.387	3.335	16.751	3	1.278	.558	.732	1.152	1.126	2.351
	.000	46.94	450.61	4	.833	.823	.933	1.534	2.274	1.577
	272.86	2.513	158.48	5	.833	.693	.300	.991	3.056	.997
	4.569	.267	.00	6	1.000	.845	.291	.973	.777	.952
	11.054	.000	11.240	7	1.278	1.811	.283	-.003	2.248	-.006
	9.882	4852.9	3.782	8	.991	1.076	1.264	.702	1.076	.702
	23.23	73.34	.000	9	.847	.800	.823	1.079	.440	.622
	269.67	2.007	164.06	10	.701	1.180	3.552	.945	2.097	1.411
	292.90	.000	231.17	11	.679	.027	1.067	1.264	.030	.823
	2.451	2.079	3.644	12	1.550	.469	1.244	.823	.551	.720
	7.439	17.100	.000	13	.745	.449	.172	1.897	.130	
	.399	.000	6.523	14	.820	.932	1.375	1.897	.031	km

(d)

Figure 4-8 (cont.)

Figure 4-8*b* shows changes in the significant system ratios. The underemployed/job ratio drops slightly at first because of the jobs created by construction of low-cost housing. But as soon as the population begins to increase to fill the newly available housing, the underemployed/job ratio rises sharply from the initial value of 1.81 to become 2.14 at the tenth year and 2.35 at the fiftieth year. Because underemployed housing increases while at the same time rising economic pressures cause the population to decline, the underemployed/housing ratio falls steadily over the 50-year period. Because of the rising ratio of underemployed to other classes of population, and the declining tax base, the tax ratio needed increases as a result of the low-cost-housing program.

Figure 4-8*c* shows some of the system rates. Slum-housing demolition increases to reach a new equilibrium consistent with the rate of construction of low-cost housing coupled with the continued inflow of dwelling units from the aging process in the worker-housing category. Between year 0 and year 10 the underemployed-arrival rate into the area increases while the underemployed-departure rate temporarily decreases. This causes an increase in the underemployed population until the worsening economic conditions cause a reversal.

Figure 4-9 shows values of variables before and after 50 years of low-cost-housing-program construction and the percentage change occurring over the 50-year period. The slum-housing-demolition rate increases because, eventually in equilibrium, all of the new construction is matched by old units that are taken down. The underemployed population falls 1% while underemployed housing rises 45%. Worker housing declines 31% while the labor population falls 30%. The underemployed/job ratio worsens by rising 30%. The underemployed/housing ratio, which was already below normal, falls another 32%. The tax ratio needed increases 36% while new enterprise falls 49%, mature business falls 45%, and declining industry falls 6%.

The low-cost-housing program brings additional pressure on the land area. It attracts people in the underemployed category, making the population proportions within the urban area even more unfavorable than in the normal stagnant condition. The higher land occupancy, unfavorable population ratio, and rising tax rate all combine to reduce the kinds of new construction the city needs most. An examination of Figure 4-9 shows remarkably large changes in an unfavorable direction. In comparison to what sounds like an innocuous 2.5% housing-construction rate for the underemployed, the results are unfavorable for all categories of population. The housing program, aimed at ameliorating conditions for the underemployed, has increased unemployment and has reduced upward economic mobility both in absolute numbers and as a percentage of population. Figure 4-9 shows that the net underemployed-to-labor flow rate UTLN has fallen 31%. Upward mobility as a percentage of the underemployed has decreased from 1.5% in the normal stagnant city to 1% after inauguration of the low-cost-housing program.

The preceding computer runs have examined programs that provide jobs, training, an external tax subsidy, and low-cost housing for the underemployed.

	Variable	Symbol	Time (years)		Change (%)
			−5	50	
a.	Low-cost-housing program	LCHP	0	11,100	—
b.	Worker-housing obsolescence	WHO	9,100	6,500	−28.
c.	Slum-housing demolition	SHD	9,100	17,100	+88.
d.	UH/SHD = underemployed-housing life		34.	26.	−24.
e.	Underemployed to labor	UTL	16,800	11,200	−33.
f.	Labor to underemployed	LTU	11,300	7,400	−35.
g.	Underemployed arrivals	UA	17,300	14,300	−17.
h.	Underemployed departures	UD	17,300	16,800	−3.
i.	Labor arrivals	LA	7,400	4,600	−38.
j.	Labor departures	LD	13,200	9,900	−25.
k.	L/U		1.04	.73	−30.
1.	New enterprise	NE	4,900	2,500	−49.
2.	Mature business	MB	7,800	4,300	−45.
3.	Declining industry	DI	16,500	15,500	−6.
4.	Premium housing	PH	110,900	73,300	−34.
5.	Worker housing	WH	335,600	231,200	−31.
6.	Underemployed housing	UH	310,100	450,600	+45.
7.	Managerial-professional	MP	71,100	46,900	−34.
8.	Labor	L	392,600	272,900	−30.
9.	Underemployed	U	377,300	372,600	−1.
10.	Manager/housing ratio	MHR	1.07	1.07	0
11.	Labor/housing ratio	LHR	1.17	1.18	+1.
12.	Underemployed/housing ratio	UHR	.81	.55	−32.
13.	Manager/job ratio	MR	1.38	1.38	0
14.	Labor/job ratio	LR	.97	.93	−4.
15.	Underemployed/job ratio	UR	1.81	2.35	+30.
16.	Tax ratio needed	TRN	2.25	3.06	+36.
17.	Underemployed to labor net	UTLN	5,500	3,800	−31.

Figure 4-9 Changes caused by low-cost-housing program that builds for about 2.5% of the underemployed each year (LCHPC = .05).

The results range from neutral to detrimental. These computer runs disclose possible reasons for the futility and frustration that characterize urban-development programs. They demonstrate the counterintuitive nature of complex social systems by showing that intuitively sensible policies can affect adversely the very problems they are designed to alleviate. Commonly in complex systems a vicious cycle develops in which the action erroneously assumed to be corrective makes the problem worse and the worsening calls forth still more of the presumed remedial action, which only further aggravates the situation.

5 Urban Revival

This chapter explores policies that might reverse urban decay. The preceding chapter showed the harmful effects of constructing low-cost housing. This chapter shows that constructing worker housing and premium housing can be detrimental too, but less so than constructing low-cost housing. The problem of the stagnant urban area is one of too much housing compared to employment opportunities and too much old industry and housing compared to new. This chapter, after exploring several policies, concludes that urban revival requires demolition of slum housing and replacement with new business enterprise. Only by this shift from slum housing to new business will the internal mix become healthy.

5.1 Worker-Housing Construction

Figure 4-8 showed how construction of low-cost housing can cause deterioration. Figure 4-8*b* exhibits a higher-than-normal labor/housing ratio and raises the possibility that construction of worker housing might increase the attractiveness to labor and lead to improving population balance and readjusting conditions in the area. The results are disappointing, as shown in Figure 5-1, where the changing conditions are caused by a worker-housing-construction program that builds for slightly more than 2% of labor families per year. The amount of desired construction is expressed as a fraction of total housing units and is influenced by the worker-housing land multiplier WHLM and the labor availability LCR (Equations 82, 86, and 138 in Appendix A). As a result the construction varies some from year to year. In Figure 5-1*a* worker housing rises initially and then declines. The decline is caused by the reduction in the total number of labor families, the resulting increased vacancy rate, and the more rapid deterioration of worker housing into underemployed housing. Figure 5-1*a* illustrates the result of regenerative interactions caused by the housing program. Housing construction increases the land fraction occupied. Land crowding causes a slight reduction in the construction of new enterprise. Declining enterprise reduces the number of jobs, which in turn reduces skilled labor. The addition of worker housing has worsened a fundamental condition already caused by housing for more people than can find economic opportunity.

71

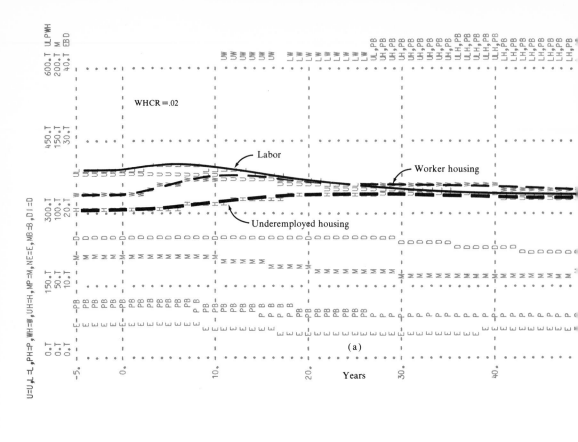

(a)

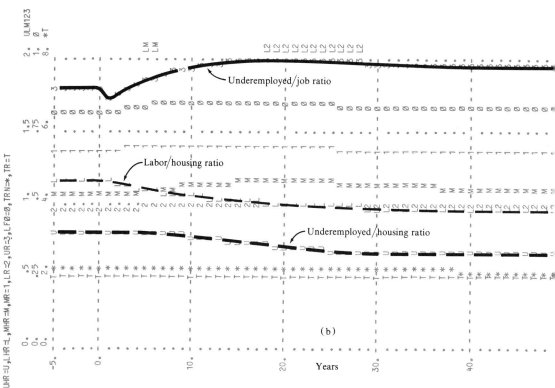

(b)

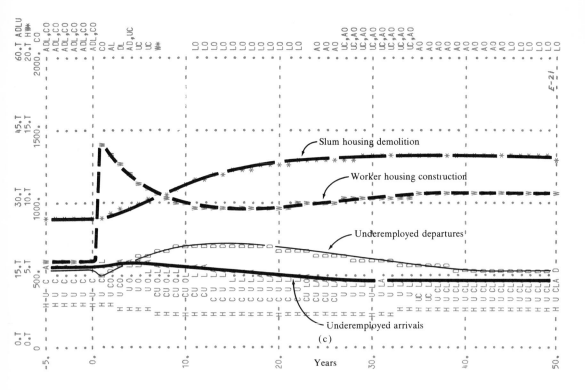

Figure 5-1 Worker-housing-construction program for about 2.1% per year of the labor families.

Figure 5-1*b* shows an initial small dip in the underemployed/job ratio caused by the work available from the housing-construction program. But as the new housing becomes available, the increasing worker housing reduces occupancy and causes a more rapid decline of worker housing into underemployed housing, which attracts underemployed. Because of reduced new-enterprise construction, industrial activity and available jobs decline in comparison to underemployed workers. As a natural accompaniment to the falling job opportunities, there is a relative increase in the amount of underemployed housing as seen in the declining underemployed/housing ratio. Because of relatively more housing and relatively fewer jobs, the city probably will show an even more accentuated condition of underemployed crowding into some dwellings and vacancy in others. Financial realities force crowding into a fraction of the housing, while the other housing becomes idle and deteriorates rapidly, though it may remain standing.

In Figure 5-1*c*, as a result of worsening conditions, the underemployed-departure rate increases while the underemployed-arrival rate decreases, leading to the falling population seen in Figure 5-1*a*.

In Figure 5-1*c* the worker-housing-construction rate jumps when the program is inaugurated and then declines as the land fraction occupied increases and as normal construction, which was taking place before the special program began, decreases. As tabulated in Figure 5-2, the special worker-housing-construction program at year 50 is building 8,340 units per year, but the total worker-housing-

TIME	AV	MB	U	1	AMM	LAJM	LSM	MSM	SHLM	UMM
	DI	MBD	UA	2	AMMP	LAM	LUM	NEGR	TCM	UMMP
	DID	MD	UD	3	BDM	LAMP	LUR	PEM	TPCR	UR
	DI DP	MP	UH	4	DI DM	LATM	MAHM	PHAM	TR	WHAM
	L	NE	UJ	5	DI EM	LAUM	MAJM	PHEM	TRN	WHEM
	LA	NEC	UJP	6	DI LM	LCR	MAM	PHGM	UAMM	WHGM
	LCHP	NECP	UTL	7	EDM	LDM	MAMP	PHGR	UDM	WHGR
	LD	P	UTLN	8	EGM	LEM	MAPM	PHLM	UEM	WHLM
	LDC	PH	UTP	9	ELJM	LFØ	MATM	PHM	UFW	WHM
	LDI	PHC	UW	10	ELV	LHR	MDM	PHØM	UHM	WHØM
	LJ	PHCP	WH	11	EM	LLF	MHR	PHPM	UHPR	WHTM
	LTM	PHØ	WHC	12	EMM	LMM	MLM	PHTM	UHR	WHUM
	LTU	SHD	WHCP	13	ETM	LMMP	MLR	SHAM	UJM	
	MA	SHDP	WHØ	14	LAHM	LR	MR	SHDM	UM	

	thousands				units					
-5.	16336.	7.806	377.31	1	.452	1.087	1.054	.344	1.060	.805
	16.474	.465	17.283	2	.449	.623	.712	.000	1.284	.802
	.464	4.849	17.275	3	1.190	.625	1.040	1.145	1.121	1.811
	.000	71.13	310.08	4	.939	.854	.931	1.549	1.966	1.542
	392.55	4.866	208.35	5	.886	.808	.296	1.000	2.248	1.000
	7.360	.462	.00	6	1.060	.878	.306	1.000	.936	1.000
	.000	.000	16.847	7	1.190	1.681	.307	.000	2.289	.000
	13.201	5729.4	5.497	8	1.000	1.073	1.300	.625	1.073	.625
	24.38	110.94	.000	9	.935	.815	.854	1.075	.557	.665
	379.15	3.142	210.06	10	.655	1.170	3.408	.948	1.529	1.352
	403.53	.000	335.65	11	.768	.029	1.069	1.300	.000	.854
	3.643	3.155	5.885	12	1.556	.466	1.262	.854	.811	.808
	11.349	9.054	.000	13	.805	.464	.181	1.378	.276	
	.655	.000	9.075	14	.830	.973	1.380	1.460	.045	
10.	16283.	7.599	375.94	1	.381	.978	.989	.306	1.219	.757
	16.714	.513	16.992	2	.442	.636	.713	-.012	1.282	.793
	.483	5.299	20.867	3	1.350	.635	1.045	1.145	1.121	1.949
	.000	68.78	322.59	4	.964	.854	.874	2.007	1.965	1.188
	392.73	4.200	192.86	5	.790	.809	.270	.906	2.244	.965
	7.487	.362	.00	6	1.219	.904	.262	.945	.931	1.044
	.000	.000	15.358	7	1.350	1.651	.292	-.007	2.775	.006
	12.967	5707.8	3.421	8	.906	1.073	1.300	.438	1.073	.438
	24.11	101.81	.000	9	.974	.852	.854	.836	.515	.362
	365.11	2.308	193.69	10	.543	1.059	3.853	1.257	1.625	1.785
	389.23	.000	370.99	11	.615	.031	1.126	1.300	.000	.854
	3.544	3.840	9.935	12	1.594	.410	1.250	.854	.777	.809
	12.277	11.377	6.966	13	.805	.451	.175	1.446	.220	
	.603	.000	13.247	14	.941	1.009	1.412	1.763	.044	
50.	14953.	6.068	333.80	1	.434	1.004	1.003	.349	1.135	.778
	14.260	.357	14.093	2	.418	.702	.706	.006	1.292	.772
	.434	4.050	16.068	3	1.176	.687	1.020	1.199	1.166	1.956
	.000	58.49	341.62	4	1.016	.856	.903	1.776	1.951	.887
	340.35	4.027	170.64	5	.895	.804	.299	1.046	2.166	1.012
	7.012	.399	.00	6	1.135	.899	.301	1.010	.876	.997
	.000	.000	13.222	7	1.176	1.510	.296	.001	2.407	-.000
	10.278	5004.9	3.020	8	1.046	1.099	1.300	.531	1.099	.531
	26.61	88.86	.000	9	.999	.834	.856	1.108	.513	.327
	314.17	2.656	171.29	10	.599	.960	3.462	.926	1.897	1.844
	340.77	.000	354.63	11	.783	.030	1.097	1.300	.000	.856
	3.186	2.469	10.620	12	1.551	.477	1.244	.856	.651	.804
	10.193	13.164	8.336	13	.808	.468	.172	1.697	.218	
	.520	.000	13.080	14	1.016	.999	1.376	1.927	.040	

(d)

Figure 5-1 (cont.)

| | | Time (years) | | |
	Variable	Symbol	−5	50	Change (%)
a.	Worker-housing-construction program	WHCP	0	8,340	—
b.	Worker-housing construction	WHC	5,880	10,620	+81.
c.	Premium-housing construction	PHC	3,140	2,660	−15.
1.	New enterprise	NE	4,900	4,030	−18.
2.	Mature business	MB	7,800	6,070	−22.
3.	Declining industry	DI	16,500	14,260	−13.
4.	Premium housing	PH	110,900	88,900	−20.
5.	Worker housing	WH	335,600	354,600	+6.
6.	Underemployed housing	UH	310,100	341,600	+10.
7.	Managerial-professional	MP	71,100	58,500	−18.
8.	Labor	L	392,600	340,400	−13.
9.	Underemployed	U	377,300	333,800	−12.
10.	Manager/housing ratio	MHR	1.07	1.10	+3.
11.	Labor/housing ratio	LHR	1.17	.96	−18.
12.	Underemployed/housing ratio	UHR	.81	.65	−20.
13.	Manager/job ratio	MR	1.38	1.38	0
14.	Labor/job ratio	LR	.97	1.00	+3.
15.	Underemployed/job ratio	UR	1.81	1.96	+8.
16.	Tax ratio needed	TRN	2.25	2.17	−4.
17.	Underemployed to labor net	UTLN	5,500	3,020	−45.

Figure 5-2 Changes caused by a worker-housing-construction program (WHCR = .02).

construction rate has increased only 4,740 units per year. This means that the normal processes of worker-housing construction within the area have declined by 2,600 units per year. The decline in normal construction illustrates a rather general characteristic of systems. A positive program to generate some rate of flow will change the system balance and cause a depression in the normal processes generating that same rate. The new program is only partly effective because much of it simply displaces normal processes.

Although in Figure 5-2 worker-housing construction has risen 81%, total worker housing has risen only 6%. The small rise in worker housing is explained by a reduction in average housing life* (shown in Figure 5-3). Because of the lower

	at − 5 years	at 50 years
Premium-housing life	35 years	36 years
Worker-housing life	37 years	27 years
Underemployed-housing life	34 years	26 years

Figure 5-3 Average housing life before and after the worker-housing-construction program.

*Housing life is the reciprocal of normal-housing-obsolescence rate multiplied by the obsolescence multiplier. For example, premium-housing life is the reciprocal of (PHON) (PHOM). These are given in Equations 79 and 80 of Appendix A. PHON = .03 and, from Figure 5-1d, PHOM = .948 at −5 years. The product is .0285, the reciprocal of which is 35 years. Similarly, worker-housing life comes from Equations 93 and 94 and underemployed-housing life from Equations 96 and 97.

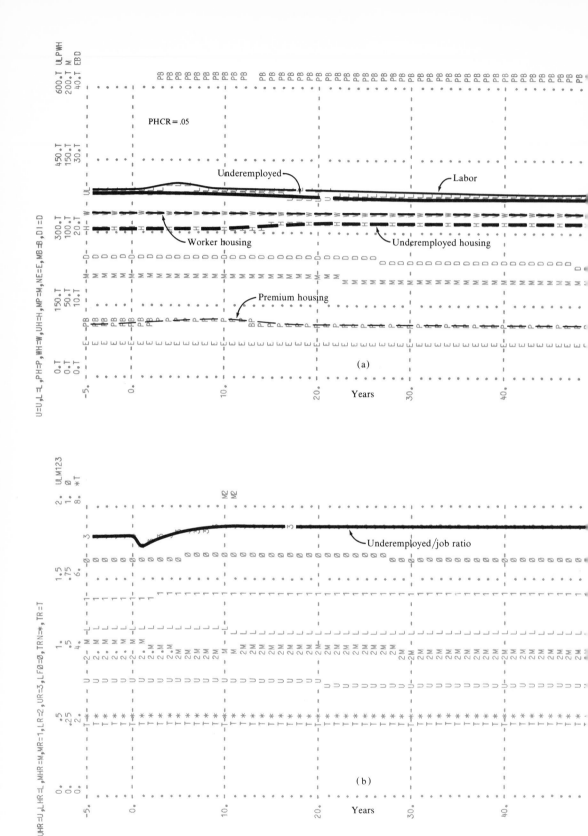

PHCR = .05

Underemployed

Labor

Worker housing

Underemployed housing

Premium housing

(a)

Years

Underemployed/job ratio

(b)

Years

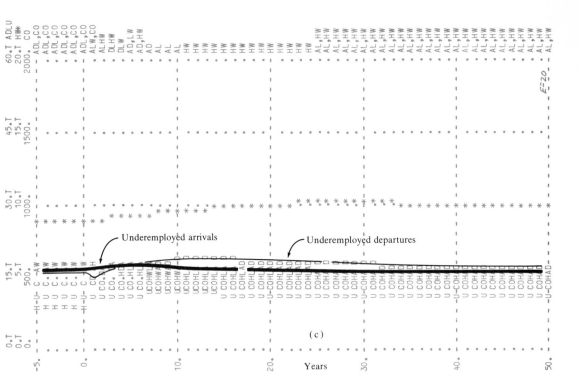

Figure 5-4 Premium-housing-construction program for about 4.7% per year of the managerial-professional families.

occupancy ratios, the housing is declining more rapidly. Although the rate of housing flow through the worker and underemployed categories is higher, the actual housing in existence has risen much less than the construction rate might suggest.

In Figure 5-2 all classes of population have declined. All classes of enterprise have declined even more. Housing has become more available, but the employment situation for labor and the underemployed has worsened.

Before starting the worker-housing-construction program, the stagnant city already had too high a level of housing and population in comparison to its industrial opportunities. The worker-housing construction has shifted this balance even further in the wrong direction. The results were not so serious as for the low-cost-housing program but still do not lead to urban improvement.

5.2 Premium-Housing Construction

To complete the examination of housing construction, Figure 5-4 shows the consequence of introducing a premium-housing-construction program. Very little change is evident except for slight decreases in population and industry and some increase in the underemployed/job ratio. The changes are small but detrimental. Figure 5-5 summarizes the changes in the principal system variables.

TIME	AV	MB	U	#	AMM	LAJM	LSM	MSM	SHLM	UMM
	AV	MB	U	1	AMM	LAJM	LSM	MSM	SHLM	UMM
	DI	MBD	UA	2	AMMP	LAM	LUM	NEGR	TCM	UMMP
	DID	MD	UD	3	BDM	LAMP	LUR	PEM	TPCR	UR
	DIDP	MP	UH	4	DIDM	LATM	MAHM	PHAM	TR	WHAM
	L	NE	UJ	5	DIEM	LAUM	MAJM	PHEM	TRN	WHEM
	LA	NEC	UJP	6	DILM	LCR	MAM	PHGM	UAMM	WHGM
	LCHP	NECP	UTL	7	EDM	LDM	MAMP	PHGR	UDM	WHGR
	LD	P	UTLN	8	EGM	LEM	MAPM	PHLM	UEM	WHLM
	LDC	PH	UTP	9	ELJM	LFØ	MATM	PHM	UFW	WHM
	LDI	PHC	UW	10	ELM	LHR	MDM	PHØM	UHM	WHØM
	LJ	PHCP	WH	11	EM	LLF	MHR	PHPM	UHPR	WHTM
	LTM	PHØ	WHC	12	EMM	LMM	MLM	PHTM	UHR	WHUM
	LTU	SHD	WHCP	13	ETM	LMMP	MLR	SHAM	UJM	UJM
	MA	SHDP	WHØ	14	LAHM	LR	MR	SHDM	UM	UM

	thousands			#	units					
−5.	16336.	7.806	377.31	1	.452	1.087	1.054	.344	1.060	.805
	16.474	.465	17.283	2	.449	.623	.712	.000	1.284	.802
	.464	4.849	17.275	3	1.190	.625	1.040	1.145	1.121	1.811
	.000	71.13	310.08	4	.939	.854	.931	1.549	1.966	1.542
	392.55	4.866	208.35	5	.886	.808	.296	1.000	2.248	1.000
	7.360	.462	.00	6	1.060	.878	.306	1.000	.936	1.000
	.000	.000	16.847	7	1.190	1.681	.307	.000	2.289	.000
	13.201	5729.4	5.497	8	1.000	1.073	1.300	.625	1.073	.625
	24.38	110.94	.000	9	.935	.815	.854	1.075	.557	.665
	379.15	3.142	210.06	10	.655	1.170	3.408	.948	1.529	1.352
	403.53	.000	335.65	11	.768	.029	1.069	1.300	.000	.854
	3.643	3.155	5.885	12	1.556	.466	1.262	.854	.811	.808
	11.349	9.054	.000	13	.805	.464	.181	1.378	.276	
	.655	.000	9.075	14	.830	.973	1.380	1.460	.045	
10.	16466.	7.718	378.63	1	.427	1.053	1.033	.309	1.115	.791
	16.547	.478	17.336	2	.449	.617	.712	−.004	1.284	.804
	.474	4.956	18.546	3	1.239	.624	1.039	1.151	1.126	1.856
	.000	71.06	312.42	4	.955	.854	.985	1.122	1.965	1.483
	393.57	4.610	204.06	5	.857	.808	.273	.968	2.237	.988
	7.372	.428	.00	6	1.115	.887	.298	1.016	.936	1.010
	.000	.000	16.533	7	1.239	1.696	.307	.002	2.449	.001
	13.350	5745.8	5.083	8	.968	1.076	1.300	.556	1.076	.556
	26.74	116.66	.000	9	.942	.829	.854	.682	.543	.568
	373.45	4.993	205.73	10	.614	1.151	3.487	1.552	1.538	1.488
	400.18	3.245	341.92	11	.718	.029	1.015	1.300	.000	.854
	3.565	5.431	5.171	12	1.591	.419	1.261	.854	.808	.808
	11.547	9.643	.000	13	.805	.453	.181	1.384	.258	E20
	.654	.000	10.176	14	.849	.983	1.409	1.543	.045	
50.	16068.	7.295	367.78	1	.444	1.064	1.040	.330	1.087	.796
	15.610	.432	16.437	2	.441	.643	.708	.002	1.289	.794
	.453	4.503	17.190	3	1.184	.638	1.027	1.163	1.135	1.864
	.000	67.83	317.94	4	.967	.855	.991	1.068	1.960	1.392
	377.77	4.635	197.32	5	.890	.805	.287	1.012	2.225	1.003
	7.228	.444	.00	6	1.087	.884	.316	1.003	.915	.999
	.000	.000	15.802	7	1.184	1.637	.315	.000	2.337	−.000
	12.368	5548.0	4.769	8	1.012	1.081	1.300	.592	1.081	.592
	27.20	112.09	.000	9	.952	.822	.855	.713	.541	.568
	358.23	5.050	198.91	10	.635	1.122	3.319	1.488	1.641	1.489
	385.44	3.316	336.56	11	.775	.029	1.009	1.300	.000	.855
	3.380	5.003	5.070	12	1.570	.449	1.259	.855	.771	.805
	11.032	10.072	.000	13	.806	.447	.180	1.458	.254	E20
	.641	.000	10.021	14	.878	.980	1.392	1.584	.043	

(d)

Figure 5-4 (cont.)

	Variable	Symbol	Time (years)		Change (%)
			−5	50	
a.	Premium-housing-construction program	PHCP	0	3,320	—
b.	Premium-housing construction total	PHC	3,140	5,050	+61.
1.	New enterprise	NE	4,900	4,640	−5.
2.	Mature business	MB	7,800	7,300	−6.
3.	Declining industry	DI	16,500	15,610	−5.
4.	Premium housing	PH	110,900	112,100	+1.
5.	Worker housing	WH	335,600	336,600	0
6.	Underemployed housing	UH	310,100	317,900	+3.
7.	Managerial-professional	MP	71,100	67,800	−5.
8.	Labor	L	392,600	377,800	−4.
9.	Underemployed	U	377,300	367,800	−3.
10.	Manager/housing ratio	MHR	1.07	1.01	−6.
11.	Labor/housing ratio	LHR	1.17	1.12	−4.
12.	Underemployed/housing ratio	UHR	.81	.77	−5.
13.	Manager/job ratio	MR	1.38	1.39	+1.
14.	Labor/job ratio	LR	.97	.98	+1.
15.	Underemployed/job ratio	UR	1.81	1.86	+3.
16.	Tax ratio needed	TRN	2.25	2.22	+1.
17.	Underemployed to labor net	UTLN	5,500	4,770	−13.

Figure 5-5 Changes produced by premium-housing program (PHCR = .05).

Construction of housing in any price class through externally imposed programs seems detrimental to the stagnant city. The reason is fairly clear if the fundamental problem of the city is too much housing and too high a population, particularly in the lower economic groups. Additional housing fills land and makes new industry more difficult to initiate.

5.3 New-Enterprise Construction

Now that we have seen that the construction of housing moves the stagnant urban area in the wrong direction, we will examine the consequences of constructing new enterprise. The results are favorable but taken alone are not sufficient to overcome the difficulties.

Figure 5-6 shows the influence of a new-enterprise-construction program. It is here assumed that the new enterprise can be created directly as a result of a positive applied program. As a practical matter a city probably can not accomplish this by any direct action; indirect action would be more realistic. However, we want to understand the influence new industry might have, and creating it by a direct-action program within the model system shows the consequences.

In Figure 5-6 the new industry being generated is equal to about 1.2% each year of the total productive units in the area. Figure 5-6a shows rises in all population classes and all business categories. Housing increases except for a slight

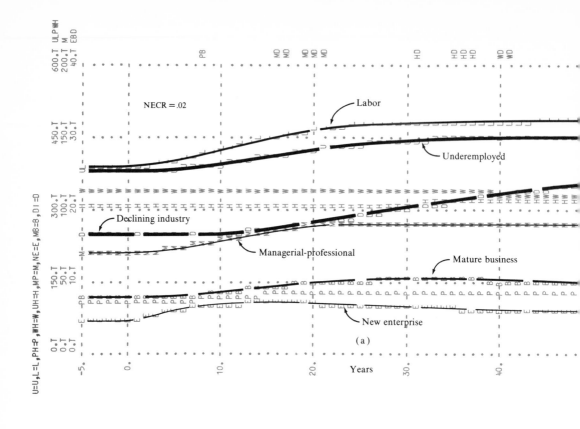

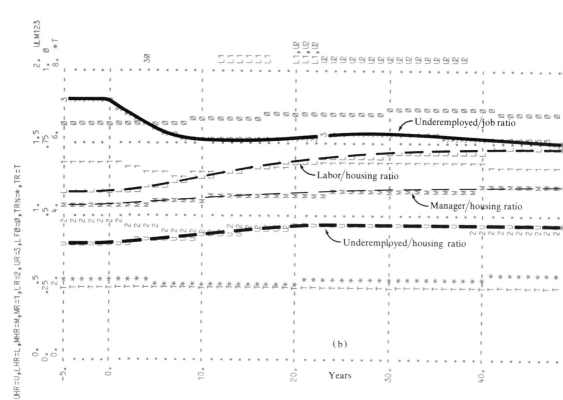

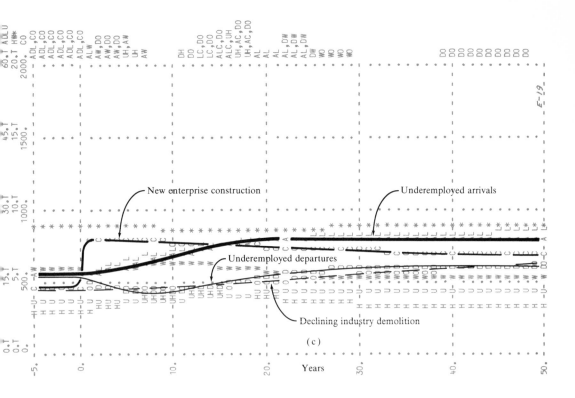

Figure 5-6 New-enterprise-construction program that produces new each year about 1.2% of the total productive units in the city.

decline in worker housing. Figure 5-6*b* shows a modest decrease, representing improvement, in the underemployed/job ratio. Figure 5-6*c* shows that the area becomes more attractive to the underemployed, causing a rise in underemployed arrivals and a decline in underemployed departures. Figure 5-7 summarizes the changes caused by the new-enterprise-construction program. In the fiftieth year the direct-action-construction program is producing 418 new-enterprise units per year. Yet the total new-enterprise-construction rate has risen only 242 units per year. Nearly half of the direct-action program is required to replace normal construction, which has been suppressed by the changed economic mix within the area.

The new-enterprise-construction program produces favorable changes. However, these changes are not sufficient to correct the economic imbalance. Furthermore, it is unlikely that new-enterprise construction can be forced by any city-government program. It is more important therefore to look at direct-action programs that conceivably lie within the authority of a city and that will indirectly generate a rebalancing of those variables that can not be directly influenced.

5.4 Declining-Industry Demolition

If the mix within the city tends toward too high a proportion of old structures, the city might establish land-clearing programs or a tax structure that provides

TIME	AV	MB	U		AMM	LAJM	LSM	MSM	SHLM	UMM
	DI	MBD	UA	2	AMMP	LAM	LUM	NEGR	TCM	UMMP
	DID	MD	UD	3	BDM	LAMP	LUR	PEM	TPCR	UR
	DIDP	MP	UH	4	DIDM	LATM	MAHM	PHAM	TR	WHAM
	L	NE	UJ	5	DIEM	LAUM	MAJM	PHEM	TRN	WHEM
	LA	NEC	UJP	6	DILM	LCR	MAM	PHGM	UAMM	WHGM
	LCHP	NECP	UTL	7	EDM	LDM	MAMP	PHGR	UDM	WHGR
	LD	P	UTLN	8	EGM	LEM	MAPM	PHLM	UEM	WHLM
	LDC	PH	UTP	9	ELJM	LFØ	MATM	PHM	UFW	WHM
	LDI	PHC	UW	10	ELM	LHR	MDM	PHØM	UHM	WHØM
	LJ	PHCP	WH	11	EM	LLF	MHR	PHPM	UHPR	WHTM
	LTM	PHØ	WHC	12	EMM	LMM	MLM	PHTM	UHR	WHUM
	LTU	SHD	WHCP	13	ETM	LMMP	MLR	SHAM	WJM	
	MA	SHDP	WHØ	14	LAHM	LR	MR	SHDM	UM	

TIME	AV	MB	U		AMM	LAJM	LSM	MSM	SHLM	UMM
-5.	16336.	7.806	377.31	1	.452	1.087	1.054	.344	1.060	.805
	16.474	.465	17.283	2	.449	.623	.712	.000	1.284	.802
	.464	4.849	17.275	3	1.190	.625	1.040	1.145	1.121	1.811
	.000	71.13	310.08	4	.939	.854	.931	1.549	1.966	1.542
	392.55	4.866	208.35	5	.886	.808	.296	1.000	2.248	1.000
	7.360	.462	.00	6	1.060	.878	.306	1.000	.936	1.000
	.000	.000	16.847	7	1.190	1.681	.307	.000	2.289	.000
	13.201	5729.4	5.497	8	1.000	1.073	1.300	.625	1.073	.625
	24.38	110.94	.000	9	.935	.815	.854	1.075	.557	.665
	379.15	3.142	210.06	10	.655	1.170	3.408	.948	1.529	1.352
	403.53	.000	335.65	11	.768	.029	1.069	1.300	.000	.854
	3.643	3.155	5.885	12	1.556	.466	1.262	.854	.811	.808
	11.349	9.054	.000	13	.805	.464	.181	1.378	.276	
	.655	.000	9.075	14	.830	.973	1.380	1.460	.045	
10.	17796.	8.595	394.51	1	.621	1.279	1.174	.453	1.109	.923
	16.695	.550	20.555	2	.500	.654	.725	.018	1.266	.862
	.462	4.593	13.305	3	1.281	.650	1.084	1.167	1.139	1.525
	.000	78.81	307.50	4	.922	.855	.888	1.899	1.958	1.842
	427.79	6.812	258.78	5	.832	.817	.369	1.142	2.162	1.035
	8.348	.783	.00	6	1.109	.830	.364	1.039	.970	1.004
	.000	.397	21.843	7	1.281	1.612	.341	.005	1.686	.001
	13.789	6116.9	10.270	8	1.142	1.084	1.300	.564	1.084	.564
	36.48	118.08	.000	9	.822	.827	.855	1.411	.643	.754
	432.11	4.149	253.53	10	.618	1.268	2.914	.752	1.405	1.244
	468.59	.000	337.48	11	.677	.027	1.112	1.300	.000	.855
	4.493	2.665	6.337	12	1.447	.623	1.268	.855	.855	.817
	11.344	8.795	.000	13	.806	.525	.184	1.289	.390	
	.807	.000	8.398	14	.732	.913	1.289	1.430	.048	
50.	18681.	9.928	451.59	1	.520	1.305	1.190	.388	1.259	.892
	23.727	.751	23.955	2	.511	.484	.723	-.004	1.270	.883
	.620	6.412	17.541	3	1.513	.510	1.075	1.074	1.061	1.510
	.000	90.38	320.45	4	.870	.852	.809	2.527	1.982	2.319
	485.64	5.928	299.03	5	.692	.815	.326	.967	2.358	.988
	7.437	.704	.00	6	1.259	.824	.292	.993	1.046	.992
	.000	.418	25.804	7	1.513	2.091	.292	-.001	1.942	-.001
	20.310	6978.5	13.011	8	.967	1.037	1.300	.413	1.037	.413
	32.00	126.49	.000	9	.782	.857	.852	1.111	.647	.652
	504.74	3.473	292.16	10	.528	1.466	3.547	.924	1.169	1.369
	536.75	.000	331.25	11	.485	.026	1.191	1.300	.000	.852
	4.932	3.507	5.339	12	1.512	.512	1.272	.852	.939	.815
	12.720	9.044	.000	13	.803	.508	.186	1.121	.396	
	.792	.000	9.072	14	.534	.905	1.343	1.411	.056	

(d)

Figure 5-6 (cont.)

	Variable	Symbol	Time (years) −5	50	Change (%)
a.	New-enterprise-construction program	NECP	0	418	—
b.	New-enterprise-construction rate total	NEC	462	704	+52.
1.	New enterprise	NE	4,900	5,930	+21.
2.	Mature business	MB	7,800	9,930	+27.
3.	Declining industry	DI	16,500	23,730	+44.
4.	Premium housing	PH	110,900	126,500	+14.
5.	Worker housing	WH	335,600	331,200	−1.
6.	Underemployed housing	UH	310,100	320,400	+3.
7.	Managerial-professional	MP	71,100	90,400	+27.
8.	Labor	L	392,600	485,600	+24.
9.	Underemployed	U	377,300	451,600	+20.
10.	Manager/housing ratio	MHR	1.07	1.19	+11.
11.	Labor/housing ratio	LHR	1.17	1.47	+26.
12.	Underemployed/housing ratio	UHR	.81	.94	+16.
13.	Manager/job ratio	MR	1.38	1.34	−3.
14.	Labor/job ratio	LR	.97	.90	−7.
15.	Underemployed/job ratio	UR	1.81	1.51	−17.
16.	Tax ratio needed	TRN	2.25	2.36	+5.
17.	Underemployed to labor net	UTLN	5,500	13,010	+136.

Figure 5-7 Changes caused by the new-enterprise-construction program (NECR = .02).

incentive for removal of aging structures. Without exploring how the removal of old structures might be initiated, let us examine the influence of such removal within the simulation model.

Figure 5-8 shows the effect of demolishing 5% of declining industry each year. There are improvements in some variables. Figure 5-9 shows the changes caused by this program. Opening up land by demolition of decaying industry has reduced substantially the amount of such industry. Both new enterprise and mature business have increased. Housing has declined slightly, population has declined more. The increase in new enterprise and the reduction in population have reduced the tax load so that the tax rate needed has declined 9%.

In Figure 5-8d underemployed jobs UJ have fallen more than the number of underemployed U so that the underemployed/job ratio in Figure 5-8b is slightly higher than before the demolition program started. The changes are of mixed merit.

5.5 Slum-Housing Demolition

To change the city toward having more industry and away from being an economically ineffective concentration of underemployed housing and underemployed population, one measure might be the demolition of slum housing. This could provide area for industrial expansion and might help to rebalance

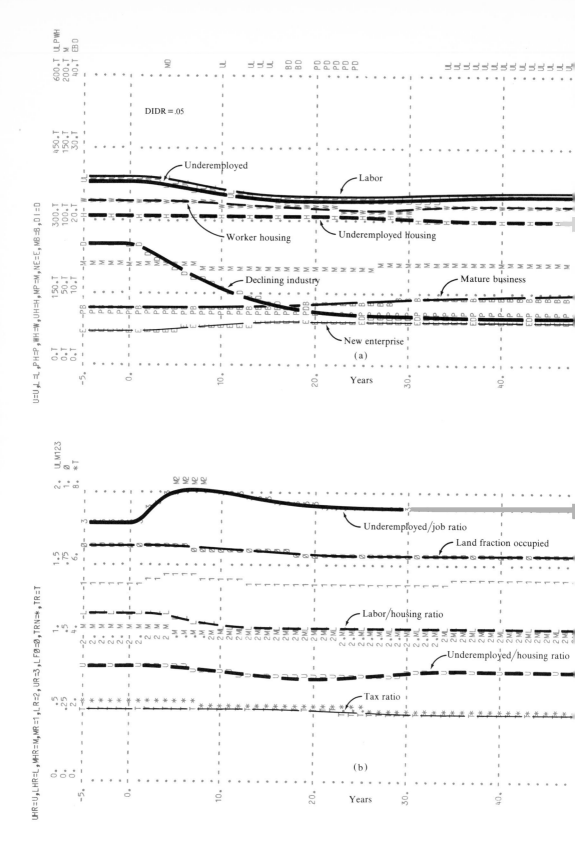

DIDR = .05

Underemployed

Labor

Worker housing

Underemployed Housing

Declining industry

Mature business

New enterprise

(a)

Years

Underemployed/job ratio

Land fraction occupied

Labor/housing ratio

Underemployed/housing ratio

Tax ratio

(b)

Years

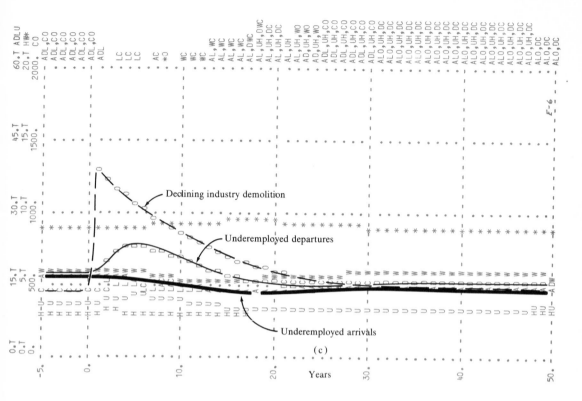

Figure 5-8 Declining-industry-demolition program that removes 5% of declining industry each year.

the population proportions so that the city could escape from its stagnant condition. To determine whether slum-housing demolition results in favorable changes for the city, the consequences for the original populations must be examined.

Figure 5-10 shows the extensive changes created by a slum-housing-demolition program that removes 5% of the underemployed housing each year. Discussion of such a program does not imply that the demolition of slum housing should result from active intervention by the city. It might better be accomplished by changes in tax laws and land zoning.

In Figure 5-10 the slum-housing-demolition program reduces the underemployed housing to a new equilibrium after 50 years at about half its beginning value. As land becomes available, new industrial construction is induced and creates more jobs. Also there is an upsurge in the construction of worker housing which, along with the additional industry, supports a larger labor force. The underemployed-arrival rate UA in Figure 5-10c changes relatively little, meaning that the attractiveness of the city is about the same at the end of 50 years as it was before the beginning of the slum-housing-demolition program. However, Figure 5-10b shows a substantial compensating change in two of the components of city attractiveness for the underemployed. The underemployed/housing ratio UHR has increased, indicating less housing availability. At the same time the

TIME									
AV	MB	U	1	AMM	LAJM	LSM	MSM	SHLM	UMM
DI	MBD	UA	2	AMMP	LAM	LUM	NEGR	TCM	UMMP
DI D	MD	UD	3	BDM	LAMP	LUR	PEM	TPCR	UR
DI DP	MP	UH	4	DIDM	LATM	MAHM	PHAM	TR	WHAM
L	NE	UJ	5	DIEM	LAUM	MAJM	PHEM	TRN	WHEM
LA	NEC	UJP	6	DILM	LCR	MAM	PHGM	UAMM	WHGM
LCHP	NECP	UTL	7	EDM	ⱠDM	MAMP	PHGR	UDM	WHGR
LD	P	UTLN	8	EGM	LEM	MAPM	PHLM	UEM	WHLM
LDC	PH	UTP	9	ELJM	LFØ	MATM	PHM	UFW	WHM
LDI	PHC	UW	10	ELM	LHR	MDM	PHØM	UHM	WHØM
LJ	PHCP	WH	11	EM	LLF	MHR	PHPM	UHPR	WHTM
LTM	PHØ	WHC	12	EMM	LMM	MLM	PHTM	UHR	WHUM
LTU	SHD	WHCP	13	ETM	LMMP	MLR	SHAM	UJM	
MA	SHDP	WHØ	14	LAHM	LR	MR	SHDM	UM	

thousands				units					

-5.									
16336.	7.806	377.31	1	.452	1.087	1.054	.344	1.060	.805
16.474	.465	17.283	2	.449	.623	.712	.000	1.284	.802
.464	4.849	17.275	3	1.190	.625	1.040	1.145	1.121	1.811
.000	71.13	310.08	4	.939	.854	.931	1.549	1.966	1.542
392.55	4.866	208.35	5	.886	.808	.296	1.000	2.248	1.000
7.360	.462	.00	6	1.060	.878	.306	1.000	.936	1.000
.000	.000	16.847	7	1.190	1.681	.307	.000	2.289	.000
13.201	5729.4	5.497	8	1.000	1.073	1.300	.625	1.073	.625
24.38	110.94	.000	9	.935	.815	.854	1.075	.557	.665
379.15	3.142	210.06	10	.655	1.170	3.408	.948	1.529	1.352
403.53	.000	335.65	11	.768	.029	1.069	1.300	.000	.854
3.643	3.155	5.885	12	1.556	.466	1.262	.854	.811	.808
11.349	9.054	.000	13	.805	.464	.181	1.378	.276	
.655	.000	9.075	14	.830	.973	1.380	1.460	.045	

10.									
15971.	7.899	355.33	1	.366	.968	.984	.319	1.012	.766
10.704	.410	14.935	2	.416	.611	.706	.007	1.292	.775
.853	4.638	20.578	3	1.037	.605	1.019	1.206	1.172	2.016
.535	67.20	311.36	4	.989	.854	.971	1.230	1.963	1.260
362.04	5.371	176.24	5	.978	.804	.280	1.059	2.165	1.015
6.573	.539	.00	6	1.012	.905	.302	.987	.924	.998
.000	.000	13.698	7	1.037	1.710	.293	-.002	2.896	-.000
12.385	5350.8	1.968	8	1.059	1.103	1.300	.685	1.103	.685
24.31	108.88	.000	9	1.019	.803	.854	.978	.497	.600
332.94	2.891	176.69	10	.691	1.081	3.451	1.033	1.670	1.441
357.26	.000	334.79	11	.950	.032	1.029	1.300	.000	.854
3.196	3.373	5.458	12	1.581	.448	1.271	.854	.761	.804
11.539	9.316	.000	13	.806	.441	.186	1.478	.197	
.591	.000	9.649	14	.919	1.013	1.400	1.496	.044	

50.									
16516.	9.696	346.04	1	.438	1.032	1.020	.333	1.000	.800
6.486	.521	15.475	2	.441	.665	.708	-.001	1.289	.806
.510	4.672	16.458	3	1.075	.664	1.027	1.214	1.179	1.906
.324	70.18	302.29	4	.955	.864	.970	1.237	1.874	1.239
355.34	6.160	181.59	5	.955	.805	.289	.994	2.044	.998
7.080	.521	.00	6	1.000	.892	.315	1.003	.912	1.005
.000	.000	14.734	7	1.075	1.588	.317	.000	2.378	.001
11.288	5251.3	4.234	8	.994	1.107	1.300	.762	1.107	.762
25.40	113.59	.000	9	.973	.791	.864	1.055	.528	.659
333.51	3.208	182.82	10	.726	1.075	3.329	.961	1.663	1.361
358.91	.000	330.63	11	.901	.030	1.030	1.300	.000	.864
3.459	3.275	5.827	12	1.567	.478	1.295	.864	.763	.805
10.519	8.910	.000	13	.819	.487	.197	1.474	.238	
.668	.000	8.999	14	.925	.990	1.389	1.474	.043	

(d)

Figure 5-8 (cont.)

| | | Time (years) | | |
Variable	Symbol	−5	50	Change (%)
a. Declining-industry-demolition program	DIDP	0	324	—
b. Declining-industry demolition total	DID	464	510	+10.
1. New enterprise	NE	4,900	6,200	+26.
2. Mature business	MB	7,800	9,700	+24.
3. Declining industry	DI	16,500	6,500	−61.
4. Premium housing	PH	110,900	113,600	+2.
5. Worker housing	WH	335,600	330,600	−2.
6. Underemployed housing	UH	310,100	302,300	−3.
7. Managerial-professional	MP	71,100	70,200	−1.
8. Labor	L	392,600	355,300	−10.
9. Underemployed	U	377,300	346,000	−8.
10. Manager/housing ratio	MHR	1.07	1.03	−4.
11. Labor/housing ratio	LHR	1.17	1.08	−8.
12. Underemployed/housing ratio	UHR	.81	.76	−6.
13. Manager/job ratio	MR	1.38	1.39	+1.
14. Labor/job ratio	LR	.97	.99	+2.
15. Underemployed/job ratio	UR	1.81	1.91	+6.
16. Tax ratio needed	TRN	2.25	2.04	−9.
17. Underemployed to labor net	UTLN	5,500	4,200	−24.

Figure 5-9 Changes caused by a declining-industry-demolition program (DIDR = .05).

underemployed/job ratio UR has declined, indicating improved economic opportunities for the underemployed that are present. Except for the rising underemployed/housing ratio UHR, with its implied shortage of housing, it would not be possible to maintain the more favorable employment conditions represented by the falling underemployed/job ratio UR. Were housing readily available, the improved economic conditions in the urban area would attract additional underemployed from the outside environment until economic conditions had fallen so far that no additional net inward flow would occur.

Figure 5-11 shows the changes produced by the slum-housing-demolition program. New enterprise and mature business increase 45%. Declining industry increases only 9% because the more favorable circumstances for new-enterprise construction encourage the abandonment and demolition of declining industry. Premium housing increases 30% and worker housing 34%, while underemployed housing is down 44%. The underemployed/housing ratio has risen 49%, a necessary crowding accompaniment to the improved underemployed/job ratio reduction of 33%. The tax ratio needed TRN has fallen 33%.

Against these improvements in the city as a whole, one must ask what the slum-demolition program has done to the underemployed population. In the first 10 years, the underemployed population U has dropped from 377,310 to 345,420 (Figure 5-10d), or 8.5%. This has occurred because of the accumulated effects

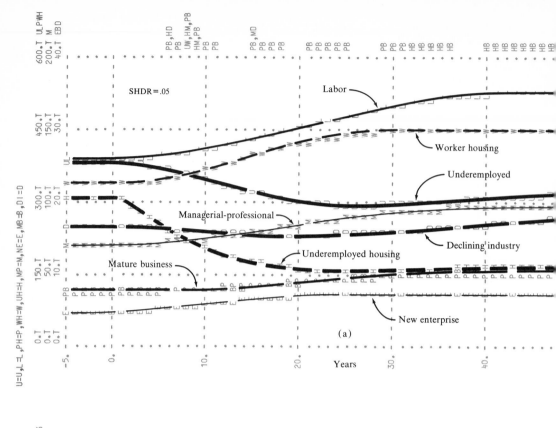

(a)

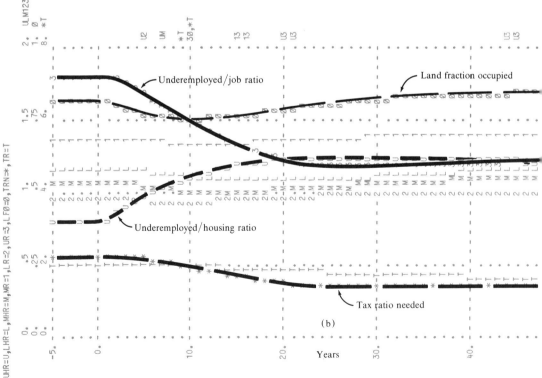

(b)

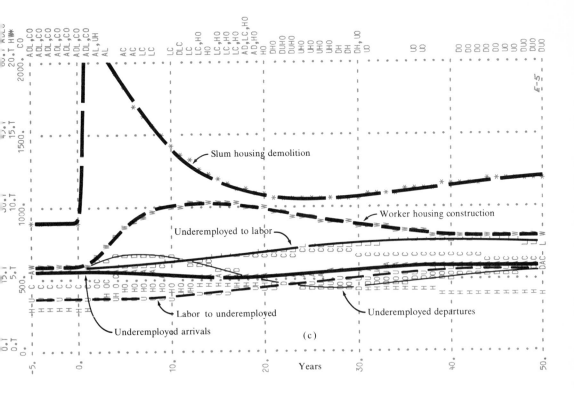

Figure 5-10 Slum-housing demolition that removes 5% of underemployed housing each year.

of changed flow rates which are, in the tenth year, a decrease of 1,050 men per year arriving UA, an increase of 2,450 men per year leaving UD, and an increase of 1,840 men per year in upward mobility UTLN from underemployed to labor. The population adjustment of 8.5% can be estimated roughly in the same proportion—1.7% change owing to fewer arrivals, 3.9% change owing to more departures, and 2.9% change owing to greater transfer to the labor catagory. Only the value of the increased departure rate could be questioned. Other policies, discussed in Section 5.7, appear to revitalize a city without forcing a net outward migration of underemployed.

This slum-housing-demolition program does not incorporate any rebuilding activity. The natural vitality of the city generates rebuilding once land area becomes available and various processes start to move toward creating a healthier economic balance.

But even with the demolition program, the land fraction occupied at the end of 50 years has risen by 2%. Furthermore, worker housing has increased as well as premium housing. In Figure 5-10c the worker-housing-construction rate WHCR rose steeply and remained high through the second decade as land area became available. This suggests that the city is still tending to generate housing more readily than industry and that some further suppression of housing in favor of industrial expansion should be explored.

TIME	AV	MB	U	#	AMM	LAJM	LSM	MSM	SHLM	UMM
	DI	MBD	UA	2	AMMP	LAM	LUM	NEGR	TCM	UMMP
	DID	MD	UD	3	BDM	LAMP	LUR	PEM	TPCR	UR
	DIDP	MP	UH	4	DIDM	LATM	MAHM	PHAM	TR	WHAM
	L	NE	UJ	5	DIEM	LAUM	MAJM	PHEM	TRN	WHEM
	LA	NEC	UJP	6	DILM	LCR	MAM	PHGM	UAMM	WHGM
	LCHP	NECP	UTL	7	EDM	LDM	MAMP	PHGR	UDM	WHGR
	LD	P	UTLN	8	EGM	LEM	MAPM	PHLM	UEM	WHLM
	LDC	PH	UTP	9	ELJM	LFØ	MATM	PHM	UFW	WHM
	LDI	PHC	UW	10	ELM	LHR	MDM	PHØM	UHM	WHØM
	LJ	PHCP	WH	11	EM	LLF	MHR	PHPM	UHPR	WHTM
	LTM	PHØ	WHC	12	EMM	LMM	MLM	PHTM	UHR	WHUM
	LTU	SHD	WHCP	13	ETM	LMMP	MLR	SHAM	UJM	
	MA	SHDP	WHØ	14	LAHM	LR	MR	SHDM	UM	

	thousands					units				
-5.	16336.	7.806	377.31	1	.452	1.087	1.054	.344	1.060	.805
	16.474	.465	17.283	2	.449	.623	.712	.000	1.284	.802
	.464	4.849	17.275	3	1.190	.625	1.040	1.145	1.121	1.811
	.000	71.13	310.08	4	.939	.854	.931	1.549	1.966	1.542
	392.55	4.866	208.35	5	.886	.808	.296	1.000	2.248	1.000
	7.360	.462	.00	6	1.060	.878	.306	1.000	.936	1.000
	.000	.000	16.847	7	1.190	1.681	.307	.000	2.289	.000
	13.201	5729.4	5.497	8	1.000	1.073	1.300	.625	1.073	.625
	24.38	110.94	.000	9	.935	.815	.854	1.075	.557	.665
	379.15	3.142	210.06	10	.655	1.170	3.408	.948	1.529	1.352
	403.53	.000	335.65	11	.768	.029	1.069	1.300	.000	.854
	3.643	3.155	5.885	12	1.556	.466	1.262	.854	.811	.808
	11.349	9.054	.000	13	.805	.464	.181	1.378	.276	
	.655	.000	9.075	14	.830	.973	1.380	1.460	.045	
10.	17122.	8.001	345.42	1	.371	1.169	1.106	.388	1.000	.934
	16.021	.404	16.229	2	.430	.739	.756	.012	1.225	.841
	.478	4.388	19.732	3	1.009	.651	1.187	1.235	1.196	1.501
	.000	74.21	208.36	4	.995	.855	.989	1.085	1.953	1.375
	409.86	5.808	230.12	5	.995	.837	.326	1.098	1.970	1.025
	8.010	.619	.00	6	1.000	.858	.358	1.055	1.006	1.053
	.000	.000	18.873	7	1.009	1.435	.324	.007	2.856	.007
	11.761	5593.5	7.341	8	1.098	1.117	1.300	.999	1.117	.999
	36.38	122.38	.000	9	.890	.757	.855	1.398	.650	1.061
	396.38	4.401	224.42	10	.828	1.117	2.956	.759	.748	.974
	432.76	.000	366.85	11	.988	.028	1.011	1.300	.000	.855
	3.956	2.786	10.019	12	1.512	.548	1.262	.855	1.105	.837
	11.428	14.235	.000	13	.807	.483	.181	.916	.400	
	.721	10.418	7.148	14	.883	.947	1.343	.916	.051	
50.	20728.	11.329	316.89	1	.401	.970	.985	.334	1.169	.929
	18.027	.669	17.940	2	.423	.668	.903	-.003	1.065	.964
	.564	6.626	16.700	3	1.181	.696	1.675	1.090	1.075	1.224
	.000	96.02	174.31	4	1.042	.897	.894	1.845	1.608	1.572
	530.81	7.118	258.91	5	.891	.935	.289	.978	1.510	.992
	11.085	.640	.00	6	1.169	.905	.302	.999	1.165	1.005
	.000	.000	22.395	7	1.181	1.580	.305	-.000	2.635	.001
	16.773	6200.1	5.578	8	.978	1.045	1.300	.489	1.045	.489
	31.75	144.74	.000	9	1.026	.842	.897	1.028	.733	.643
	492.56	4.039	232.22	10	.573	1.179	3.450	.980	.491	1.382
	524.31	.000	450.28	11	.777	.032	1.106	1.300	.000	.897
	4.949	4.256	7.855	12	1.566	.440	1.262	.897	1.212	.935
	16.846	12.100	.000	13	.863	.466	.181	.830	.642	
	.879	8.716	12.448	14	.821	1.012	1.388	.971	.071	

(d)

Figure 5-10 (cont.)

	Variable	Symbol	Time (years) −5	50	Change (%)
a.	Slum-housing-demolition program	SHDP	0	8,720	—
b.	Slum-housing demolition total rate	SHD	9,050	12,100	+34.
c.	Worker-housing construction	WHC	5,880	7,860	+34.
d.	Land fraction occupied	LFO	.82	.84	+2.
1.	New enterprise	NE	4,900	7,100	+45.
2.	Mature business	MB	7,800	11,300	+45.
3.	Declining industry	DI	16,500	18,000	+9.
4.	Premium housing	PH	110,900	144,700	+30.
5.	Worker housing	WH	335,600	450,300	+34.
6.	Underemployed housing	UH	310,100	174,300	−44.
7.	Managerial-professional	MP	71,100	96,000	+35.
8.	Labor	L	392,600	530,800	+35.
9.	Underemployed	U	377,300	316,900	−16.
10.	Manager/housing ratio	MHR	1.07	1.11	+4.
11.	Labor/housing ratio	LHR	1.17	1.18	+1.
12.	Underemployed/housing ratio	UHR	.81	1.21	+49.
13.	Manager/job ratio	MR	1.38	1.39	+1.
14.	Labor/job ratio	LR	.97	1.01	+4.
15.	Underemployed/job ratio	UR	1.81	1.22	−33.
16.	Tax ratio needed	TRN	2.25	1.51	−33.
17.	Underemployed to labor net	UTLN	5,500	5,580	+1.

Figure 5-11 Changes caused by a slum-housing-demolition program (SHDR = .05).

5.6 Discouraging Housing Construction

In Figure 5-1 the construction of worker housing depressed activity within the city. This suggests that less housing construction might be beneficial. Figure 5-12 shows results when a slum-housing-demolition program is pursued and in addition construction of new worker housing is restrained. The 5% slum-demolition program is the same as in Figure 5-10. In addition the worker-housing normal coefficient WHCN has been reduced from .03 to .015. This means, if all other conditions remained identical, that the worker-housing-construction rate would be reduced by a factor of 2. Of course, other conditions do not remain constant but shift to partly compensate for the restrictions on new construction. The reduced coefficient WHCN (see Equation 83 in Appendix A) implies less favorable conditions for new construction. In practice these might mean zoning restrictions, increasing standards of building construction, a tax structure unfavorable to such construction, or other urban policies designed to shift the balance from housing to productive business activity.

A comparison of Figures 5-12 and 5-10 shows that the restriction on worker-housing construction has increased the labor force, decreased the underemployed, increased the managerial population, and increased business activity. Figure 5-13 shows the changes from the equilibrium city caused by the slum-demolition program and the restriction on worker-housing construction. New enterprise and

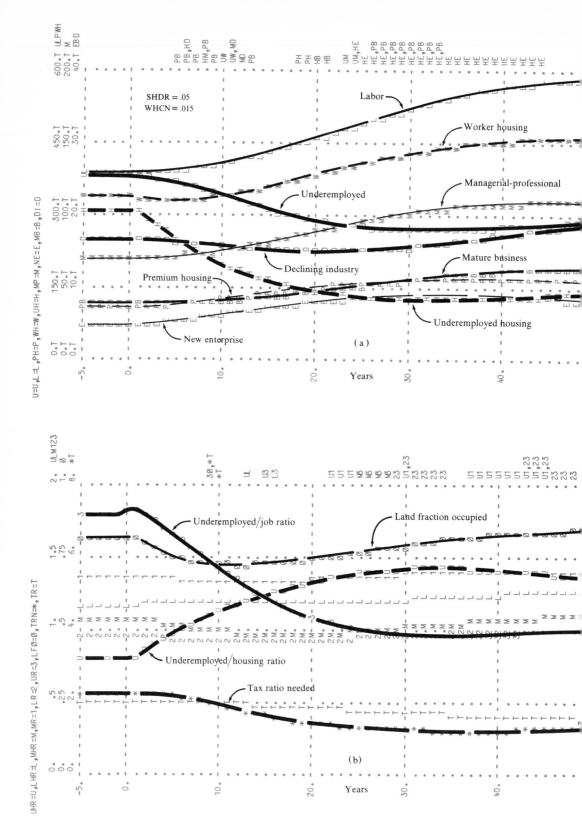

(a)

(b)

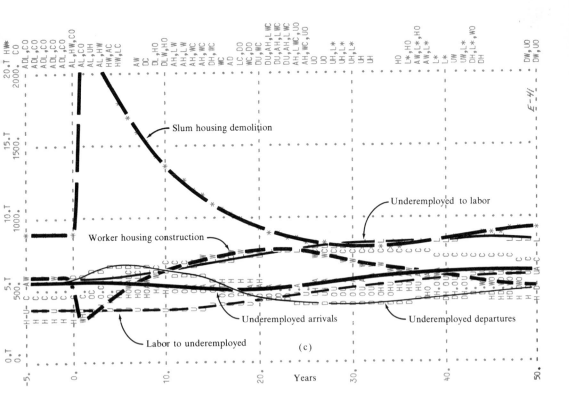

Figure 5-12   Slum-housing demolition of 5% of the underemployed housing each year and restrictions that reduce to half the normal worker-housing-construction rate.

mature business are up substantially more than declining industry. Premium housing has increased 48% and worker housing 36%, while underemployed housing has declined 54%. In spite of the 23% decrease in the underemployed population, the net upward economic mobility UTLN has risen 29%, indicating that the city has become a more effective converter of the underemployed into people matched to modern business activity. Because of the changed internal mix in the city, the tax ratio needed TRN has fallen 41%.

Figure 5-14 shows the changes caused by restrictions on worker-housing construction only, when added to slum-housing demolition. The figure compares the fiftieth year from Figure 5-10 with the fiftieth year from Figure 5-12. The difference between the two is caused by a halving of the worker-housing-construction rate for any particular set of urban conditions. Figure 5-14 contains some rather surprising results. Although there is half the tendency to construct worker housing, the amount of worker housing has risen by 1%. Premium housing has increased 13% and underemployed housing has decreased 18%. All of these changes are in comparison to the conditions caused by a slum-demolition program only. New enterprise and mature business have increased 14% each and declining industry is up 6%. The restriction on worker housing has increased the labor

TIME	AV	MB	U		AMM	LAJM	LSM	MSM	SHLM	UMM
	DI	MBD	UA	2	AMMP	LAM	LUM	NEGR	TCM	UMMP
	DID	MD	UD	3	BDM	LAMP	LUR	PEM	TPCR	UR
	DIDP	MP	UH	4	DIDM	LATM	MAHM	PHAM	TR	WHAM
	L	NE	UJ	5	DIEM	LAUM	MAJM	PHEM	TRN	WHEM
	LA	NEC	UJP	6	DILM	LCR	MAM	PHGM	UAMM	WHGM
	LCHP	NECP	UTL	7	EDM	LDM	MAMP	PHGR	UDM	WHGR
	LD	P	UTLN	8	EGM	LEM	MAPM	PHLM	UEM	WHLM
	LDC	PH	UTP	9	ELJM	LFØ	MATM	PHM	UFW	WHM
	LDI	PHC	UW	10	ELM	LHR	MDM	PHØM	UHM	WHØM
	LJ	PHCP	WH	11	EM	LLF	MHR	PHPM	UHPR	WHTM
	LTM	PHØ	WHC	12	EMM	LMM	MLM	PHTM	UHR	WHUM
	LTU	SHD	WHCP	13	ETM	LMMP	MLR	SHAM	UJM	
	MA	SHDP	WHØ	14	LAHM	LR	MR	SHDM	UM	
	thousands				units					
-5.	16336.	7.806	377.31	1	.452	1.087	1.054	.344	1.060	.805
	16.474	.465	17.283	2	.449	.623	.712	.000	1.284	.802
	.464	4.849	17.275	3	1.190	.625	1.040	1.145	1.121	1.811
	.000	71.13	310.08	4	.939	.854	.931	1.549	1.966	1.542
	392.55	4.866	208.35	5	.886	.808	.296	1.000	2.248	1.000
	7.360	.462	.00	6	1.060	.878	.306	1.000	.936	1.000
	.000	.000	16.847	7	1.190	1.681	.307	.000	2.289	.000
	13.201	5729.4	5.497	8	1.000	1.073	1.300	.625	1.073	.625
	24.38	110.94	.000	9	.935	.815	.854	1.075	.557	.665
	379.15	3.142	210.06	10	.655	1.170	3.408	.948	1.529	1.352
	403.53	.000	335.65	11	.768	.029	1.069	1.300	.000	.854
	3.643	3.155	5.885	12	1.556	.466	1.262	.854	.811	.808
	11.349	9.054	.000	13	.805	.464	.181	1.378	.276	
	.655	.000	9.075	14	.830	.973	1.380	1.460	.045	
10.	16984.	8.082	342.20	1	.390	1.233	1.146	.409	1.000	.968
	15.768	.390	16.070	2	.429	.706	.757	.016	1.225	.847
	.507	4.211	18.556	3	.964	.639	1.188	1.234	1.195	1.435
	.000	75.20	202.20	4	1.071	.855	1.003	.973	1.954	1.641
	406.66	6.194	238.44	5	1.071	.838	.339	1.129	1.970	1.032
	7.798	.684	.00	6	1.000	.842	.378	1.073	1.011	1.014
	.000	.000	19.396	7	.964	1.500	.331	.009	2.711	.002
	12.204	5553.6	8.109	8	1.129	1.117	1.300	1.207	1.117	1.207
	35.79	126.42	.000	9	.871	.728	.855	1.581	.669	1.486
	402.78	5.047	229.09	10	.917	1.200	2.800	.670	.692	.829
	438.58	.000	338.80	11	1.086	.027	.991	1.300	.000	.855
	3.986	2.542	6.355	12	1.491	.580	1.270	.855	1.128	.838
	11.016	13.739	.000	13	.807	.490	.185	.897	.452	
	.748	10.110	5.617	14	.800	.927	1.326	.897	.051	
50.	22317.	12.908	290.28	1	.411	.977	.988	.323	1.172	1.032
	18.990	.764	18.976	2	.435	.644	1.002	-.004	.998	1.097
	.594	7.497	14.885	3	1.184	.690	2.008	1.085	1.071	1.016
	.000	108.07	142.27	4	1.043	.909	.901	1.795	1.526	1.861
	582.83	8.130	285.80	5	.889	1.002	.282	.969	1.322	.988
	12.066	.710	.00	6	1.172	.904	.300	.995	1.245	1.020
	.000	.000	25.323	7	1.184	1.634	.310	-.001	2.564	.003
	19.044	6359.6	7.118	8	.969	1.043	1.300	.484	1.043	.484
	31.10	163.84	.000	9	1.011	.843	.909	.990	.795	.827
	546.11	4.398	230.86	10	.571	1.276	3.469	1.015	.312	1.164
	577.21	.000	456.94	11	.774	.031	1.099	1.300	.000	.909
	5.509	4.988	5.126	12	1.577	.428	1.271	.909	1.360	1.002
	18.280	9.488	.000	13	.878	.473	.185	.712	.975	
	1.005	7.114	10.634	14	.724	1.010	1.398	.835	.086	

(d)

Figure 5-12 (cont.)

		Time (years)		
Variable	Symbol	−5	50	Change (%)
a. Slum-housing-demolition program	SHDP	0	7,100	—
b. Slum-housing demolition total rate	SHD	9,100	9,500	+4.
c. Worker-housing construction	WHC	5,900	5,100	−14.
1. New enterprise	NE	4,900	8,100	+65.
2. Mature business	MB	7,800	12,900	+65.
3. Declining industry	DI	16,500	19,000	+15.
4. Premium housing	PH	110,900	163,800	+48.
5. Worker housing	WH	335,600	456,900	+36.
6. Underemployed housing	UH	310,100	142,300	−54.
7. Managerial-professional	MP	71,100	108,100	+52.
8. Labor	L	392,600	582,800	+48.
9. Underemployed	U	377,300	290,300	−23.
10. Manager/housing ratio	MHR	1.07	1.10	+3.
11. Labor/housing ratio	LHR	1.17	1.28	+9.
12. Underemployed/housing ratio	UHR	.81	1.36	+68.
13. Manager/job ratio	MR	1.38	1.40	+1.
14. Labor/job ratio	LR	.97	1.01	+4.
15. Underemployed/job ratio	UR	1.81	1.02	−44.
16. Tax ratio needed	TRN	2.25	1.32	−41.
17. Underemployed to labor net	UTLN	5,500	7,120	+29.

Figure 5-13 Changes caused by slum-housing-demolition (SHDR = .05) and restriction of worker-housing construction (WHCN = .015).

occupying the housing by 10%. The restriction on housing construction has caused the underemployed/job ratio to decrease 16% and the tax ratio needed to decrease another 13% compared to what the slum-housing-demolition program alone produced. As a social converter from underemployed to labor, the new conditions with the worker-housing restriction have caused a 28% increase in underemployed-to-labor net UTLN.

Figure 5-14 requires some explanation. The results of restricting worker-housing construction are spread widely through the urban system, many in unexpected directions. This internal rebalancing to readjust for a policy change is typical of complex systems. It is also common that the results may be opposite those expected, as here finding an increase in worker housing when the construction rate has been restrained. The biggest changes often occur in quite remote places. In Figure 5-14 the largest percentage change has occurred in the net upward mobility UTLN. The next largest change is downward, not in worker housing, which was directly affected, but in underemployed housing, which is indirectly influenced. The third largest change is a decline in the ratio of underemployed to available jobs, indicating more favorable economic opportunities. And the next largest changes are increases in new enterprise and mature business. Worker housing, which is directly influenced by worker-housing construction, is one of the four variables least affected.

Variable	Symbol	Year 50 Fig. 5-10	Year 50 Fig. 5-12	Change (%)
1. New enterprise	NE	7,100	8,100	+14.
2. Mature business	MB	11,300	12,900	+14.
3. Declining industry	DI	18,000	19,000	+6.
4. Premium housing	PH	144,700	163,800	+13.
5. Worker housing	WH	450,300	456,900	+1.
6. Underemployed housing	UH	174,300	142,300	−18.
7. Managerial-professional	MP	96,000	108,100	+13.
8. Labor	L	530,800	582,800	+10.
9. Underemployed	U	316,900	290,300	−8.
10. Manager/housing ratio	MHR	1.11	1.10	−1.
11. Labor/housing ratio	LHR	1.18	1.28	+8.
12. Underemployed/housing ratio	UHR	1.21	1.36	+12.
13. Manager/job ratio	MR	1.39	1.40	+1.
14. Labor/job ratio	LR	1.01	1.01	0
15. Underemployed/job ratio	UR	1.22	1.02	−16.
16. Tax ratio needed	TRN	1.51	1.32	−13.
17. Underemployed to labor net	UTLN	5,580	7,120	+28.

Figure 5-14 Changes caused by restriction on worker-housing construction only, when added to a slum-housing-demolition program.

Worker-housing construction is determined by Equation 82 and associated Equations 83 and 84 (discussed in Appendix A but reproduced here).

$$WHC.KL = (WHCD.K)(LCR.K) \qquad\qquad 82,R$$

    WHC   – WØRKER-HØUSING CØNSTRUCTIØN (HØUSING UNITS/
            YEAR)
    WHCD – WØRKER-HØUSING CØNSTRUCTIØN DESIRED
            (HØUSING UNITS/YEAR)
    LCR   – LABØR CØNSTRUCTIØN RATIØ (DIMENSIØNLESS)

$$WHCD.K = (WHCN)(WH.K)(WHM.K) + WHCP.K \qquad 83,A$$

$$WHCN = .03 \qquad\qquad 83.1,C$$

    WHCD – WØRKER-HØUSING CØNSTRUCTIØN DESIRED
            (HØUSING UNITS/YEAR)
    WHCN – WØRKER-HØUSING CØNSTRUCTIØN NØRMAL
            (FRACTIØN/YEAR)
    WH   – WØRKER HØUSING (HØUSING UNITS)
    WHM   – WØRKER-HØUSING MULTIPLIER (DIMENSIØNLESS)
    WHCP – WØRKER-HØUSING-CØNSTRUCTIØN PRØGRAM
            (HØUSING UNITS/YEAR)

$$WHM.K = (WHAM.K)(WHLM.K)(WHUM.K)(WHTM.K)(WHEM.K)(WHGM.K) \quad 84,A$$
$$(WHF)$$

$$WHF = 1 \qquad\qquad 84.1,C$$

    WHM   – WØRKER-HØUSING MULTIPLIER (DIMENSIØNLESS)

```
WHAM  - WØRKER-HØUSING-ADEQUACY MULTIPLIER
        (DIMENSIØNLESS)
WHLM  - WØRKER-HØUSING LAND MULTIPLIER
        (DIMENSIØNLESS)
WHUM  - WØRKER-HØUSING UNDEREMPLØYED MULTIPLIER
        (DIMENSIØNLESS)
WHTM  - WØRKER-HØUSING TAX MULTIPLIER
        (DIMENSIØNLESS)
WHEM  - WØRKER-HØUSING ENTERPRISE MULTIPLIER
        (DIMENSIØNLESS)
WHGM  - WØRKER-HØUSING-GRØWTH MULTIPLIER
        (DIMENSIØNLESS)
WHF   - WØRKER-HØUSING FACTØR (DIMENSIØNLESS)
```

The dominant variables are given in Equation 83 determining the worker-housing construction desired as the product of WHCN, WH, and WHM. Worker-housing construction is proportional to the existing housing (representing the size of the urban area) and to the normal construction rate WHCN. This normal rate is then modified by the multiplier WHM, which combines the influences of the urban system on the housing-construction rate. These influences are given by the multiple product in Equation 84.

Figure 5-15 shows several changes caused when the value of WHCN is reduced from .03 to .015. When a new equilibrium has been reached, the worker-housing multiplier WHM has increased 29% to compensate for nearly a third of the reduction in WHCN. The major changes affecting the multiplier are the worker-housing-adequacy multiplier WHAM, which has risen 18%, and the worker-housing underemployed multiplier WHUM, which has increased 7%. The adequacy multiplier has risen because the ratio of labor to worker housing has increased, producing a higher demand for housing. The underemployed multiplier is derived from the ratio of labor to underemployed and indicates a more favorable city environment for the construction of worker housing. The net result of these changes is that worker-housing construction WHC has fallen 35% compared to

Variable	Symbol	Year 50 Fig. 5-10	Year 50 Fig. 5-12	Change (%)
Worker-housing multiplier	WHM	.643	.827	+29.
Worker-housing-adequacy multiplier	WHAM	1.57	1.86	+18.
Worker-housing underemployed multiplier	WHUM	.935	1.00	+7.
Worker-housing construction	WHC	7,860	5,130	−35.
Premium-housing obsolescence	PHO	4,260	4,990	+17.
Total rate entering worker housing		12,120	10,120	−17.
Worker-housing-obsolescence multiplier	WHOM	1.382	1.164	−16.
Worker-housing life		36 years	43 years	+19.

Figure 5-15 Changes in the worker-housing variables caused by restricting construction.

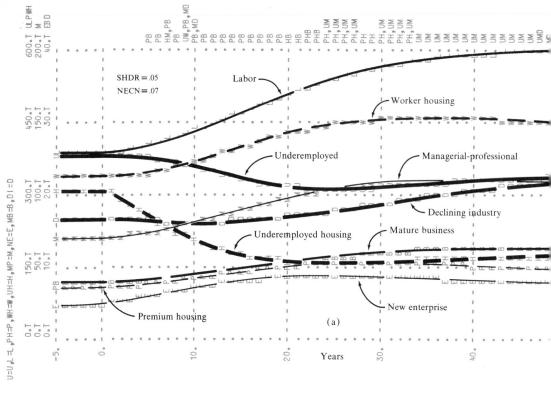

(a)

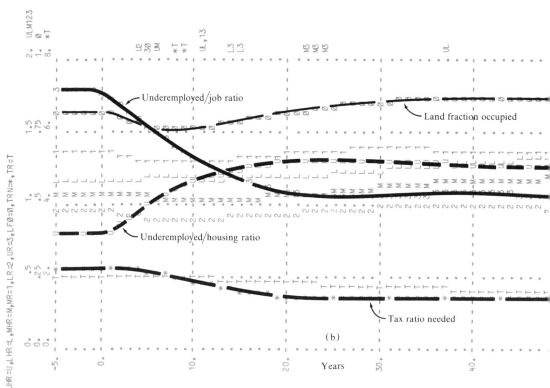

(b)

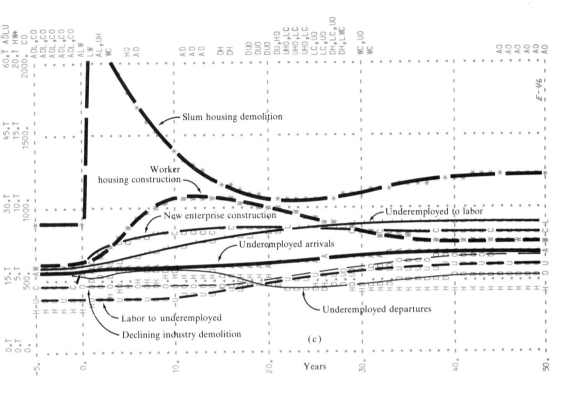

Figure 5-16 Demolition of 5% of slum housing each year and business encouragement that increases new-enterprise construction 40% over what would have occurred under the same conditions without added incentive.

its rate under a policy of slum-housing demolition alone. However, the premium-housing obsolescence PHO has increased as a result of the higher rate of construction of premium housing. This aging of premium housing represents a flow into the worker-housing category so that the total rate of flow into worker housing has declined only 17%. But Figure 5-14 showed an increase in the total worker housing in existence. The difference is explained by Figure 5-15, which shows a 19% increase in worker-housing life. The greater pressure to build worker housing caused by the restrictions on such construction has caused the housing to be maintained in the worker-housing category and used by the labor population for a longer period of time. As was seen in Figure 3-4, the total units in an age category are proportional to the rate of flow and to the length of time in the category. The smaller flow rate of worker housing multiplied by the longer life in the worker-housing category leads to a slight increase in total worker housing.

In Figure 5-12b the slum-housing demolition and the restriction on worker-housing construction lead initially during the first 10 years to a reduction in the land fraction occupied LFO. This encourages a rise in new-enterprise construction which is supported by the rising labor population, the latter generated by new industry, and by the changing ratio of labor to underemployed. The improving tax rate, which in Figure 5-13 falls 41%, encourages still more new-enterprise

TIME	AV	MB	U		AMM	LAJM	LSM	MSM	SHLM	UMM
	DI	MBD	UA	2	AMMP	LAM	LUM	NEGR	TCM	UMMP
	DID	MD	UD	3	BDM	LAMP	LUR	PEM	TPCR	UR
	DIDP	MP	UH	4	DIDM	LATM	MAHM	PHAM	TR	WHAM
	L	NE	UJ	5	DIEM	LAUM	MAJM	PHEM	TRN	WHEM
	LA	NEC	UJP	6	DILM	LCR	MAM	PHGM	UAMM	WHGM
	LCHP	NECP	UTL	7	EDM	LDM	MAMP	PHGR	UDM	WHGR
	LD	P	UTLN	8	EGM	LEM	MAPM	PHLM	UEM	WHLM
	LDC	PH	UTP	9	ELJM	LFØ	MATM	PHM	UFW	WHM
	LDI	PHC	UW	10	ELM	LHR	MDM	PHØM	UHM	WHØM
	LJ	PHCP	WH	11	EM	LLF	MHR	PHPM	UHPR	WHTM
	LTM	PHØ	WHC	12	EMM	LMM	MLM	PHTM	UHR	WHUM
	LTU	SHD	WHCP	13	ETM	LMMP	MLR	SHAM	UJM	
	MA	SHDP	WHØ	14	LAHM	LR	MR	SHDM	UM	

	thousands				units					

TIME	AV	MB	U		AMM	LAJM	LSM	MSM	SHLM	UMM
-5.	16336.	7.806	377.31	1	.452	1.087	1.054	.344	1.060	.805
	16.474	.465	17.283	2	.449	.623	.712	.000	1.284	.802
	.464	4.849	17.275	3	1.190	.625	1.040	1.145	1.121	1.811
	.000	71.13	310.08	4	.939	.854	.931	1.549	1.966	1.542
	392.55	4.866	208.35	5	.886	.808	.296	1.000	2.248	1.000
	7.360	.462	.00	6	1.060	.878	.306	1.000	.936	1.000
	.000	.000	16.847	7	1.190	1.681	.307	.000	2.289	.000
	13.201	5729.4	5.497	8	1.000	1.073	1.300	.625	1.073	.625
	24.38	110.94	.000	9	.935	.815	.854	1.075	.557	.665
	379.15	3.142	210.06	10	.655	1.170	3.408	.948	1.529	1.352
	403.53	.000	335.65	11	.768	.029	1.069	1.300	.000	.854
	3.643	3.155	5.885	12	1.556	.466	1.262	.854	.811	.808
	11.349	9.054	.000	13	.805	.464	.181	1.378	.276	
	.655	.000	9.075	14	.830	.973	1.380	1.460	.045	
10.	18224.	8.556	358.46	1	.429	1.300	1.188	.455	1.000	1.021
	16.244	.467	17.988	2	.453	.766	.765	.022	1.214	.883
	.461	4.252	17.484	3	1.091	.671	1.215	1.248	1.207	1.340
	.000	80.06	207.63	4	.945	.856	.965	1.276	1.948	1.587
	435.63	7.209	267.45	5	.945	.843	.370	1.173	1.922	1.043
	8.767	.832	.00	6	1.000	.825	.398	1.084	1.021	1.055
	.000	.000	22.094	7	1.091	1.383	.349	.011	2.439	.007
	12.053	5881.7	10.451	8	1.173	1.124	1.300	.919	1.124	.919
	45.80	128.97	.000	9	.811	.769	.856	1.659	.698	1.158
	434.95	5.296	250.17	10	.794	1.183	2.655	.635	.638	.937
	480.75	.000	368.10	11	.881	.026	1.035	1.300	.000	.856
	4.576	2.458	10.549	12	1.445	.649	1.268	.856	1.151	.843
	11.434	14.033	.000	13	.808	.525	.184	.879	.528	
	.839	10.382	6.895	14	.817	.906	1.287	.879	.053	
50.	22300.	12.843	335.93	1	.428	1.063	1.040	.368	1.318	.998
	22.171	.851	20.884	2	.446	.611	.936	-.002	1.043	1.021
	.705	7.608	16.431	3	1.326	.646	1.786	1.052	1.044	1.072
	.000	108.72	175.32	4	1.060	.899	.814	2.488	1.598	1.996
	599.99	8.023	313.33	5	.804	.957	.312	.985	1.504	.994
	11.630	.830	.00	6	1.318	.884	.297	.995	1.215	1.001
	.000	.000	26.690	7	1.326	1.708	.297	-.001	2.446	.000
	20.501	6831.0	9.164	8	.985	1.026	1.300	.376	1.026	.376
	37.29	152.78	.000	9	.964	.865	.899	1.072	.778	.643
	574.82	4.343	261.48	10	.506	1.332	3.499	.950	.378	1.382
	612.11	.000	450.58	11	.636	.029	1.186	1.300	.000	.899
	5.865	4.355	7.680	12	1.532	.477	1.262	.899	1.277	.957
	17.524	12.362	.000	13	.865	.489	.181	.778	.885	
	.968	8.766	12.455	14	.668	.980	1.360	1.026	.079	

(d)

Figure 5-16 (cont.)

construction and more management and labor residing in the area. The individual influences are slight, but their multiple regeneration on each other can have a substantial effect on the delicate equilibrium of a system poised between growth and decline.

5.7   Encouraging Industry

The natural tendency toward imbalance in which housing dominates industry might be corrected by urban policies that encourage industry as well as by policies that discourage construction of excess worker housing. Figure 5-16 shows the effect of policies that combine slum-housing demolition with active encouragement for new-enterprise construction. The slum-housing-demolition rate of 5% is the same as that in Figures 5-10 and 5-12. In the basic model the new-enterprise construction normal NECN is .05 per year (as described in Equation 102 in Appendix A). As with the other normal rates of flow, the actual rate is modulated by conditions within the urban area. In Figure 5-16 the coefficient NECN has been increased from .05 to .07 which means that, all other circumstances being equal, the new-enterprise-construction rate would be increased 40%. Of course such a change in the propensity to build new enterprise will produce reactions throughout the system. A comparison of Figures 5-16 and 5-12 shows only a few

	Variable	Symbol	Time (years)		Change (%)
			−5	50	
a.	Slum-housing-demolition program	SHDP	0	8,770	—
b.	Slum-housing demolition total rate	SHD	9,100	12,360	+36.
c.	Worker-housing construction	WHC	5,900	7,700	+31.
d.	New-enterprise construction	NEC	462	830	+80.
1.	New enterprise	NE	4,900	8,000	+63.
2.	Mature business	MB	7,800	12,000	+64.
3.	Declining industry	DI	16,500	22,200	+35.
4.	Premium housing	PH	110,900	152,800	+38.
5.	Worker housing	WH	335,600	450,600	+34.
6.	Underemployed housing	UH	310,100	175,300	−43.
7.	Managerial-professional	MP	71,100	108,700	+53.
8.	Labor	L	392,600	600,000	+53.
9.	Underemployed	U	377,300	335,900	−11.
10.	Manager/housing ratio	MHR	1.07	1.19	+11.
11.	Labor/housing ratio	LHR	1.17	1.33	+14.
12.	Underemployed/housing ratio	UHR	.81	1.28	+58.
13.	Manager/job ratio	MR	1.38	1.36	−1.
14.	Labor/job ratio	LR	.97	.98	+1.
15.	Underemployed/job ratio	UR	1.81	1.07	−41.
16.	Tax ratio needed	TRN	2.25	1.50	−33.
17.	Underemployed to labor net	UTLN	5,500	9,200	+67.

Figure 5-17   Changes caused by combined policies of slum-housing demolition (SHDR = .05) and encouragement of new-enterprise construction (NECN = .07).

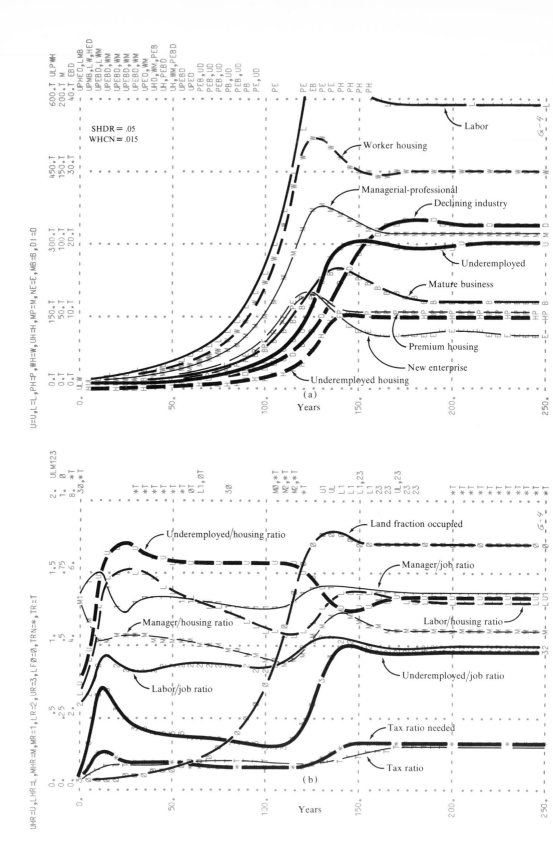

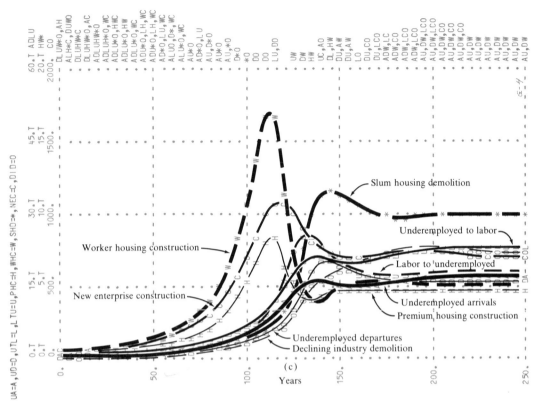

Figure 5-18 Urban-area development with continuous application from the beginning of policies for 5% per year slum demolition and discouragement of worker-housing construction.

substantial differences between the results obtained here from encouraging new enterprise and those obtained by discouraging worker-housing construction.

Figure 5-17, compared to Figure 5-13, shows a larger increase, 67%, in upward mobility UTLN. Underemployed population and underemployed housing have not declined so much.

In Figure 5-17 the number of underemployed has declined 11%. Figure 5-16d shows how this has been accomplished. During the first 10 years there is almost no change in either the underemployed-arrival rate UA or the underemployed-departure rate UD (arrivals have actually increased a little more than departures). The change in underemployed population is accounted for almost entirely by the increased net upward mobility UTLN, which in the first 10 years has risen from 5,497 men per year to 10,451. After the population stabilizes at 50 years, net arrivals (UA − UD) have increased by about 4,400 men per year, indicating that the city has become substantially more effective in accepting underemployed and providing an economic climate to generate upward economic mobility into the labor group.

References here to encouraging new enterprise must be considered in the context of the particular geographical area to be revived. New enterprise at a

TIME	AV	MB	U		AMM	LAJM	LSM	MSM	SHLM	UMM
	DI	MBD	UA	2	AMMP	LAM	LUM	NEGR	TCM	UMMP
	DID	MD	UD	3	BDM	LAMP	LUR	PEM	TPCR	UR
	DIDP	MP	UH	4	DIDM	LATM	MAHM	PHAM	TR	WHAM
	L	NE	UJ	5	DIEM	LAUM	MAJM	PHEM	TRN	WHEM
	LA	NEC	UJP	6	DILM	LCR	MAM	PHGM	UAMM	WHGM
	LCHP	NECP	UTL	7	EDM	LDM	MAMP	PHGR	UDM	WHGR
	LD	P	UTLN	8	EGM	LEM	MAPM	PHLM	UEM	WHLM
	LDC	PH	UTP	9	ELJM	LFØ	MATM	PHM	UFW	WHM
	LDI	PHC	UW	10	ELM	LHR	MDM	PHØM	UHM	WHØM
	LJ	PHCP	WH	11	EM	LLF	MJR	PHPM	UHPR	WHTM
	LTM	PHØ	WHC	12	EMM	LMM	MLM	PHTM	UHR	WHUM
	LTU	SHD	WHCP	13	ETM	LMMP	MLR	SHAM	UJM	
	MA	SHDP	WHØ	14	LAHM	LR	MR	SHDM	UM	

	thousands				units					
0.	881.	1.000	1.20	1	2.891	2.142	1.785	.386	1.000	2.035
	.100	.032	.760	2	1.000	3.524	1.400	.030	.800	1.000
	.005	.227	.009	3	.650	1.000	11.667	.753	.691	.071
	.000	3.90	1.10	4	1.802	1.117	.700	3.320	.444	.233
	14.00	.200	16.94	5	1.802	1.300	.324	1.240	.411	1.060
	.420	.051	.00	6	1.000	.586	.364	1.240	1.100	1.240
	.000	.000	.107	7	.650	.297	1.000	.030	.368	.030
	.083	113.1	-.093	8	1.240	.815	1.300	.548	.815	.548
	3.04	5.00	.000	9	1.000	.030	1.234	4.066	.893	.244
	20.00	.357	1.07	10	1.045	.667	2.911	.298	1.745	2.006
	23.04	.000	21.00	11	2.386	.014	1.300	1.300	.000	1.117
	.280	.045	.045	12	1.514	.409	1.300	1.117	.727	1.300
	.200	.034	.000	13	1.217	1.000	.279	1.545	2.000	ω≠
	.117	.000	.842	14	1.133	.608	1.345	1.545	.063	
50.	2379.	1.435	14.63	1	.336	1.451	1.282	.416	1.000	1.367
	1.123	.064	1.283	2	.367	1.193	1.277	.016	.800	1.325
	.041	.526	.919	3	.890	1.090	3.774	.780	.725	.389
	.000	11.90	6.22	4	1.221	1.037	.968	1.258	.774	2.110
	55.23	1.256	37.58	5	1.221	1.277	.344	1.125	.742	1.031
	1.806	.117	.00	6	1.000	.787	.464	1.133	1.282	1.161
	.000	.000	1.670	7	.890	.873	.462	.017	3.139	.020
	.964	508.0	.321	8	1.125	.835	1.300	.766	.835	.766
	6.43	19.22	.000	9	.649	.073	1.074	1.655	.861	2.562
	57.86	.751	12.60	10	1.110	1.379	2.209	.637	.173	.629
	64.29	.000	40.04	11	1.291	.024	1.032	1.300	.000	1.037
	.498	.367	1.212	12	1.484	.451	1.300	1.037	1.568	1.277
	1.346	.383	.000	13	1.074	.451	.215	.573	1.944	ω≠
	.165	.311	.504	14	.621	.859	1.320	.573	.096	
100.	11443.	5.406	52.57	1	.357	1.485	1.303	.490	1.000	1.551
	2.942	.206	5.242	2	.353	1.787	1.365	.029	.800	1.507
	.130	1.811	3.123	3	.763	1.598	4.647	.829	.787	.309
	.000	50.64	22.21	4	1.475	1.044	1.040	.678	.736	1.364
	244.30	6.619	170.17	5	1.475	1.300	.393	1.231	.639	1.058
	11.714	.688	.00	6	1.000	.779	.579	1.231	1.287	1.236
	.000	.000	6.885	7	.763	.582	.555	.029	2.970	.030
	2.844	2139.5	1.005	8	1.231	.872	1.300	1.731	.872	1.731
	45.04	93.84	.000	9	.640	.365	1.088	2.412	.869	4.189
	242.91	5.289	45.69	10	1.433	1.114	1.788	.446	.169	.494
	287.95	.000	219.38	11	1.732	.024	.899	1.300	.000	1.044
	2.579	1.257	10.734	12	1.410	.555	1.300	1.044	1.578	1.300
	5.848	1.363	.000	13	1.088	.528	.207	.569	1.976	ω≠
	.843	1.111	2.166	14	.886	.848	1.259	.569	.097	

(d)

Figure 5-18 (cont.)

thousands				units					
150. 23014.	15.480	304.20	1	.335	.999	1.000	.370	1.253	.803
18.795	.955	15.392	2	.334	.635	1.006	-.018	.994	.814
.608	6.987	19.166	3	1.233	.810	2.028	.731	.664	.987
.000	112.51	161.50	4	1.078	1.005	.828	2.376	.966	2.090
616.99	8.264	308.34	5	.860	1.006	.313	.852	1.344	.945
14.985	.704	.00	6	1.253	.900	.340	.976	1.122	.967
.000	.000	19.843	7	1.233	1.653	.340	-.003	3.150	-.004
20.397	6698.1	1.039	8	.852	.798	1.300	.417	.798	.417
31.41	160.00	.000	9	1.036	.857	1.010	1.076	.801	.804
585.43	4.650	243.77	10	.530	1.371	3.105	.947	.395	1.189
616.83	.000	450.09	11	.723	.030	1.172	1.300	.000	1.005
4.509	4.545	4.883	12	1.530	.373	1.265	1.005	1.256	1.006
18.532	11.294	.000	13	1.010	.365	.182	.795	1.032	↩↩
1.149	8.075	10.703	14	.629	1.000	1.359	.997	.065	
250. 22059.	12.194	296.44	1	.393	1.044	1.027	.352	1.171	.973
22.890	.717	17.275	2	.391	.670	.995	-.000	1.003	.971
.719	6.816	15.962	3	1.176	.671	1.984	.935	.919	.978
.000	106.72	147.66	4	1.047	.937	.899	1.808	1.341	1.951
588.24	7.609	303.13	5	.895	.997	.301	1.000	1.362	1.000
11.849	.716	.00	6	1.171	.889	.330	1.000	1.210	1.000
.000	.000	23.082	7	1.176	1.577	.330	-.000	2.692	-.000
18.551	6434.6	5.752	8	1.000	.952	1.300	.486	.952	.486
32.44	161.56	.000	9	.967	.843	.937	1.070	.802	.886
563.99	4.611	237.81	10	.572	1.313	3.194	.951	.329	1.105
596.44	.000	448.11	11	.783	.029	1.101	1.300	.000	.937
4.957	4.610	5.293	12	1.548	.423	1.263	.937	1.338	.997
17.324	9.905	.000	13	.916	.421	.181	.729	1.053	↩↩
1.058	7.383	9.902	14	.687	.986	1.373	.854	.078	

(e)

Figure 5-18 (cont.)

remote point, for example in an industrial belt beyond the suburbs of a city, is not sufficiently related to the decaying areas to have substantial effect. New enterprise must compete in the specific aging area with the tendency for excess decaying housing. The policies discussed in this section must be exercised on a local basis, not on the basis of a metropolitan area as a whole. Otherwise some areas will be economically balanced while others will be isolated and decay. Balance should occur within an area small enough to have communication within the school system between different economic categories of population. It would be an area that can be crossed by available transportation during a rush period in 20 minutes. It appears that a larger area will tend to break up into isolated blocks of population and industry that are segregated by building age and economic effectiveness.

5.8 Preventing Urban Decline

Reviving blighted areas is a task forced on us by earlier failures in urban management. Preventing blight would of course be better than having to cure it.

Many metropolitan areas that are not now conspicuously in trouble are nevertheless following a pattern of full land occupancy with consequent aging and stagnation that will turn them into the slum areas of the future. More specifically, this is a future that can be anticipated for the low-cost suburban housing developments that sprang up after World War II.

Policies used for reviving a decayed area should, if continuously applied, prevent decay. With rare and very special exceptions, the ultimate equilibrium in a system does not depend on the system's history. It depends only on those policies and system parameters that act during the period when equilibrium is being established. This means that the revival policies in this chapter could be applied to a city throughout its growth period and should produce the same final equilibrium conditions as they do when applied to a stagnant city.

Figure 5-18 demonstrates how equilibrium is not dependent on history. In this figure the entire growth history of the urban area has occurred under the same policies that were used for revival in Figure 5-12. The final conditions in year 250 in Figure 5-18 and the final conditions in year 50 in Figure 5-12 are substantially identical. The small differences arise because complete equilibrium has not been reached, particularly in Figure 5-12. The new policies during growth in Figure 5-18 have produced some effect on the growth pattern (as seen by comparing this figure with Figure 3-1 representing growth in the basic system). Because of slum demolition and restrictions on worker-housing construction, the growth rate has been retarded slightly. But in Figure 5-18 the area enters directly into a more healthy state of equilibrium without going through the high underemployment conditions and the high ratio of underemployed to labor that occurred in Figure 3-1.

New and more satisfactory urban-development policies can be initiated at any point in the growth-maturity-stagnation cycle. Transient conditions will be affected, but the final equilibrium depends on the policies themselves and not the initial conditions at the time the policies are implemented.

6 Notes on Complex Systems

This chapter is an interlude to comment on the general nature of complex systems. Chapter 7 will return to specific consideration of the city and interpret the material of Chapters 2 through 6 in terms of urban management.

6.1 Nature of Complex Systems

Complex systems have special responses which cause many of the failures and frustrations experienced in trying to improve their behavior. As used here the phrase "complex system" refers to a high-order, multiple-loop, nonlinear feedback structure. All social systems belong to this class. The management structure of a corporation has all the characteristics of a complex system. Similarly, an urban area, a national government, economic processes, and international trade all are complex systems. Complex systems have many unexpected and little understood characteristics.

Like all systems, the complex system is an interlocking structure of feedback loops. "Feedback loop" is the technical term describing the environment around any decision point in a system. The decision leads to a course of action that changes the state of the surrounding system and gives rise to new information on which future decisions are based. This loop structure surrounds all decisions public or private, conscious or unconscious. The processes of man and nature, of psychology and physics, of medicine and engineering all fall within this structure. But the complex system has some special characteristics.

The complex system is of high order. The "order" of a system is determined by the number of level equations (that is, integrations or states) in the system description. A company might have separate level variables representing the employees, the bank balance, the finished inventory, the in-process inventory, the physical machinery, various psychological attitudes, components of reputation, and elements of tradition. A system of greater than fourth or fifth order begins to enter the range here defined as a complex system. An adequate representation of a social system, even for a very limited purpose, can be tenth to hundredth order. The urban system in this book is twentieth order.

A complex system is multiple loop. It will have upward of three or four interacting feedback loops. The interplay among these loops and the shifting dominance from one to the other gives the complex system much of its character.

The complex system has both positive- and negative-feedback loops. The negative-feedback loop is the one most commonly found in the literature of systems theory and is almost the only one discussed in engineering. But it is the positive-feedback loop that generates all growth processes, whether they be biological or economic. Negative-feedback loops are goal-seeking, tending to regulate the system toward some objective. Positive-feedback loops are goal-divergent, tending to depart exponentially from some point of unstable equilibrium. But the positive-feedback character, which gives the positive loop its growth behavior, comes not only from structure but also from numerous variable factors around the loop. These factors are often set and controlled by other loops in the system. As these factors change, the positive-growth loop can be depressed in its regenerative characteristics and brought to a neutral point marking the boundary between positive- and negative-feedback behavior. If the loop is pushed into the negative-feedback region, the loop begins to generate exponential collapse toward the original reference point from which it was diverging. The behavior of social systems is intimately related to this interaction between positive- and negative-feedback processes. For example, the large changes seen in Figure 4-9 result from the shift of positive loops into a collapsing mode that finds a new and much lower equilibrium.

The complex system is nonlinear. Modern mathematics deals almost exclusively with linear processes. Life and society deal almost entirely with nonlinear processes. Nonlinear coupling allows one feedback loop to dominate the system for a time and then can cause this dominance to shift to another part of the system where behavior is so different that the two seem unrelated. Multiple-loop realignment along various nonlinear functions makes the complex system highly insensitive to most system parameters. The same nonlinear behavior makes the system resistant to efforts to change its behavior. The nonlinearities, when understood, make it relatively easy to produce system models with realistic dynamic characteristics. Much of our knowledge about system components resides in the range of nonlinear relationships. Only by dealing forthrightly with the nonlinearities in systems will we begin to understand the dynamics of social behavior. Nonlinearity is necessary to represent the behavior of complex systems. Nonlinearity is easy to handle once we stop demanding analytical solutions to systems of equations and accept the less elegant and more empirical approach of system simulation. Acceptance of the nonlinear nature of systems shifts our attention away from the futile effort to measure accurately the parameters of social systems and instead focuses attention on the far more important matter of system structure.

Complex systems have characteristics that are commonly unknown. Complex systems behave far differently from the simple systems on which our intuitive responses have been sharpened. They are different from the behavior studied in science and mathematics, where only simple systems have received orderly attention and analysis.

Complex social systems bring together many factors which, by quirks of history, have been compartmentalized into isolated intellectual fields. The barriers between disciplines must melt away if we are successfully to cope with complex systems. Within the same system we must admit the interactions of the psychological, the economic, the technical, the cultural, and the political. The interactions among these are often more important than the internal content of any one alone. Yet, if these separate disciplines are isolated in our study and in our thinking, the interactions will never come into view.

Complex systems have many important behavior characteristics that we must understand if we expect to design systems with better behavior. Complex systems: (1) are counterintuitive; (2) are remarkably insensitive to changes in many system parameters; (3) stubbornly resist policy changes; (4) contain influential pressure points, often in unexpected places, from which forces will radiate to alter system balance; (5) counteract and compensate for externally applied corrective efforts by reducing the corresponding internally generated action (the corrective program is largely absorbed in replacing lost internal action); (6) often react to a policy change in the long run in a way opposite to how they react in the short run; (7) tend toward low performance. Each of these seven characteristics will now be examined in more detail.

6.2 Counterintuitive Behavior

The counterintuitive behavior to be expected from complex systems was mentioned in Chapter 1 as a major reason for undertaking this study of urban dynamics. All complex systems—whether in engineering, biology, economics, management, or politics—can be expected to exhibit this devious behavior.

Chapter 3 has shown, perhaps as a surprise to some, that the rather obvious processes of growth, aging, and population movements create urban decay. Chapter 4 suggests the even more unexpected result that past programs designed to solve urban problems may well be making matters worse. Chapter 5 suggests that policy changes in exactly the opposite direction from present trends are needed if the decaying inner city is to be revived.

Intuition and judgment, generated by a lifetime of experience with the simple systems that surround one's every action, create a network of expectations and perceptions that could hardly be better designed to mislead the unwary when he moves into the realm of complex systems. One's life and mental processes have been conditioned almost exclusively by experience with first-order, negative-feedback loops. Such loops are goal-seeking and contain a single important system level variable. For example, one can pick up an object from the table because he senses the difference in position between hand and object and controls movement to close the gap. While many nervous and muscular responses are involved, the system is dominated by the level variable representing the position of the hand.

From all normal personal experience one learns that cause and effect are closely related in time and space. A difficulty or failure of the simple system is observed at once. The cause is obvious and immediately precedes the consequence. But in complex systems all of these facts become fallacies. Cause and effect are not closely related either in time or in space. Causes of a symptom may actually lie in some far distant sector of a social system. Furthermore, symptoms may appear long after the primary causes.

But the complex system is far more devious and diabolical than merely being different from the simple systems with which we have experience. Although it is truly different, it appears to be the same. The complex system presents an apparent cause that is close in time and space to the observed symptoms. But the relationship is usually not one of cause and effect. Instead both are coincident symptoms arising from the dynamics of the system structure. Almost all variables in a complex system are highly correlated, but time correlation means little in distinguishing cause from effect. Much statistical and correlation analysis is futilely pursuing this will-o'-the-wisp.

In a situation where coincident symptoms appear to be causes, a person acts to dispel the symptoms. But the underlying causes remain. The treatment is either ineffective or actually detrimental. With a high degree of confidence we can say that the intuitive solutions to the problems of complex social systems will be wrong most of the time. Here lies much of the explanation for the problems of faltering companies, disappointments in developing nations, foreign-exchange crises, and troubles of urban areas.

6.3   Insensitivity to Parameter Changes

Complex systems are remarkably insensitive to changes in many of the system parameters (constants in the equations). Social science attempts to measure to a high degree of accuracy many of the characteristics of psychological and economic systems. Yet closed, nonlinear feedback models of those same systems show little change in behavior even from parameter changes of severalfold. Contemplating our social systems indicates that this must be true. The life cycle of companies follows similar patterns in very different industries and even in different countries. Problems in economic development are much the same regardless of continent, social heritage, or even availability of raw materials. Economic systems have behaved in about the same way over the last hundred years even though the developed countries have shifted from agricultural to urban societies, from independent to central banking, from individual entrepreneurship to large corporations, and from communication delays of weeks to seconds. In fact, social systems are dominated by natural and psychological factors that change very little.

6.4   Resistance to Policy Changes

Complex systems resist most policy changes. When a change, even a substantial one, is made in a system, behavior often remains the same. The reasons lie in the counterintuitive nature of complex systems and in their insensitivity to parameter changes.

A policy is composed of both a structure (that is, what information sources are selected and how they are used) and parameters (determining how much influence from the information and how much action). "Policy" here means the rule that describes how the available information will be used to determine action. The insensitivity of a system to most of its parameters means that the system is also insensitive to most modifications that would be called policy changes, because often the policy changes are only changes in degree of information influence or action. Here lies the explanation for the stubborn nature of social systems. When a policy is changed, the many system levels shift slightly and offer a new ensemble of information to the policy point in the system. The new information, processed through the new policy, gives nearly the old results.

6.5 Control Through Influence Points

Complex systems have a high sensitivity to changes in a few parameters and to some changes in structure. Thus the converse of parameter insensitivity is true too.

There are a few points in any system to which behavior is sensitive. If a policy at one of these points is changed, pressures radiate throughout the system. Behavior everywhere seems different. But people have not been persuaded or forced to react differently. As they respond in the old way to new information, their actions change. (Examples of these have been seen in Chapter 5.)

The parameters and structural changes to which a system is sensitive are usually not self-evident. They must be discovered through careful examination of system dynamics.

6.6 Corrective Programs Counteracted by the System

Active corrective programs imposed on a social system can have far less than their anticipated effect because they tend to displace the corresponding internal processes. As seen repeatedly in Chapters 4 and 5, the active corrective programs shift the system balance so that the corresponding natural processes encounter more resistance and reduce the load they were previously carrying. For example, in Figure 4-4 the underemployed-training program processed 19,100 people per year, and yet the net upward flow from underemployed to labor increased only 11,300. The 60% efficiency of the new program is explained by the decline in the natural upward mobility that existed previously. This tendency of a system to resist and to counteract an applied force must be carefully considered. Compensating counteraction can be disastrous if the applied programs are expensive. The external financing required may be impossible to sustain. Only applied programs of intrinsic low cost are feasible. Probably no active, externally imposed program is superior to a system modification that changes internal incentives and leaves the burden of system improvement to internal processes.

6.7   Long-Term Versus Short-Term Response

Change in a complex system commonly causes short-term responses in the opposite direction from the long-term effect. These "worse-before-better" sequences will be particularly troublesome to the political leader faced with reviving an urban system. The conflict between the short run and the long run is found repeatedly. In Figure 4-3*a* the underemployed-training program first reduced the number of underemployed and then led to a reversal, with a final value slightly higher than at the beginning. In Figure 4-8*c* the low-cost-housing program produced an initial attractiveness, with rising underemployed-arrival rate which eventually fell 17% below the initial value. In the slum-housing-demolition programs of Figures 5-10 through 5-17, the unfavorable political aspects of housing reduction and the counterpressures caused by the necessary relocation of people within the area will appear faster than the more favorable aspects of job availability and economic improvement.

This conflict between short-term and long-term system responses partly accounts for the unhappy state of our present urban systems. As voter pressure and political expediency combine to favor short-run considerations, the stage is set for long-term degeneration.

6.8   Drift to Low Performance

Complex social systems tend toward a condition of poor performance. Their counterintuitive nature causes detrimental design changes. Also, the opposite direction of short-term and long-term responses leads to policies that produce a less satisfactory system. For example, a particular change in policy may improve matters for a period of a year or two while setting the stage for changes that lower performance and desirability further in the future. But the natural interpretation is to observe that good resulted from the change and when matters become worse the original efforts are redoubled. The intensified action produces another short-term improvement and still deeper long-term difficulty. Again the complex system is cunning in its ability to mislead.

6.9   On Modeling

A Model. A simulation model is a theory describing the structure and interrelationships of a system. The fact that the simulation process is to be used does not of itself make the theory correct. Models can be useful or useless. They can be soundly conceived, inadequate, or wrong. They can be concise and clear and describe only those characteristics of the real system necessary to give the behavior characteristics of interest, or they can be verbose, obscure, and cluttered with unimportant detail so that they confuse rather than inform. They can be structured with recognition of the dynamic principles of feedback-system behavior, or they can simply be a catchall for observed fragments of the system while omitting the essential structure. Correct concepts of structure must guide model-building.*

*See References 1, 4, and 6.

Everyone uses models. A written description is a model that presents one aspect of reality. A mental image used in thinking is a model, it is not the real system. The simulation model differs in being logically complete. It describes a dynamic process and can manipulate rates and levels to generate a time history in accordance with the statements of which the model is composed.

Model Validity. A model should always be created for a purpose. The adequacy of the model can only be judged in terms of that purpose. There is no possibility of absolute proof that a model is appropriate for its objective. But the model can be evaluated in several stages.* The basic assumptions (in Appendix A) can be checked against available experience and data. The dynamic behavior of a model (as in Chapter 3) can be compared with the real systems it should represent. Changes in the model (as in Chapter 4) can be related to similar changes that have occurred in reality.

Modeling to Create Symptoms. The first step in modeling is to generate a model that creates the problem. Only if we understand the processes leading to the difficulties can we hope to restructure the system so that the internal processes lead in a different direction. If the model is to create the difficulties, it must contain all the interacting relationships necessary to lead the system into trouble. The troubles are not imposed on the system from outside the structure being modeled. The model will be a closed model which is not dependent for its inherent characteristic behavior on any variables transmitted across its boundary from the external world.

The concept of the closed boundary and the development of a simulation model which has within itself all of the generating mechanisms for the problems of the system is essential to successful investigation of complex systems. A system study should start without emphasis on the correction of difficulties. Instead it focuses attention on the causes of difficulty and their removal. Removing causes may take action quite different from that aimed at alleviating symptoms. The cost of removing causes is often far less, the influence is much deeper, and the improvements last longer.

Adequacy of Information. In the social sciences failure to understand systems is often blamed on inadequate data. The barrier to progress in social systems is not lack of data. We have vastly more information than we use in an orderly and organized way. The barrier is deficiency in the existing theories of structure. The conventional forms of data-gathering will seldom produce new insights into the details of system structure. Those insights come from an intimate working knowledge of the actual systems. Furthermore, the structuring of a proper system theory must be done without regard to the boundaries of conventional intellectual disciplines. One must interrelate within a single system the economic, the psy-

---

*See Reference 5 and Chapter 13 of Reference 1 for discussions of model validity.

chological, and the physical. When this is properly done, the resulting structure provides nooks and corners to receive fragments of our fabulous store of knowledge, experience, and observation.

Much of the behavior of systems rests on relationships and interactions that are believed, and probably correctly so, to be important but that for a long time will evade quantitative measure. Unless we take our best estimates of these relationships and include them in a system model, we are in effect saying that they make no difference and can be omitted. It is far more serious to omit a relationship that is believed to be important than to include it at a low level of accuracy that fits within the plausible range of uncertainty. In this particular aspect the kind of modeling discussed here follows the philosophy of the manager or political leader more than that of the scientist.* If one believes a relationship to be important, he acts accordingly and makes the best use he can of the information available. He is willing to let his reputation rest on his keenness of perception and interpretation.

A shortage of information is not a major barrier to understanding urban dynamics. One can say the same for other complex systems. The barrier is the lack of willingness and ability to organize the information that already exists into a structure that represents the structure of the actual system and therefore has an opportunity to behave as the real system would. When structure is properly represented, parameter values are of secondary importance. Parameter values must not be crucial because cities have much the same character and life cycle regardless of the era and the society within which they exist. Similar patterns emerge in cities having quite different economic constraints and social traditions.

---

*This reference to the difference between an operating man and a scientist is made in the spirit of the conventional image of science. Of course, the successful scientist also operates on subjective observation and moves ahead in his work on the basis of available information, gathering such facts as he can and making assumptions where he must.

7 Interpretations

This book is more an opening of a subject than it is a package of final results and recommendations. The primary objective is to improve understanding of the complexities of our social systems. However, one always draws conclusions as he goes along. How to use the results of a system study is an important part of the learning process. The cities and their problems are here today. They will not wait for ultimate answers. Because one must act on the best evidence available, it seems entirely proper to interpret as one proceeds, but to remain open to new evidence and changing conclusions. This chapter presents opinions arising from the urban-dynamics study. As stated earlier, these conclusions should be accepted only after establishing that the assumptions used here fit the particular situation.

An Implicit Goal. These recommendations assume that the most desirable way to reverse the present condition of cities is to restore economic vitality and to absorb the present underemployed groups into the main stream of productive activity. Some might argue to the contrary that today's underemployed Negro minority is less apt to rise in status by diffusion into existing economic activity than by coalescing into a self-respecting, self-disciplining, and self-leading group. Were the latter the more promising course of action, Negro concentration in high-density slum areas might be a necessary prelude to self-generating social change. This study assumes that extreme concentration of economic and social groups is detrimental and that success will be more easily achieved in a single economic system than in two separate and parallel systems.

7.1 Outside the City

This book focuses on an urban area and its improvement. But no conflict need exist between the well-being of that area and the health of the surrounding urban and rural areas. A healthy city is a more effective economic converter for upgrading the underemployed than is a decaying city. A healthy city generates new industry, managers, and skilled labor beyond those who can remain employed within the city area. These men and enterprises leave to start nuclei of rising economic activity at other places.

The policies for controlling population balance that the city must establish are not antisocial. No purpose is served by operating a city so that it is a drain on the economy of the country and a disappointment and frustration to its occupants. An urban area that maintains effective internal balance can absorb poor people from other areas at a faster rate than can one that is operating in deep stagnation. The healthy area does not act as a drag on the other parts of the country by requiring assistance from the outside. Furthermore, the well-balanced urban area can contribute to raising the standard of living of the entire country.

7.2   The City in Its Environment

Urban Evolution. A city starts with empty land area having intrinsic economic potential. Business develops. People move to the new economic opportunities. Housing is built to support the growing population. During the growth period the average age of housing is relatively low. The housing is occupied by those employed in the growing business activity.

When the first land area has become filled, the city geographical pattern has become a central commercial core surrounded by dwelling units. The housing stands as a barrier to expansion of the area devoted to business. In time the ring of housing deteriorates until it is no longer attractive to those who are fully employed with satisfactory income.

Then a second phase of housing construction starts outside the old city as the managerial and labor classes build a new ring of housing in the available land area outside the first ring of housing, which is now deteriorating. Until this time housing available for the underemployed had been so limited that the under-employed population could not rise above what the city system could absorb. But as the deteriorating inner ring of housing is vacated by management and labor, the housing near the center of the city is occupied by those with the lowest skills and the smallest income. Their presence in the dwelling units prevents demolition, and the housing continues to restrict expansion of the commercial area. The declining housing and its occupants generate city expenditures, cause tax rates to rise, and decrease the likelihood of new industrial activity. The central city becomes progressively more unattractive to the kind of manufacturing activity that could provide upward mobility for the underemployed. The central city begins to be dominated by office and professional activities, which place a premium on proximity to each other and to transportation systems.

After a period of adjustment the outer suburbs with their skilled labor and managerial talent begin to be self-sufficient, with the development of industrial activity within their borders and in the ring of open country outside the suburban boundary.

The stage is then set for a second phase of deterioration. The oldest housing in the central city will eventually reach the point where it must come down and at that time it will be replaced with new structures, probably tending toward premium housing for those engaged in the managerial and professional activities still located in the central city. As this replacement of the slum areas with new structures proceeds, the nearest suburban areas age and deteriorate and become technologically less attractive than new construction. The managerial and labor populations will move to new buildings. These inner suburban areas will then become the outward-moving slum-housing ring of the future.

The urban dynamics discussed in this book do not apply solely to the present core city. The concepts apply to all areas. Each is in some phase of the growth and stagnation life cycle. Each, given past circumstances and policies, can be expected to complete the cycle into decay. If decline is to be avoided in areas that now appear healthy, urban dynamics must become better understood. Quite different urban-management policies must be accepted.

The Limitless Environment. This study conceives an urban area as an organic living complex set in an unlimited environment. This implies that the urban area and its internal policies determine its own condition and evolution. The unlimited environment means that people are available from outside for migration into the area whenever the area appears more attractive than the point from which people may come. Conversely, the environment will absorb those who find the area less attractive. This relation between a particular urban area and its surroundings has existed throughout the history of the United States. For any particular area relative to the remainder of the country, it will continue to be true. The surrounding environment may be represented by other urban as well as rural areas, and mobility between urban areas may supersede the more dominant past mobility from country to city.

The Attractiveness Concept. Unrestricted mobility between the urban area and its environment has an important corollary. For any class of person, conditions in the area must be approximately equal in attractiveness to conditions elsewhere. As an example, conditions in a city for people in the lowest economic class will not be substantially better or worse than the conditions in other parts of the country from which there is free mobility.* If the city is more attractive, inward migration will occur until it is overloaded. Unable to cope with the influx, the city falls to the lowest attractiveness level with which it communicates. Any hope for changing the conditions in a city rests on an examination of total attractiveness and its components.

The term "attractiveness" is used here to describe the variable that modulates the flow of people to and from an urban area. As the area becomes more attractive, the inward flow increases and the outward flow decreases. Attractiveness is perceived in different ways by different people. The components of attractive-

---

*As used here, there is free mobility between all areas. Attractiveness is a multidimensional concept and includes factors such as legal restrictions, prejudice, racial and ethnic groupings, and anything else that influences a person to move. Some of these are represented explicitly as variables in the urban model. All others are combined into the mobility coefficients on the basis that they can be treated as constants and are not involved as dynamic variables in the modes of urban change here being explored.

ness are weighted differently. But the distribution of all perceptions of attractiveness, as seen by the distribution of all kinds of people, results in the flow of population. This net composite effect in the model generates "average" attractiveness, which regulates movement of "average" people.

Attractiveness is a composite concept combining a large number of influences. Attractiveness in the model is defined by such variables as upward mobility, available housing, public-expenditure rate, accessible jobs, and special government programs. Other attractiveness factors obviously exist. Climate may affect the attractiveness of a particular city, but this would not usually be a dynamic variable which itself is affected by the internal conditions of the city. Remoteness may affect attractiveness. Political restrictions may be considered a form of unattractiveness. Immigration restrictions may detract from an otherwise attractive city.* Attractiveness components of the city shift with the city's conditions. They vary with the stage in the city's growth and stagnation life cycle. The internally generated attractiveness is a concept essential to the theory of urban behavior presented here.

The free population exchange with a limitless environment means that the city is powerless to change its composite total attractiveness. However, because the attractiveness is made of many components, there is a wide range of choice as to the separate values of these components. Some attractiveness components can be improved if others are simultaneously made less favorable so that the composite remains the same. It is in adjusting the components of attractiveness, while keeping the total attractiveness the same, that the opportunities for the city rest.

The Stagnant Urban Condition. The urban area that has passed its phase of population growth and internal development and has settled into equilibrium exhibits a set of characteristics here called the "stagnant condition." In this stagnant condition the area has an excessive housing/industry ratio. The excess housing is in the underemployed-housing category, including housing in declining areas, slum dwellings, and abandoned housing. The amount of housing is too large compared to industry because the number of housing and industrial structures each tends to be the same as when the area was in healthy economic balance. But aging has reduced the population employed in the industrial structures while at the same time increasing and changing the character of the population occupying the housing. Even in terms of population, the housing may be excessive. When the economic potential of the area falls far enough, the population may decline below what the housing could accommodate at the normal population densities of the economic class that occupies the housing. In the underemployed category there can simultaneously be excessive housing and very crowded living conditions.

---

*West Berlin illustrates the point. It has no slums in the United States, South American, and Asian meaning of the word. First, it communicates only with West Germany whose high economic level and superior standard of living is protected by severe immigration restrictions. Second, West Berlin is practically a new city so that economic vitality has attracted the managerial and labor classes who occupy and maintain at a high standard of repair even the older structures that remain. Third, the political stress inherent in West Berlin is a strong negative factor which must be balanced by superior physical and economic attractiveness if a population is to be maintained.

The crowding, however, is not a reflection of housing unavailability but of economic conditions. Some dwelling units are abandoned, while others are crowded because the tenants are unable to pay for maintaining and operating the total available housing.

The stagnant urban area has too high a ratio of old industry and housing to new. This happens because the economic life of a new unit is shorter than that of a declining unit. As shown in Figure 3-4 the number of buildings in various economic categories is proportional to the average lifetime in each category. The city that attempts to save old structures to extend their remaining small contribution speeds its own decline.

The stagnant urban area has too high a ratio of underemployed to labor. This is a direct consequence of the high proportion of industry and housing in the oldest-age categories. Until there is continued renewal through aggressive repair and demolition, the area will inexorably sink into stagnation.

The declining condition of a city is accelerated by policies or conditions that encourage concentration of any one economic group. For example, an effective transportation system which brings people into the central city from remote suburbs contributes to the blighting of the area it traverses. Without the transportation system the rebuilding of inlying areas would be more likely to occur. Concentration allows industry to be located in one place, labor in another, management in a third, and the marginal underemployed group in a fourth. The mobility multipliers that depend on population ratios in the model (such as Equations 25 and 38 in Appendix A) assume that the populations are in close proximity and communication with one another. This communication sets one of the land-area limits on the validity of the model. Some aspects of the model do not apply to areas so large that different groups have no contact through normal living activities and school systems.

Soaring Municipal Costs. The increase of costs as the urban area ages is a reflection of the shifting balance that results from laws and administration that permit and encourage excessive immigration of the poor and speed the exit of the more affluent. As the poor begin to dominate, their political power is felt. Their short-term interests increasingly dominate their own long-term welfare and that of the city. As shown in Appendix B, if this political power is too great, the rising taxes and the accelerating decline can continue to the point where the urban area begins to collapse economically and all population classes decline.

7.3 Alternatives Open to the City

Pursuing unachievable goals can lead only to frustration. Much urban planning fails to distinguish the possible from the impossible. Until the difference is clearly understood, the future of cities remains in doubt. Attempting the impossible can foreclose even those goals that might have been achieved.

Two quite different kinds of action can be chosen in dealing with a complex system such as an urban area. One is to make a frontal assault with direct-action programs aimed at correcting deficiencies. A quite different approach is to alter the internal system which has created the deficiencies.

It is often said that only a massive federal commitment of money will solve urban problems. But if the city is unable to help itself, where is this massive federal commitment to come from in a country that is already largely urbanized and where many sections seem destined to become as blighted as present ghetto areas? Even if the massive financial support were available, there is no certainty that it would have the desired effect. Chapter 4 showed sufficient adverse effects from common urban-development programs to suggest that the intuitive selection of massive programs may be ineffective at best and a waste of money and actively detrimental at worst.

A properly conceived system study aimed at the improvement of a complex system should start by developing a clear understanding of how and why the difficulties have been created. If this is well done, one discovers the causes of the observed symptoms. When the system behavior is understood, the internal incentives that are creating difficulty can usually be altered at much less expense than would be necessary for direct-action programs aimed at reducing symptoms. Furthermore, the massive action program, if it does nothing about the underlying causes of difficulty, simply comes into conflict with the operation of a system already set at cross purposes. The internal forces in most social systems are so powerful that they will likely dominate any effort to treat symptoms, if treatment does not reach the true structural causes. Conversely, if the causes can be reversed, an internally generated revival can proceed faster and with more lasting effect than if the treatment comes from the outside.

Outside help for the city cannot be sustained forever if the effort is directed toward an unnatural goal that the city itself cannot even maintain, to say nothing of achieve on its own.

If the dynamic structure suggested in this book is correct, the city, because of population interchange with its environment, cannot hope to improve simultaneously all aspects of life for its inhabitants. The total attractiveness of a city can improve only as the entire communicating environment improves.

On the other hand, the city can exchange improvement in one attractiveness component for decline in another and thereby alter its economic and social effectiveness. The character of a city is determined by its population. At any time population is a result of past movement to and from the city and the social and economic conversions that have occurred within. The two components that seem most influential in determining movement to the city and upward economic mobility inside are jobs and housing. Much of this book has focused on the interplay between work opportunities and housing. There appears to be little possibility of increasing the availability of both simultaneously. In special situations other attractiveness factors might be unfavorable enough so that both jobs and housing could simultaneously exist in excess and remain so in equilibrium. These unfavorable factors would most likely take the form of strong legal or psychological forces repulsing immigration. In the absence of such conditions, housing and jobs appear to be the most powerful influences in determining the equilibrium condition of an urban area.

The natural condition of the aging city tends toward too much housing and too few jobs for the underemployed population. In such condition an urban area fails to operate effectively. It attracts an unskilled population but then offers little opportunity. It traps the underemployed in a low economic condition from which few escape.

The cities have reached their present condition by following policies that look attractive for the short run. But because long-run effects are often the opposite, short-run emphasis eventually leads to difficulty. Education to increase public understanding of urban dynamics and generate popular support of long-range goals might allow changes that would reverse the decline of metropolitan areas. Decaying regions move. Our past programs that try to rebuild the physical area without integrating the underemployed into an economic revival merely shift the troubled area to a new location. Given time, a disintegrated area will certainly be rebuilt if the area has economic potential, but the next-oldest bordering area will then fall victim to concentration of the underemployed population.

If the concept of attractiveness equilibrium between areas is correct, a city will not be able to outrun the needs of the underemployed by providing ever more low-cost housing and welfare. The city that attempts this will inundate itself with the less fortunate of the world in a cycle where effort does not improve conditions but only increases population without in fact improving the lot of that population. In an effort to improve short-run conditions by alleviating symptoms of a defective social system, the city does long-run harm to the very group it is trying to help.

In taking the longer view, a city must recognize the slowness with which change will come. Time scales are probably about correct in the simulation profiles in Chapter 5. If so, even after appropriate policies are adopted substantial change will not occur for one or two decades. The greatest danger is that impatience will reverse the policies before they have a chance to be effective. Political leaders will face another problem. Policies that lead to urban revival will give the superficial appearance of favoring upper-income groups and industry at the expense of the underemployed. If the city has already reached the point where the under-employed are numerous and politically powerful, these programs for restoring the economic health of a city may not be open for practical political considera-tion.

The urban system is a complex interlocking network of positive- and negative-feedback loops. Equilibrium is a condition wherein growth in the positive loops has been arrested. But such a positive loop is in precarious balance between growth on one side and conversion into a negative loop with intrinsic declining characteristics on the other. Internal shifts in the incentive structure of the system can be powerful in determining the path that is followed.

A city in better economic balance than the decayed areas would have a lower underemployed population at any one time but a higher flow from the outside through the underemployed group into the labor group. The balanced city would serve all sectors of the population more effectively. By accepting a larger flow of underemployed, the balanced city would contribute more to raising the standard of living of the surrounding environment by taking in the underemployed and giving back skilled labor, managers, and industrial activity generated in the urban area.

It appears from the model simulation results in this book that a better urban balance can be achieved by altering the laws and policies under which our cities operate. The change would aim at encouraging a revised pattern of using land area and replacing old structures. The changes needed in laws and administrative practices would not require a more coercive legal structure. A new system should be able to operate with less government encroachment by eminent-domain proceedings than employed at present for urban renewal. Our present system is characterized by tax and zoning regulations that encourage private enterprise to act in ways that have produced the present degeneration in the older urban areas. A different tax and legal system should be devised so that actions in self-interest by land and building owners will produce a city that evolves toward a new and better equilibrium condition.

7.4   Maintaining Economic Balance

If the city is to survive as a healthy economic unit and as a satisfactory place to live, it must be managed under an ensemble of policies that induce constant renewal at a rate that matches the relentless march of deterioration. By contrast, present laws, zoning regulations, and tax structures all conspire to produce a city with declining industry, slum housing, and a population mix that inhibits economic revival.

The city, by shifting taxes off those who are already too numerous, encourages a still greater influx of the underemployed, who tip the balance downward in a spiral of urban decline. By shifting the tax burden onto those who generate the least municipal costs, who have the greatest mobility, who need not live in the aging structures, and who have the least reason to remain in the city, the city encourages the departure of the people and industries most necessary for its revival.

By favoring rent ceilings the city often accelerates the deterioration of housing into the housing classes that are already too large for the well-being of the city.

By believing that the problems of the city are beyond its control, the city lays its problems at the doorstep of a higher level of government and corrective action is deferred. By asserting that the city is the inevitable recipient of the underemployed and the misfits from other parts of the country, one creates the impression that the city is a victim of circumstances. By accepting old structures and their consequences as a condition of nature rather than as reflections of the legal and tax structure, people fail to see the true causes of decline. These attitudes are then used to justify ignoring the fact that the city is creating its own condition.

Kinds of Industry. The theory of urban dynamics presented here indicates that the relationship between working and living is basic to urban evolution. If so, the kinds of commercial activity in the area are important.

By encouraging the wrong kinds of industry, the city establishes an unfavorable "balance of trade" in some of its poorer areas. In these areas there is insufficient product manufactured and service sold to the outside to maintain the inner community. Local merchants and professional activities, while "commercial" in nature, do not serve the purpose. They end up selling to the inside and buying from the outside without themselves generating an "export." The area tends to be a net purchaser until the standard of living is driven down to be in balance with the "export" flow. The "foreign-exchange" problem is similar to that faced by a developing country. Some commercial activities, such as warehouses, occupy land area but generate very little in payrolls to the community.

Policies need to favor industries that are profitable, pay a high wage rate, and carry on labor-intensive activity. Such industries should be perceived as a great service to the community rather than as ones to be penalized and saddled with the burden of carrying the cost of the urban area they alone are able to revive. The declining urban area needs to be made an effective part of commercial interchange. If the people in these areas begin to contribute economically, they acquire the purchasing power to become consumers and indirectly justify and generate their own jobs.

Taxes. Taxes, in the representation of an urban system presented here, affect mobility of people of all classes and the construction of housing and industry.

City administration has generally not been based on any cost-benefit concept relating revenue to expenditures within segments of the city. The tax structure tends to penalize those who can contribute most to the well-being of the city, while favoring those who generate costs to the city. Such a strong bias tips the city too far toward population and, within the population, disproportionately increases the group least able to contribute to a successful city. In the short run, the conventional tax policies seem humanitarian and appear to be a desirable social force. But in the long run the policies produce economic decline and trap in poverty the very people they are designed to serve. And as the balance in the city shifts toward the underemployed population, the political power shifts too, giving further dominance to the downward forces. It is characteristic of our complex social systems that actions that appear to alleviate difficulties in fact often produce trouble. As the trouble deepens, the presumed treatment is intensified in a well-motivated but misguided effort to reverse the process. A spiral develops which drives the system harder and harder against the crisis limit.

This urban-system study suggests that, if economic balance of the city is to be realigned, there must be a revision in attitude toward various classes of city activity.

People are the fundamental generator of municipal expenditure. People require welfare. People require police and fire departments. People require transportation.

People use schools. People demand city services. Unless the people are economically able to support these services and politically responsible for authorizing them, the urban system is almost sure to be self-defeating. The one facet of a city most closely identified with people is housing. If the urban theory of behavior proposed here withstands wider examination and criticism, the present trend to shift taxation away from housing will need to be thoroughly re-examined. Only if cost and revenue are closely coupled will the city be responsible in its expenditure. Only if the revenue is highly correlated with the people who require the expenditure will the city have a self-regulating system which generates a population able to sustain a healthy city and to pay for the urban services they desire.

The most significant variables seem to be various ratios between industry and housing, which suggest that the attitude toward industry needs to be substantially reversed. Industry has been perceived as a politically impotent sector of the city onto which to load rising demands for revenue. But industry is not without retaliatory power. It can leave, and it does. It can also shift its mix, leaving the city with the kinds of industry that contribute least to maintaining urban vitality. Desirable types of industry should be seen as an asset, as an essential element in solving the city's problems, and as a sector of the city to be encouraged through favorable administrative regulations, zoning practices, and tax policy. Enterprise of the right kind costs the city very little by its presence. It polices its own internal land area. It buys water and other utilities. In modern construction built to proper standards, it demands little of fire departments. Industry of itself does not require schools. But on the favorable side, industry exports the products and services that generate a favorable balance of trade and make it possible for the area to generate the revenue necessary for importing the goods needed for survival and gracious living.

Tax-exempt institutions need to be re-examined. They too should be judged on the basis of how they contribute to the city's cost and revenue balance. It is neither sufficient nor proper simply to contrast the lack of tax revenue from a tax-exempt institution with the tax revenue which might conceivably come from a highly taxed industrial complex on the same land area. If the tax-exempt institution causes the city no expense in its own right and produces no revenue, then it could almost be perceived as nonexistent. The land area might simply be subtracted from what is considered to be the city and the institution would be perceived as neutral. On the other hand, if a tax-exempt institution is established in areas that would otherwise contain deteriorated housing, the creation of the tax-exempt institution may help correct the land-area imbalance of the city. But, if the institution attracts a population that creates a cost load on the city and does not pay its own way, the institution could be considered detrimental. In other words, classes of institutions differ markedly in how they affect the cost-revenue balance of the city. The presence of such institutions, the regulations under which they operate, and their relation to the city should be examined in terms of what they do to the long-term revitalization and maintenance of the city.

If industrial taxation is seen as a means of encouraging the proper kinds of industry and the proper industrial behavior, quite different tax structures would evolve. Taxation should favor high-employment industries that pay high wage rates. Present taxation on the basis of falling property value defeats the goal of replacing declining industry. This suggests a tax rate based on occupied land area or on factory floor area. The marginal business, which has already amortized and recovered its costs, would be unable to pay the taxes and would be forced to clear the land. If the objective is to redress the balance between industrial and residential land in the declining areas, commercial tax rates should be reduced relative to residential rates.

Quite the opposite of moving toward a payroll tax, the city should consider a tax credit based on salaries and wages paid to residents of the local community. This would serve multiple purposes. It would improve the balance-of-trade position of the local area by favoring high-wage industries. By encouraging employment of those living nearby, it would help reverse the city trend toward ever-increasing costs of public transportation.

This urban study suggests the desirability of reversing residential tax trends. The high taxation of undeveloped land may force housing construction in areas where it should not occur. Reduced assessments on aging structures favor the survival of the very structures that should be removed. A flat tax per dwelling unit, regardless of age or condition, might do much to create internal incentives that would maintain a favorable residential balance in the urban area. Some form of personal-residence-amortization deduction against personal income tax might produce a favorable bias in housing renewal. Assessing the residential tax more nearly in proportion to the city costs generated by the different classes of population would help to control the proportions of population classes so that the city can better serve the needs of all classes.

These comments about tax structure are included to illustrate the type of exploration into causes that should be precipitated by a system study. The form of the final conclusions should come from the resolution of doubts and counter-proposals. Tax structure realignments should be devised to help make the city self-sustaining. The city does not serve an effective social function for any population class by putting itself in a position where desirable industry leaves and the disadvantaged population comes. Such evolution as has occurred in the past moves the underemployed away from sparsely settled areas that have potential for economic development into old and declining areas that cannot revive under the existing mode of operation.

Land Zoning. Just as the tax laws need re-examination, so do the land-zoning regulations. At the present time zoning favors excess ratios of housing to economic activity and favors segregation of activities into blocks that are too large for favorable interaction.

There should be a reconsideration of property rights. Do the property rights of the landowner include the right to generate decay which blights the entire urban system? Through zoning and taxation it should be possible to design a system that encourages owners to take self-protective actions that generate renewal.

Zoning tends now toward limiting areas where industry is permitted. These areas permit both industry and housing, with industry sharply restricted and housing virtually unlimited. But should not the reverse attitude exist? Suppose residence were restricted to particular areas. Other areas, even in metropolitan regions, could be restricted to agriculture only and taxed at appropriate low rates to maintain open areas. Industrial areas would be specified but would not be open to residential construction. The blocks for each of these would be smaller and more intertwined than in present land usage. Zoning might specify proximity of high- and low-density housing areas to bring different economic classes closer together and to enhance the opportunity for upward mobility.

7.5   Choice of Urban Pressures

A complex system can operate in any one of many different modes. Some modes are desirable, others are not. Some modes are firmly self-sustaining, others tend to terminate their own existence.

If a mode of behavior is to be sustained, there must be some restraint against which the system presses to locate and maintain the particular mode and to anchor the system against drifting into some other mode of operation. This pressure against a restraining force will appear as some form of social, psychological, or economic pressure within the system. Each decisive and sustainable mode of operation is characterized by its own pattern of pressures. A system without internal pressures is probably one whose behavior mode will drift in an uncontrolled manner until it is captured by a set of pressures that represent a self-sustaining mode.

The life cycle of an urban area (as in Figure 3-1) carries the area through several sequential modes. In the early growth mode, the growth forces are restrained by pressures from shortage of capital and lack of management and labor. As the land area becomes filled, these pressures decline and the mode of behavior begins to drift toward equilibrium and stagnation. In equilibrium a new set of pressures appear that tend to maintain the mode: (1) buildings become old, (2) industry declines, (3) population balance shifts, and (4) taxes rise. This mode is highly stable. It does not within itself contain natural or psychological processes that will shift the mode to one of revival (as illustrated in Figure 5-16).

But the revival mode of Figure 5-16 is also one that generates pressures. The new equilibrium of Figure 5-16 exhibits an excess of jobs and a shortage of housing. The mode encourages more industry when excess industry is already visible. The mode continues slum-housing demolition even though that housing is in demand and is not in extreme decay. Everyone within the system will see these pressures and will be unanimous in wanting to relieve them. Managers will see economic opportunities for which they need more employees. Potential employees will exert pressures for more apartment construction so they can move to the work opportunities. But with the elimination of the housing pressure comes a period of drifting between modes and almost certainly the capture of the system by the old stagnation mode with its excess housing and declining industry.

Growth modes are not forever sustainable, so we must always look toward the choice of some equilibrium mode. Each equilibrium mode that is sharply definable and free of indecisive drifting will generate its characteristic pressures. In choosing a mode, we are choosing the ensemble of pressures under which we want to live. To sustain that mode we must be willing to accept and, in fact, maintain the corresponding pressures.

The more desirable equilibrium modes of a system seem to exhibit pressures that are easy to alleviate, and alleviating them eliminates the desirable mode. The undesirable modes will often have pressure patterns from which escape is difficult. The equilibrium toward which urban areas now move is stable, undesirable, and accompanied by pressures that do not yield to intuitively chosen corrective programs. The revival mode in Figure 5-16 depends for its existence on pressures that can be easily eliminated by obvious changes in policy.

These shifting equilibrium modes with their associated pressures are seen in all complex systems. For example, a family, by its spending pattern, can choose the solvent mode where it must resist the pressure to overspend its income, or it can yield to consumption pressures, move into a debtor mode, and must then resist the pressure of creditors trying to collect. As another example, a company can resist the pressure to overcommit itself in sales promises, but if it does not it must accept the pressures resulting from late delivery, falling quality, and narrowing profit margins. Another example of shifting from one equilibrium to another is probably illustrated by the response to unemployment pressures in an economic system whereby the corrective action permits a drift into a price-wage spiral and inflation mode.

The suggestion here proposed that population in an area be maintained in balance by limiting housing is directly the opposite of some proposals that depend on limiting work opportunities to control population.

Urban Transportation. The assumptions incorporated here in the model of an urban system contain implications about urban transportation systems. The transportation system is intimately involved in how population classes, industrial classes, and housing classes interact. The model coefficients and nonlinear tables imply, even if indirectly, statements about spatial interaction within the system.

Urban transportation systems can encourage land separation into large nonintercommunicating sectors. The better the transportation system, the less the interleaving of population classes and the less the proximity of housing to industry. As sector separations increase, commuting cost rises rapidly in transportation cost, in psychological trauma, and in time lost from productive activity. Furthermore, transportation can span the deteriorating areas, helping to hide them and making renewal less pressing and less likely. This suggests that urban transportation planning might better be focused on transportation between industrial centers.

Interindustry communication would favor industrial decentralization into numerous islands that interleave residential and open areas. The transportation would serve the communication needs of effective economic activity but would not be primarily for long-distance commuting from home to work.

The urban planner must plan in terms of the pressures his system is to generate. We now yield to economic pressures, allow and encourage excessive construction in response to high–land–price pressures, and exchange these economic pressures for psychological pressures that come from congestion and commuting. But an urban plan that aspires to a different equilibrium than we now have must be firmly based on a public understanding and willingness to live with the corresponding pressures.

7.6   The City—Master of Its Own Destiny

It has become popular to talk of massive financial aid from the federal government to solve the problems of American cities. But, if the system analysis in this book contains the proper concepts, money, even if available, may be no solution. Given present laws and administrative practices, the problems of a city may respond by growing in size and difficulty to match any available financial support.

But the urban dynamics exposed by this investigation imply that the city can change from the inside. Whether or not it will, assuming that the validity of the study is sustained, depends primarily on political leadership and improved public understanding leading to support for policies that can reverse urban decline. A city need not wait for the national problems of poverty and the underemployed to be solved.

The city, by influencing the type and availability of housing, can delay an increase in the immigration rate until internal balance is re-established. The city must press for removal of aging housing before deterioration creates an imbalance in the urban system. Because aging is continuous, the renewal process should be continuous instead of occurring in waves several decades apart. At the same time industrial parks should be established within present decayed residential areas to generate jobs for those already living in the city. Favorable city regulations and new tax policies should be designed to attract the kinds of industry most needed for revival. The ensemble of new policies would be aimed at restraining the processes of urban stagnation.

The proposed new policies of urban management do not imply additional hardships on present urban residents except for relocation within the area. Relocation will be caused by three streams of change:

1. Slum demolition for gradually consolidating land into parcels large enough for the needed industrial centers (and any associated landscaping, parks, etc.).

2. Voluntary relocation from underemployed housing to worker housing as upward economic mobility makes such improvements in living conditions possible.

3. Economic relocation arising from revival activity as older housing is replaced by new housing and declining industry by new enterprise.

The city has been presented here as a living, self-regulating system which generates its own evolution through time. It is not a victim of outside circumstances but of its own internal practices. As long as present practices continue, infusion of outside money can produce only fleeting benefit, if any. If the city needs outside help, it may be legislative action to force on the city those practices that will lead to long-term revival. Such outside pressure may be necessary if internal short-term considerations make the reversal of present trends politically impossible. The revival of the city depends not on massive programs of external aid but on changed internal administration.

Appendixes

A The Model—A Theory of Urban Interactions

This appendix describes the model used in this book to represent an urban area. The model is stated in mathematical equations. These equations provide a specific and precise notation. They say nothing that could not be said in English, but mathematical symbols have precise definitions and are far less ambiguous than words. Relationships between variables are shown pictorially in flow diagrams.*

A brief discussion of general system structure and the specific structure used here for an urban area is in Chapter 2, which should be reread before continuing.

Figure 2-4 shows the principal system levels and associated rates of flow. The choices of the degree of aggregation and of the principal levels and rates are critical to the success of system modeling. There are as yet no explicit rules for guiding such choices. But it is usually necessary and sufficient to penetrate into the system one or two layers of detail below the point at which the trouble symptoms appear. If the symptoms involve housing and employment, the processes of building housing, generating jobs, and representing population flows will need to be included. Figure 2-4 illustrates the basic framework of the urban model. The flow diagrams in this appendix show each system rate and the inputs that control it. As each flow diagram is encountered the reader may want to refer to Figure 2-4 to maintain his over-all perspective.

A.1 Underemployed Sector

Figure A-1 contains somewhat more detail than was first encountered in Figure 2-7. The figure shows the underemployed level U by the upper rectangle and

---

*For more explanation of equation structure, the appropriate solution interval DT, and the flow-diagram symbolism, see References 1 and 6. Equations are in the format recognized by the DYNAMO compiler in the DYNAMO II version. The manual for DYNAMO II has not yet been published, but the reader is referred to Alexander Pugh, *DYNAMO User's Manual* (The M.I.T. Press, Cambridge, Massachusetts, 1963) for a general explanation. The new DYNAMO contains an algebraic translator and does not limit the choice of equations as did the earlier version.

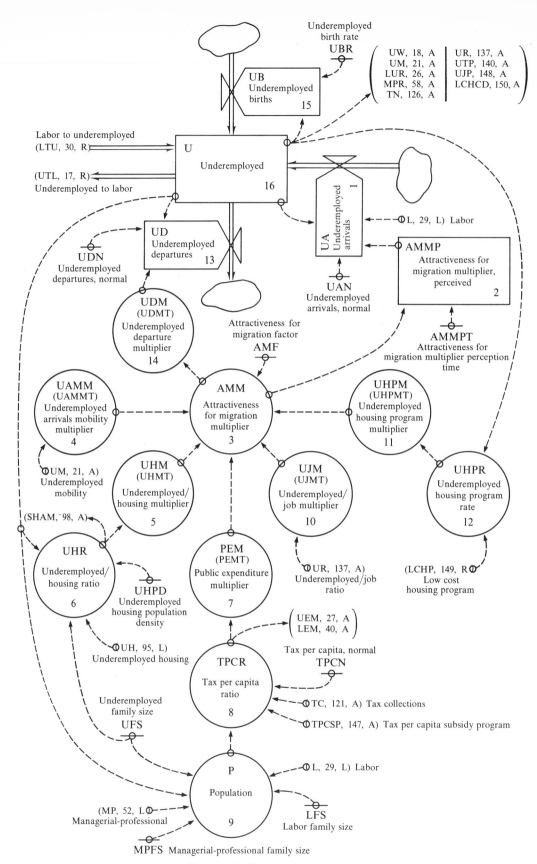

Figure A-1 Underemployed sector.

the five rates of flow that communicate with it. The details are shown for three of the flow rates—underemployed arrivals, underemployed departures, and underemployed births. In the diagrams, levels are shown as rectangles and rates are shown as valve symbols. The auxiliary equations in the circles are algebraic subdivisions of the rate equations. They are part of the rate equations and can be substituted into the rate equations and made to disappear. They are kept separate because they have individual conceptual meaning and represent identifiable aspects of the urban system. Explanation of the model will follow the sequence of the equation numbers.

A compact listing of equations as actually entered in the computer will be found in Appendix E. The same equations appear in the same sequence in this appendix but with explanation and with the definitions of symbols following the equations.*

Equation 1 is the rate equation describing the arrival of underemployed into the area. The underemployed, as used here, are the potential wage earners. Total underemployed population will, in Equation 9, be computed as underemployed multiplied by underemployed family size.

$$UA.KL=(U.K+L.K)(UAN)(AMMP.K) \qquad 1,R$$

$$UAN=.05 \qquad 1.1,C$$

UA	–	UNDEREMPLØYED ARRIVALS (MEN/YEAR)
U	–	UNDEREMPLØYED (MEN)
L	–	LABØR (MEN)
UAN	–	UNDEREMPLØYED ARRIVALS NØRMAL (FRACTIØN/YEAR)
AMMP	–	ATTRACTIVENESS–FØR–MIGRATIØN MULTIPLIER PERCEIVED (DIMENSIØNLESS)

Equation 1 is a product of three terms. The first is the sum of underemployed and labor populations, which is here taken to represent the size and activity of the urban area which attract people from the outside. The second term UAN is a "normal" multiplier which represents the fraction of existing inhabitants U + L that would come to the area each year. With a UAN value of .05 in Equation 1.1, the statement is made that under normal circumstances the inflow to the area would represent 5% of the underemployed plus labor inhabitants. As we will see in Appendix B, numerical values for these coefficients are not critical to the results obtained in this book. The "normal" area is best thought of as one nearing the end of its growth phase. It has neither the dynamic vitality of maximum growth rate nor the depressed activity of the stagnation phase.

Equation 1 contains the third term AMMP. This is a modulating term representing the attractiveness of the area compared to normal. The normal value of AMMP is 1. A more attractive area will have a multiplier higher than 1 and

---

*The format of the equations with related definitions has been generated by the "DOCUMENTOR" program, which merges the model file in Appendix E with the file of definitions in Appendix C.

a less attractive area will have a multiplier lower than 1. As the area becomes more or less attractive relative to its surrounding environment, the multiplier value changes.

In Equation 1 the letters K and L, after the period following the symbol group for a variable, represent points in time. The equation system is evaluated at uniformly spaced intervals in time. The "present time" at any particular point in the computation is known as time K. Time L is the forthcoming period at which the equations are next evaluated and time J is the previous instant at which they were last evaluated. Rates of flow are presumed to be constant during the intervening time intervals* and cause the levels to change from the value at one time period to the value at the next time period. The rate of flow UA.KL is the underemployed-arrival rate that will exist during the forthcoming time interval from time K to time L. As a rate of flow, it depends on constants and on system levels, not on other rates. All three of the variables on the right-hand side of Equation 1 are system levels.

Equation 2 describes the perception by the outside underemployed of the attractiveness of the particular urban area. The perceived value will be different from the true value when attractiveness is changing. The true value is generated in Equation 3, but Equation 2 generates a time delay representing the time for the image of the urban area to change in the minds of those who might migrate from a distant point. The perception-time delay is here taken in Equation 2.2 as 20 years. In an earlier day the delay would perhaps have been longer. At the present time, with television and more rapid communication, the time might be somewhat shorter.

$$AMMP.K = AMMP.J + (DT/AMMPT)(AMM.J - AMMP.J) \qquad 2,L$$

$$AMMP = 1 \qquad 2.1,N$$

$$AMMPT = 20 \qquad 2.2,C$$

AMMP — ATTRACTIVENESS-FØR-MIGRATIØN MULTIPLIER
         PERCEIVED (DIMENSIØNLESS)
AMMPT — ATTRACTIVENESS-FØR-MIGRATIØN-MULTIPLIER
         PERCEPTIØN TIME (YEARS)
AMM   — ATTRACTIVENESS-FØR-MIGRATIØN MULTIPLIER
         (DIMENSIØNLESS)

Equation 2 is listed as a level equation but actually combines within itself a rate equation which causes the level AMMP to change. The perceived value AMMP is always moving toward the true value AMM. The rate at which it moves depends on the difference between AMM and the value of AMMP. This difference is divided by the perception time AMMPT to create the rate of change in the perceived value.

All level equations must be given initial values. The level equations fully

---

*The time interval between successive evaluations of the equation set is made short enough so that the assumption of constant rates in the intervening interval is satisfactory.

determine the existing condition of the system and must have values from which to start the computation sequence. Equation 2.1 with a value of 1 says that the perceived attractiveness of the city is initially normal.

Equation 2 describing a system level is not represented in Figure 2-4 showing the principal levels. The perception delays will affect the transient responses of the system but will have no effect on equilibrium values. In equilibrium the perceived value AMMP will be equal to the true value AMM, because, if AMM does not change, the delayed value AMMP will move toward it and take on essentially the same value.

The true present value of attractiveness to the underemployed is described by Equation 3. This is the actual, but not the perceived, attractiveness. As seen in the flow diagram of Figure A-1 the attractiveness-for-migration multiplier AMM is generated by 6 inputs. Five of these are active system variables and the sixth is a coefficient AMF which is available for system experimentation.

In Equation 3 multiplication has been chosen as the most appropriate way to combine the components of attractiveness. This asserts that if one component doubles in value the attractiveness variable doubles, regardless of the values of the other variables. Under extreme conditions this formulation might be open to some question. However, it seems far more suitable than combination by addition. Some of the components of attractiveness are sufficiently influential that by themselves they can effectively suppress inward migration. A linear additive formulation would not be able to give this dominant position to one of the component influences. As written in Equation 3, any one of the multipliers becoming 0 will cause the attractiveness multiplier AMM to become 0 regardless of the values taken on by the other inputs.

$$\text{AMM.K} = (\text{UAMM.K})\,(\text{UHM.K})\,(\text{PEM.K})\,(\text{UJM.K})\,(\text{UHPM.K})\,(\text{AMF}) \qquad \text{3,A}$$

$$\text{AMF} = 1 \qquad \text{3.1,C}$$

AMM — ATTRACTIVENESS–FØR–MIGRATIØN MULTIPLIER
    (DIMENSIØNLESS)
UAMM — UNDEREMPLØYED–ARRIVALS–MØBILITY MULTIPLIER
    (DIMENSIØNLESS)
UHM — UNDEREMPLØYED/HØUSING MULTIPLIER
    (DIMENSIØNLESS)
PEM — PUBLIC–EXPENDITURE MULTIPLIER
    (DIMENSIØNLESS)
UJM — UNDEREMPLØYED/JØB MULTIPLIER
    (DIMENSIØNLESS)
UHPM — UNDEREMPLØYED–HØUSING–PRØGRAM MULTIPLIER
    (DIMENSIØNLESS)
AMF — ATTRACTIVENESS–FØR–MIGRATIØN FACTØR
    (DIMENSIØNLESS)

All system formulations are to some extent a compromise. The test is one of adequacy and a balance between the simplicity of modeling and the complexity of real life. The multiplicative arrangement of Equation 3 seems to be a sub-

stantial improvement over linear addition in matching the system being represented. Going further into some form of multidimensional arbitrary table of
values does not appear justified.

The input multipliers to the attractiveness-for-migration multiplier AMM are
generated in table look-up operations to allow for nonlinear relationships between
the source variables and their influence on attractiveness.

Equation 4, which describes the effect of upward economic mobility on attractiveness of the area, is such a table function.

UAMM.K =TABLE(UAMMT,UM.K,0,.15,.025)   4,A

UAMMT=.3/.7/1/1.2/1.3/1.4/1.5   4.1,T

    UAMM — UNDEREMPLØYED-ARRIVALS-MØBILITY MULTIPLIER
           (DIMENSIØNLESS)
    UAMMT — UNDEREMPLØYED-ARRIVALS-MØBILITY-MULTIPLIER
           TABLE
    UM   — UNDEREMPLØYED MØBILITY (FRACTIØN/YEAR)

Equation 4 is not the usual algebraic computation. It designates a procedure.
The word "TABLE" which is not in parentheses and not separated by an asterisk
(used as a multiply sign) is read by the DYNAMO compiler as an instruction.
It says that the table of values UAMMT is to be entered with the variable UM.
The table range is from 0 to .15 in steps of .025 in the variable UM. The output
of the table yields the underemployed-arrivals-mobility multiplier UAMM. This
table appears graphically in Figure A-2. The value of UM, available from elsewhere in the system, is used to enter along the horizontal axis. Going vertically
to the curve and reading the value on the vertical axis yields a value of UAMM.
Interpolation between values in the table is done along straight lines connecting
the recorded points. The table UAMMT called for in Equation 4 is specified in
Equation 4.1. The successive values correspond to the range of UM from 0 to
.15 in the specified steps of .025.

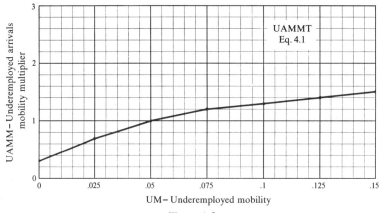

Figure A-2

Figure A-2, like most of the functional relationships used, revolves around the concept of a normal system. At the normal operating condition the value of the multiplier is 1. Here an upward mobility of .05 per year is taken as normal. This means that 5% of the underemployed each year move into the labor category. As the mobility declines toward 0, the attractiveness multiplier falls from 1 to a value of .3. This says that lack of upward mobility can make the urban area only 30% as attractive as normal but that this variable by itself is not capable of exerting enough influence to stop inward migration.

In Figure A-2 the upper section of the curve has been taken as having decreasing slope with increases in the underemployed mobility UM. It is with respect to these functional curves that research data and practical opinion can most readily be brought to bear on model formulation. For example, one might argue that the relationship in Figure A-2 should be curved in the opposite direction. This would imply that low upward mobility has no decisive effect but that high upward mobility becomes increasingly influential. If such a different relationship were suspected, the efficient procedure would be to put the alternative assumption in the model to discover what influence it has. If the result turns out to affect the conclusions drawn from the model, then the assumed relationship must be approached with greater care and refined as far as justified on the basis of the probable consequences measured against the effort required.

The attractiveness of an urban area in generating inward mobility is seen as being sensitive to available housing under conditions of housing shortage. Equation 5 is a table function giving the relationship illustrated in Figure A-3. For a normal ratio of underemployed to available housing, the multiplier is again 1. The input variable UHR to the table is the ratio of the underemployed population to the number of people considered normal for the underemployed housing. As the ratio UHR becomes smaller it indicates fewer people relative to the housing. As shown in the table, this makes the area more attractive up to some point where excess housing is available. If UHR falls still further it does not create still greater attraction because more than adequate housing is already available. At the right end of the curve, when UHR takes on higher values, the severe crowding and housing shortage becomes a strong influence toward reducing inward migration. The meaning of "housing" in this context must be taken relative to the social situation under consideration. If economic and housing circumstances in the surrounding areas are desperate, housing in the particular area might be construed as a place to sleep in the street. The meaning of housing in an

UHM.K =TABHL(UHMT, UHR.K, 0, 2, .25) 5,A

UHMT=2.5/2.4/2.2/1.7/1/.4/.2/.1/.05 5.1,T

UHM — UNDEREMPLØYED/HØUSING MULTIPLIER
(DIMENSIØNLESS)
UHMT — UNDEREMPLØYED-HØUSING-MULTIPLIER TABLE
UHR — UNDEREMPLØYED/HØUSING RATIØ (DIMENSIØNLESS)

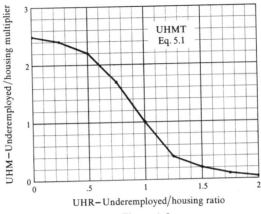

Figure A-3

underdeveloped country might be quite different from the meaning of housing in an American city. Similarly, were the model to be used to represent a gold-rush camp, housing might mean a tent and would be represented by a table having relatively less influence compared to the economic promise.

Some social scientists who read the typescript of this book have objected to this housing multiplier on the basis that studies show that housing is not a strong determinant in regulating urban migration of the underemployed. Such an empirical fact and the curve in Figure A-3 are not necessarily contradictory. The computer runs for the stagnant city show operation toward the upper knee of the curve in the left-hand region where there is unoccupied housing in the city at the low end of the economic scale. In this region to the upper left, the curve in Figure A-3 levels out and migration is not sensitive to housing. The observed lack of sensitivity appears to come, not from lack of potential influence from housing, but from the tendency of the stagnant system to operate in a region where housing has lost its dominance.

Equation 6 defines the underemployed/housing ratio UHR on which Equation 5 depends. It is the ratio of the underemployed population to the total number of people that could normally be housed in the existing underemployed housing. The underemployed family size UFS is defined in Equation 9. It has a value of 8, representing the ratio of total underemployed population to those defined as underemployed for job-seeking purposes. The underemployed-housing population density is taken as 12 persons per housing unit. A housing unit is the same

$$UHR.K = (U.K * UFS) / (UH.K * UHPD)$$ 6,A

$$UHPD = 12$$ 6.1,C

UHR   — UNDEREMPLØYED/HØUSING RATIØ (DIMENSIØNLESS)
U   — UNDEREMPLØYED (MEN)
UFS   — UNDEREMPLØYED FAMILY SIZE (PEØPLE/MAN)
UH   — UNDEREMPLØYED HØUSING (HØUSING UNITS)
UHPD — UNDEREMPLØYED-HØUSING PØPULATIØN DENSITY
        (PEØPLE/HØUSING UNIT)

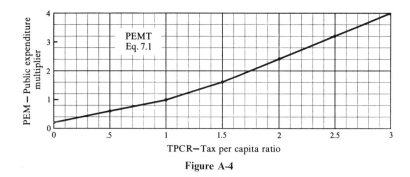

Figure A-4

physical piece of floor space as it moves from premium housing into worker housing and deteriorates into underemployed housing. However, its use changes in the different categories to represent the crowding imposed by economic pressures. The housing unit is taken as normally accommodating 12 persons in the underemployed population, 6 persons in the labor population, and 3 persons in the managerial-professional population.

The attractiveness of the urban area has been made to depend on the rate of per capita public expenditure. Equation 7, which is illustrated in the table of Figure A-4, shows the assumed dependence. The tax per capita ratio TPCR with a value of 1 is taken to represent the public-expenditure rate in the outside environment. The tax expenditure within the area is relative to the outside standard. A ratio of 1 gives a multiplier of 1. The curve suggests that the tax per capita ratio is influential and curves upward. In other words, a tax per capita ratio of 3 would raise the multiplier to 4. At the low end one can argue that the curve might be drawn more steeply and actually intercept the horizontal axis before TPCR falls to 0. At 0, there is no public expenditure. Chaos and anarchy might characterize the area and effectively repel further immigration to the area.

$$PEM.K = TABHL(PEMT, TPCR.K, 0, 3, .5) \hspace{4cm} 7, A$$

$$PEMT = .2/.6/1/1.6/2.4/3.2/4 \hspace{4cm} 7.1, T$$

        PEM   — PUBLIC-EXPENDITURE MULTIPLIER
                   (DIMENSIØNLESS)
        PEMT — PUBLIC-EXPENDITURE-MULTIPLIER TABLE
        TPCR — TAX PER CAPITA RATIØ (DIMENSIØNLESS)

Equation 8 computes the tax per capita ratio. First the tax collections within the area are divided by the total population. To this is added any tax per capita subsidy to the area from outside the system. This total expenditure rate per capita is then divided by the value taken as normal in the outside environment. The normal is represented as $250 per year per person to cover all public services.

Equation 9 gives total population for use in Equation 8. It takes the three categories of wage-earning population, multiplies each by its family size, and totals the three categories.

$$TPCR.K = ((TC.K/P.K) + TPCSP.K)/TPCN \qquad\qquad 8,A$$

$$TPCN = 250 \qquad\qquad 8.1,C$$

```
TPCR   - TAX PER CAPITA RATIØ (DIMENSIØNLESS)
TC     - TAX CØLLECTIØNS (DØLLARS/YEAR)
P      - PØPULATIØN (MEN)
TPCSP  - TAX-PER-CAPITA-SUBSIDY PRØGRAM (DØLLARS/
         PERSØN/YEAR)
TPCN   - TAX PER CAPITA NØRMAL (DØLLARS/YEAR/PERSØN)
```

$$P.K = (MP.K)(MPFS) + (L.K)(LFS) + (U.K)(UFS) \qquad\qquad 9,A$$

$$MPFS = 5 \qquad\qquad 9.1,C$$

$$LFS = 6 \qquad\qquad 9.2,C$$

$$UFS = 8 \qquad\qquad 9.3,C$$

```
P     - PØPULATIØN (MEN)
MP    - MANAGERIAL-PRØFESSIØNAL (MEN)
MPFS  - MANAGERIAL-PRØFESSIØNAL FAMILY SIZE
        (PEØPLE/MAN)
L     - LABØR (MEN)
LFS   - LABØR FAMILY SIZE (PEØPLE/MAN)
U     - UNDEREMPLØYED (MEN)
UFS   - UNDEREMPLØYED FAMILY SIZE (PEØPLE/MAN)
```

The underemployed/job multiplier in Equation 10 is an important relationship in the urban system. Available evidence suggests that job opportunities are strongly influential in determining regional attractiveness.

$$UJM.K = TABHL(UJMT, UR.K, 0, 3, .25) \qquad\qquad 10,A$$

$$UJMT = 2/2/1.9/1.6/1/.6/.4/.3/.2/.15/.1/.05/.02 \qquad\qquad 10.1,T$$

```
UJM   - UNDEREMPLØYED/JØB MULTIPLIER
        (DIMENSIØNLESS)
UJMT  - UNDEREMPLØYED/JØB MULTIPLIER TABLE
UR    - UNDEREMPLØYED/JØB RATIØ (DIMENSIØNLESS)
```

Equation 10 as shown in Figure A-5 has the standard value of 1 when the underemployed/job ratio is 1. The curve is steep in this normal region. As the underemployed decline compared to available jobs (at the left) the multiplier rises until, when there are sufficient excess jobs, additional jobs have little more effect. The curve should therefore level out at low values of UR. In the opposite direction, the curve descends steeply but with reducing slope. An underemployed/job ratio of 2 reduces to .2 the attractiveness. At a ratio of 3, inward mobility has been effectively suppressed. As seen in Figure 3-1*b*, the city during its growth phase tends to have insufficient housing and excess jobs. By contrast, the situation reverses rather quickly as the land area becomes filled and as aging of the housing increases the available underemployed housing and underemployed population, while aging industry reduces available jobs.

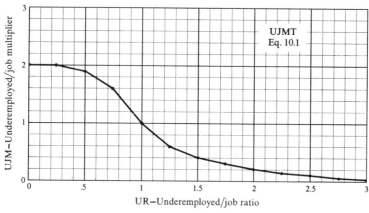

Figure A-5

Equation 11 describes the influence of a low-cost-housing program. Living spaces were accounted for in Equation 5. Here in Equation 11 the attractiveness arises from the low-cost-housing-construction activity and the image of aid to the underemployed which this creates. It says that active low-cost-housing construction creates attractiveness above and beyond what arises from the physical housing units. This is partly because of the atmosphere of activity in behalf of the underemployed and also because the living units will be seen as more attractive than the deteriorated units composing much of the underemployed-housing pool itself.

UHPM.K=TABHL(UHPMT, UHPR.K,0,.05,.01)   11,A

UHPMT=1/1.2/1.5/1.9/2.4/3   11.1,T

    UHPM — UNDEREMPLØYED-HØUSING-PRØGRAM MULTIPLIER
          (DIMENSIØNLESS)
    UHPMT — UNDEREMPLØYED-HØUSING-PRØGRAM-MULTIPLIER
          TABLE
    UHPR — UNDEREMPLØYED-HØUSING-PRØGRAM RATE (HØUSES/
          YEAR/MAN)

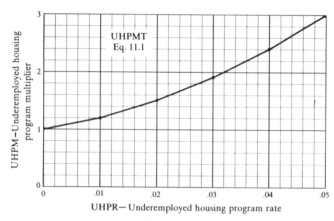

Figure A-6

Figure A-6 illustrates the relationship in Equation 11. Normal is taken as no low-cost-housing program. As the program increases in terms of the fraction per year of the underemployed who are given new housing, the attractiveness of the area rises progressively more steeply.

The input to Equation 11 is the underemployed-housing-program rate UHPR computed in Equation 12. This divides the low-cost-housing units per year being built by the number of underemployed to yield the fraction per year receiving new housing.

$$\text{UHPR.K} = \text{LCHP.JK/U.K} \qquad\qquad 12,A$$

UHPR — UNDEREMPLØYED-HØUSING-PRØGRAM RATE (HØUSES/
    YEAR/MAN)
LCHP — LØW-CØST-HØUSING PRØGRAM (HØUSING UNITS/
    YEAR)
U — UNDEREMPLØYED (MEN)

At all times a social system can be expected to have simultaneously an inward flow and an outward flow. All people are not identical in their preferences. Urban attractiveness is not seen the same way by everyone. A given level of attractiveness may be drawing some people in while pushing others out.

$$\text{UD.KL} = (\text{UDN})(\text{U.K})(\text{UDM.K}) \qquad\qquad 13,R$$

$$\text{UDN} = .02 \qquad\qquad 13.1,C$$

UD — UNDEREMPLØYED DEPARTURES (MEN/YEAR)
UDN — UNDEREMPLØYED DEPARTURES NØRMAL (FRACTIØN/
    YEAR)
U — UNDEREMPLØYED (MEN)
UDM — UNDEREMPLØYED-DEPARTURE MULTIPLIER
    (DIMENSIØNLESS)

Equation 13 has the same structure as Equation 1. It is the outward flow rate expressed in terms of the fraction of the existing underemployed population that would normally leave each year. This normal is then multiplied by the factor UDM, which determines how the actual outward flow at any particular time is related to the normal. An outward flow of 2% per year has been inserted to represent the normal.

The underemployed-departure multiplier UDM is described by Equation 14 and Figure A-7. For lack of more specific evidence the relationship is taken as the reciprocal of the inward attractiveness AMM. When AMM doubles, the outward flow is reduced by half and vice versa.

Equation 14 has a technical complication that will be encountered in several of the other tables. The relationship has a symmetry not on an arithmetic linear scale but in terms of ratios both above and below 1. In other words, doubling and quadrupling the value of AMM has the inverse effect of halving and quarter-

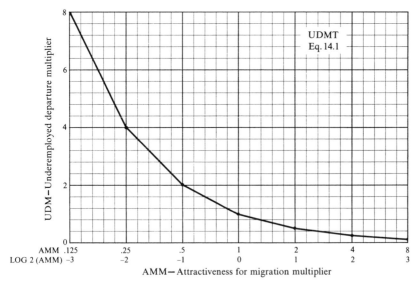

Figure A-7

ing. The appropriate scale to give proper weighting to the function table is logarithmic. The term "LOGN" in Equation 14 is a function indicator as is the TABLE designator itself. It causes the DYNAMO compiler to take the natural logarithm of the variable AMM. The multiplier 1.44 converts from the natural logarithm (base e) to a logarithm on the base 2. The table look-up then proceeds in terms of the value of the base-2 logarithm of AMM. Figure A-7 shows both the logarithm used in the table and the corresponding value of AMM.

UDM.K=TABHL(UDMT,1.44*LØGN(AMM.K),-3,3,1)	14,A
UDMT=8/4/2/1/.5/.25/.125	14.1,T

    UDM   - UNDEREMPLØYED-DEPARTURE MULTIPLIER
            (DIMENSIØNLESS)
    UDMT - UNDEREMPLØYED-DEPARTURE-MULTIPLIER TABLE
    AMM   - ATTRACTIVENESS-FØR-MIGRATIØN MULTIPLIER
            (DIMENSIØNLESS)

Equation 15 is described as the underemployed birth rate but is actually the net difference between birth rate and death rate. It is one of the flows into the underemployed level and has the value of .015 of the underemployed each year.

UB.KL=(U.K) (UBR)	15,R
UBR=.015	15.1,C

    UB   - UNDEREMPLØYED BIRTHS (MEN/YEAR)
    U   - UNDEREMPLØYED (MEN)
    UBR   - UNDEREMPLØYED BIRTH RATE (FRACTIØN/YEAR)

Equation 16 is the level equation which accumulates the flow into and out of the underemployed pool. It is one of the principal system levels appearing in Figure 2-4.

$$U.K = U.J + (DT)(UA.JK + UB.JK + LTU.JK - UD.JK - UTL.JK) \qquad 16, L$$

$$U = 1200 \qquad 16.1, N$$

U	—	UNDEREMPLØYED (MEN)
UA	—	UNDEREMPLØYED ARRIVALS (MEN/YEAR)
UB	—	UNDEREMPLØYED BIRTHS (MEN/YEAR)
LTU	—	LABØR TØ UNDEREMPLØYED (MEN/YEAR)
UD	—	UNDEREMPLØYED DEPARTURES (MEN/YEAR)
UTL	—	UNDEREMPLØYED TØ LABØR (MEN/YEAR)

The level equations are integrations. They accumulate the rates of flow to generate the changing system states. The level equations change the time shape of variables, that is, a constant rate of flow becomes a uniformly changing level, a straight line rising flow rate becomes a parabolic increase in the level, etc. The level equations are essential to creating time-varying behavior in a system. The rate equations and their associated auxiliaries are algebraic equations which would instantly reach their final values without time transients if there were no level equations.

The solution interval DT in Equation 16 represents the interval between evaluations of the equations of the system. In a proper model formulation the interval DT has no intrinsic relationship to the real behavior of the system except that it must be short enough not to influence the behavior of the simulated system. It should not be used to introduce time delays. It need not be equal to the basic unit of time measure except by coincidence. A rule of thumb for selecting the solution interval is to make it half or less of the shortest delay in the system. One year is used here because only much longer dynamic responses are involved in this system study.*

Equation 16, being a level equation, must have an initial value as given in Equation 16.1. The initial values are arbitrary and not important. They are chosen to be compatible with an early stage of growth when 3% of the land area is occupied.

Two positive-feedback loops are visible in Figure A-1 and the preceding equations. One is the birth rate involving Equations 15 and 16, where the underemployed generate a birth rate that increases the underemployed. The other positive loop is the one involving the underemployed in Equation 16 and the underemployed arrivals in Equation 1. The underemployed attract more underemployed, who further increase the underemployed.

The effective positive-feedback loop involving the underemployed operates on the difference between the underemployed arrivals and the underemployed departures. As the multiplier AMM shifts, these two loops can be converted from

*See References 1 and 6.

a composite positive loop in which growth increases size to further increase the growth rate into a set of loops with neutral net consequence when the arrival rate equals the departure rate. As the multiplier AMM becomes still smaller, the loops pass through the transition point and become a net negative loop in which the decrease rate of underemployed is proportional to the underemployed group and, if this effect were to run to completion, the underemployed group would move exponentially toward zero in the typical decay pattern of a negative-feedback loop. In operation this set of loops maintain their positive-feedback character during the internal growth phase of an area and then in stagnation take on values which, along with the other three flows, hold the number of underemployed at a constant value.

A.2 Labor Sector

The flow diagram of Figure A-8 shows the structure of flows between labor and the underemployed, and the labor birth rate. The labor pool is influenced by 6 flow rates—upward mobility from the underemployed, downward mobility back to the underemployed, labor arrivals from outside the area, labor departures, upward mobility from labor to the managerial-professional group, and labor births.

The flow from underemployed to labor represents upward economic mobility in Equation 17. It is taken to depend on the underemployed actually working UW. Of this working group a normal fraction of .1 per year make the transition to the labor class. This normal value is modulated by the multiplier UMMP, which combines the influences of the various economic and social conditions of the city. The last term of Equation 17 is the upward mobility produced by an underemployed-training program. The underemployed-training program UTP is not itself dependent on the condition of the urban area. It is one of a number of special programs that can be applied from the outside in an effort to modify the condition of the area. (These programs are described later in Equations 140 through 150.)

$$\text{UTL.KL} = (\text{UMN})(\text{UW.K})(\text{UMMP.K}) + \text{UTP.K} \qquad\qquad 17,\text{R}$$

$$\text{UMN} = .1 \qquad\qquad 17.1,\text{C}$$

>   UTL   — UNDEREMPLØYED TØ LABØR (MEN/YEAR)
>   UMN   — UNDEREMPLØYED MØBILITY NØRMAL (FRACTIØN/
>   YEAR)
>   UW   — UNDEREMPLØYED WØRKING (MEN)
>   UMMP   — UNDEREMPLØYED-MØBILITY MULTIPLIER PERCEIVED
>   (DIMENSIØNLESS)
>   UTP   — UNDEREMPLØYED-TRAINING PRØGRAM (MEN/YEAR)

Equation 18 gives the number of underemployed that are working in terms of the total underemployed multiplied by the fraction of the underemployed that hold jobs.

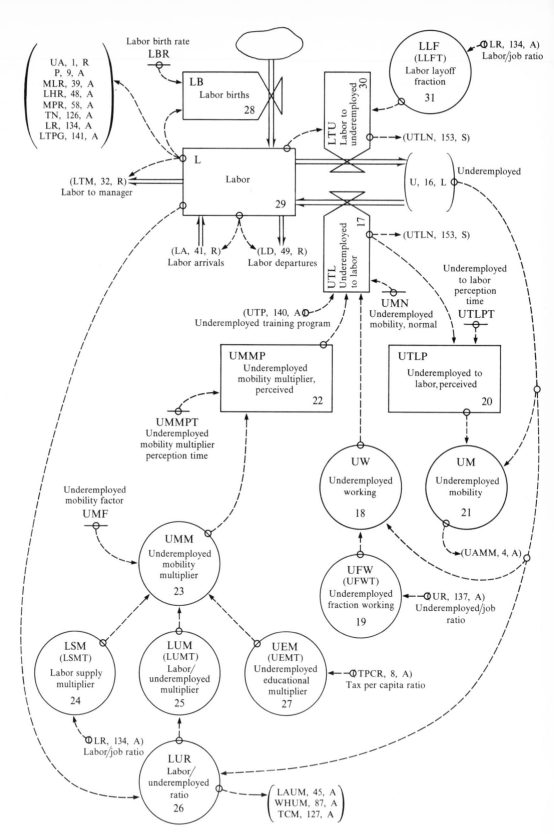

Figure A-8 Labor mobility and birth rate.

$$UW.K = (U.K)(UFW.K) \qquad\qquad 18,A$$

UW — UNDEREMPLØYED WØRKING (MEN)
U — UNDEREMPLØYED (MEN)
UFW — UNDEREMPLØYED FRACTIØN WØRKING
(DIMENSIØNLESS)

The fraction of the underemployed working UFW is expressed in Equation 19 and Figure A-9 in terms of the underemployed/job ratio.

$$UFW.K = TABHL(UFWT,UR.K,0,4,1) \qquad\qquad 19,A$$

$$UFWT = .9/.8/.5/.33/.25 \qquad\qquad 19.1,T$$

UFW — UNDEREMPLØYED FRACTIØN WØRKING
(DIMENSIØNLESS)
UFWT — UNDEREMPLØYED-FRACTIØN-WØRKING TABLE
UR — UNDEREMPLØYED/JØB RATIØ (DIMENSIØNLESS)

In Figure A-9 the assertion is made that when the underemployed outnumber available jobs by a factor of 2, all available jobs will be filled and therefore half of the underemployed will be occupied. Similarly, when there are three times as many underemployed as jobs, one-third will be occupied and when there are four times as many underemployed as jobs one-quarter will have employment.

Figure A-9

Going downward in the value of UR from UR = 2, the same inverse relationship does not hold. When UR equals 0, it implies an overwhelming excess of jobs compared to the underemployed. Even under such circumstances only 90% of the underemployed will be working rather than all. At the 1 to 1 ratio, with jobs and people exactly in balance, the matching of the two and incentive and ability to work will decrease employment to 80%.

Equation 20 is a first-order exponential delay like Equation 2 and produces a 10-year perception delay between actual upward mobility and that which influences AMM in Equation 3.

Equation 21 gives the fraction of underemployed observed as making the upward transition each year. It is the upward rate perceived divided by the total number of underemployed.

UTLP.K=UTLP.J+(DT/UTLPT)(UTL.JK-UTLP.J)   20,L

UTLP=75   20.1,N

UTLPT=10   20.2,C

    UTLP - UNDEREMPLØYED TØ LABØR PERCEIVED
           (DIMENSIØNLESS)
    UTLPT - UNDEREMPLØYED-TØ-LABØR PERCEPTIØN TIME
           (YEARS)
    UTL   - UNDEREMPLØYED TØ LABØR (MEN/YEAR)

UM.K=UTLP.K/U.K   21,A

    UM   - UNDEREMPLØYED MØBILITY (FRACTIØN/YEAR)
    UTLP - UNDEREMPLØYED TØ LABØR PERCEIVED
          (DIMENSIØNLESS)
    U   - UNDEREMPLØYED (MEN)

Equation 22 defines a variable UMMP called the underemployed-mobility multiplier perceived. "Effective" in this context might be a better term than "perceived." The equation produces a 10-year delay between the inputs from Equations 24, 25, and 27 before they effectively create the flow rate from underemployed to labor. This delay represents training time and time necessary for social influences to become effective. Like the other perception times, it has no influence on the equilibrium conditions of the system and rather minor influence on transient behavior.

UMMP.K=UMMP.J+(DT/UMMPT)(UMM.J-UMMP.J)   22,L

UMMP=1   22.1,N

UMMPT=10   22.2,C

    UMMP - UNDEREMPLØYED-MØBILITY MULTIPLIER PERCEIVED
          (DIMENSIØNLESS)
    UMMPT - UNDEREMPLØYED-MØBILITY-MULTIPLIER
          PERCEPTIØN TIME (YEARS)
    UMM   - UNDEREMPLØYED-MØBILITY MULTIPLIER
          (DIMENSIØNLESS)

The multiplier UMM in Equation 23 combines three system conditions that influence upward mobility. The fourth term UMF is not a part of the real-life system but a technical parameter permitting experimentation with the effect of this equation.

UMM.K=(LSM.K)(LUM.K)(UEM.K)(UMF)   23,A

UMF=1   23.1,C

    UMM   - UNDEREMPLØYED-MØBILITY MULTIPLIER
          (DIMENSIØNLESS)
    LSM   - LABØR-SUPPLY MULTIPLIER (DIMENSIØNLESS)

```
LUM   - LABØR/UNDEREMPLØYED MULTIPLIER
        (DIMENSIØNLESS)
UEM   - UNDEREMPLØYED EDUCATIØNAL MULTIPLIER
        (DIMENSIØNLESS)
UMF   - UNDEREMPLØYED-MØBILITY FACTØR
        (DIMENSIØNLESS)
```

Equation 24 and Figure A-10 describe a relationship between the labor/job ratio and upward mobility from underemployed to labor. Its purpose is to increase upward mobility when there is a labor shortage and an excess of labor jobs and to decrease upward mobility when there is a labor excess and a shortage of the more skilled positions.

$$LSM.K=TABHL(LSMT,LR.K,0,2,.5) \qquad\qquad 24,A$$

$$LSMT=2.4/2/1/.4/.2 \qquad\qquad 24.1,T$$

```
LSM   - LABØR-SUPPLY MULTIPLIER (DIMENSIØNLESS)
LSMT  - LABØR-SUPPLY-MULTIPLIER TABLE
LR    - LABØR/JØB RATIØ (DIMENSIØNLESS)
```

The normal condition is taken for a labor/job ratio of 1, at which point the multiplier has a value of 1. As the ratio LR declines, indicating fewer in the labor group compared to available jobs, upward mobility increases to 2.4 times normal. At the right-hand extreme, when labor is double the number of available jobs, upward mobility is reduced to one-fifth of normal.

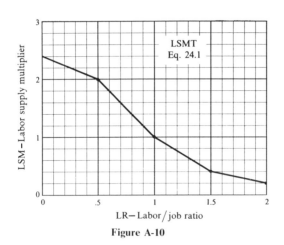

Figure A-10

Equation 25 and Figure A-11 describe an influence on upward mobility owing to the ratio of labor to underemployed. This curve asserts that, as the labor group decreases relative to the underemployed, there is less skilled labor in evidence, and fewer jobs to serve as examples for the underemployed. Under these circum-

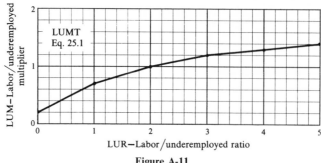

Figure A-11

stances upward mobility is more difficult. This is the factor that represents the influence of dominant blocks of underemployed in one area where they are not intermingled with other economic groups. It covers all social effects including school segregation and the unavailability of more affluent groups to emulate. Once the underemployed/labor ratio is high enough, increasing it further has little effect. As it falls off, the influence increases.

```
LUM.K =TABHL(LUMT,LUR.K,0,5,1)                          25,A

LUMT=.2/.7/1/1.2/1.3/1.4                                25.1,T

    LUM    - LABØR/UNDEREMPLØYED MULTIPLIER
             (DIMENSIØNLESS)
    LUMT   - LABØR/UNDEREMPLØYED MULTIPLIER TABLE
    LUR    - LABØR/UNDEREMPLØYED RATIØ (DIMENSIØNLESS)
```

Equation 26 provides the labor/underemployed ratio LUR needed in Equation 25.

```
LUR.K=L.K/U.K                                           26,A

    LUR    - LABØR/UNDEREMPLØYED RATIØ (DIMENSIØNLESS)
    L      - LABØR (MEN)
    U      - UNDEREMPLØYED (MEN)
```

Upward economic mobility has been made a function of the tax per capita ratio TPCR. This is intended to reflect primarily the effect of education in upgrading economic skills. Equation 27 and Figure A-12 show the extent of dependence that has been assumed. Falling tax expenditure has an increasingly adverse effect, while rising expenditures begin to saturate and show progressively less effect.

```
UEM.K =TABHL(UEMT,TPCR.K,0,3,.5)                        27,A

UEMT=.2/.7/1/1.3/1.5/1.6/1.7                            27.1,T

    UEM    - UNDEREMPLØYED EDUCATIØNAL MULTIPLIER
             (DIMENSIØNLESS)
    UEMT   - UNDEREMPLØYED-EDUCATIØNAL-MULTIPLIER TABLE
    TPCR   - TAX PER CAPITA RATIØ (DIMENSIØNLESS)
```

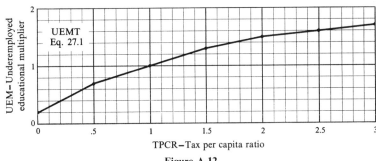

Figure A-12

Equation 28 gives the labor birth rate as the net of births minus deaths at a slightly smaller annual increase rate than used in Equation 15 for the underemployed.

LB.KL=(L.K)(LBR)   28,R

LBR=.01   28.1,C

> LB   - LABØR BIRTHS (MEN/YEAR)
> L   - LABØR (MEN)
> LBR - LABØR BIRTH RATE (FRACTIØN/YEAR)

Equation 29 is a level equation accumulating the flow rates into and out of the labor pool.

L.K=L.J+(DT)(UTL.JK+LB.JK-LTM.JK+LA.JK-LD.JK-LTU.JK)   29,L

L=14000   29.1,N

> L   - LABØR (MEN)
> UTL - UNDEREMPLØYED TØ LABØR (MEN/YEAR)
> LB   - LABØR BIRTHS (MEN/YEAR)
> LTM - LABØR TØ MANAGER (MEN/YEAR)
> LA   - LABØR ARRIVALS (MEN/YEAR)
> LD   - LABØR DEPARTURES (MEN/YEAR)
> LTU - LABØR TØ UNDEREMPLØYED (MEN/YEAR)

Equation 30 provides a dropout rate from the labor category into the underemployed category contingent on the labor/job ratio.

LTU.KL=(L.K)(LLF.K)   30,R

> LTU - LABØR TØ UNDEREMPLØYED (MEN/YEAR)
> L   - LABØR (MEN)
> LLF - LABØR-LAYØFF FRACTIØN (FRACTIØN/YEAR)

Equation 31 and Figure A-13 describe a sharply increasing dropout rate as the labor population exceeds available jobs. Under sustained, severe unemployment

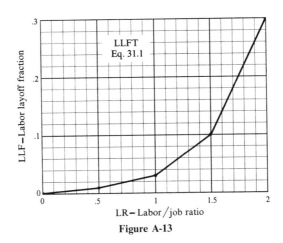

Figure A-13

it is assumed that the marginal individual in the labor category is forced economically into the underemployed category, that as he stays there his skills decline in relation to the economy, and that he does not represent a special pool having preferred access back to the labor category. Under normal conditions, with labor and jobs in balance, the dropout rate is taken as 3% per year. At a 2 to 1 excess of labor to jobs this rises to 30%.

$$\text{LLF.K =TABLE(LLFT,LR.K,0,2,.5)} \qquad\qquad 31,\text{A}$$

$$\text{LLFT=0/.01/.03/.1/.3} \qquad\qquad 31.1,\text{T}$$

```
LLF   - LABØR-LAYØFF FRACTIØN (FRACTIØN/YEAR)
LLFT  - LABØR-LAYØFF-FRACTIØN TABLE
LR    - LABØR/JØB RATIØ (DIMENSIØNLESS)
```

Figure A-14 shows how the upward mobility from labor to the managerial-professional group is generated.

Equation 32 defines the flow rate. As with most of the other flow rates it is described in terms of a normal fraction of the labor group. This is modulated by the multiplier LMMP, which represents the more important economic and social influences. The added term LTPG provides the possibility of an externally applied training program to increase this flow rate.

$$\text{LTM.KL=(LMN)(L.K)(LMMP.K)+LTPG.K} \qquad\qquad 32,\text{R}$$

$$\text{LMN=.02} \qquad\qquad 32.1,\text{C}$$

```
LTM   - LABØR TØ MANAGER (MEN/YEAR)
LMN   - LABØR MØBILITY NØRMAL (FRACTIØN/YEAR)
L     - LABØR (MEN)
LMMP  - LABØR-MØBILITY MULTIPLIER PERCEIVED
        (DIMENSIØNLESS)
LTPG  - LABØR-TRAINING PRØGRAM (MEN/YEAR)
```

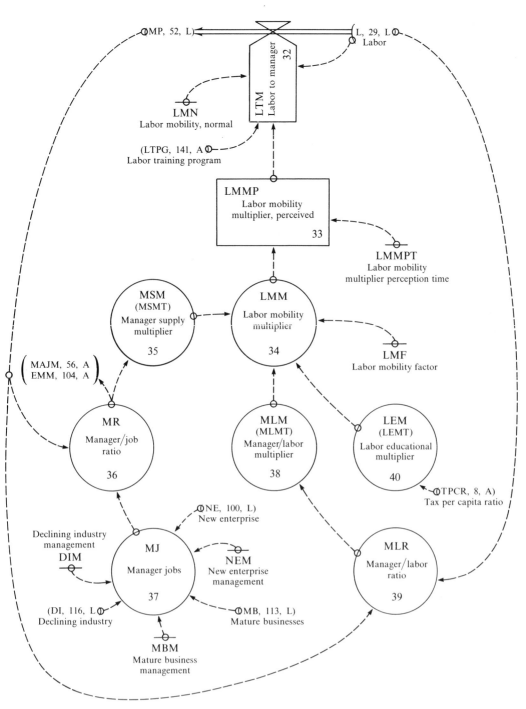

Figure A-14 Labor-to-manager mobility.

Equation 33, like Equation 22, provides for a delay between changes in the system levels and their influence in changing the mobility rate from labor to management. Although called a perception delay, it is more in the nature of a functional delay involving training and adaptation to social conditions. On the basis that the transition from labor to management takes longer conditioning than that from underemployed to labor, the delay is taken as 15 years instead of 10.

$$LMMP.K=LMMP.J+(DT/LMMPT)(LMM.J-LMMP.J) \qquad\qquad 33,L$$

$$LMMP=1 \qquad\qquad 33.1,N$$

$$LMMPT=15 \qquad\qquad 33.2,C$$

```
    LMMP   - LABØR-MØBILITY MULTIPLIER PERCEIVED
               (DIMENSIØNLESS)
    LMMPT  - LABØR-MØBILITY-MULTIPLIER PERCEPTIØN TIME
               (YEARS)
    LMM    - LABØR-MØBILITY MULTIPLIER (DIMENSIØNLESS)
```

Equation 34, following the pattern already described, combines the three multipliers influencing labor mobility and includes a technical factor LMF for model experimentation.

$$LMM.K=(MSM.K)(MLM.K)(LEM.K)(LMF) \qquad\qquad 34,A$$

$$LMF=1 \qquad\qquad 34.1,C$$

```
    LMM    - LABØR-MØBILITY MULTIPLIER (DIMENSIØNLESS)
    MSM    - MANAGER-SUPPLY MULTIPLIER (DIMENSIØNLESS)
    MLM    - MANAGER/LABØR MULTIPLIER (DIMENSIØNLESS)
    LEM    - LABØR EDUCATIØNAL MULTIPLIER
               (DIMENSIØNLESS)
    LMF    - LABØR-MØBILITY FACTØR (DIMENSIØNLESS)
```

Equation 35 and Figure A-15 describe the influence of management availability on labor mobility in the same way that Equation 24 influenced mobility from underemployed to labor. In a manager shortage upward labor mobility is easier than in a manager excess.

$$MSM.K=TABHL(MSMT,MR.K,0,2,.25) \qquad\qquad 35,A$$

$$MSMT=2.3/2.2/2/1.6/1/.5/.2/.1/.05 \qquad\qquad 35.1,T$$

```
    MSM    - MANAGER-SUPPLY MULTIPLIER (DIMENSIØNLESS)
    MSMT   - MANAGER-SUPPLY-MULTIPLIER TABLE
    MR     - MANAGER/JØB RATIØ (DIMENSIØNLESS)
```

Equation 36 gives the ratio needed in Equation 35 computed as managers divided by available managerial jobs.

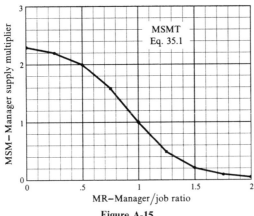

Figure A-15

$$MR.K = MP.K / MJ.K \qquad\qquad 36,A$$

MR - MANAGER/JØB RATIØ (DIMENSIØNLESS)
MP - MANAGERIAL-PRØFESSIØNAL (MEN)
MJ - MANAGER JØBS (MEN)

Equation 37 computes the available managerial jobs in terms of industry units in the three age categories and the number of managers assumed to be needed in each type of productive unit.

$$MJ.K = (NE.K)(NEM) + (MB.K)(MBM) + (DI.K)(DIM) \qquad 37,A$$

$$NEM = 4 \qquad\qquad 37.1,C$$

$$MBM = 2 \qquad\qquad 37.2,C$$

$$DIM = 1 \qquad\qquad 37.3,C$$

MJ   - MANAGER JØBS (MEN)
NE   - NEW ENTERPRISE (PRØDUCTIVE UNITS)
NEM - NEW-ENTERPRISE MANAGEMENT (MEN/PRØDUCTIVE
       UNIT)
MB   - MATURE BUSINESS (PRØDUCTIVE UNITS)
MBM - MATURE-BUSINESS MANAGEMENT (MEN/PRØDUCTIVE
       UNIT)
DI   - DECLINING INDUSTRY (PRØDUCTIVE UNITS)
DIM - DECLINING-INDUSTRY MANAGEMENT (MEN/
       PRØDUCTIVE UNIT)

A new-enterprise productive unit in Equation 37 is characterized as needing twice as many managers as the same unit when it enters the mature-business category, and the mature-business unit uses twice as many managers as a declining-industry unit. Shifting relationships of this kind define aging units and lie behind the changing system ratios which appear as the phases of growth and stagnation progress.

The manager/labor multiplier MLM in Equation 38 and Figure A-16 is similar

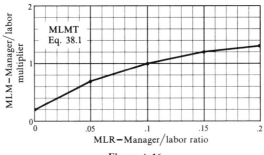

Figure A-16

to the multiplier in Equation 25. It describes the effect on upward labor mobility of social proximity between the labor group and the managerial group.

MLM.K=TABHL(MLMT,MLR.K,0,.2,.05)   38,A

MLMT=.2/.7/1/1.2/1.3   38.1,T

    MLM   - MANAGER/LABØR MULTIPLIER (DIMENSIØNLESS)
    MLMT - MANAGER/LABØR MULTIPLIER TABLE
    MLR   - MANAGER/LABØR RATIØ (DIMENSIØNLESS)

The manager/labor ratio is computed in Equation 39.

MLR.K=MP.K/L.K   39,A

    MLR   - MANAGER/LABØR RATIØ (DIMENSIØNLESS)
    MP   - MANAGERIAL-PRØFESSIØNAL (MEN)
    L   - LABØR (MEN)

Equation 40 and Figure A-17 state an influence of tax expenditures through education on labor mobility. The relationship is similar to that in Equation 27.

LEM.K=TABHL(LEMT,TPCR.K,0,3,.5)   40,A

LEMT=.2/.7/1/1.3/1.5/1.6/1.7   40.1,T

    LEM   - LABØR EDUCATIØNAL MULTIPLIER
           (DIMENSIØNLESS)
    LEMT - LABØR-EDUCATIØNAL-MULTIPLIER TABLE
    TPCR - TAX PER CAPITA RATIØ (DIMENSIØNLESS)

Figure A-18 illustrates the network of relationships that control labor arrivals and departures.

In Equation 41 the labor-arrival rate is a normal fraction of the labor level multiplied by the modulating term LAMP.

In Equation 42 a perception-time delay of 15 years is used between the actual conditions of the city and the perceived value, which controls arrival rate.

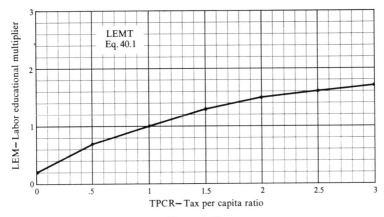

Figure A-17

LA.KL=(LAN)(L.K)(LAMP.K)   41,R

LAN=.03   41.1,C

     LA   - LABØR ARRIVALS (MEN/YEAR)
     LAN - LABØR ARRIVALS NØRMAL (FRACTIØN/YEAR)
     L   - LABØR (MEN)
     LAMP - LABØR-ARRIVAL MULTIPLIER PERCEIVED
          (DIMENSIØNLESS)

LAMP.K=LAMP.J+(DT/LAMPT)(LAM.J-LAMP.J)   42,L

LAMP=1   42.1,N

LAMPT=15   42.2,C

     LAMP - LABØR-ARRIVAL MULTIPLIER PERCEIVED
           (DIMENSIØNLESS)
     LAMPT - LABØR-ARRIVAL-MULTIPLIER PERCEPTIØN TIME
           (YEARS)
     LAM - LABØR-ARRIVAL MULTIPLIER (DIMENSIØNLESS)

The labor-arrival multiplier in Equation 43 is a product of four active terms and the experimental factor LAF.

LAM.K=(LAJM.K)(LAUM.K)(LATM.K)(LAHM.K)(LAF)   43,A

LAF=1   43.1,C

     LAM   - LABØR-ARRIVAL MULTIPLIER (DIMENSIØNLESS)
     LAJM - LABØR-ARRIVAL JØB MULTIPLIER
           (DIMENSIØNLESS)
     LAUM - LABØR-ARRIVAL UNDEREMPLØYED MULTIPLIER
           (DIMENSIØNLESS)
     LATM - LABØR-ARRIVAL TAX MULTIPLIER
           (DIMENSIØNLESS)
     LAHM - LABØR-ARRIVAL HØUSING MULTIPLIER
           (DIMENSIØNLESS)
     LAF   - LABØR-ARRIVAL FACTØR (DIMENSIØNLESS)

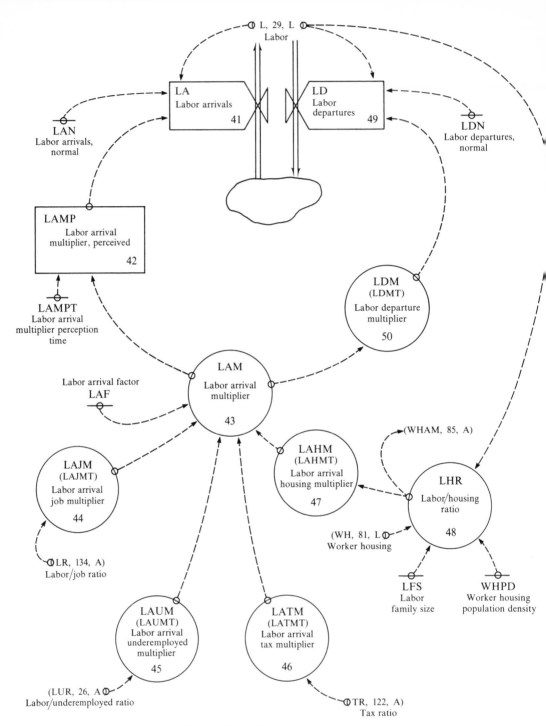

Figure A-18 Labor arrivals and departures.

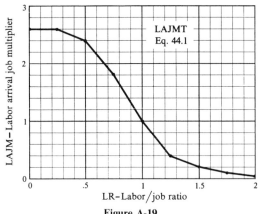

Figure A-19

Equation 44 is similar to Equation 10; it describes the influence of job availability in making the city attractive to labor. The relationship is illustrated in Figure A-19.

LAJM.K =TABLE(LAJMT,LR.K,0,2,.25)   44,A

LAJMT=2.6/2.6/2.4/1.8/1/.4/.2/.1/.05   44.1,T

    LAJM - LABØR-ARRIVAL JØB MULTIPLIER
           (DIMENSIØNLESS)
    LAJMT - LABØR-ARRIVAL-JØB-MULTIPLIER TABLE
    LR   - LABØR/JØB RATIØ (DIMENSIØNLESS)

Equation 45 and Figure A-20 describe the social attractiveness of the city in terms of the ratio of labor to underemployed. When the ratio of labor to underemployed is 2, the multiplier value is taken as 1. A higher proportion of labor makes the city slightly more attractive. A lower percentage of labor makes the city progressively less attractive as a place into which labor desires to move.

LAUM.K =TABHL(LAUMT,LUR.K,0,5,1)   45,A

LAUMT=.4/.8/1/1.2/1.3/1.3   45.1,T

    LAUM - LABØR-ARRIVAL UNDEREMPLØYED MULTIPLIER
           (DIMENSIØNLESS)
    LAUMT - LABØR-ARRIVAL-UNDEREMPLØYED-MULTIPLIER
           TABLE
    LUR   - LABØR/UNDEREMPLØYED RATIØ (DIMENSIØNLESS)

The labor-arrival tax multiplier LATM in Equation 46 and Figure A-21 represents the influence of the city tax rate on the inclination of labor to move into the city. When rates are reasonable, they have little effect, but should they become unusually high, they have a depressing effect.

Figure A-20

LATM.K =TABLE(LATMT,1.44* LØGN(TR.K) ,-2,4,2)   46,A

LATMT=1.2/1/.7/.3   46.1,T

    LATM - LABØR-ARRIVAL TAX MULTIPLIER
         (DIMENSIØNLESS)
    LATMT - LABØR-ARRIVAL-TAX-MULTIPLIER TABLE
    TR   - TAX RATIØ (DIMENSIØNLESS)

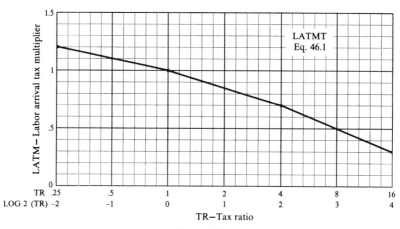

Figure A-21

Just as housing in Equation 5 influenced the arrival of the underemployed, so housing in Equation 47 and Figure A-22 influences the arrival of labor. The relationship is represented as rather steep above a labor/housing ratio of one. At a ratio of 3, inward migration is almost suppressed.

LAHM.K =TABLE(LAHMT,LHR.K,0,3,.5)   47,A

LAHMT=1.3/1.2/1/.5/.2/.1/.05   47.1,T

    LAHM - LABØR-ARRIVAL HØUSING MULTIPLIER
         (DIMENSIØNLESS)
    LAHMT - LABØR-ARRIVAL-HØUSING-MULTIPLIER TABLE
    LHR   - LABØR/HØUSING RATIØ (DIMENSIØNLESS)

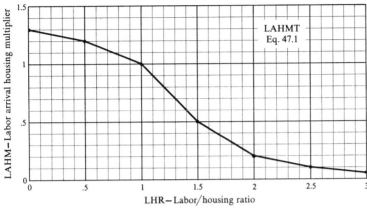

Figure A-22

The labor/housing ratio in Equation 48 is labor multiplied by family size and divided by available housing and housing density. At the worker level a housing unit is assumed to be occupied by six persons.

LHR.K=(L.K*LFS)/(WH.K*WHPD)   48,A

WHPD=6   48.1,C

    LHR   - LABØR/HØUSING RATIØ (DIMENSIØNLESS)
    L   - LABØR (MEN)
    LFS   - LABØR FAMILY SIZE (PEØPLE/MAN)
    WH   - WØRKER HØUSING (HØUSING UNITS)
    WHPD   - WØRKER-HØUSING PØPULATIØN DENSITY (PEØPLE/
             HØUSING UNIT)

Equation 49, which applies to labor departures, is the standard form of the basic rate equation. Normal departures per year are expressed as a fraction of the labor population. This normal fraction is then modified by a multiplier that describes whether the urban area is causing a departure rate greater or less than normal.

LD.KL=(LDN)(L.K)(LDM.K)   49,R

LDN=.02   49.1,C

    LD   - LABØR DEPARTURES (MEN/YEAR)
    LDN   - LABØR DEPARTURES NØRMAL (FRACTIØN/YEAR)
    L   - LABØR (MEN)
    LDM   - LABØR-DEPARTURE MULTIPLIER (DIMENSIØNLESS)

Like Equation 14, Equation 50 as shown in Figure A-23 sets departure influence as the reciprocal of arrival influence. As the city becomes more attractive to labor, arrivals increase and departures decrease.

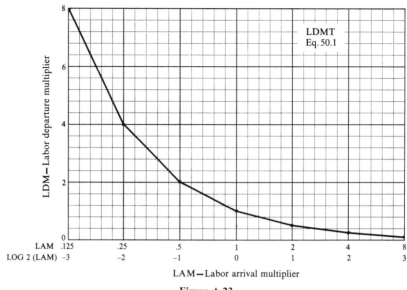

Figure A-23

LDM.K =TABHL(LDMT, 1.44*LØGN(LAM.K) ,-3,3,1)   50,A

LDMT=8/4/2/1/.5/.25/.125   50.1,T

    LDM   - LABØR-DEPARTURE MULTIPLIER (DIMENSIØNLESS)
    LDMT - LABØR-DEPARTURE-MULTIPLIER TABLE
    LAM   - LABØR-ARRIVAL MULTIPLIER (DIMENSIØNLESS)

A.3   Managerial-Professional Sector

The flow diagram in Figure A-24 shows the managerial-professional level, its related flow rates, and the structure controlling birth rate and managerial arrivals and departures.

Equation 51 is the net birth rate (births minus deaths) in this population sector with three-quarters the value found in the labor sector and half the value in the underemployed sector.

MPB.KL=(MP.K) (MPBR)   51,R

MPBR=.0075   51.1,C

    MPB   - MANAGERIAL-PRØFESSIØNAL BIRTHS (MEN/YEAR)
    MP   - MANAGERIAL-PRØFESSIØNAL (MEN)
    MPBR - MANAGERIAL-PRØFESSIØNAL BIRTH RATE
           (FRACTIØN/YEAR)

The level equation which accumulates the managerial flows is given in Equation 52. The initial value, as for the others in the model, is selected to give an internally consistent set for starting the system with the land area 3% filled.

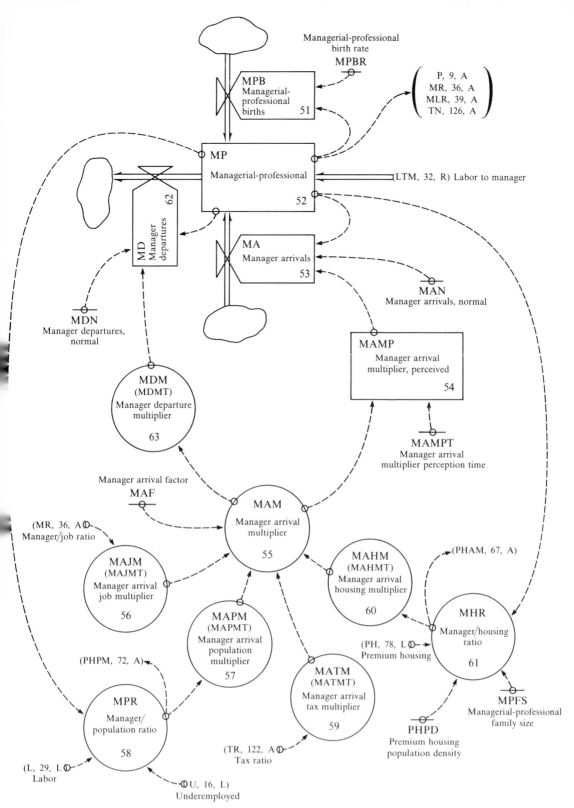

Figure A-24 Managerial-professional sector.

```
MP.K=MP.J+(DT)(LTM.JK+MPB.JK+MA.JK-MD.JK)                    52,L

MP=3900                                                     52.1,N

      MP   - MANAGERIAL-PRØFESSIØNAL (MEN)
      LTM  - LABØR TØ MANAGER (MEN/YEAR)
      MPB  - MANAGERIAL-PRØFESSIØNAL BIRTHS (MEN/YEAR)
      MA   - MANAGER ARRIVALS (MEN/YEAR)
      MD   - MANAGER DEPARTURES (MEN/YEAR)
```

Normal managerial arrivals are defined in Equation 53 as 3% per year of the managerial group.

```
MA.KL=(MAN)(MP.K)(MAMP.K)                                    53,R

MAN=.03                                                     53.1,C

      MA   - MANAGER ARRIVALS (MEN/YEAR)
      MAN  - MANAGER ARRIVALS NØRMAL (FRACTIØN/YEAR)
      MP   - MANAGERIAL-PRØFESSIØNAL (MEN)
      MAMP - MANAGER-ARRIVAL MULTIPLIER PERCEIVED
             (DIMENSIØNLESS)
```

Equation 54 gives the perception-time delay between the true state of the city and its condition as perceived by arriving managerial-professional persons. The delay of 10 years is smaller than in the other population sectors on the assumption that communication and awareness in this group will cause perception to follow reality more rapidly.

```
MAMP.K=MAMP.J+(DT/MAMPT)(MAM.J-MAMP.J)                       54,L

MAMP=1                                                      54.1,N

MAMPT=10                                                    54.2,C

      MAMP  - MANAGER-ARRIVAL MULTIPLIER PERCEIVED
              (DIMENSIØNLESS)
      MAMPT - MANAGER-ARRIVAL-MULTIPLIER PERCEPTIØN TIME
              (YEARS)
      MAM   - MANAGER-ARRIVAL MULTIPLIER (DIMENSIØNLESS)
```

The manager-arrival multiplier in Equation 55 consists of the product of the four active terms representing urban conditions, and the experimental test factor MAF.

```
MAM.K=(MAJM.K)(MAPM.K)(MATM.K)(MAHM.K)(MAF)                  55,A

MAF=1                                                      55.1,C

      MAM  - MANAGER-ARRIVAL MULTIPLIER (DIMENSIØNLESS)
      MAJM - MANAGER-ARRIVAL JØB MULTIPLIER
             (DIMENSIØNLESS)
      MAPM - MANAGER-ARRIVAL PØPULATIØN MULTIPLIER
             (DIMENSIØNLESS)
```

MATM – MANAGER–ARRIVAL TAX MULTIPLIER
       (DIMENSIONLESS)
MAHM – MANAGER–ARRIVAL HOUSING MULTIPLIER
       (DIMENSIONLESS)
MAF   – MANAGER–ARRIVAL FACTOR (DIMENSIONLESS)

As in Equations 10 and 44 available work conditions here influence managerial arrival, as described in Equation 56 and Figure A-25. The relationship is a rather steep function of job availability. In this relationship more than pure job count is involved. The central, steep section of the curve extends from a manager/job

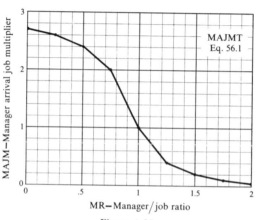

Figure A-25

ratio MR of .75 up to 1.25. Varying degrees of underloading and overloading of managers, as well as varying degrees of using full competence and ability, can occur. Less than fully effective employment can exist even though every individual may hold a position.

MAJM.K =TABLE(MAJMT,MR.K,0,2,.25)   56,A

MAJMT=2.7/2.6/2.4/2/1/.4/.2/.1/.05   56.1,T

    MAJM   – MANAGER–ARRIVAL JOB MULTIPLIER
            (DIMENSIONLESS)
    MAJMT – MANAGER–ARRIVAL-JOB-MULTIPLIER TABLE
    MR   – MANAGER/JOB RATIO (DIMENSIONLESS)

As in Equation 45 the manager's desire to come to the city is asserted to depend on the population mix, as expressed in Equation 57 and Figure A-26. As the

MAPM.K =TABHL(MAPMT,MPR.K,0,.1,.02)   57,A

MAPMT=.3/.7/1/1.2/1.3/1.3   57.1,T

    MAPM   – MANAGER–ARRIVAL POPULATION MULTIPLIER
            (DIMENSIONLESS)
    MAPMT – MANAGER–ARRIVAL-POPULATION-MULTIPLIER TABLE
    MPR   – MANAGER/POPULATION RATIO (DIMENSIONLESS)

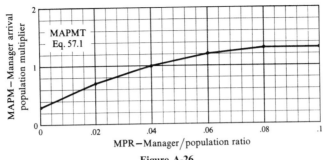

Figure A-26

ratio of the managerial-professional group to the population MPR falls too low, the area is seen as socially unattractive and inward mobility is depressed.

Equation 58 computes the ratio of managers to labor-plus-underemployed classes for use in Equation 57.

$$MPR.K = MP.K/(L.K+U.K)$$ 58,A

MPR	— MANAGER/PØPULATIØN RATIØ (DIMENSIØNLESS)
MP	— MANAGERIAL-PRØFESSIØNAL (MEN)
L	— LABØR (MEN)
U	— UNDEREMPLØYED (MEN)

Equation 59 is similar to Equation 46; it describes the influence of the city tax rate on manager willingness to move into or stay in the city. The tax-rate influences are illustrated in Figure A-27.

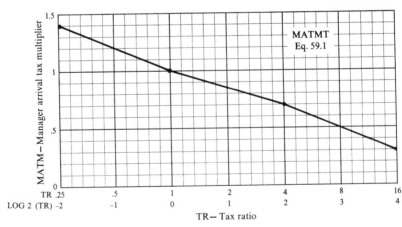

Figure A-27

Availability of housing is introduced as another influence on manager movement, as given in Equation 60 and Figure A-28.

MATM.K =TABLE(MATMT,1.44*LØGN(TR.K) ,-2,4,2)   59,A

MATMT=1.4/1/.7/.3   59.1,T

    MATM - MANAGER-ARRIVAL TAX MULTIPLIER
           (DIMENSIØNLESS)
   MATMT - MANAGER-ARRIVAL-TAX-MULTIPLIER TABLE
   TR   - TAX RATIØ (DIMENSIØNLESS)

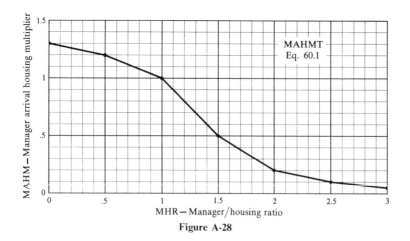

Figure A-28

MAHM.K =TABLE(MAHMT,MHR.K,0,3,.5)   60,A

MAHMT=1.3/1.2/1/.5/.2/.1/.05   60.1,T

   MAHM - MANAGER-ARRIVAL HØUSING MULTIPLIER
          (DIMENSIØNLESS)
   MAHMT - MANAGER-ARRIVAL-HØUSING-MULTIPLIER TABLE
   MHR   - MANAGER/HØUSING RATIØ (DIMENSIØNLESS)

For use in the preceding equation, Equation 61 computes the relationship between the management population and the population that normally could be housed in a premium-housing residence. At this point in the system a housing unit is assumed normally to serve three persons.

MHR.K=(MP.K*MPFS)/(PH.K*PHPD)   61,A

PHPD=3   61.1,C

   MHR   - MANAGER/HØUSING RATIØ (DIMENSIØNLESS)
   MP   - MANAGERIAL-PRØFESSIØNAL (MEN)
   MPFS - MANAGERIAL-PRØFESSIØNAL FAMILY SIZE
         (PEØPLE/MAN)
   PH   - PREMIUM HØUSING (HØUSING UNITS)
   PHPD - PREMIUM-HØUSING PØPULATIØN DENSITY (PEØPLE/
         HØUSING UNIT)

Manager departures are defined in Equation 62 as having a normal value of 2% per year of the manager group.

MD.KL=(MDN)(MP.K)(MDM.K)   62,R

MDN=.02   62.1,C

MD   – MANAGER DEPARTURES (MEN/YEAR)
MDN – MANAGER DEPARTURES NØRMAL (FRACTIØN/YEAR)
MP   – MANAGERIAL-PRØFESSIØNAL (MEN)
MDM – MANAGER-DEPARTURE MULTIPLIER
       (DIMENSIØNLESS)

The manager-departure multiplier MDM is the inverse of the manager-arrival multiplier MAM, as produced by Equation 63 and illustrated in Figure A-29.

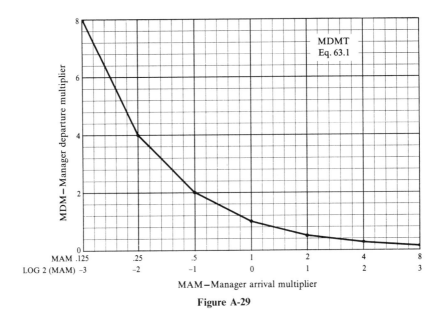

Figure A-29

MDM.K =TABHL(MDMT,1.44*LØGN(MAM.K),-3,3,1)   63,A

MDMT=8/4/2/1/.5/.25/.125   63.1,T

MDM – MANAGER-DEPARTURE MULTIPLIER
       (DIMENSIØNLESS)
MDMT – MANAGER-DEPARTURE-MULTIPLIER TABLE
MAM – MANAGER-ARRIVAL MULTIPLIER (DIMENSIØNLESS)

A.4   Premium-Housing Sector
Figure A-30 shows the structure of relationships causing the construction and obsolescence of premium housing.

Equation 64 defines the rate of premium-housing construction PHC in terms of premium-housing construction desired PHCD multiplied by the factor LCR

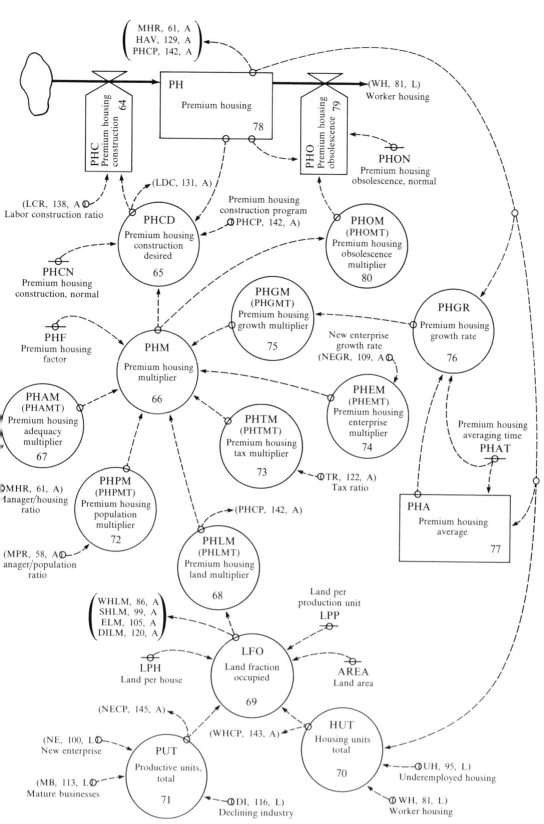

Figure A-30 Premium-housing sector.

coming from the job sector and causing limitation in the actual construction rate below that desired if the labor shortage in the city does not permit full construction activity.

```
PHC.KL=(PHCD.K)(LCR.K)                                        64,R
```

    PHC   - PREMIUM-HOUSING CONSTRUCTION (HOUSING
              UNITS/YEAR)
    PHCD - PREMIUM-HOUSING CONSTRUCTION DESIRED
              (HOUSING UNITS/YEAR)
    LCR   - LABOR CONSTRUCTION RATIO (DIMENSIONLESS)

The premium-housing construction desired in Equation 65 contains the structure seen earlier for flow rates. It describes the desired construction rate as 3% per year of existing premium housing. This normal rate is influenced by the premium-housing multiplier PHM. An externally imposed premium-housing-construction program can be added through the last term. Desired construction is first generated in this manner so that it can be influenced in Equation 64 by the availability of construction labor.

```
PHCD.K=(PHCN)(PH.K)(PHM.K)+PHCP.K                           65,A

PHCN=.03                                                   65.1,C
```

    PHCD - PREMIUM-HOUSING CONSTRUCTION DESIRED
              (HOUSING UNITS/YEAR)
    PHCN - PREMIUM-HOUSING CONSTRUCTION NORMAL
              (HOUSING UNITS/YEAR)
    PH   - PREMIUM HOUSING (HOUSING UNITS)
    PHM   - PREMIUM-HOUSING MULTIPLIER (DIMENSIONLESS)
    PHCP - PREMIUM-HOUSING-CONSTRUCTION PROGRAM
              (HOUSING UNITS/YEAR)

The premium-housing multiplier in Equation 66 is composed of six terms and the factor PHF, which is again included for experimental purposes to allow introducing test changes into the equation.

```
PHM.K=(PHAM.K)(PHLM.K)(PHPM.K)(PHTM.K)(PHEM.K)(PHGM.K)   66,A
   (PHF)

PHF=1                                                     66.1,C
```

    PHM   - PREMIUM-HOUSING MULTIPLIER (DIMENSIONLESS)
    PHAM - PREMIUM-HOUSING-ADEQUACY MULTIPLIER
              (DIMENSIONLESS)
    PHLM - PREMIUM-HOUSING LAND MULTIPLIER
              (DIMENSIONLESS)
    PHPM - PREMIUM-HOUSING POPULATION MULTIPLIER
              (DIMENSIONLESS)
    PHTM - PREMIUM-HOUSING TAX MULTIPLIER
              (DIMENSIONLESS)
    PHEM - PREMIUM-HOUSING ENTERPRISE MULTIPLER
              (DIMENSIONLESS)

PHGM   –   PREMIUM-HØUSING-GRØWTH MULTIPLIER
             (DIMENSIØNLESS)
PHF   –   PREMIUM-HØUSING FACTØR (DIMENSIØNLESS)

The premium-housing-adequacy multiplier as defined in Equation 67 and shown in Figure A-31 is one of two strong influences on the construction rate. The adequacy multiplier has a value of 1 when the manager/housing ratio is

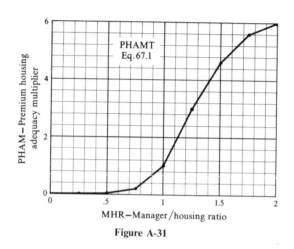

Figure A-31

at its normal value of 1. As MHR falls, indicating fewer managers than housing, the construction rate falls rapidly because of lack of need. On the other hand, as the managerial population exceeds available housing, there is pressure to increase the rate of construction.

PHAM.K=TABLE(PHAMT,MHR.K,0,2,.25)   67,A

PHAMT=0/.001/.01/.2/1/3/4.6/5.6/6   67.1,T

     PHAM   –   PREMIUM-HØUSING-ADEQUACY MULTIPLIER
               (DIMENSIØNLESS)
     PHAMT   –   PREMIUM-HØUSING-ADEQUACY-MULTIPLIER TABLE
     MHR   –   MANAGER/HØUSING RATIØ (DIMENSIØNLESS)

The land multiplier in Equation 68 and Figure A-32 illustrates the influence of land availability on the construction flows within the model. At very low levels of land occupancy, the area has not yet shown economic importance and the nearly empty land tends to discourage aggressive construction. As land occupancy increases toward the middle region, the rising multiplier indicates economic excitement and potential. Also, all of the common urban activities and services are now present to support further expansion. But as the area approaches the fully occupied condition, the more favorable construction sites have already been used. The less and less attractive locations begin to depress the tendency to build

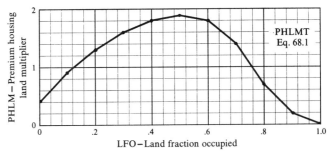

Figure A-32

until the absolute unavailability of land drives the construction rate to 0 at full land occupancy.

PHLM.K=TABHL(PHLMT,LFØ.K,0,1,.1)   68,A

PHLMT=.4/.9/1.3/1.6/1.8/1.9/1.8/1.4/.7/.2/0   68.1,T

   PHLM – PREMIUM-HØUSING LAND MULTIPLIER
      (DIMENSIØNLESS)
   PHLMT – PREMIUM-HØUSING-LAND-MULTIPLIER TABLE
   LFØ   – LAND FRACTIØN ØCCUPIED (DIMENSIØNLESS)

As the land fills, the changing values of the land multipliers begin to suppress the growth of industrial and housing structures in the original land area and to set the stage for the other variables to interact into the stagnation phase.

Equation 69 generates the land fraction occupied as the sum of the land used for housing plus the land used for productive units divided by the land area.

LFØ.K=(HUT.K*LPH+PUT.K*LPP)/AREA   69,A

LPH=.1   69.1,C

LPP=.2   69.2,C

AREA=100000   69.3,C

   LFØ   – LAND FRACTIØN ØCCUPIED (DIMENSIØNLESS)
   HUT   – HØUSING UNITS TØTAL (HØUSING UNITS)
   LPH   – LAND PER HØUSE (ACRES/HØUSING UNIT)
   PUT   – PRØDUCTIVE UNITS TØTAL (PRØDUCTIVE UNITS)
   LPP   – LAND PER PRØDUCTIØN UNIT (ACRES/PRØDUCTIØN
      UNIT)
   AREA – LAND AREA (ACRES)

Equation 70 totals the number of housing units in the system. Equation 71 totals the productive units.

HUT.K=PH.K+WH.K+UH.K   70,A

   HUT – HØUSING UNITS TØTAL (HØUSING UNITS)
   PH   – PREMIUM HØUSING (HØUSING UNITS)

WH   – WØRKER HØUSING (HØUSING UNITS)
UH   – UNDEREMPLØYED HØUSING (HØUSING UNITS)

$$PUT.K = NE.K + MB.K + DI.K \qquad\qquad\qquad 71,A$$

PUT   – PRØDUCTIVE UNITS TØTAL (PRØDUCTIVE UNITS)
NE   – NEW ENTERPRISE (PRØDUCTIVE UNITS)
MB   – MATURE BUSINESS (PRØDUCTIVE UNITS)
DI   – DECLINING INDUSTRY (PRØDUCTIVE UNITS)

In Equation 72 the premium-housing population multiplier illustrated in Figure A-33 reflects the social composition of the city. It tends to depress premium-

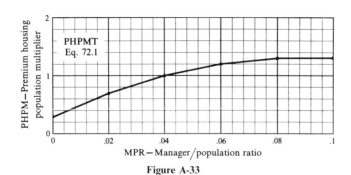

Figure A-33

housing construction if the city is heavily oriented toward labor and under-employed groups. Under such circumstances the city becomes a less desirable place for construction of premium housing.

$$PHPM.K = TABHL(PHPMT, MPR.K, 0, .1, .02) \qquad\qquad 72,A$$

$$PHPMT = .3/.7/1/1.2/1.3/1.3 \qquad\qquad\qquad 72.1,T$$

PHPM   – PREMIUM-HØUSING PØPULATIØN MULTIPLIER
            (DIMENSIØNLESS)
PHPMT – PREMIUM-HØUSING-PØPULATIØN-MULTIPLIER TABLE
MPR   – MANAGER/PØPULATIØN RATIØ (DIMENSIØNLESS)

Equation 73 in Figure A-34 shows the depressing effects of a high tax rate on premium-housing construction.

$$PHTM.K = TABHL(PHTMT, 1.44 * LØGN(TR.K), -2, 4, 2) \qquad 73,A$$

$$PHTMT = 1.2/1/.7/.3 \qquad\qquad\qquad\qquad 73.1,T$$

PHTM   – PREMIUM-HØUSING TAX MULTIPLIER
           (DIMENSIØNLESS)
PHTMT – PREMIUM-HØUSING-TAX-MULTIPLIER TABLE
TR   – TAX RATIØ (DIMENSIØNLESS)

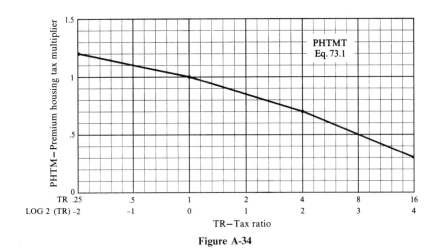

Figure A-34

The premium-housing enterprise multiplier PHEM in Equation 74 and Figure A-35 provides a speculative or momentum factor which increases premium-housing construction if there has been a recent history of above-average growth in

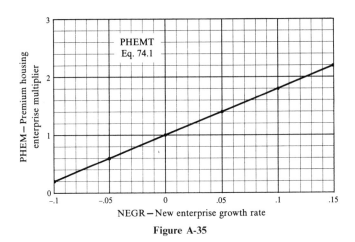

Figure A-35

new enterprise. In other words, establishment of new enterprise tends to encourage construction of new premium housing for the managerial-professional class associated with the industrial expansion.

```
PHEM.K=TABHL(PHEMT,NEGR.K,-.1,.15,.05)                          74,A

PHEMT=.2/.6/1/1.4/1.8/2.2                                       74.1,T

      PHEM  - PREMIUM-HØUSING ENTERPRISE MULTIPLER
              (DIMENSIØNLESS)
      PHEMT - PREMIUM-HØUSING-ENTERPRISE-MULTIPLIER TABLE
      NEGR  - NEW-ENTERPRISE GRØWTH RATE (FRACTIØN/YEAR)
```

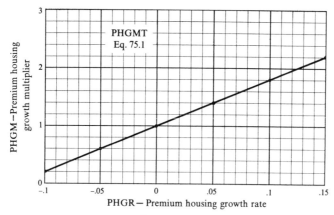

Figure A-36

Also, the momentum of recent construction in premium housing itself tends to carry forward and cause still more premium-housing construction. Equation 75 and Figure A-36 provide a link in what is essentially a positive-feedback loop from premium housing through growth rate and back into premium-housing construction.

$$PHGM.K = TABHL(PHGMT, PHGR.K, -.1, .15, .05) \qquad 75,A$$

$$PHGMT = .2/.6/1/1.4/1.8/2.2 \qquad 75.1,T$$

    PHGM - PREMIUM-HØUSING-GRØWTH MULTIPLIER
             (DIMENSIØNLESS)
    PHGMT - PREMIUM-HØUSING-GRØWTH-MULTIPLIER TABLE
    PHGR - PREMIUM-HØUSING GRØWTH RATE (FRACTIØN/YEAR)

Equation 76 computes the premium-housing growth rate used in Equation 75. It is generated by taking present premium housing, subtracting an earlier value of premium housing PHA, dividing this by the time delay PHAT to obtain the number of housing units constructed per year, and then dividing by premium housing to convert to a fractional growth rate. The formulation might also have been made by averaging PHC from Equation 64 and dividing by premium housing.

$$PHGR.K = (PH.K - PHA.K)/(PH.K*PHAT) \qquad 76,A$$

    PHGR - PREMIUM-HØUSING GRØWTH RATE (FRACTIØN/YEAR)
    PH   - PREMIUM HØUSING (HØUSING UNITS)
    PHA   - PREMIUM-HØUSING AVERAGE (HØUSING UNITS)
    PHAT - PREMIUM-HØUSING AVERAGING TIME (YEARS)

Equation 77 is a first-order exponential smoothing or averaging equation which generates the delayed version of premium housing needed in Equation 76. The initial value of PHA is computed so that it will generate an initial premium-housing growth rate of 3% per year.

$$PHA.K=PHA.J+(DT/PHAT)(PH.J-PHA.J) \qquad \text{77,L}$$

$$PHA=PH-(PHGRI)(PHAT)(PH) \qquad \text{77.1,N}$$

$$PHAT=10 \qquad \text{77.2,C}$$

$$PHGRI=.03 \qquad \text{77.3,C}$$

PHA   – PREMIUM–HØUSING AVERAGE (HØUSING UNITS)
PHAT   – PREMIUM–HØUSING AVERAGING TIME (YEARS)
PH   – PREMIUM HØUSING (HØUSING UNITS)
PHGRI – PREMIUM–HØUSING GRØWTH RATE INITIAL
         (FRACTIØN/YEAR)

The level Equation 78 accumulates the amount of premium housing by adding construction and subtracting obsolescence.

$$PH.K=PH.J+(DT)(PHC.JK-PHØ.JK) \qquad \text{78,L}$$

$$PH=5000 \qquad \text{78.1,N}$$

PH   – PREMIUM HØUSING (HØUSING UNITS)
PHC   – PREMIUM–HØUSING CØNSTRUCTIØN (HØUSING
        UNITS/YEAR)
PHØ   – PREMIUM–HØUSING ØBSØLESCENCE (HØUSING
        UNITS/YEAR)

Premium-housing obsolescence is defined in Equation 79 as having a normal value of 3% per year. This means that premium housing is taken to have the reciprocal of .03, or 33 years of normal active life in the premium category. But the multiplier PHOM can modify this average age depending on the demand for housing. In periods of high demand, housing will be maintained and will continue to be occupied by the managerial-professional group beyond its normal life. As the managerial group decreases relative to housing and housing becomes excessive, the housing drifts more rapidly into the worker-housing category.

$$PHØ.KL=(PHØN)(PH.K)(PHØM.K) \qquad \text{79,R}$$

$$PHØN=.03 \qquad \text{79.1,C}$$

PHØ   – PREMIUM–HØUSING ØBSØLESCENCE (HØUSING
         UNITS/YEAR)
PHØN   – PREMIUM–HØUSING ØBSØLESCENCE NØRMAL
         (FRACTIØN/YEAR)
PH   – PREMIUM HØUSING (HØUSING UNITS)
PHØM   – PREMIUM–HØUSING–ØBSØLESCENCE MULTIPLIER
         (DIMENSIØNLESS)

The premium-housing-obsolescence multiplier in Equation 80 and Figure A-37 is derived from the premium-housing multiplier PHM. To the right, as the urgency of new premium-housing construction increases, the obsolescence rate declines and the average life of premium housing increases. At the extreme left the

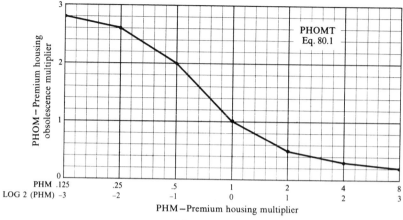

Figure A-37

obsolescence rate can climb to almost three times normal, indicating an average life of about ten years under some imaginary extreme circumstances where there is no managerial-professional population to occupy the dwellings.

$$\text{PHØM.K} = \text{TABHL(PHØMT}, 1.44 * \text{LØGN(PHM.K)}, -3, 3, 1) \qquad \text{80,A}$$

$$\text{PHØMT} = 2.8/2.6/2/1/.5/.3/.2 \qquad \text{80.1,T}$$

    PHØM   - PREMIUM-HØUSING-ØBSØLESCENCE MULTIPLIER
               (DIMENSIØNLESS)
    PHØMT - PREMIUM-HØUSING-ØBSØLESCENCE-MULTIPLIER
               TABLE
    PHM   - PREMIUM-HØUSING MULTIPLIER (DIMENSIØNLESS)

A.5 Worker-Housing Sector

Construction of worker housing in Figure A-38 depends on a group of factors equivalent to those explained in relation to premium housing.

The level of worker housing is given by Equation 81, which accumulates housing becoming available from premium-housing obsolescence, worker housing being constructed, and outflow of worker housing through obsolescence.

$$\text{WH.K} = \text{WH.J} + (\text{DT}) (\text{PHØ.JK} + \text{WHC.JK} - \text{WHØ.JK}) \qquad \text{81,L}$$

$$\text{WH} = 2\ 1000 \qquad \text{81.1,N}$$

    WH   - WØRKER HØUSING (HØUSING UNITS)
    PHØ   - PREMIUM-HØUSING ØBSØLESCENCE (HØUSING
               UNITS/YEAR)
    WHC   - WØRKER-HØUSING CØNSTRUCTIØN (HØUSING UNITS/
               YEAR)
    WHØ   - WØRKER-HØUSING ØBSØLESCENCE (HØUSING UNITS/
               YEAR)

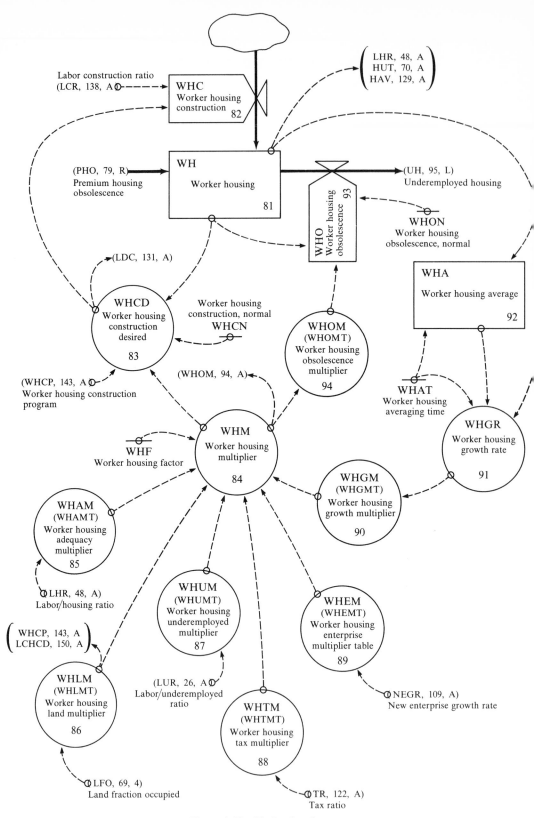

Figure A-38 Worker-housing sector.

Equation 82, like Equation 64, gives the construction rate in terms of the construction rate desired, multiplied by a factor that depends on construction labor availability.

$$WHC.KL=(WHCD.K)(LCR.K) \qquad\qquad 82,R$$

WHC	–	WORKER-HOUSING CONSTRUCTION (HOUSING UNITS/YEAR)
WHCD	–	WORKER-HOUSING CONSTRUCTION DESIRED (HOUSING UNITS/YEAR)
LCR	–	LABOR CONSTRUCTION RATIO (DIMENSIONLESS)

Desired worker-housing construction in Equation 83 is a normal 3% per year multiplied by the worker-housing multiplier WHM, plus any external program of worker-housing construction.

$$WHCD.K =(WHCN)(WH.K)(WHM.K)+WHCP.K \qquad\qquad 83,A$$

$$WHCN=.03 \qquad\qquad 83.1,C$$

WHCD	–	WORKER-HOUSING CONSTRUCTION DESIRED (HOUSING UNITS/YEAR)
WHCN	–	WORKER-HOUSING CONSTRUCTION NORMAL (FRACTION/YEAR)
WH	–	WORKER HOUSING (HOUSING UNITS)
WHM	–	WORKER-HOUSING MULTIPLIER (DIMENSIONLESS)
WHCP	–	WORKER-HOUSING-CONSTRUCTION PROGRAM (HOUSING UNITS/YEAR)

The worker-housing multipliers reflect the influence of the city system on worker-housing construction and are combined in Equation 84.

$$WHM.K =(WHAM.K)(WHLM.K)(WHUM.K)(WHTM.K)(WHEM.K)(WHGM.K) \qquad 84,A$$
$$(WHF)$$

$$WHF=1 \qquad\qquad 84.1,C$$

WHM	–	WORKER-HOUSING MULTIPLIER (DIMENSIONLESS)
WHAM	–	WORKER-HOUSING-ADEQUACY MULTIPLIER (DIMENSIONLESS)
WHLM	–	WORKER-HOUSING LAND MULTIPLIER (DIMENSIONLESS)
WHUM	–	WORKER-HOUSING UNDEREMPLOYED MULTIPLIER (DIMENSIONLESS)
WHTM	–	WORKER-HOUSING TAX MULTIPLIER (DIMENSIONLESS)
WHEM	–	WORKER-HOUSING ENTERPRISE MULTIPLIER (DIMENSIONLESS)
WHGM	–	WORKER-HOUSING-GROWTH MULTIPLIER (DIMENSIONLESS)
WHF	–	WORKER-HOUSING FACTOR (DIMENSIONLESS)

The worker-housing-adequacy multiplier in Equation 85 and Figure A-39 shows the strong influence of housing shortage to the right, and housing excess to the left, on the worker-housing-construction rate.

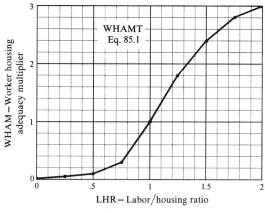

Figure A-39

```
WHAM.K =TABHL(WHAMT,LHR.K,0,2,.25)                    85,A

WHAMT=0/.05/.1/.3/1/1.8/2.4/2.8/3                     85.1,T

     WHAM  - WØRKER-HØUSING-ADEQUACY MULTIPLIER
                (DIMENSIØNLESS)
     WHAMT - WØRKER-HØUSING-ADEQUACY-MULTIPLIER TABLE
     LHR   - LABØR/HØUSING RATIØ (DIMENSIØNLESS)
```

The land multiplier of Equation 86 and Figure A-40 operates as explained in connection with Equation 68.

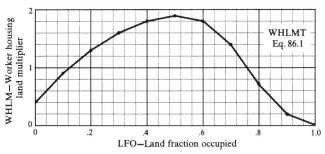

Figure A-40

```
WHLM.K=TABHL(WHLMT,LFØ.K,0,1,.1)                      86,A

WHLMT=.4/.9/1.3/1.6/1.8/1.9/1.8/1.4/.7/.2/0           86.1,T

     WHLM  - WØRKER-HØUSING LAND MULTIPLIER
                (DIMENSIØNLESS)
     WHLMT - WØRKER-HØUSING-LAND-MULTIPLIER TABLE
     LFØ   - LAND FRACTIØN ØCCUPIED (DIMENSIØNLESS)
```

Equation 87, as illustrated in Figure A-41, shows the influence of the social balance of the area on the tendency to construct new housing. When the ratio

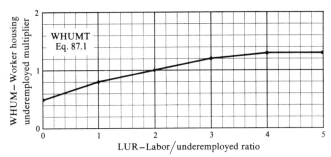

Figure A-41

of labor to underemployed falls, the willingness to construct additional housing declines because the area has become blighted, obsolete, and undesirable.

WHUM.K =TABHL(WHUMT,LUR.K,0,5,1)   87,A

WHUMT=.5/.8/1/1.2/1.3/1.3   87.1,T

>   WHUM   - WØRKER-HØUSING UNDEREMPLØYED MULTIPLIER
>   (DIMENSIØNLESS)
>   WHUMT - WØRKER-HØUSING-UNDEREMPLØYED-MULTIPLIER
>   TABLE
>   LUR   - LABØR/UNDEREMPLØYED RATIØ (DIMENSIØNLESS)

The tax multiplier in Equation 88 and Figure A-42 provides a depressing influence on construction as the tax rate rises.

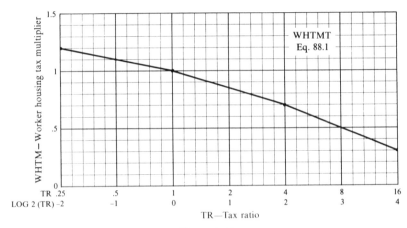

Figure A-42

WHTM.K =TABHL(WHTMT,1.44*LØGN(TR.K) ,-2,4,2)   88,A

WHTMT=1.2/1/.7/.3   88.1,T

>   WHTM   - WØRKER-HØUSING TAX MULTIPLIER
>   (DIMENSIØNLESS)
>   WHTMT - WØRKER-HØUSING-TAX-MULTIPLIER TABLE
>   TR   - TAX RATIØ (DIMENSIØNLESS)

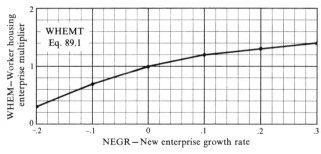

Figure A-43

As with premium housing, an industrial growth factor has been introduced into the willingness to construct worker housing. Equation 89, as shown in Figure A-43, relates new-enterprise growth rates to the worker-housing multiplier.

```
WHEM.K=TABHL(WHEMT,NEGR.K,-.2,.3,.1)                    89,A

WHEMT=.3/.7/1/1.2/1.3/1.4                               89.1,T
```

```
WHEM   - WØRKER-HØUSING ENTERPRISE MULTIPLIER
           (DIMENSIØNLESS)
WHEMT  - WØRKER-HØUSING-ENTERPRISE-MULTIPLIER TABLE
NEGR   - NEW-ENTERPRISE GRØWTH RATE (FRACTIØN/YEAR)
```

Equation 90, as diagramed in Figure A-44, provides the momentum factor of worker housing on construction of worker housing. A history of successful housing construction, and the building industry organized to provide the construction, tends to maintain the construction rate.

Figure A-44

```
WHGM.K=TABHL(WHGMT,WHGR.K,-.1,.15,.05)                  90,A

WHGMT=.2/.6/1/1.4/1.8/2.2                               90.1,T
```

```
WHGM   - WØRKER-HØUSING-GRØWTH MULTIPLIER
           (DIMENSIØNLESS)
```

```
WHGMT - WORKER-HOUSING-GROWTH-MULTIPLIER TABLE
WHGR  - WORKER-HOUSING GROWTH RATE (FRACTION/YEAR)
```

Equations 91 and 92 calculate the worker-housing growth rate through the same procedure used in Equations 76 and 77.

```
WHGR.K =(WH.K-WHA.K)/(WH.K*WHAT)                         91,A

    WHGR  - WORKER-HOUSING GROWTH RATE (FRACTION/YEAR)
    WH    - WORKER HOUSING (HOUSING UNITS)
    WHA   - WORKER-HOUSING AVERAGE (HOUSING UNITS)
    WHAT  - WORKER-HOUSING AVERAGING TIME (YEARS)


WHA.K=WHA.J+(DT/WHAT)(WH.J-WHA.J)                        92,L

WHA=WH-(WHGRI)(WHAT)(WH)                                 92.1,N

WHAT=10                                                  92.2,C

WHGRI=.03                                                92.3,C

    WHA   - WORKER-HOUSING AVERAGE (HOUSING UNITS)
    WHAT  - WORKER-HOUSING AVERAGING TIME (YEARS)
    WH    - WORKER HOUSING (HOUSING UNITS)
    WHGRI - WORKER-HOUSING GROWTH RATE INITIAL
            (FRACTION/YEAR)
```

Worker-housing obsolescence in Equation 93 is taken as having a normal value of 2% per year, implying that housing remains in this category 50 years.

```
WHO.KL=(WHON)(WH.K)(WHOM.K)                              93,R

WHON=.02                                                 93.1,C

    WHO   - WORKER-HOUSING OBSOLESCENCE (HOUSING UNITS/
            YEAR)
    WHON  - WORKER-HOUSING OBSOLESCENCE NORMAL
            (FRACTION/YEAR)
    WH    - WORKER HOUSING (HOUSING UNITS)
    WHOM  - WORKER-HOUSING-OBSOLESCENCE MULTIPLIER
            (DIMENSIONLESS)
```

The obsolescence multiplier in Equation 94 and Figure A-45 modifies the lifetime of worker housing depending on the need for such housing as indicated

```
WHOM.K =TABHL(WHOMT,1.44*LOGN(WHM.K),-3,3,1)            94,A

WHOMT=2.2/2/1.6/1/.7/.5/.4                              94.1,T

    WHOM  - WORKER-HOUSING-OBSOLESCENCE MULTIPLIER
            (DIMENSIONLESS)
    WHOMT - WORKER-HOUSING-OBSOLESCENCE-MULTIPLIER
            TABLE
    WHM   - WORKER-HOUSING MULTIPLIER (DIMENSIONLESS)
```

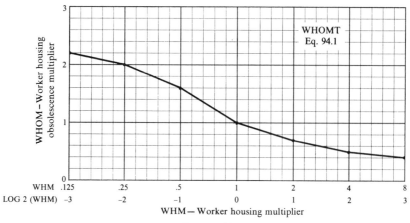

Figure A-45

by the worker-housing multiplier WHM. A higher value of WHM leads to a lower obsolescence rate and a correspondingly longer life and vice versa.

A.6 Underemployed-Housing Sector

Figure A-46 shows the flows associated with underemployed housing. Obsolescent worker housing, as well as construction resulting from an externally generated low-cost-housing program, enters the underemployed-housing category. The underemployed housing disappears from the system through demolition.

The amount of underemployed housing is accumulated in level Equation 95.

The slum-housing-demolition rate in Equation 96 is specified as 2% per year

$$UH.K=UH.J+(DT)(WHØ.JK-SHD.JK+LCHP.JK) \qquad 95,L$$

$$UH=1100 \qquad 95.1,N$$

UH	– UNDEREMPLØYED HØUSING (HØUSING UNITS)
WHØ	– WØRKER-HØUSING ØBSØLESCENCE (HØUSING UNITS/ YEAR)
SHD	– SLUM-HØUSING DEMØLITIØN (HØUSING UNITS/ YEAR)
LCHP	– LØW-CØST-HØUSING PRØGRAM (HØUSING UNITS/ YEAR)

$$SHD.KL=(SHDN)(UH.K)(SHDM.K)+SHDP.K \qquad 96,R$$

$$SHDN=.02 \qquad 96.1,C$$

SHD	– SLUM-HØUSING DEMØLITIØN (HØUSING UNITS/ YEAR)
SHDN	– SLUM-HØUSING DEMØLITIØN NØRMAL (FRACTIØN/ YEAR)
UH	– UNDEREMPLØYED HØUSING (HØUSING UNITS)
SHDM	– SLUM-HØUSING-DEMØLITIØN MULTIPLIER (DIMENSIØNLESS)
SHDP	– SLUM-HØUSING-DEMØLITIØN PRØGRAM (HØUSING UNITS/YEAR)

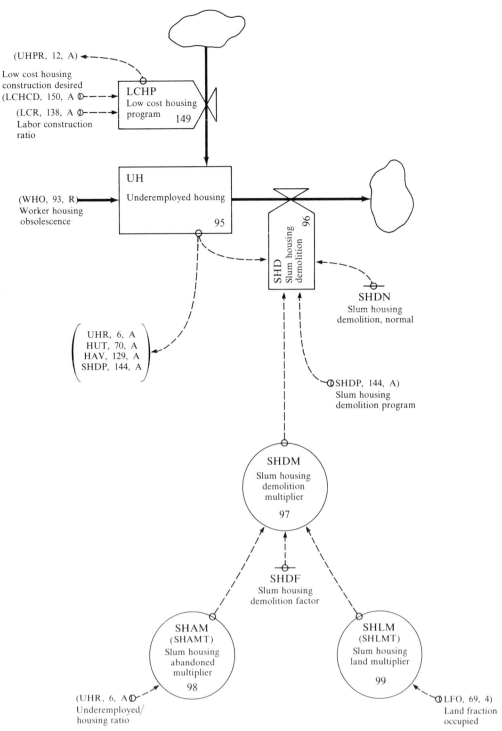

Figure A-46 Underemployed-housing sector.

of the underemployed housing, meaning a 50-year life in this category. A multiplier introduces the effects of occupancy and pressures on land. The addition of the term SHDP provides for an externally introduced slum-housing-demolition program.

The slum-housing-demolition multiplier in Equation 97 contains the two active variables and an experimental factor that can be changed to explore the behavior of the system.

SHDM.K=(SHAM.K)(SHLM.K)(SHDF)   97,A

SHDF=1   97.1,C

    SHDM — SLUM-HØUSING-DEMØLITIØN MULTIPLIER
              (DIMENSIØNLESS)
    SHAM — SLUM-HØUSING-ABANDØNED MULTIPLIER
              (DIMENSIØNLESS)
    SHLM — SLUM-HØUSING LAND MULTIPLIER
              (DIMENSIØNLESS)
    SHDF — SLUM-HØUSING-DEMØLITIØN FACTØR
              (DIMENSIØNLESS)

Equation 98 and Figure A-47 show the effect of occupancy on the demolition rate. The demolition rate is normal when the ratio of underemployed to housing

SHAM.K=TABLE(SHAMT,UHR.K,0,2,.5)   98,A

SHAMT=3.6/2/1/.6/.4   98.1,T

    SHAM — SLUM-HØUSING-ABANDØNED MULTIPLIER
              (DIMENSIØNLESS)
    SHAMT — SLUM-HØUSING-ABANDØNED-MULTIPLIER TABLE
    UHR   — UNDEREMPLØYED/HØUSING RATIØ (DIMENSIØNLESS)

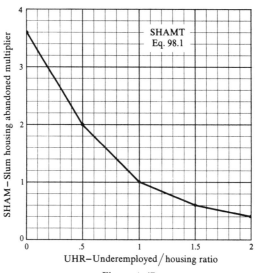

Figure A-47

is 1. Deterioration and the demolition rate rise rapidly as occupancy falls, and decline (meaning longer housing life) when occupancy is above normal.

Equation 99 and Figure A-48 show the assumed relation between land fraction occupied and demolition rate. In the occupancy interval from .8 to .95, demolition rises gradually, indicating the tendency to tear down old buildings for replacement as the remaining land area becomes less suitable. The rapid rise in the curve

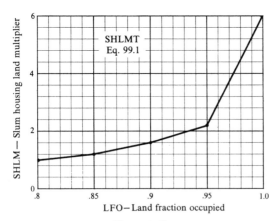

Figure A-48

as the land fraction occupied reaches 1 is to couple the demolition and construction under any circumstances where a massive forced construction program might drive land occupancy up to and possibly beyond full occupancy. In other words, if construction is to take place in this region, demolition must occur.

```
SHLM.K=TABHL(SHLMT,LFØ.K,.8,1,.05)                                99,A

SHLMT=1/1.2/1.6/2.2/6                                            99.1,T

      SHLM  - SLUM-HØUSING LAND MULTIPLIER
              (DIMENSIØNLESS)
      SHLMT - SLUM-HØUSING-LAND-MULTIPLIER TABLE
      LFØ   - LAND FRACTIØN ØCCUPIED (DIMENSIØNLESS)
```

A.7 New-Enterprise Sector

The new-enterprise sector in Figure A-49 is very similar to the premium-housing sector in Figure A-30.

```
NE.K=NE.J+(DT)(NEC.JK-NED.JK)                                   100,L

NE=200                                                         100.1,N

      NE    - NEW ENTERPRISE (PRØDUCTIVE UNITS)
      NEC   - NEW-ENTERPRISE CØNSTRUCTIØN (PRØDUCTIVE
              UNITS/YEAR)
      NED   - NEW-ENTERPRISE DECLINE (PRØDUCTIVE UNITS/
              YEAR)
```

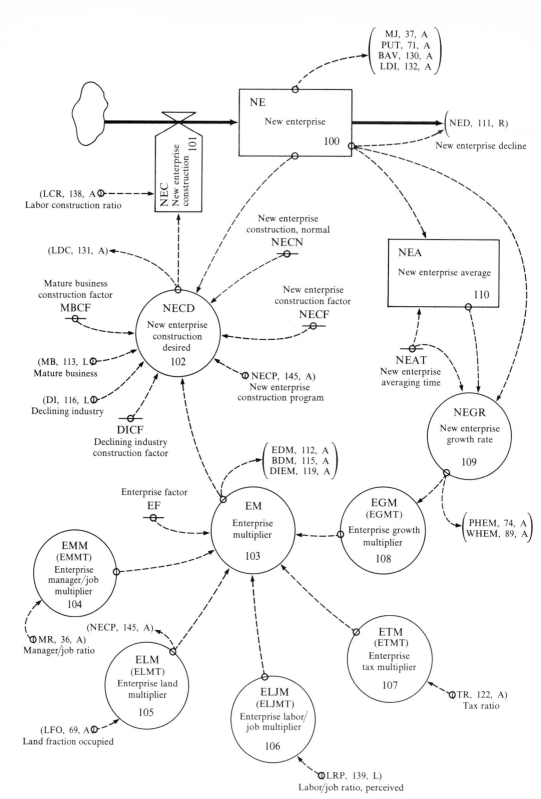

Figure A-49 New-enterprise sector.

The accumulation of net construction minus decline is generated by the level Equation 100.

New-enterprise construction in Equation 101 is similar in form to Equation 64. Desired construction is modified by labor availability.

$$NEC.KL=(NECD.K)(LCR.K) \qquad 101,R$$

NEC — NEW-ENTERPRISE CØNSTRUCTIØN (PRØDUCTIVE
      UNITS/YEAR)
NECD — NEW-ENTERPRISE CØNSTRUCTIØN DESIRED
      (PRØDUCTIVE UNITS/YEAR)
LCR — LABØR CØNSTRUCTIØN RATIØ (DIMENSIØNLESS)

New-enterprise construction desired NECD is taken as 5% per year of a weighted combination of the different business categories. New enterprise has a weighting factor of one, meaning that a unit of new enterprise is most likely to form another new unit. Mature business has a weighting factor of .5 and declining industry .3. Quite possibly the latter coefficient is too high because it does not appear that declining industry is often a source of new business creation.

$$NECD.K=(NECN)(NECF*NE.K+MBCF*MB.K+DICF*DI.K)(EM.K)+ \qquad 102,A$$
$$NECP.K$$

$$NECF=1 \qquad 102.1,C$$

$$MBCF=.5 \qquad 102.2,C$$

$$DICF=.3 \qquad 102.3,C$$

$$NECN=.05 \qquad 102.4,C$$

NECD — NEW-ENTERPRISE CØNSTRUCTIØN DESIRED
      (PRØDUCTIVE UNITS/YEAR)
NECN — NEW-ENTERPRISE CØNSTRUCTIØN NØRMAL
      (FRACTIØN/YEAR)
NECF — NEW-ENTERPRISE-CØNSTRUCTIØN FACTØR
      (DIMENSIØNLESS)
NE — NEW ENTERPRISE (PRØDUCTIVE UNITS)
MBCF — MATURE-BUSINESS-CØNSTRUCTIØN FACTØR
      (DIMENSIØNLESS)
MB — MATURE BUSINESS (PRØDUCTIVE UNITS)
DICF — DECLINING-INDUSTRY-CØNSTRUCTIØN FACTØR
      (DIMENSIØNLESS)
DI — DECLINING INDUSTRY (PRØDUCTIVE UNITS)
EM — ENTERPRISE MULTIPLIER (DIMENSIØNLESS)
NECP — NEW-ENTERPRISE-CØNSTRUCTIØN PRØGRAM
      (PRØDUCTIVE UNITS/YEAR)

The enterprise multiplier in Equation 103 is the product of the five component multipliers and of the system experimental factor EF.

EM.K =(EMM.K)(ELM.K)(ELJM.K)(ETM.K)(EGM.K)(EF)   103,A

EF=1   103.1,C

    EM   — ENTERPRISE MULTIPLIER (DIMENSIØNLESS)
    EMM   — ENTERPRISE MANAGER/JØB MULTIPLIER
            (DIMENSIØNLESS)
    ELM   — ENTERPRISE LAND MULTIPLIER (DIMENSIØNLESS)
    ELJM — ENTERPRISE LABØR/JØB MULTIPLIER
            (DIMENSIØNLESS)
    ETM   — ENTERPRISE TAX MULTIPLIER (DIMENSIØNLESS)
    EGM   — ENTERPRISE-GRØWTH MULTIPLIER
            (DIMENSIØNLESS)
    EF   — ENTERPRISE FACTØR (DIMENSIØNLESS)

Equation 104 in Figure A-50 states that increasing managers in proportion to managerial jobs increases the likelihood of establishing new enterprise. As the

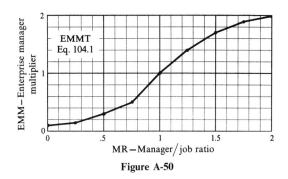

Figure A-50

managerial-professional population grows in proportion to the existing needs of the city, more time, skill, and incentive are available to start new activities.

EMM.K =TABHL(EMMT,MR.K,0,2,.25)   104,A

EMMT=.1/.15/.3/.5/1/1.4/1.7/1.9/2   104.1,T

    EMM   — ENTERPRISE MANAGER/JØB MULTIPLIER
            (DIMENSIØNLESS)
    EMMT — ENTERPRISE MANAGER/JØB MULTIPLIER TABLE
    MR   — MANAGER/JØB RATIØ (DIMENSIØNLESS)

The land multiplier ELM in Equation 105 and Figure A-51 describes an economic incentive to build as a function of total land area occupied. The con-

ELM.K =TABHL(ELMT,LFØ.K,0,1,.1)   105,A

ELMT=1/1.15/1.3/1.4/1.45/1.4/1.3/1/.7/.4/0   105.1,T

    ELM   — ENTERPRISE LAND MULTIPLIER (DIMENSIØNLESS)
    ELMT — ENTERPRISE-LAND-MULTIPLIER TABLE
    LFØ   — LAND FRACTIØN ØCCUPIED (DIMENSIØNLESS)

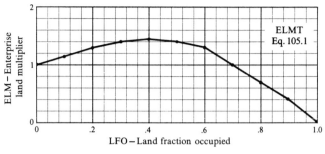

Figure A-51

cepts are the same discussed for Equation 68. When land becomes completely occupied, construction must cease unless demolition takes place.

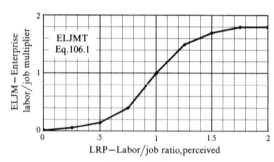

Figure A-52

Equation 106 and Figure A-52 describe the inclination to build new enterprise in terms of the availability of labor. If the labor/job ratio is low, indicating a shortage of labor, new-enterprise construction is depressed. An excess of labor encourages new construction.

```
ELJM.K=TABHL(ELJMT,LRP.K,0,2,.25)                    106,A

ELJMT=0/.05/.15/.4/1/1.5/1.7/1.8/1.8                 106.1,T

      ELJM  - ENTERPRISE LABØR/JØB MULTIPLIER
              (DIMENSIØNLESS)
      ELJMT - ENTERPRISE LABØR/JØB MULTIPLIER TABLE
      LRP   - LABØR/JØB RATIØ PERCEIVED (DIMENSIØNLESS)
```

The tax multiplier in Equation 107 and Figure A-53 is similar in purpose to those discussed earlier but represents a more decisive effect at the high tax end

```
ETM.K=TABHL(ETMT,1.44*LØGN(TR.K),-2,4,1)             107,A

ETMT=1.3/1.2/1/.8/.5/.25/.1                          107.1,T

      ETM   - ENTERPRISE TAX MULTIPLIER (DIMENSIØNLESS)
      ETMT  - ENTERPRISE-TAX-MULTIPLIER TABLE
      TR    - TAX RATIØ (DIMENSIØNLESS)
```

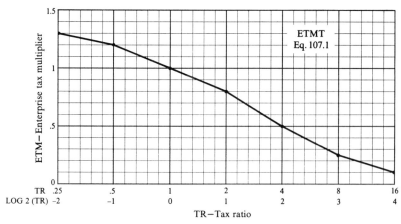

Figure A-53

than was assumed for housing. The multiplier declines to where a tax rate of 16 times normal cuts construction by a factor of 10.

The enterprise-growth multiplier in Equation 108 and Figure A-54 is a speculative and momentum factor tending to encourage construction during a period

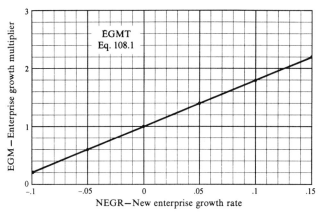

Figure A-54

of active construction and tending to depress construction during a period when obsolescence exceeds new construction.

```
EGM.K=TABHL( EGMT,NEGR.K,-.1,.15,.05)                    108,A

EGMT=.2/.6/1/1.4/1.8/2.2                                108.1,T

    EGM   - ENTERPRISE-GRØWTH MULTIPLIER
            ( DIMENSIØNLESS)
    EGMT  - ENTERPRISE-GRØWTH-MULTIPLIER TABLE
    NEGR  - NEW-ENTERPRISE GRØWTH RATE (FRACTIØN/YEAR)
```

The new-enterprise growth rate is computed in Equations 109 and 110 in the same way as discussed for Equations 76 and 77.

$$\text{NEGR.K} = (\text{NE.K} - \text{NEA.K}) / (\text{NE.K} * \text{NEAT}) \qquad\qquad 109, A$$

    NEGR - NEW-ENTERPRISE GRØWTH RATE (FRACTIØN/YEAR)
    NE   - NEW ENTERPRISE (PRØDUCTIVE UNITS)
    NEA   - NEW-ENTERPRISE AVERAGE (PRØDUCTIVE UNITS)
    NEAT - NEW-ENTERPRISE AVERAGING TIME (YEARS)

$$\text{NEA.K} = \text{NEA.J} + (\text{DT/NEAT})(\text{NE.J} - \text{NEA.J}) \qquad\qquad 110, L$$

$$\text{NEA} = \text{NE} - (\text{NEGRI})(\text{NEAT})(\text{NE}) \qquad\qquad 110.1, N$$

$$\text{NEAT} = 10 \qquad\qquad 110.2, C$$

$$\text{NEGRI} = .03 \qquad\qquad 110.3, C$$

    NEA   - NEW-ENTERPRISE AVERAGE (PRØDUCTIVE UNITS)
    NEAT - NEW-ENTERPRISE AVERAGING TIME (YEARS)
    NE   - NEW ENTERPRISE (PRØDUCTIVE UNITS)
    NEGRI - NEW-ENTERPRISE GRØWTH RATE INITIAL
            (FRACTIØN/YEAR)

A.8 Mature-Business Sector

Figure A-55 illustrates the structure surrounding the mature-business level.

New-enterprise decline in Equation 111 represents the aging of new enterprise into mature business. The normal value of .08 per year implies an average life of 12 years in the new-enterprise category. This is modified by the enterprise-decline multiplier.

$$\text{NED.KL} = (\text{NEDN})(\text{NE.K})(\text{EDM.K}) \qquad\qquad 111, R$$

$$\text{NEDN} = .08 \qquad\qquad 111.1, C$$

    NED   - NEW-ENTERPRISE DECLINE (PRØDUCTIVE UNITS/
            YEAR)
    NEDN - NEW-ENTERPRISE DECLINE NØRMAL (FRACTIØN/
            YEAR)
    NE   - NEW ENTERPRISE (PRØDUCTIVE UNITS)
    EDM   - ENTERPRISE-DECLINE MULTIPLIER
            (DIMENSIØNLESS)

The enterprise-decline multiplier in Equation 112 and Figure A-56 adjusts the decline rate of new enterprise in response to the enterprise multiplier EM. When

$$\text{EDM.K} = \text{TABHL}(\text{EDMT}, 1.44 * \text{LØGN}(\text{EM.K}), -3, 3, 1) \qquad\qquad 112, A$$

$$\text{EDMT} = 2/1.8/1.5/1/.7/.5/.5 \qquad\qquad 112.1, T$$

    EDM   - ENTERPRISE-DECLINE MULTIPLIER
            (DIMENSIØNLESS)
    EDMT - ENTERPRISE-DECLINE-MULTIPLIER TABLE
    EM   - ENTERPRISE MULTIPLIER (DIMENSIØNLESS)

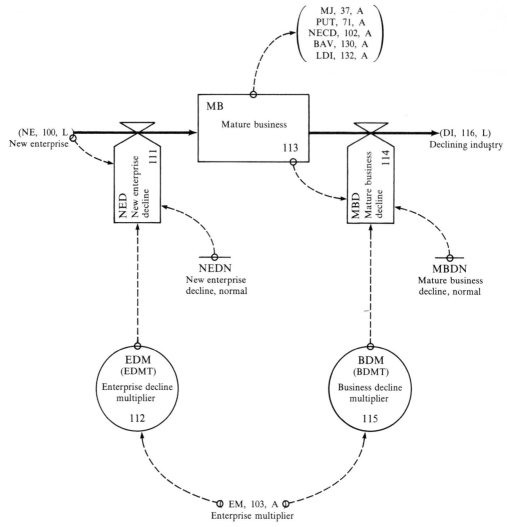

Figure A-55 Mature-business sector.

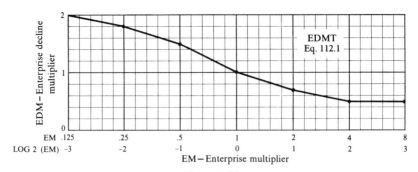

Figure A-56

there is active demand for new enterprise, it is assumed that the existing new enterprise will retain its vitality for a longer period than when there is no incentive for new construction.

Equation 113 accumulates the level of mature business, taking in the decline from new enterprise and giving up mature-business decline into the category of declining industry.

$$MB.K=MB.J+(DT)(NED.JK-MBD.JK) \qquad\qquad 113,L$$

$$MB=1000 \qquad\qquad 113.1,N$$

MB	- MATURE BUSINESS (PRØDUCTIVE UNITS)
NED	- NEW-ENTERPRISE DECLINE (PRØDUCTIVE UNITS/ YEAR)
MBD	- MATURE-BUSINESS DECLINE (PRØDUCTIVE UNITS/ YEAR)

The initial value of 1,000 mature-business units in Equation 113.1 is selected, along with initial conditions of the other levels, to get a reasonably balanced economy at the beginning of the growth phase.

Mature-business decline into the declining-industry category is established by the rate in Equation 114. It is taken with a normal value representing a life of 20 years.

$$MBD.KL=(MBDN)(MB.K)(BDM.K) \qquad\qquad 114,R$$

$$MBDN=.05 \qquad\qquad 114.1,C$$

MBD	- MATURE-BUSINESS DECLINE (PRØDUCTIVE UNITS/ YEAR)
MBDN	- MATURE-BUSINESS DECLINE NØRMAL (FRACTIØN/ YEAR)
MB	- MATURE BUSINESS (PRØDUCTIVE UNITS)
BDM	- BUSINESS-DECLINE MULTIPLIER (DIMENSIØNLESS)

Life in the mature-business category is varied in Equation 115 and Figure A-57 depending on the enterprise multiplier EM. This is done on the basis that an

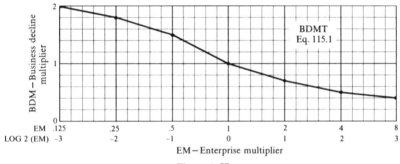

Figure A-57

economy very much in need of new enterprise will retain the vitality of existing business longer than one in a state of deterioration.

$$BDM.K = TABHL(BDMT, 1.44*L\emptyset GN(EM.K), -3, 3, 1) \qquad 115, A$$

$$BDMT = 2/1.8/1.5/1/.7/.5/.4 \qquad 115.1, T$$

    BDM   — BUSINESS-DECLINE MULTIPLIER (DIMENSIØNLESS)
    BDMT — BUSINESS-DECLINE-MULTIPLIER TABLE
    EM   — ENTERPRISE MULTIPLIER (DIMENSIØNLESS)

A.9   Declining-Industry Sector

Figure A-58 shows declining industry and its demolition rate.

Equation 116 generates the number of declining-industry productive units by accumulating the difference between mature-business decline and declining-industry demolition.

$$DI.K = DI.J + (DT)(MBD.JK - DID.JK) \qquad 116, L$$

$$DI = 100 \qquad 116.1, N$$

    DI   — DECLINING INDUSTRY (PRØDUCTIVE UNITS)
    MBD — MATURE-BUSINESS DECLINE (PRØDUCTIVE UNITS/
             YEAR)
    DID — DECLINING-INDUSTRY DEMØLITIØN (PRØDUCTIVE
             UNITS/YEAR)

The declining-industry demolition rate DID in Equation 117 has a normal value representing a 33-year life in this category, modulated by a multiplier representing the influence of the demand for new enterprise and the influence of land shortage. The added factor DIDP allows for an externally determined declining-industry-demolition program.

$$DID.KL = (DIDN)(DI.K)(DIDM.K) + DIDP.K \qquad 117, R$$

$$DIDN = .03 \qquad 117.1, C$$

    DID — DECLINING-INDUSTRY DEMØLITIØN (PRØDUCTIVE
             UNITS/YEAR)
    DIDN — DECLINING-INDUSTRY DEMØLITIØN NØRMAL
             (FRACTIØN/YEAR)
    DI   — DECLINING INDUSTRY (PRØDUCTIVE UNITS)
    DIDM — DECLINING-INDUSTRY-DEMØLITIØN MULTIPLIER
             (DIMENSIØNLESS)
    DIDP — DECLINING-INDUSTRY-DEMØLITIØN PRØGRAM
             (PRØDUCTIVE UNITS/YEAR)

The declining-industry multiplier contains the two active variables and an experimental factor.

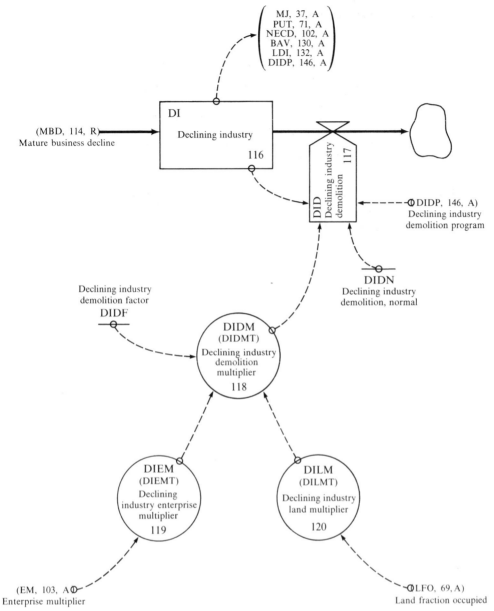

Figure A-58   Declining-industry sector.

DI DM.K =(DI EM.K)(DI LM.K)(DI DF)   118,A

DI DF=1   118.1,C

DI DM - DECLINING-INDUSTRY-DEMØLITIØN MULTIPLIER
           (DIMENSIØNLESS)
DI EM - DECLINING-INDUSTRY ENTERPRISE MULTIPLIER
           (DIMENSIØNLESS)
DI LM - DECLINING-INDUSTRY LAND MULTIPLIER
           (DIMENSIØNLESS)
DI DF - DECLINING-INDUSTRY-DEMØLITIØN FACTØR
           (DIMENSIØNLESS)

In Equation 119 and Figure A-59 the assumed effect of demand for new enterprise on declining-industry demolition is given. This assumes that the more active the new-enterprise-construction rate, the higher will be the declining-indus-

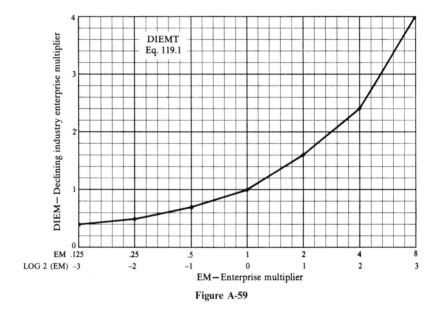

Figure A-59

try demolition rate. This presumes that much of the new enterprise that is constructed will be on the geographical site of old enterprise that has reached the end of its effective life.

DI EM.K =TABLE(DI EMT,1.44*LØGN(EM.K),-3,3,1)   119,A

DI EMT=.4/.5/.7/1/1.6/2.4/4   119.1,T

DI EM - DECLINING-INDUSTRY ENTERPRISE MULTIPLIER
           (DIMENSIØNLESS)
DI EMT - DECLINING-INDUSTRY-ENTERPRISE-MULTIPLIER
           TABLE
EM   - ENTERPRISE MULTIPLIER (DIMENSIØNLESS)

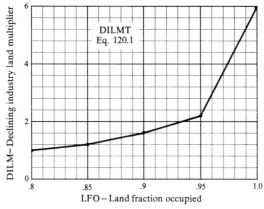

Figure A-60

The declining-industry land multiplier in Equation 120 and Figure A-60 is similar to the slum-housing land multiplier in Equation 99. It shows a natural tendency for demolition to increase as land usage becomes more nearly complete, and forced demolition at very high land usage, should land fill up and reach such a point. Actually, in the computer runs in this book, land occupied has never reached the .95 region.

```
DILM.K=TABHL( DILMT,LFØ.K,.8,1,.05)                    120,A

DILMT=1/1.2/1.6/2.2/6                                  120.1,T

     DILM  - DECLINING-INDUSTRY LAND MULTIPLIER
              (DIMENSIØNLESS)
     DILMT - DECLINING-INDUSTRY-LAND-MULTIPLIER TABLE
     LFØ   - LAND FRACTIØN ØCCUPIED (DIMENSIØNLESS)
```

A.10   Tax Sector

Figure A-61 shows the relationships used for generating tax collections and the tax ratio which influences mobility and construction. Equation 121 computes the total tax collection per year as the product of the assessed value multiplied by tax assessment normal TAN in the outside world and multiplied by the ratio of city to outside tax rate TR.

```
TC.K=(AV.K)(TAN)(TR.K)                                 121,A

TAN=50                                                 121.1,C

     TC    - TAX CØLLECTIØNS (DØLLARS/YEAR)
     AV    - ASSESSED VALUE (THØUSAND DØLLARS)
     TAN   - TAX ASSESSMENT NØRMAL (DØLLARS/YEAR/
              THØUSAND DØLLARS)
     TR    - TAX RATIØ (DIMENSIØNLESS)
```

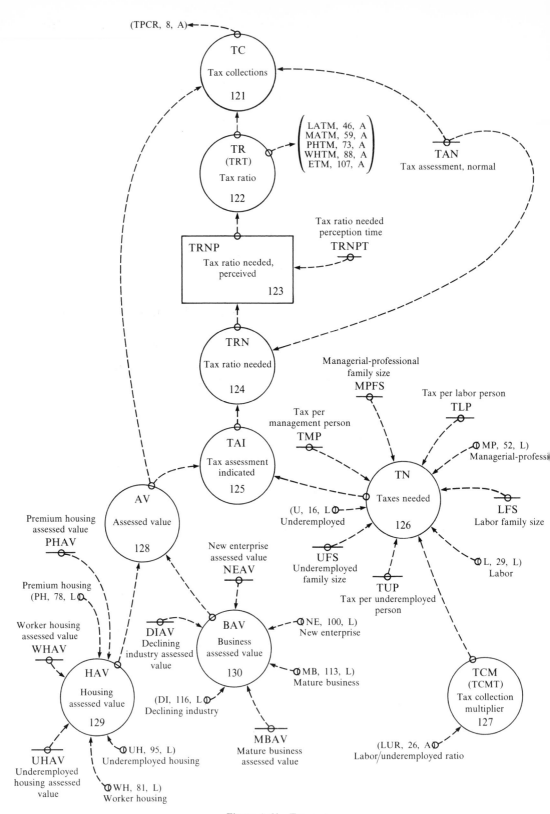

Figure A-61 Tax sector.

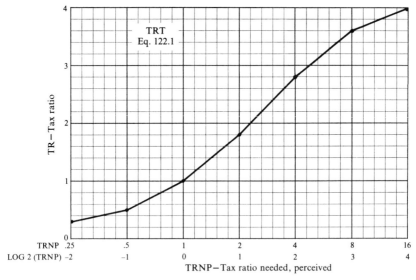

Figure A-62

The tax ratio actually assessed is based on the tax ratio which is perceived as needed, as given in Equation 122 and Figure A-62. This relationship recognizes that it may not be possible or politically practical to assess the full amount of tax which is computed according to needs of the population. In Figure A-62 the tax ratio assessed does not rise so rapidly as the tax ratio need perceived. This relationship can be changed in the model as can all other functional relationships. It can be used to see the effect of more or less aggressive tax assessment to meet the needs of the city.

$$TR.K = TABHL(TRT, 1.44*L\emptyset GN(TRNP.K), -2, 4, 1) \qquad 122, A$$

$$TRT = .3/.5/1/1.8/2.8/3.6/4 \qquad 122.1, T$$

> TR   - TAX RATI∅ (DIMENSI∅NLESS)
> TRT   - TAX-RATI∅ TABLE
> TRNP - TAX RATI∅ NEEDED PERCEIVED (DIMENSI∅NLESS)

Equation 123 represents a time delay between the perception of tax need and the actual need. Here perceptions mean not only awareness of the need but political support and voter acceptance of the need. With the 30-year time lag

$$TRNP.K = TRNP.J + (DT/TRNPT)(TRN.J - TRNP.J) \qquad 123, L$$

$$TRNP = TRN \qquad 123.1, N$$

$$TRNPT = 30 \qquad 123.2, C$$

> TRNP   - TAX RATI∅ NEEDED PERCEIVED (DIMENSI∅NLESS)
> TRNPT - TAX-RATI∅-NEEDED PERCEPTI∅N TIME (YEARS)
> TRN   - TAX RATI∅ NEEDED (DIMENSI∅NLESS)

in Equation 123, about a third of the discrepancy between perceived need and actual need will be closed each decade.

In equation 124 the tax ratio needed is computed by dividing the tax assessment indicated by the tax assessment normal.

$$TRN.K = TAI.K/TAN \qquad\qquad 124,A$$

TRN – TAX RATIØ NEEDED (DIMENSIØNLESS)
TAI – TAX ASSESSMENT INDICATED (DØLLARS/YEAR/
        THØUSAND DØLLARS)
TAN – TAX ASSESSMENT NØRMAL (DØLLARS/YEAR/
        THØUSAND DØLLARS)

In Equation 125 the tax assessment indicated is computed as the ratio of the tax needed divided by the assessed value of the property in the city.

$$TAI.K = TN.K/AV.K \qquad\qquad 125,A$$

TAI – TAX ASSESSMENT INDICATED (DØLLARS/YEAR/
        THØUSAND DØLLARS)
TN   – TAXES NEEDED (DØLLARS/YEAR)
AV   – ASSESSED VALUE (THØUSAND DØLLARS)

Equation 126 generates taxes needed on a per capita basis, with different assumed needs generated by each population class. For example, the first term is the tax per management person multiplied by the management family size times the number of managers. The tax per management person is taken as $150.00 a year, for a labor person as $200.00, and for an unemployed person as $300.00.

$$TN.K = (TMP*MPFS*MP.K + TLP*LFS*L.K + TUP*UFS*U.K)(TCM.K) \qquad 126,A$$

$$TMP = 150 \qquad\qquad 126.1,C$$

$$TLP = 200 \qquad\qquad 126.2,C$$

$$TUP = 300 \qquad\qquad 126.3,C$$

TN   – TAXES NEEDED (DØLLARS/YEAR)
TMP – TAX PER MANAGEMENT PERSØN (DØLLARS/PERSØN/
        YEAR)
MPFS – MANAGERIAL-PRØFESSIØNAL FAMILY SIZE
        (PEØPLE/MAN)
MP   – MANAGERIAL-PRØFESSIØNAL (MEN)
TLP – TAX PER LABØR PERSØN (DØLLARS/PERSØN/YEAR)
LFS – LABØR FAMILY SIZE (PEØPLE/MAN)
L   – LABØR (MEN)
TUP – TAX PER UNDEREMPLØYED PERSØN (DØLLARS/
        PERSØN/YEAR)
UFS – UNDEREMPLØYED FAMILY SIZE (PEØPLE/MAN)
U   – UNDEREMPLØYED (MEN)
TCM – TAX-CØLLECTIØN MULTIPLIER (DIMENSIØNLESS)

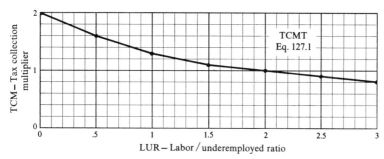

Figure A-63

Equation 127 and Figure A-63 provide a political factor that relates taxes to the labor/underemployed ratio. To the left, as the labor population declines in proportion to the underemployed, the political power moves more and more toward the underemployed group who use tax expenditures but pay less of the tax assessments, and the asserted tax needs of the city rise.

$$\text{TCM.K =TABHL(TCMT,LUR.K ,0,3,.5)} \qquad\qquad 127,A$$

$$\text{TCMT=2/1.6/1.3/1.1/1/.9/.8} \qquad\qquad 127.1,T$$

    TCM   - TAX-CØLLECTIØN MULTIPLIER (DIMENSIØNLESS)
    TCMT   - TAX-CØLLECTIØN-MULTIPLIER TABLE
    LUR   - LABØR/UNDEREMPLØYED RATIØ (DIMENSIØNLESS)

Equation 128 is the total assessed valuation of the city as the sum of housing and business.

$$\text{AV.K =(HAV.K+BAV.K)} \qquad\qquad 128,A$$

    AV   - ASSESSED VALUE (THØUSAND DØLLARS)
    HAV   - HØUSING ASSESSED VALUE (THØUSAND DØLLARS)
    BAV   - BUSINESS ASSESSED VALUE (THØUSAND DØLLARS)

Equation 129 computes the total assessed value of housing. Each premium-housing unit is assessed at $30,000, worker housing at $15,000, and underemployed housing at $5,000.

$$\text{HAV.K =PHAV*PH.K+WHAV*WH.K+ UHAV*UH.K} \qquad\qquad 129,A$$

$$\text{PHAV=30} \qquad\qquad 129.1,C$$

$$\text{WHAV=15} \qquad\qquad 129.2,C$$

$$\text{UHAV=5} \qquad\qquad 129.3,C$$

    HAV   - HØUSING ASSESSED VALUE (THØUSAND DØLLARS)
    PHAV   - PREMIUM-HØUSING ASSESSED VALUE (THØUSAND
             DØLLARS/HØUSING UNIT)
    PH   - PREMIUM HØUSING (HØUSING UNITS)

WHAV — WØRKER-HØUSING ASSESSED VALUE (THØUSAND
        DØLLARS/HØUSING UNIT)
WH   — WØRKER HØUSING (HØUSING UNITS)
UHAV — UNDEREMPLØYED-HØUSING ASSESSED VALUE
        (THØUSAND DØLLARS/HØUSING UNIT)
UH   — UNDEREMPLØYED HØUSING (HØUSING UNITS)

Equation 130 tallies the assessed valuation of business units with a value of $500,000 for a new-enterprise unit, $300,000 for a mature-business unit, and $100,000 for a declining-industry unit.

$$BAV.K = NEAV*NE.K + MBAV*MB.K + DIAV*DI.K \qquad 130,A$$

$$NEAV = 500 \qquad 130.1,C$$

$$MBAV = 300 \qquad 130.2,C$$

$$DIAV = 100 \qquad 130.3,C$$

BAV   — BUSINESS ASSESSED VALUE (THØUSAND DØLLARS)
NEAV — NEW-ENTERPRISE ASSESSED VALUE (THØUSAND
        DØLLARS/PRØDUCTIVE UNIT)
NE   — NEW ENTERPRISE (PRØDUCTIVE UNITS)
MBAV — MATURE-BUSINESS ASSESSED VALUE (THØUSAND
        DØLLARS/PRØDUCTIVE UNIT)
MB   — MATURE BUSINESS (PRØDUCTIVE UNITS)
DIAV — DECLINING-INDUSTRY ASSESSED VALUE (THØUSAND
        DØLLARS/PRØDUCTIVE UNIT)
DI   — DECLINING INDUSTRY (PRØDUCTIVE UNITS)

A.11 Job Sector

Figure A-64 relates the variables involved in computing the employment ratios and then creating the multiplier which makes construction rates dependent on available labor.

Equation 131 gives the labor desired for construction by multiplying the construction rate per year in each category of housing and enterprise by the labor man-years involved in constructing the unit.

$$LDC.K = PHCD.K*PHCL + WHCD.K*WHCL + NECD.K*NECL + LCHCD.K* \qquad 131,A$$
$$LCHCL$$

$$PHCL = 2 \qquad 131.1,C$$

$$WHCL = 1 \qquad 131.2,C$$

$$NECL = 20 \qquad 131.3,C$$

$$LCHCL = .6 \qquad 131.4,C$$

LDC   — LABØR DESIRED FØR CØNSTRUCTIØN (MEN)
PHCD — PREMIUM-HØUSING CØNSTRUCTIØN DESIRED
        (HØUSING UNITS/YEAR)
PHCL — PREMIUM-HØUSING-CØNSTRUCTIØN LABØR (MAN-
        YEARS/HØUSING UNIT)

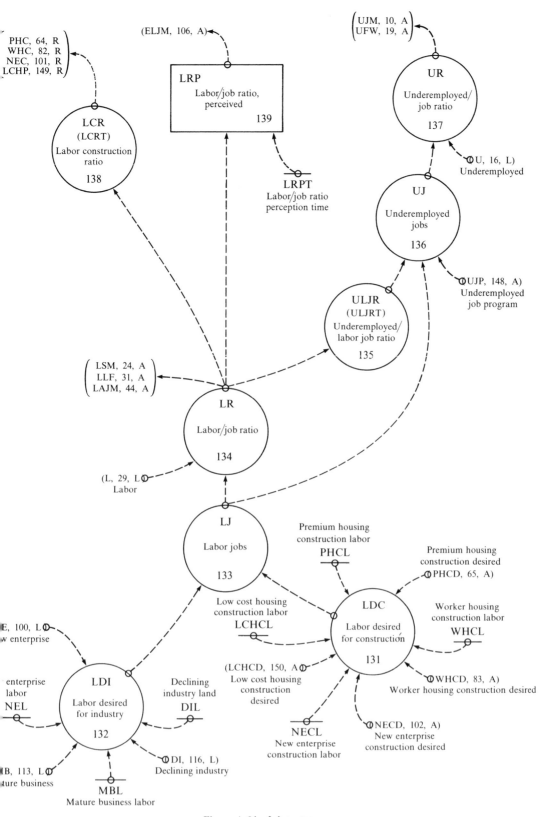

Figure A-64 Job sector.

```
WHCD   - WØRKER-HØUSING CØNSTRUCTIØN DESIRED
           (HØUSING UNITS/YEAR)
WHCL   - WØRKER-HØUSING-CØNSTRUCTIØN LABØR (MAN-
           YEARS/HØUSING UNIT)
NECD   - NEW-ENTERPRISE CØNSTRUCTIØN DESIRED
           (PRØDUCTIVE UNITS/YEAR)
NECL   - NEW-ENTERPRISE-CØNSTRUCTIØN LABØR (MAN-
           YEARS/PRØDUCTIVE UNIT)
LCHCD  - LØW-CØST-HØUSING CØNSTRUCTIØN DESIRED
           (HØUSING UNITS/YEAR)
LCHCL  - LØW-CØST-HØUSING-CØNSTRUCTIØN LABØR (MAN-
           YEARS/HØUSING UNIT)
```

The labor desired for industry in Equation 132 totals the normal labor employment for each industry class.

```
LDI.K=NE.K*NEL+MB.K*MBL+DI.K*DIL                        132,A

NEL=20                                                 132.1,C

MBL=15                                                 132.2,C

DIL=10                                                 132.3,C
```

```
LDI   - LABØR DESIRED FØR INDUSTRY (MEN)
NE    - NEW ENTERPRISE (PRØDUCTIVE UNITS)
NEL   - NEW-ENTERPRISE LABØR (MEN/PRØDUCTIVE UNIT)
MB    - MATURE BUSINESS (PRØDUCTIVE UNITS)
MBL   - MATURE-BUSINESS LABØR (MEN/PRØDUCTIVE UNIT)
DI    - DECLINING INDUSTRY (PRØDUCTIVE UNITS)
DIL   - DECLINING-INDUSTRY LABØR (MEN/PRØDUCTIVE
          UNIT)
```

Equation 133 adds construction and industry labor desired to give the total available jobs.

```
LJ.K=LDC.K+LDI.K                                        133,A
```

```
LJ    - LABØR JØBS (MEN)
LDC   - LABØR DESIRED FØR CØNSTRUCTIØN (MEN)
LDI   - LABØR DESIRED FØR INDUSTRY (MEN)
```

The labor/job ratio LR is given by Equation 134.

```
LR.K=L.K/LJ.K                                           134,A
```

```
LR    - LABØR/JØB RATIØ (DIMENSIØNLESS)
L     - LABØR (MEN)
LJ    - LABØR JØBS (MEN)
```

Equation 135 and Figure A-65 relate labor jobs and underemployed jobs. When the labor ratio is 1, the table states that there is half a job available for the underemployed for each job in the labor category. If the labor/job ratio is low, more of the available labor jobs become open to the underemployed; as the

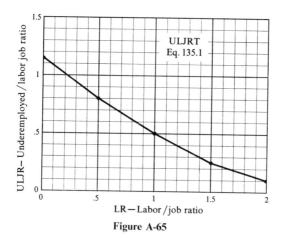

Figure A-65

labor/job ratio increases, the jobs for underemployed decline on the assumption that, under the condition of labor unemployment, the work goes first to the more skilled labor class, leaving less for the underemployed.

ULJR.K=TABHL(ULJRT,LR.K,0,2,.5)   135,A

ULJRT=1.15/.8/.5/.25/.1   135.1,T

    ULJR   - UNDEREMPLØYED/LABØR JØB RATIØ
                (DIMENSIØNLESS)
    ULJRT - UNDEREMPLØYED/LABØR JØB-RATIØ TABLE
    LR   - LABØR/JØB RATIØ (DIMENSIØNLESS)

The actual underemployed jobs are then given by multiplying the total labor jobs by the underemployed/labor job ratio as in Equation 136. The added term UJP provides for an externally generated underemployed-job program.

UJ.K=LJ.K*ULJR.K+UJP.K   136,A

    UJ   - UNDEREMPLØYED JØBS (MEN)
    LJ   - LABØR JØBS (MEN)
    ULJR   - UNDEREMPLØYED/LABØR JØB RATIØ
                (DIMENSIØNLESS)
    UJP   - UNDEREMPLØYED-JØB PRØGRAM (MEN)

The underemployed/job ratio can then be computed in Equation 137 as the underemployed divided by available jobs.

UR.K=U.K/UJ.K   137,A

    UR   - UNDEREMPLØYED/JØB RATIØ (DIMENSIØNLESS)
    U   - UNDEREMPLØYED (MEN)
    UJ   - UNDEREMPLØYED JØBS (MEN)

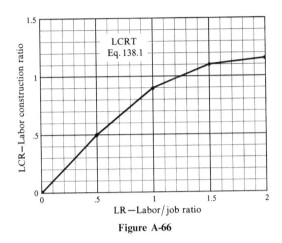

Figure A-66

Equation 138 and Figure A-66 express the influence of available labor on housing and enterprise construction. When the labor/job ratio is 1, 90% of desired construction is possible. As labor falls in relation to job openings, labor is shared by construction and industry, with a proportionate decrease in the fraction of desired construction possible. At the upper end there is a tendency for an excess of labor to encourage more construction than would otherwise be undertaken.

LCR.K=TABHL(LCRT,LR.K,0,2,.5)   138,A

LCRT=0/.5/.9/1.1/1.15   138.1,T

      LCR   - LABØR CØNSTRUCTIØN RATIØ (DIMENSIØNLESS)
      LCRT - LABØR-CØNSTRUCTIØN-RATIØ TABLE
      LR   - LABØR/JØB RATIØ (DIMENSIØNLESS)

Equation 139 introduces a perception delay between labor availability and new-enterprise construction. This is the time taken to perceive the availability of a labor supply as a factor in locating new enterprise. This level equation is also necessary from a technical standpoint to avoid a closed loop of simultaneous auxiliary equations running from Equation 134 to 106, 103, 102, back to 131 and 133, and returning to 134. Such a loop would not be a permissible formulation.

LRP.K =LRP.J+(DT/LRPT) (LR.J-LRP.J)   139,L

LRP=1   139.1,N

LRP T=5   139.2,C

      LRP   - LABØR/JØB RATIØ PERCEIVED (DIMENSIØNLESS)
      LRPT - LABØR/JØB RATIØ PERCEPTIØN TIME (YEARS)
      LR   - LABØR/JØB RATIØ (DIMENSIØNLESS)

A.12 Urban-Development Programs

The following equations shown in Figure A-67 represent externally generated influences on the urban system that allow testing the influence of various externally supported efforts to improve the urban condition.

Equation 140 describes an underemployed-training program. The coefficient UTR, if set to a value other than the normal 0, gives the fraction of underemployed transferred to the labor category each year. The CLIP function allows the training program to be activated at any point during the simulation run. The function has a value of zero until TIME reaches the time set for the value SWT1. After that time the multiplier of 1 brings into existence the first two terms of the equation.

$$UTP.K = UTR*U.K*CLIP(0,1,SWT1,TIME.K) \hspace{2cm} 140,A$$

$$UTR = 0 \hspace{4cm} 140.1,C$$

$$SWT1 = 0 \hspace{4cm} 140.2,C$$

    UTP   — UNDEREMPLOYED-TRAINING PROGRAM (MEN/YEAR)
    UTR   — UNDEREMPLOYED-TRAINING RATE (FRACTION/YEAR)
    U   — UNDEREMPLOYED (MEN)
    SWT1 — SWITCH TIME 1 (YEARS)

A labor-training program is given in Equation 141 with the same format as the preceding equation.

$$LTPG.K = LTR*L.K*CLIP(0,1,SWT2,TIME.K) \hspace{2cm} 141,A$$

$$LTR = 0 \hspace{4cm} 141.1,C$$

$$SWT2 = 0 \hspace{4cm} 141.2,C$$

    LTPG — LABOR-TRAINING PROGRAM (MEN/YEAR)
    LTR   — LABOR-TRAINING RATE (FRACTION/YEAR)
    L   — LABOR (MEN)
    SWT2 — SWITCH TIME 2 (YEARS)

$$PHCP.K = PHCR*PH.K*PHLM.K*CLIP(0,1,SWT3,TIME.K) \hspace{1cm} 142,A$$

$$PHCR = 0 \hspace{4cm} 142.1,C$$

$$SWT3 = 0 \hspace{4cm} 142.2,C$$

    PHCP — PREMIUM-HOUSING-CONSTRUCTION PROGRAM
              (HOUSING UNITS/YEAR)
    PHCR — PREMIUM-HOUSING-CONSTRUCTION RATE
              (FRACTION/YEAR)
    PH   — PREMIUM HOUSING (HOUSING UNITS)
    PHLM — PREMIUM-HOUSING LAND MULTIPLIER
              (DIMENSIONLESS)
    SWT3 — SWITCH TIME 3 (YEARS)

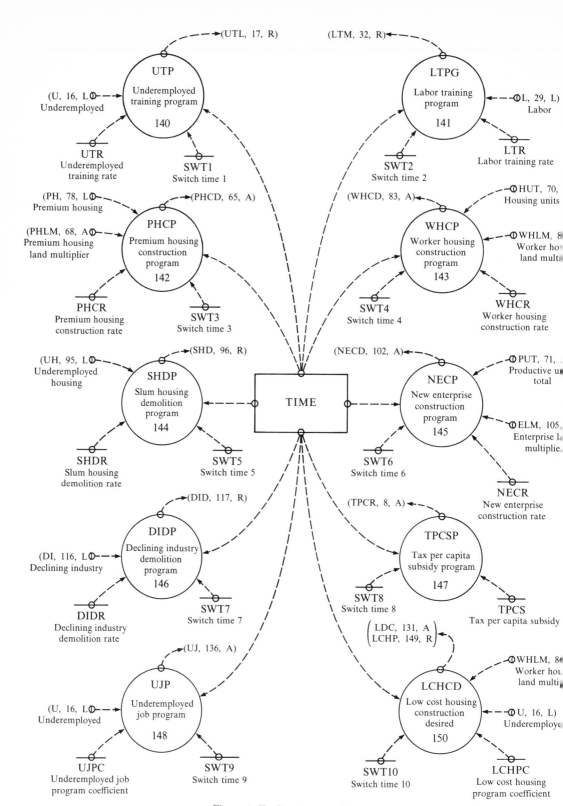

Figure A-67 Development Programs.

Equation 142 describes a premium-housing-construction program. It builds each year the fraction PHCR of the existing premium housing, multiplied by the premium-housing land multiplier PHLM from Equation 68 so that this equation cannot overfill the land area. The CLIP function again determines the time at which the program becomes effective.

The worker-housing-construction program in Equation 143 has the same form. It is set up in terms of a fraction of total housing units in the area.

$$\text{WHCP.K} = \text{WHCR} * \text{HUT.K} * \text{WHLM.K} * \text{CLIP}(0,1,\text{SWT4},\text{TIME.K}) \qquad 143,\text{A}$$

$$\text{WHCR} = 0 \qquad 143.1,\text{C}$$

$$\text{SWT4} = 0 \qquad 143.2,\text{C}$$

WHCP — WØRKER-HØUSING-CØNSTRUCTIØN PRØGRAM
(HØUSING UNITS/YEAR)
WHCR — WØRKER-HØUSING-CØNSTRUCTIØN RATE (FRACTIØN/
YEAR)
HUT — HØUSING UNITS TØTAL (HØUSING UNITS)
WHLM — WØRKER-HØUSING LAND MULTIPLIER
(DIMENSIØNLESS)
SWT4 — SWITCH TIME 4 (YEARS)

Equation 144 provides for a slum-housing-demolition program in which the coefficient SHDR determines the fraction per year of underemployed housing that will be removed from the system. SWT5 gives the time in which the coefficient changes from 0 to the new value.

$$\text{SHDP.K} = \text{SHDR} * \text{UH.K} * \text{CLIP}(0,1,\text{SWT5},\text{TIME.K}) \qquad 144,\text{A}$$

$$\text{SHDR} = 0 \qquad 144.1,\text{C}$$

$$\text{SWT5} = 0 \qquad 144.2,\text{C}$$

SHDP — SLUM-HØUSING-DEMØLITIØN PRØGRAM (HØUSING
UNITS/YEAR)
SHDR — SLUM-HØUSING-DEMØLITIØN RATE (FRACTIØN/
YEAR)
UH — UNDEREMPLØYED HØUSING (HØUSING UNITS)
SWT5 — SWITCH TIME 5 (YEARS)

In Equation 145 a forced construction of new enterprise can be generated. This is for the purpose of seeing what a new-enterprise-construction program would do for the system. It makes no provision for ways of creating the new enterprise except that, by entering through Equation 102 and thence to Equation 131, the construction does have its normal impact on the labor situation. The coefficient NECR gives the new-enterprise-construction rate as a fraction per year of total productive units. Actual construction from this program is modified by the enterprise land multiplier ELM which prevents overfilling of the land area.

$$NECP.K = NECR*PUT.K*ELM.K*CLIP(0,1,SWT6,TIME.K) \qquad 145,A$$

$$NECR = 0 \qquad 145.1,C$$

$$SWT6 = 0 \qquad 145.2,C$$

    NECP   – NEW-ENTERPRISE-CONSTRUCTION PROGRAM
             (PRODUCTIVE UNITS/YEAR)
    NECR   – NEW-ENTERPRISE-CONSTRUCTION RATE (FRACTION/
             YEAR)
    PUT   – PRODUCTIVE UNITS TOTAL (PRODUCTIVE UNITS)
    ELM   – ENTERPRISE LAND MULTIPLIER (DIMENSIONLESS)
    SWT6   – SWITCH TIME 6 (YEARS)

In a manner similar to that of Equation 144, Equation 146 provides a program for the demolition of the declining industry.

$$DIDP.K = DIDR*DI.K*CLIP(0,1,SWT7,TIME.K) \qquad 146,A$$

$$DIDR = 0 \qquad 146.1,C$$

$$SWT7 = 0 \qquad 146.2,C$$

    DIDP   – DECLINING-INDUSTRY-DEMOLITION PROGRAM
             (PRODUCTIVE UNITS/YEAR)
    DIDR   – DECLINING-INDUSTRY-DEMOLITION RATE
             (FRACTION/YEAR)
    DI   – DECLINING INDUSTRY (PRODUCTIVE UNITS)
    SWT7   – SWITCH TIME 7 (YEARS)

Equation 147 provides an externally supplied tax subsidy to the area. It enters the system through Equation 8 and affects area attractiveness and education, which influences upward mobility from underemployed to labor and from labor to managerial-professional. It does not directly operate to reduce taxes needed or the tax assessment.

$$TPCSP.K = TPCS*CLIP(0,1,SWT8,TIME.K) \qquad 147,A$$

$$TPCS = 0 \qquad 147.1,C$$

$$SWT8 = 0 \qquad 147.2,C$$

    TPCSP – TAX-PER-CAPITA-SUBSIDY PROGRAM (DOLLARS/
             PERSON/YEAR)
    TPCS   – TAX PER CAPITA SUBSIDY (DOLLARS/PERSON/
             YEAR)
    SWT8   – SWITCH TIME 8 (YEARS)

An underemployed-job program can be created through Equation 148, which provides jobs for a specified fraction of the underemployed.

Equations 149 and 150 generate a low-cost-housing program which creates construction directly into the category of underemployed housing. The fraction per year of the underemployed to be housed is entered in Equation 150. The

```
UJP.K=UJPC*U.K*CLIP(0,1,SWT9,TIME.K)                          148,A

UJPC=0                                                        148.1,C

SWT9=0                                                        148.2,C

    UJP    - UNDEREMPLØYED-JØB PRØGRAM (MEN)
    UJPC   - UNDEREMPLØYED-JØB-PRØGRAM CØEFFICIENT
             (DIMENSIØNLESS)
    U      - UNDEREMPLØYED (MEN)
    SWT9   - SWITCH TIME 9 (YEARS)


LCHP.KL=(LCHCD.K)(LCR.K)                                      149,R

    LCHP   - LØW-CØST-HØUSING PRØGRAM (HØUSING UNITS/
             YEAR)
    LCHCD  - LØW-CØST-HØUSING CØNSTRUCTIØN DESIRED
             (HØUSING UNITS/YEAR)
    LCR    - LABØR CØNSTRUCTIØN RATIØ (DIMENSIØNLESS)


LCHCD.K=LCHPC*U.K*WHLM.K*CLIP(0,1,SWT10,TIME.K)              150,A

LCHPC=0                                                       150.1,C

SWT10=0                                                       150.2,C

    LCHCD  - LØW-CØST-HØUSING CØNSTRUCTIØN DESIRED
             (HØUSING UNITS/YEAR)
    LCHPC  - LØW-CØST-HØUSING-PRØGRAM CØEFFICIENT
             (HØUSING UNITS/MAN/YEAR)
    U      - UNDEREMPLØYED (MEN)
    WHLM   - WØRKER-HØUSING LAND MULTIPLIER
             (DIMENSIØNLESS)
    SWT10  - SWITCH TIME 10 (YEARS)
```

worker-housing land multiplier operates at this point. Equation 149 modifies the result of Equation 150 in accordance with the available labor supply.

A.13   Simulation-Control Instructions

The following two constants specify the solution interval between successive evaluations of the system equations and the length in time of the simulation run.

```
DT=1                                                         151,C

LENGTH=250                                                   151.1,C
```

The following instruction controls the time interval between successive entries in the plotted graphs. The interval changes from the PLTMIN value to the PLTMAX value at the time specified by PLTCT. The values here give a plotting period of five years throughout the simulation run. If PLTMIN is set to 0, no plotting occurs until the transfer to PLTMAX. This, for example, is used for Figure 3-2. If both values are 0, the plotting is suppressed.

```
PLTPER.K=CLIP(PLTMIN,PLTMAX,PLTCT,TIME.K)                    152,A

PLTMIN=5                                                     152.1,C

PLTMAX=5                                                     152.2,C

PLTCT=500                                                    152.3,C
```

```
    PLTPER- PLØT PERIØD (YEARS)
    PLTMIN- PLØT PERIØD MINIMUM (YEARS)
    PLTMAX- PLØT PERIØD MAXIMUM (YEARS)
    PLTCT - PLØT-PERIØD CHANGE TIME (YEARS)
```

In the same manner the following instructions control the minimum interval between printed results, the maximum interval, the time of change over, and the ability to suppress printing by setting both intervals to 0.

```
PRTPER.K=CLIP(PRTMIN,PRTMAX,PRTCT,TIME.K)                    153,A

PRTMIN=50                                                    153.1,C

PRTMAX=100                                                   153.2,C

PRTCT=160                                                    153.3,C
```

```
    PRTPER- PRINT PERIØD (YEARS)
    PRTMIN- PRINT PERIØD MINIMUM (YEARS)
    PRTMAX- PRINT PERIØD MAXIMUM (YEARS)
    PRTCT - PRINT-PERIØD CHANGE TIME (YEARS)
```

Equation 154 is not active in the system. It is a supplementary equation "S" used only for generating values that are to be printed or plotted.

```
UTLN.K=UTL.JK-LTU.JK                                        154,S
```

```
    UTLN  - UNDEREMPLØYED TØ LABØR NET (MEN/YEAR)
    UTL   - UNDEREMPLØYED TØ LABØR (MEN/YEAR)
    LTU   - LABØR TØ UNDEREMPLØYED (MEN/YEAR)
```

In addition to the preceding active equations and control cards, the complete model contains instructions for the variables to be printed and plotted on lines 154.3 through 156.5 as given at the end of the model tabulation in Appendix E.

A.14   The Equilibrium Model

In most of the computer simulation results in this book, the urban area is examined over an interval of 50 years starting from the equilibrium condition that existed at the end of the life cycle shown in Figure 3-1. The equilibrium model is identical to the growth model described in this Appendix except for the constants that describe the initial conditions. Following are the line numbers and modified values used to give system equilibrium as a beginning point for simulations that examine how the urban area would be changed by modified policies or conditions.

2.1	AMMP	= .449	77.3	PHGRI	= 0
16.1	U	= 377310	78.1	PH	= 110940
20.1	UTLP	= 16847	81.1	WH	= 335650
22.1	UMMP	= .802	92.3	WHGRI	= 0
29.1	L	= 392550	95.1	UH	= 310080
33.1	LMMP	= .464	100.1	NE	= 4866
42.1	LAMP	= .625	110.3	NEGRI	= 0
52.1	MP	= 71130	113.1	MB	= 7806
54.1	MAMP	= .307	116.1	DI	= 16474
			139.1	LRP	= .973

B Miscellaneous

This appendix contains several computer simulation runs and miscellaneous commentary on systems which will be of interest to some readers but which do not fit in the primary chapters of the book.

B.1 Political Power

The urban model in this book is aggregated to such a high level that many of the urban processes are combined into rather general system parameters. But this does not mean that the model need be ineffective in exploring special questions. Very often a careful examination of an aggregate model leads one to those parameters that represent the conditions of interest. As an example of such a process, we might ask how political influence on tax and expenditure policies of a city might affect the urban condition.

Appendix A (in Section A.10, Tax Sector) contains two places where political considerations are reflected in the parameters of the urban model. Table TRT, Equation 122.1 (shown in Figure A-62) relates the tax rate needed to the tax actually levied. Up to a tax ratio of 1 to 1 compared to the outside environment, the tax levied has been assumed equal to the tax needed. But at higher values of tax need, the actual tax levied falls below the need to reflect a public reluctance and the political infeasibility of raising taxes to the rates needed to finance city operations. For example, in Figure A-62, when the tax ratio needed TRNP rises to 4 times that in the outside environment, the tax ratio actually levied reaches only 2.8 times that outside.

Figure A-63 shows another political relationship. The tax-collection multiplier influences the taxes needed TN in Equation 126 to represent the political influence of the underemployed population. As the labor/underemployed ratio LUR decreases, the underemployed become more and more dominant. Figure A-63 implies that as the underemployed population gains influence the taxes needed TN are raised above the normal. This reflects voting power in a population that needs tax expenditures and can vote for them yet pays a disproportionately small shares of the taxes.

218

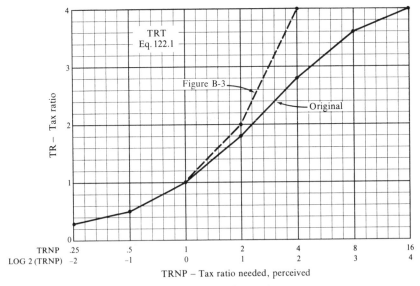

Figure B-1

In the next model simulation Figures A-62 and A-63 have been changed (as shown in Figures B-1 and B-2). In the equations of Appendix A and Appendix E these changes are:

$$TRT = .3/.5/1/2/4/8/16 \qquad 122.1, T$$
$$TCMT = 3.8/2.8/2/1.4/1/.9/.8 \qquad 127.1, T$$

In Figure B-1 the tax ratio TR is made equal to the tax ratio needed perceived TRNP, even at high values of need.

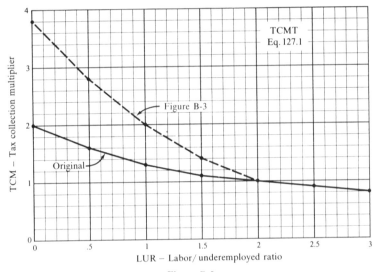

Figure B-2

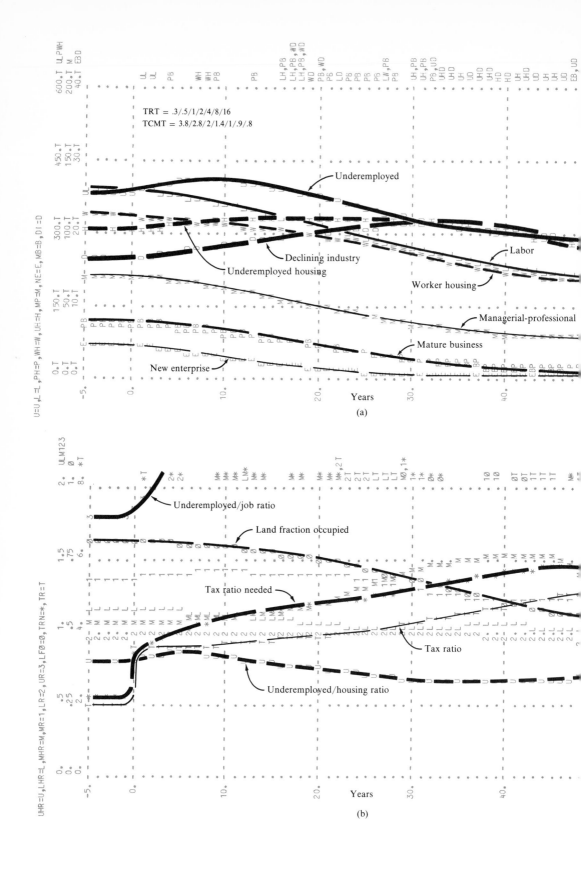

TRT = .3/.5/1/2/4/8/16
TCMT = 3.8/2.8/2/1.4/1/.9/.8

Underemployed

Declining industry

Underemployed housing

Labor

Worker housing

Managerial-professional

Mature business

New enterprise

Years

(a)

Underemployed/job ratio

Land fraction occupied

Tax ratio needed

Tax ratio

Underemployed/housing ratio

Years

(b)

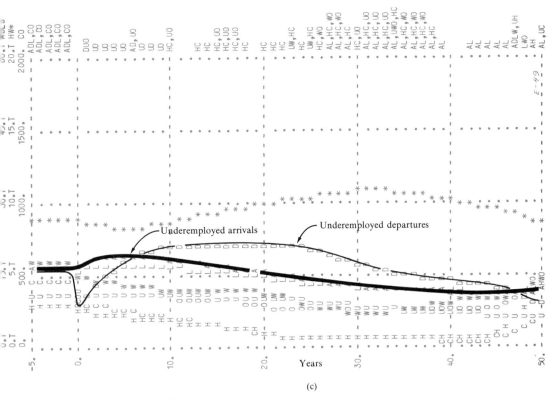

(c)

Figure B-3   Greater political power of the underemployed as expressed in higher tax rate.

In Figure B-2 political influence of the underemployed has been increased toward the left side of the graph where they dominate the voting population.

The results of these two changes appear in Figures B-3*a, b, c,* and *d*. Figure B-3*a* shows that all activity declines as the higher tax rate depresses new construction and availability of jobs. Figure B-3*b* shows the rising tax rate, the rising underemployed/job ratio, and the decrease in land fraction occupied from .82 to .56, indicating a 32% decline in occupied land.

Figure B-4 gives the changes in the most interesting system variables as a result of this assumption of more taxing power exercised by the underemployed. Declining industry shows a rise, but this is still changing, as seen in Figure B-3*a* where declining industry rises for 30 years and then starts to fall. The tax ratio needed rises 156% over the 50-year interval. The underemployed/job ratio becomes more unfavorable by rising 24%. Underemployed population declines but by only half as much as do other population classes. The power to levy higher taxes never succeeds in outrunning the shrinking tax base and declining construction, which reduces jobs. The short-term effort by the underemployed to improve their condition by raising taxes is, in this example, self-defeating throughout the 50 years.

TIME	AV	MB	U	#	AMM	LAJM	LSM	MSM	SHLM	UMM
	DI	MBD	UA	2	AMMP	LAM	LUM	NEGR	TCM	UMMP
	DID	MD	UD	3	BDM	LAMP	LUR	PEM	TPCR	UR
	DIDP	MP	UH	4	DIDM	LATM	MAHM	PHAM	TR	WHAM
	L	NE	UJ	5	DIEM	LAUM	MAJM	PHEM	TRN	WHEM
	LA	NEC	UJP	6	DILM	LCR	MAM	PHGM	UAMM	WHGM
	LCHP	NECP	UTL	7	EDM	LDM	MAMP	PHGR	UDM	WHGR
	LD	P	UTLN	8	EGM	LEM	MAPM	PHLM	UEM	WHLM
	LDC	PH	UTP	9	ELJM	LFØ	MATM	PHM	UFW	WHM
	LDI	PHC	UW	10	ELM	LHR	MDM	PHØM	UHM	WHØM
	LJ	PHCP	WH	11	EM	LLF	MHR	PHPM	UHPR	WHTM
	LTM	PHØ	WHC	12	EMM	LMM	MLM	PHTM	UHR	WHUM
	LTU	SHD	WHCP	13	ETM	LMMP	MLR	SHAM	UJM	
	MA	SHDP	WHØ	14	LAHM	LR	MR	SHDM	UM	

thousands				units					

TIME	AV	MB	U	#	AMM	LAJM	LSM	MSM	SHLM	UMM
-5.	16336.	7.806	377.31	1	.452	1.087	1.054	.344	1.060	.805
	16.474	.465	17.283	2	.449	.623	.712	.000	1.284	.802
	.464	4.849	17.275	3	1.190	.625	1.040	1.145	1.121	1.811
	.000	71.13	310.08	4	.939	.854	.931	1.549	1.966	1.542
	392.55	4.866	208.35	5	.886	.808	.296	1.000	2.248	1.000
	7.360	.462	.00	6	1.060	.878	.306	1.000	.936	1.000
	.000	.000	16.847	7	1.190	1.681	.307	.000	2.289	.000
	13.201	5729.4	5.497	8	1.000	1.073	1.300	.625	1.073	.625
	24.38	110.94	.000	9	.935	.815	.854	1.075	.557	.665
	379.15	3.142	210.06	10	.655	1.170	3.408	.948	1.529	1.352
	403.53	.000	335.65	11	.768	.029	1.069	1.300	.000	.854
	3.643	3.155	5.885	12	1.556	.466	1.262	.854	.811	.808
	11.349	9.054	.000	13	.805	.464	.181	1.378	.276	
	.655	.000	9.075	14	.830	.973	1.380	1.460	.045	
10.	14527.	6.803	407.51	1	.414	.990	.995	.298	1.000	.921
	18.533	.545	18.476	2	.482	.467	.641	-.044	2.189	.917
	.351	5.785	20.717	3	1.602	.554	.882	2.181	1.863	2.288
	.000	61.77	327.50	4	.632	.719	.893	1.854	3.672	1.410
	359.29	2.853	178.10	5	.632	.753	.265	.647	4.387	.868
	5.967	.210	.00	6	1.000	.902	.221	.894	.902	.970
	.000	.000	16.849	7	1.602	2.192	.260	-.013	2.542	-.004
	15.754	5724.7	5.933	8	.647	1.445	1.300	.732	1.445	.732
	13.32	93.03	.000	9	.991	.795	.719	.733	.451	.478
	344.43	1.845	183.80	10	.714	1.128	4.683	1.447	1.477	1.626
	357.75	.000	318.53	11	.395	.031	1.107	1.300	.000	.719
	3.706	4.038	4.115	12	1.602	.535	1.244	.719	.830	.765
	10.995	8.783	.000	13	.538	.516	.172	1.341	.142	*w 49*
	.481	.000	10.357	14	.872	1.004	1.418	1.341	.042	
50.	8065.	.931	285.82	1	.675	1.252	1.158	.457	1.000	1.030
	18.452	.055	11.503	2	.460	.528	.574	.012	2.402	.940
	.494	2.903	8.951	3	1.180	.485	.748	2.789	2.243	2.249
	.000	29.35	269.51	4	.892	.627	.766	2.870	5.169	1.123
	213.93	.626	127.11	5	.892	.699	.371	1.100	5.747	1.025
	3.112	.216	.00	6	1.000	.837	.212	1.030	.902	.915
	.000	.000	12.294	7	1.180	1.920	.167	.004	1.566	-.011
	8.213	3716.9	6.254	8	1.100	1.549	1.187	1.845	1.549	1.845
	21.23	39.65	.000	9	.893	.555	.627	4.461	.458	.882
	211.02	4.442	130.83	10	1.345	1.038	4.945	.285	1.786	1.108
	232.24	.000	206.03	11	.779	.027	1.234	1.187	.000	.627
	3.385	.339	4.563	12	1.443	.812	1.149	.627	.707	.725
	5.743	8.549	.000	13	.409	.791	.137	1.586	.150	*w 49*
	.147	.000	4.567	14	.962	.921	1.286	1.586	.042	

(d)

Figure B-3 (cont.)

Variable	Symbol	Time (years)		Change (%)
		−5	50	
1. New enterprise	NE	4,900	626	−87.
2. Mature business	MB	7,800	930	−88.
3. Declining industry	DI	16,500	18,450	+12.
4. Premium housing	PH	110,900	39,600	−64.
5. Worker housing	WH	335,600	206,000	−38.
6. Underemployed housing	UH	310,100	269,500	−13.
7. Managerial-professional	MP	71,100	29,400	−59.
8. Labor	L	392,600	213,900	−45.
9. Underemployed	U	377,300	285,800	−24.
10. Manager/housing ratio	MHR	1.07	1.23	+15.
11. Labor/housing ratio	LHR	1.17	1.04	−11.
12. Underemployed/housing ratio	UHR	.81	.71	−12.
13. Manager/job ratio	MR	1.38	1.29	−7.
14. Labor/job ratio	LR	.97	.92	−5.
15. Underemployed/job ratio	UR	1.81	2.25	+24.
16. Tax ratio needed	TRN	2.25	5.75	+156.
17. Underemployed to labor net	UTLN	5,500	6,300	+15.

Figure B-4 Changes caused by greater political power of the underemployed resulting in higher taxes.

B.2 Negative Income Tax

How would the city be affected by a form of income maintenance such as the negative income tax for those people whose income falls below an arbitrarily established minimum? Proposals for the negative income tax suggest that such a substitute for present forms of welfare would reduce the migration of low-income groups to the city.

The actual effect of a minimum income would seem to depend on how the attractiveness components are arranged in the urban areas and in the surrounding environment. In other words, what areas are made more attractive by a negative-income-tax dollar flow to the underemployed? Attractiveness might be expected

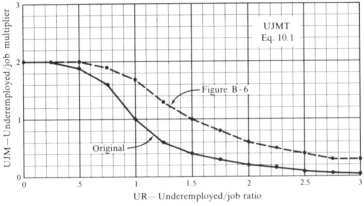

Figure B-5

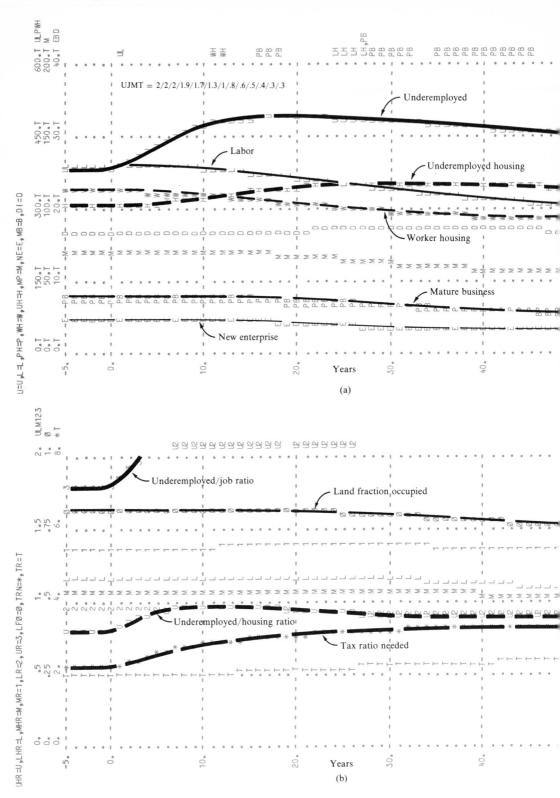

UJMT = 2/2/2/1.9/1.7/1.7/1.3/1/.8/.6/.5/.4/.3/.3

Underemployed

Labor

Underemployed housing

Worker housing

Mature business

New enterprise

(a)

Underemployed/job ratio

Land fraction occupied

Underemployed/housing ratio

Tax ratio needed

(b)

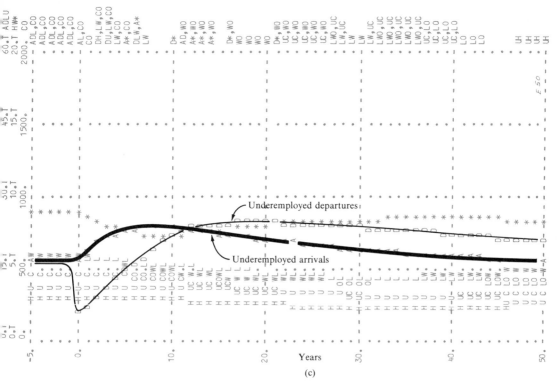

Figure B-6 Less sensitivity by the underemployed to a shortage of jobs.

to increase most in those areas where economic opportunity is the most unfavorable characteristic of the area. Consider two contrasting areas in equilibrium with each other and therefore having the same total composite attractiveness. Area A has favorable job and economic opportunities but unfavorable housing and unfavorable prejudice and ethnic factors. Area B has favorable housing opportunities and ethnic-group attractiveness but very unfavorable job and economic conditions. If an outside source of income is made available in both areas, it should enhance the attractiveness of Area B more than Area A.

The stagnant urban area is equivalent to Area B. Its primary unattractive feature that creates attractiveness balance with other areas is lack of income. In most other ways it is relatively attractive. The negative income tax might, therefore, cause a shift in the underemployed/job multiplier of a stagnant urban area (as shown in Figure B-5). The new (dotted) curve for the table UJMT says that lack of jobs is no longer so important; there is another source of income. Toward the right in Figure B-5 the new underemployed/job multiplier UJM does not fall as rapidly when the underemployed population begins to exceed job opportunities.

The change in Figure B-5 has been introduced at time $= 0$ in Figure B-6. Figure B-6a shows an increase of underemployed and underemployed housing while most other system level variables decrease. In Figure B-6b the major

TIME	AV	MB	U		AMM	LAJM	LSM	MSM	SHLM	UMM
	AV	MB	U	1	AMM	LAJM	LSM	MSM	SHLM	UMM
	DI	MBD	UA	2	AMMP	LAM	LUM	NEGR	TCM	UMMP
	DID	MD	UD	3	BDM	LAMP	LUR	PEM	TPCR	UR
	DI DP	MP	UH	4	DI DM	LATM	MAHM	PHAM	TR	WHAM
	L	NE	UJ	5	DI EM	LAUM	MAJM	PHEM	TRN	WHEM
	LA	NEC	UJP	6	DI LM	LCR	MAM	PHGM	UAMM	WHGM
	LCHP	NECP	UTL	7	EDM	LDM	MAMP	PHGR	UDM	WHGR
	LD	P	UTLN	8	EGM	LEM	MAPM	PHLM	UEM	WHLM
	LDC	PH	UTP	9	ELJM	LFØ	MATM	PHM	UFW	WHM
	LDI	PHC	UW	10	ELM	LHR	MDM	PHØM	UHM	WHØM
	LJ	PHCP	WH	11	EM	LLF	MHR	PHPM	UHPR	WH TM
	LTM	PHØ	WHC	12	EMM	LMM	MLM	PHTM	UHR	WHUM
	LTU	SHD	WHCP	13	ETM	LMMP	MLR	SHAM	UJM	
	MA	SHDP	WHØ	14	LAHM	LR	MR	SHDM	UM	

	thousands				units					
-5.	16336.	7.806	377.31	1	.452	1.087	1.054	.344	1.060	.805
	16.474	.465	17.283	2	.449	.623	.712	.000	1.284	.802
	.464	4.849	17.275	3	1.190	.625	1.040	1.145	1.121	1.811
	.000	71.13	310.08	4	.939	.854	.931	1.549	1.966	1.542
	392.55	4.866	208.35	5	.886	.808	.296	1.000	2.248	1.000
	7.360	.462	.00	6	1.060	.878	.306	1.000	.936	1.000
	.000	.000	16.847	7	1.190	1.681	.307	.000	2.289	.000
	13.201	5729.4	5.497	8	1.000	1.073	1.300	.625	1.073	.625
	24.38	110.94	.000	9	.935	.815	.854	1.075	.557	.665
	379.15	3.142	210.06	10	.655	1.170	3.408	.948	1.529	1.352
	403.53	.000	335.65	11	.768	.029	1.069	1.300	.000	.854
	3.643	3.155	5.885	12	1.556	.466	1.262	.854	.811	.808
	11.349	9.054	.000	13	.805	.464	.181	1.378	.276	
	.655	.000	9.075	14	.830	.973	1.380	1.460	.045	
10.	16185.	7.771	472.29	1	.445	1.113	1.071	.341	1.081	.657
	16.530	.480	23.622	2	.551	.568	.607	-.002	1.412	.742
	.460	4.877	22.009	3	1.236	.608	.814	1.022	1.019	2.273
	.000	70.49	324.14	4	.928	.848	.928	1.574	2.026	1.546
	384.41	4.731	207.75	5	.858	.726	.294	.981	2.874	.993
	7.011	.426	.00	6	1.081	.872	.301	.992	.822	.986
	.000	.000	15.898	7	1.236	1.815	.305	-.001	2.330	-.002
	13.951	6437.2	5.018	8	.981	1.011	1.300	.599	1.011	.599
	22.06	109.63	.000	9	.927	.820	.848	1.011	.454	.572
	376.48	2.898	214.20	10	.639	1.170	3.459	.992	1.080	1.483
	398.54	.000	328.42	11	.720	.029	1.072	1.300	.000	.848
	3.508	3.263	4.909	12	1.559	.437	1.267	.848	.971	.744
	10.987	7.409	.000	13	.795	.456	.183	1.057	.491	E_{50}
	.646	.000	9.742	14	.830	.965	1.382	1.143	.035	
50.	13591.	5.515	453.75	1	.451	1.240	1.150	.355	1.000	.668
	16.721	.337	17.119	2	.449	.612	.541	-.002	1.491	.657
	.435	3.811	20.789	3	1.221	.588	.681	1.149	1.124	2.490
	.000	55.68	341.12	4	.867	.812	.977	1.183	2.384	1.310
	309.22	3.218	182.23	5	.867	.673	.304	.987	3.296	.995
	5.458	.339	.00	6	1.000	.840	.305	.980	.738	.986
	.000	.000	12.419	7	1.221	1.707	.296	-.003	2.291	-.002
	10.559	5763.7	4.046	8	.987	1.075	1.265	.948	1.075	.948
	20.04	90.72	.000	9	.826	.765	.812	1.114	.417	.697
	314.29	2.546	189.08	10	.806	1.097	3.422	.922	1.317	1.312
	334.33	.000	281.88	11	.735	.027	1.023	1.265	.000	.812
	2.818	2.511	4.950	12	1.545	.481	1.260	.812	.887	.704
	8.348	8.367	.000	13	.725	.456	.180	1.226	.404	E_{50}
	.494	.000	7.396	14	.903	.925	1.371	1.226	.028	

(d)

Figure B-6 (cont.)

Variable	Symbol	Time (years)		Change (%)
		−5	50	
1. New enterprise	NE	4,900	3,200	−35.
2. Mature business	MB	7,800	5,500	−30.
3. Declining industry	DI	16,500	16,700	+1.
4. Premium housing	PH	110,900	90,700	−18.
5. Worker housing	WH	335,600	281,900	−16.
6. Underemployed housing	UH	310,100	341,100	+10.
7. Managerial-professional	MP	71,100	55,700	−22.
8. Labor	L	392,600	309,200	−21.
9. Underemployed	U	377,300	453,800	+20.
10. Manager/housing ratio	MHR	1.07	1.02	−5.
11. Labor/housing ratio	LHR	1.17	1.10	−6.
12. Underemployed/housing ratio	UHR	.81	.89	+10.
13. Manager/job ratio	MR	1.38	1.37	−1.
14. Labor/job ratio	LR	.97	.92	−5.
15. Underemployed/job ratio	UR	1.81	2.49	+38.
16. Tax ratio needed	TRN	2.25	3.30	+47.
17. Underemployed to labor net	UTLN	5,500	4,050	−26.

Figure B-7 Changes caused by less sensitivity by the underemployed to a shortage of jobs.

changes are a rise in the underemployed/job ratio and the tax ratio needed. Land fraction occupied declines slightly from .82 to .76. In Figure B-6c underemployed arrivals increase initially while departures drop and then rise. After the tenth year departures exceed arrivals.

Figure B-7 shows substantial decline in new enterprise, mature business, premium housing, worker housing, managerial-professional population, and labor population. There are increases in underemployed housing, underemployed, underemployed/housing ratio, underemployed/job ratio, and tax rate needed. The area becomes a less effective socioeconomic converter for raising the economic level of the underemployed, as indicated by the 26% reduction in UTLN.

B.3 Parameter Sensitivity

Earlier chapters have stated that complex systems are surprisingly insensitive to changes in parameters (the constants and table functions that describe the relationships within the system). But sensitivity to parameters differs in amount and in kind. The system can be insensitive, in any sense and degree, to some parameters. To others, the system may show sensitivity of one type but not of another type.

In examining sensitivity of a system to changes in parameters, we should consider three classifications of a parameter:

1. Does it affect either the growth, stability, or equilibrium conditions of the system?

2. Can it be controlled?

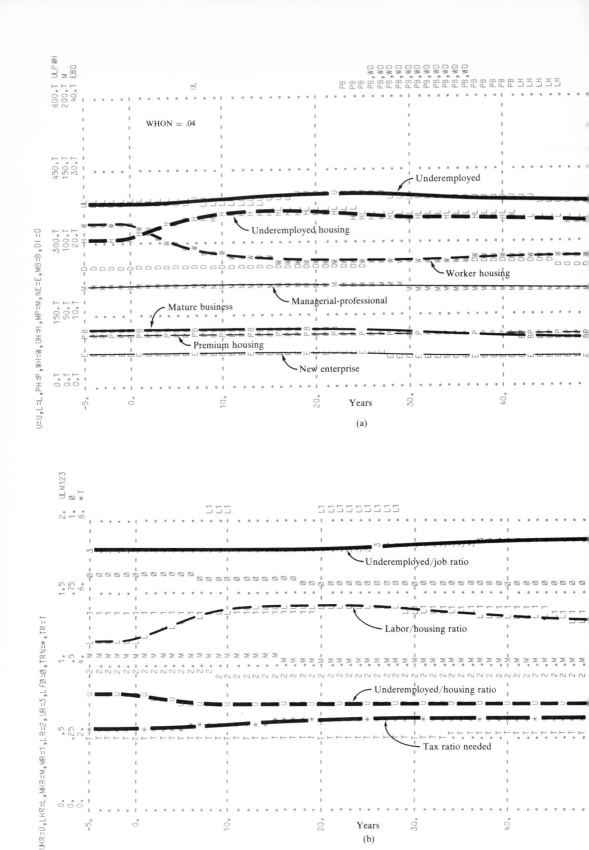

(a)

(b)

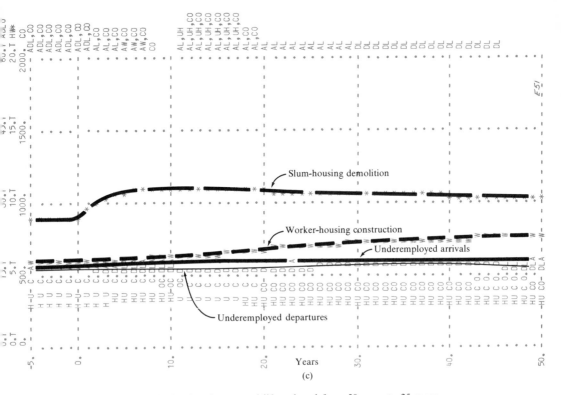

Figure B-8 Worker-housing normal life reduced from 50 years to 25 years.

3. Does a change in it affect the selection or use of those other parameters or structural modifications that are to be employed to improve the system?

With regard to the first classification, many parameters have little effect on any aspect of the system. One example is given later where the average age of worker housing is halved; another example will show that the system is not highly sensitive to the assumptions made about the employment densities in the various business units and the population densities in the housing units.

With regard to the second classification, we are most interested in that subclass of parameters that do affect the system condition *and* that can be changed or controlled. We usually search for ways to alter the undesirable characteristics of a system. Very often the most significant changes come from changes in structure, but with regard to parameter values we search for those showing sensitivity (by the test in classification 1 above) and, among these, the ones that can be controlled (by the test in classification 2 above). Examples of this subclass were examined in Chapter 5. A sensitive parameter that *cannot* be controlled (and often cannot even be measured) is of no interest unless it represents a hazard by falling on the wrong side of classification 3 above.

In the third classification, we examine sensitive parameters to see if they affect

TIME	AV	MB	U		AMM	LAJM	LSM	MSM	SHLM	UMM
	DI	MBD	UA	2	AMMP	LAM	LUM	NEGR	TCM	UMMP
	DID	MD	UD	3	BDM	LAMP	LUR	PEM	TPCR	UR
	DIDP	MP	UH	4	DIDM	LATM	MAHM	PHAM	TR	WHAM
	L	NE	UJ	5	DIEM	LAUM	MAJM	PHEM	TRN	WHEM
	LA	NEC	UJP	6	DILM	LCR	MAM	PHGM	UAMM	WHGM
	LCHP	NECP	UTL	7	EDM	LDM	MAMP	PHGR	UDM	WHGR
	LD	P	UTLN	8	EGM	LEM	MAPM	PHLM	UEM	WHLM
	LDC	PH	UTP	9	ELJM	LFØ	MATM	PHM	UFW	WHM
	LDI	PHC	UW	10	ELM	LHR	MDM	PHØM	UHM	WHØM
	LJ	PHCP	WH	11	EM	LLF	MHR	PHPM	UHPR	WHTM
	LTM	PHØ	WHC	12	EMM	LMM	MLM	PHTM	UHR	WHUM
	LTU	SHD	WHCP	13	ETM	LMMP	MLR	SHAM	UJM	
	MA	SHDP	WHØ	14	LAHM	LR	MR	SHDM	UM	
		thousands					units			

	AV	MB	U		AMM	LAJM	LSM	MSM	SHLM	UMM
-5.	16336.	7.806	377.31	1	.452	1.087	1.054	.344	1.060	.805
	16.474	.465	17.283	2	.449	.623	.712	.000	1.284	.802
	.464	4.849	17.275	3	1.190	.625	1.040	1.145	1.121	1.811
	.000	71.13	310.08	4	.939	.854	.931	1.549	1.966	1.542
	392.55	4.866	208.35	5	.886	.808	.296	1.000	2.248	1.000
	7.360	.462	.00	6	1.060	.878	.306	1.000	.936	1.000
	.000	.000	16.847	7	1.190	1.681	.307	.000	2.289	.000
	13.201	5729.4	5.497	8	1.000	1.073	1.300	.625	1.073	.625
	24.38	110.94	.000	9	.935	.815	.854	1.075	.557	.665
	379.15	3.142	210.06	10	.655	1.170	3.408	.948	1.529	1.352
	403.53	.000	335.65	11	.768	.029	1.069	1.300	.000	.854
	3.643	3.155	5.885	12	1.556	.466	1.262	.854	.811	.808
	11.349	9.054	.000	13	.805	.464	.181	1.378	.276	
	.655	.000	9.075	14	.830	.973	1.380	1.460	.045	
10.	15710.	7.796	388.85	1	.496	1.182	1.113	.350	1.012	.807
	16.509	.461	17.824	2	.463	.498	.691	-.000	1.311	.802
	.446	4.752	15.698	3	1.183	.585	.982	1.097	1.081	1.799
	.000	70.91	355.49	4	.901	.852	.941	1.475	1.981	2.102
	381.84	4.865	216.19	5	.890	.793	.300	1.000	2.411	1.000
	6.698	.455	.00	6	1.012	.855	.312	1.004	.925	.900
	.000	.000	17.484	7	1.183	2.005	.308	.000	2.019	-.012
	15.312	5756.3	6.709	8	1.000	1.049	1.300	.685	1.049	.685
	25.48	111.56	.000	9	.901	.803	.852	1.124	.560	.878
	379.33	3.215	217.91	10	.691	1.376	3.351	.916	1.742	1.112
	404.81	.000	277.56	11	.776	.028	1.059	1.300	.000	.852
	3.542	3.065	6.250	12	1.550	.466	1.271	.852	.729	.795
	10.588	11.089	.000	13	.803	.464	.186	1.542	.281	*E/51*
	.655	.000	12.347	14	.624	.943	1.375	1.560	.044	
50.	14772.	6.823	382.47	1	.478	1.227	1.142	.344	1.000	.814
	16.812	.403	17.508	2	.476	.547	.662	.000	1.346	.809
	.449	4.321	16.259	3	1.182	.528	.923	1.154	1.128	1.855
	.000	65.13	344.36	4	.891	.840	.978	1.174	2.102	1.943
	353.06	4.184	206.15	5	.891	.769	.296	1.003	2.534	1.001
	5.593	.414	.00	6	1.000	.843	.316	.989	.934	1.006
	.000	.000	16.810	7	1.182	1.869	.311	-.001	2.126	.001
	13.199	5503.8	7.220	8	1.003	1.077	1.300	.869	1.077	.869
	25.84	106.23	.000	9	.827	.776	.840	1.105	.543	1.110
	354.15	2.970	207.84	10	.773	1.310	3.317	.928	1.719	.955
	379.99	.000	269.56	11	.777	.027	1.022	1.300	.000	.840
	3.223	2.957	7.571	12	1.556	.470	1.269	.840	.740	.777
	9.591	10.462	.000	13	.779	.456	.184	1.519	.258	*E/51*
	.608	.000	10.296	14	.690	.929	1.380	1.519	.045	

(d)

Figure B-8 (cont.)

the validity of proposed policy changes. If a particular policy change always produces improvement, regardless of changes in a sensitive parameter, then the policy recommendation is not affected. The sensitive parameter might affect the absolute desirability of the final system but not the relative desirability of new versus old management policies. In other words, we may be confident that the new policies are better than the old even in the face of system parameters that are sensitive, uncontrollable, and even unmeasurable. Several examples are given later. One example shows that the detrimental changes produced by the new job multiplier in Figure B-5 as affecting Figures B-6 and B-7 still leave a system that can be markedly improved by the same policy changes regarding slum demolition and industry attraction that were examined in Figure 5-16.

We now turn to examples of various types of sensitivity.

Insensitive Parameters. Figure B-8 illustrates the urban-system insensitivity to many of the parameter values that have been assumed in the simulation model. Here the urban area starts in the condition of equilibrium stagnation as in earlier chapters. At time $= 0$ the worker-housing obsolescence normal WHON has been changed from .02 to .04 in Equation 93.1. This means that the normal life of a structure in the worker-housing category has been changed from 50 years to 25 years. Figure B-8 shows rather small change. In Figure B-8*a* worker housing has declined 20%; in Figure B-8*b* the labor/housing ratio has increased 12%; and in Figure B-8*c* worker-housing construction WHC has increased 29%. Otherwise the system has changed very little.

Policy Not Affected. Next is an example where a sensitive parameter (classification 1) does not affect the recommendation of policies that improve the system behavior (classification 3). Here the revival policies from Figure 5-16, which include slum demolition and encouragement of new industry, are initiated in the system at year 50 of Figure B-6 after the more depressed condition of stagnation has been created by the changed underemployed/job multiplier of Figure B-5. In other words, Figures B-6 and B-7 showed the equilibrium condition of the urban area to be rather sensitive to the change in the underemployed/job multiplier table in Figure 5. With the changed table the condition of the urban area became more depressed, as shown by Figures B-6 and B-7. The question is: Will the revival policies that were favorable in Figure 5-16 still produce improvement when applied to the modified system? One way to answer the question is to generate the conditions at the end of Figure B-6 and at that point in time initiate the revival policies. This will be done by "moving" Figure B-6 backward 50 years in time. The computation starts at $-$ 50 years with the standard equilibrium conditions used in Chapters 4 and 5, introduces at that $-$ 50-year point the changed curve of Figure B-5, computes the changes to reach the new state of depressed stagnation at time $= 0$ (corresponding to time $= 50$ in Figure B-6), alters the slum-

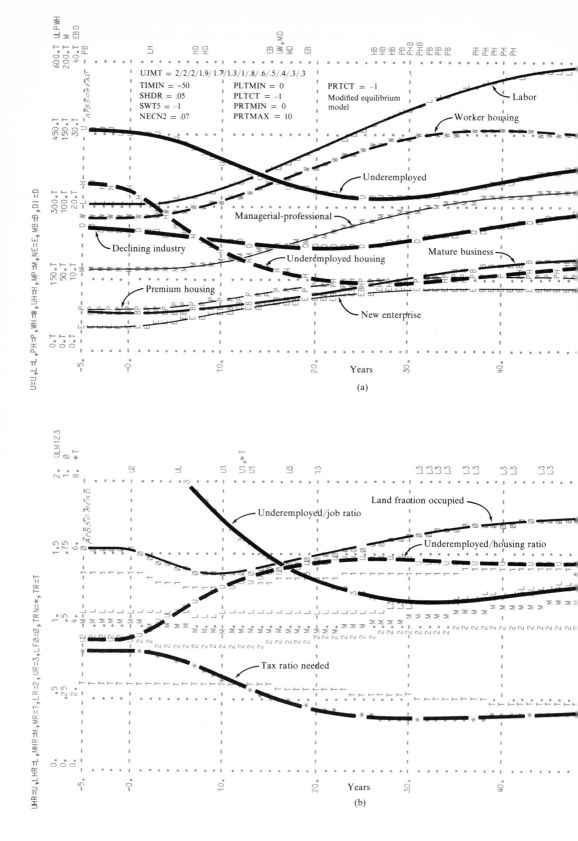

(a)

(b)

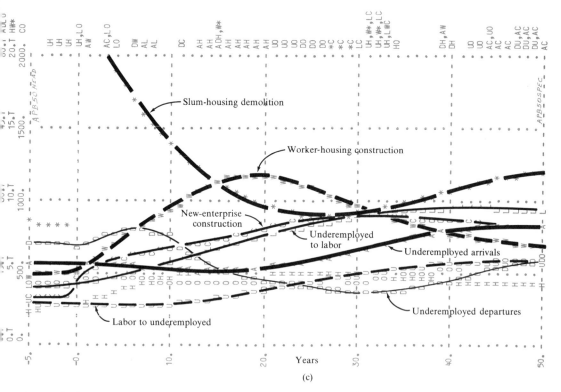

Figure B-9 Revival policies applied to system when underemployed are less sensitive to a shortage of jobs.

demolition and new-enterprise policies at time = 0, and then computes system changes for another 50 years.* (This is done in Figure B-9.)

Figure B-9 shows how the policies of Figure 5-16 revive the system from the more depressed equilibrium reached at the end of Figure B-6. The changes that

*To control the urban model in this manner requires the following changes and additions starting with original Equation 102 and ending before original Equation 103.

```
101.3   NØTE   **************************************************************
101.4   NØTE   THE FØLLØWING CHANGES ARE FØR SPECIAL RUNS IN APPENDIX B.
101.5   NØTE   **************************************************************
102     A      NECD.K=(NECN.K)(NECF*NE.K+MBCF*MB.K+DICF*DI.K)(EM.K)+NECP.K
102.1   C      NECF=1
102.2   C      MBCF=.5
102.3   C      DICF=.3
103     A      NECN.K=CLIP(NECN1,NECN2,SWT11,TIME.K)
103.1   C      NECN1=.05
103.2   C      NECN2=.05
103.3   C      SWT11=-1
103.4   N      TIME=TIMIN
103.5   C      TIMIN=0
103.8   NØTE   **************************************************************
```

These changes leave the model in its previous operating condition but provide the controls that allow the special model runs used in this appendix. Line 102 is modified to make NECN a variable. Lines 103 through 103.3 provide the switching between two values of NECN. Lines 103.4 and 103.5 permit a choice of the initial value of TIME, the internal independent variable within the DYNAMO compiler. The slum-demolition policy is already controllable in time through lines 144.1 and 144.2 in the original model (see Appendixes A and E).

TIME	AV	MB	U		AMM	LAJM	LSM	MSM	SHLM	UMM
	DI	MBD	UA	2	AMMP	LAM	LUM	NEGR	TCM	UMMP
	DI D	MD	UD	3	BDM	LAMP	LUR	PEM	TPCR	UR
	DI DP	MP	UH	4	DI DM	LATM	MAHM	PHAM	TR	WHAM
	L	NE	UJ	5	DI EM	LAUM	MAJM	PHEM	TRN	WHEM
	LA	NEC	UJP	6	DI LM	LCR	MAM	PHGM	UAMM	WHGM
	LCHP	NECP	UTL	7	EDM	LDM	MAMP	PHGR	UDM	WHGR
	LD	P	UTLN	8	EGM	LEM	MAPM	PHLM	UEM	WHLM
	LDC	PH	UTP	9	ELJM	LFØ	MATM	PHM	UFW	WHM
	LDI	PHC	UW	10	ELM	LHR	MDM	PHØM	UHM	WHØM
	LJ	PHCP	WH	11	EM	LLF	MHR	PHPM	UHPR	WHTM
	LTM	PHØ	WHC	12	EMM	LMM	MLM	PHTM	UHR	WHUM
	LTU	SHD	WHCP	13	ETM	LMMP	MLR	SHAM	UJM	
	MA	SHDP	WHØ	14	LAHM	LR	MR	SHDM	UM	

	thousands					units				
-5.	13676.	5.690	459.21	1	.444	1.233	1.146	.350	1.000	.660
	17.156	.358	17.372	2	.449	.600	.542	-.007	1.490	.652
	.435	3.924	21.498	3	1.258	.581	.684	1.125	1.104	2.493
	.000	56.41	345.98	4	.845	.815	.966	1.273	2.357	1.362
	314.14	3.125	184.20	5	.845	.674	.300	.943	3.314	.979
	5.480	.327	.00	6	1.000	.842	.299	.968	.741	.977
	.000	.000	12.463	7	1.258	1.735	.291	-.004	2.341	-.003
	10.902	5840.6	3.933	8	.943	1.062	1.265	.903	1.062	.903
	19.39	90.91	.000	9	.834	.771	.815	1.081	.416	.675
	319.41	2.481	191.11	10	.787	1.113	3.478	.944	1.322	1.339
	338.80	.000	282.22	11	.699	.027	1.265	1.265	.000	.815
	2.815	2.575	4.813	12	1.550	.469	1.259	.815	.885	.705
	8.510	8.513	.000	13	.730	.448	.180	1.230	.403	*APB 50 HAD*
	.493	.000	7.559	14	.887	.927	1.375	1.230	.028	
10.	15051.	6.073	395.00	1	.370	1.438	1.274	.465	1.000	.949
	15.246	.321	15.783	2	.430	.795	.629	.027	1.385	.753
	.441	3.294	22.602	3	1.058	.655	.858	1.368	1.307	1.727
	.000	62.85	210.33	4	.965	.812	1.012	.902	2.391	1.268
	339.09	5.437	228.77	5	.965	.743	.377	1.213	2.580	1.053
	6.659	.666	.00	6	1.000	.790	.403	1.089	.830	1.055
	.000	.000	17.313	7	1.058	1.330	.348	.011	2.861	.007
	9.020	5508.8	8.585	8	1.213	1.184	1.300	1.461	1.184	1.461
	40.64	108.06	.000	9	.701	.685	.812	1.837	.582	1.266
	352.30	4.708	229.90	10	1.046	1.084	2.621	.562	.398	.898
	392.94	.000	312.86	11	.922	.025	.969	1.300	.000	.812
	3.644	1.822	9.388	12	1.435	.700	1.271	.812	1.252	.758
	8.314	13.875	.000	13	.723	.537	.185	.798	.819	*APB 50 SPEC*
	.657	10.517	5.621	14	.916	.863	1.279	.798	.036	
50.	22256.	12.911	382.45	1	.447	1.035	1.022	.346	1.301	.946
	19.663	.855	24.513	2	.506	.563	.860	-.002	1.093	1.024
	.618	7.971	17.714	3	1.324	.648	1.534	1.153	1.127	1.273
	.000	108.69	178.80	4	1.048	.873	.830	2.356	1.804	1.949
	586.55	8.339	300.37	5	.805	.907	.297	.982	1.673	.993
	11.396	.823	.00	6	1.301	.891	.280	1.003	1.177	1.004
	.000	.000	28.115	7	1.324	1.827	.291	.000	2.316	.000
	21.427	7122.3	10.833	8	.982	1.076	1.300	.387	1.076	.387
	35.92	154.89	.000	9	.982	.863	.873	1.019	.718	.595
	557.08	4.221	274.61	10	.512	1.312	3.667	.986	.259	1.448
	593.00	.000	447.06	11	.637	.030	1.170	1.300	.000	.873
	6.145	4.583	7.114	12	1.554	.473	1.271	.873	1.426	.907
	17.341	12.006	.000	13	.830	.524	.185	.659	1.272	*APB 50 SPEC*
	.948	8.940	12.951	14	.688	.989	1.379	.857	.072	

(d)

Figure B-9 (cont.)

Variable	Symbol	Year 50 (Fig. B-6)	Year 50 (Fig. B-9)	Change (%)
1. New enterprise	NE	3,200	8,300	+160.
2. Mature business	MB	5,500	12,900	+135.
3. Declining industry	DI	16,700	19,700	+18.
4. Premium housing	PH	90,700	154,900	+71.
5. Worker housing	WH	281,900	447,100	+59.
6. Underemployed housing	UH	341,100	178,800	−48.
7. Managerial-professional	MP	55,700	108,700	+95.
8. Labor	L	309,200	586,600	+90.
9. Underemployed	U	453,800	382,400	−16.
10. Manager/housing ratio	MHR	1.02	1.17	+15.
11. Labor/housing ratio	LHR	1.10	1.31	+19.
12. Underemployed/housing ratio	UHR	.89	1.43	+61.
13. Manager/job ratio	MR	1.37	1.38	+1.
14. Labor/job ratio	LR	.92	.99	+8.
15. Underemployed/job ratio	UR	2.49	1.27	−49.
16. Tax ratio needed	TRN	3.30	1.67	−49.
17. Underemployed to labor net	UTLN	4,050	10,800	+167.

Figure B-10   Changes caused by the revival policies of Figure 5-16 when initiated in an equilibrium system having the modified underemployed/job multiplier from Figure B-5.

occur in Figure B-9 are summarized in Figure B-10. All the changes are markedly favorable (recognizing that the increases in the housing ratios are a necessary accompaniment to economic improvement). In fact, a comparison of Figures B-10 and 5-17 shows that the revival policies produce a much greater effect starting from the terminal conditions of B-6 than from the more favorable stagnation at the beginning of Figure 5-16. One can conclude that the kind of change in Figure B-5 does not alter the desirability of the revival policies that were explored in Figure 5-16.

Reducing Sensitivity of Parameters. A further comparison of Figures B-9 and 5-16 shows another important facet of complex systems. When a sensitive parameter is discovered, and it is one that might change (as suggested in Section B.2 dealing with a possible unfavorable influence of a negative income tax on decayed urban areas), the system designer should look for ways to make the system insensitive to that uncontrollable parameter. This conversion from a sensitive to an insensitive parameter has been created here by the revival policies. In Figure B-6 the system was found to be sensitive to the table change in Figure B-5. But Figure B-11 shows that the system containing the revival policies is no longer sensitive to the table change in Figure B-5. Figure B-11 compares the fiftieth year from Figure B-9 with the fiftieth year from Figure 5-16. The per cent changes calculated in Figure B-11 are caused when the new curve of Figure B-5 has been introduced in the presence of the revival policies. The changes in Figure B-11 should be compared with the changes in Figure B-7. In fact, a surprising thing has happened in going from Figure B-7 to B-11. In Figure B-7, where the change in Table UJMT

Variable	Symbol	Year 50 (Fig. 5-16)	Year 50 (Fig. B-9)	Change (%)
1. New enterprise	NE	8,000	8,300	+4.
2. Mature business	MB	12,800	12,900	+1.
3. Declining industry	DI	22,200	19,700	−11.
4. Premium housing	PH	152,800	154,900	+1.
5. Worker housing	WH	450,600	447,600	−1.
6. Underemployed housing	UH	175,300	178,800	+2.
7. Managerial-professional	MP	108,700	108,700	0
8. Labor	L	600,000	586,600	−2.
9. Underemployed	U	335,900	382,400	+14.
10. Manager/housing ratio	MHR	1.19	1.17	−2.
11. Labor/housing ratio	LHR	1.33	1.31	−2.
12. Underemployed/housing ratio	UHR	1.28	1.43	+12.
13. Manager/job ratio	MR	1.36	1.38	+1.
14. Labor/job ratio	LR	.98	.99	+1.
15. Underemployed/job ratio	UR	1.07	1.27	+19.
16. Tax ratio needed	TRN	1.50	1.67	+11.
17. Underemployed to labor net	UTLN	9,200	10,800	+17.

Figure B-11 Changes caused by the new underemployed/job multiplier from Figure B-5 when imposed on the revival policies of Figure 5-16.

was added to the original stagnation conditions, the changes are substantial and almost all detrimental. In Figure B-11, where the change in Table UJMT was added to the revival conditions, not only are the changes slight, but many are in a favorable direction. The revival policies have eliminated the hazard of changes in underemployed sensitivity to job conditions.

In reexamining Figure B-9 we see that revival comes through upgrading the area and creating upward economic mobility for the people already in it. The fall of underemployed in Figure B-9a is caused by the greater flow of underemployed to the labor class. The flow of underemployed to labor net UTLN has risen 167%. Figure B-9c shows only a very slight increase above normal in underemployed departures followed by a substantial decline, while underemployed arrivals remain about constant for 20 years and then rise.

Policy Affected by Parameters. In contrast to the parameter variations that do not influence the direction of desirable policy changes, some parameters, if they change, can affect the validity of proposed improvement policies. Usually there are very few parameters that can affect policy recommendations. The one in this example is the only one that is known to exist in this model of urban dynamics. Others may exist, or combinations of several parameter changes might react to defeat the desirability of a policy proposal.

In the following example underemployed movement to and from the urban area has been made much less dependent on availability of housing than in the original model. Figure B-12 shows the new curve for UHMT. It has no effect on the original equilibrium condition of the system because the two curves cross

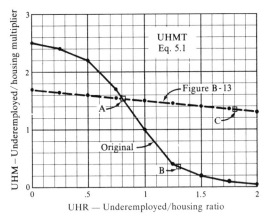

Figure B-12   Less influence of housing on underemployed arrivals.

at the equilibrium value of UHR at Point A. (Point B is the equilibrium reached at the fiftieth year in Figure 5-16. Point C is the equilibrium reached at the fiftieth year in Figure B-13.) The revival policies of Figure 5-16 cause a major shift in many system variables and make use of the underemployed/housing multiplier to control the population distribution in the area. With a housing influence as shown in Figure B-12, the revival policies are in several ways less effective (as shown in Figure B-13). Figure B-13 should be compared with Figure 5-16.

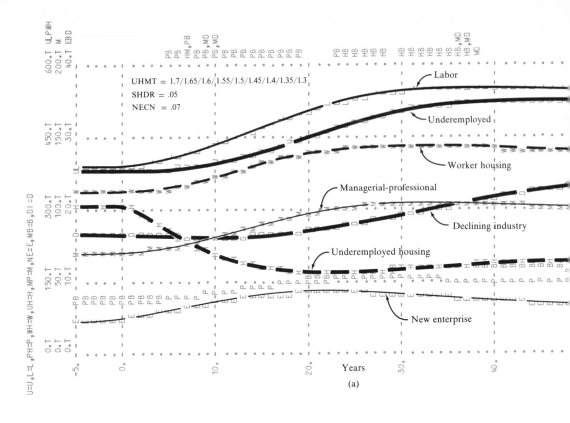

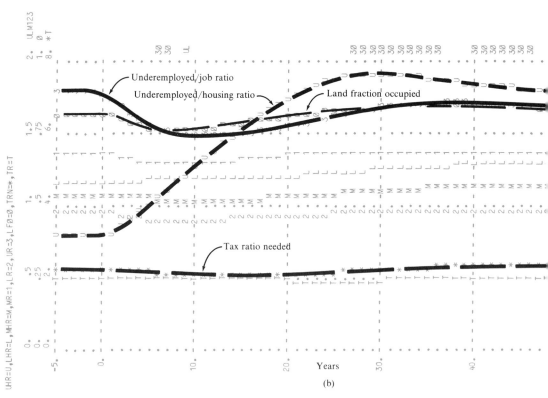

(a)

(b)

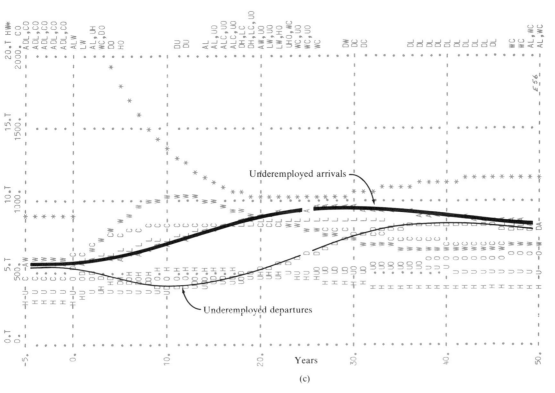

(c)

Figure B-13 Revival policies applied with the less sensitive underemployed/housing multiplier from Figure B-12.

Figure B-13*a* shows a decrease in underemployed housing similar to that in Figure 5-16*a*. But now the number of underemployed has risen rather than decreased. Figure B-13*b* shows that the underemployed/job ratio has changed very little. Low economic opportunity is still the factor controlling the population movement. With the housing influence almost removed, the underemployed move in, in spite of a very high underemployed/housing ratio. Tax rates remain about constant rather than declining. In Figure B-13*c* the underemployed-arrival rate in the middle years is higher and the departure rate is lower than in Figure 5-16.

The effectiveness of the revival policies is reduced because of the change in Figure B-12. But the example is of more technical than practical interest, at least for cities in the United States. Even the poorest people in the United States are not so desperate that they will move to available jobs where housing is unavailable. The situation may well be different in other parts of the world with different climatic, natural, or political conditions.

This subsection has illustrated that changing parameter values in nonlinear systems can shift the mode of operation so as to affect the design of new policies. A careful search for such influential parameters should be made before finally deciding on the new policies to be established.

TIME	AV	MB	U		AMM	LAJM	LSM	MSM	SHLM	UMM
	AV	MB	U	1	AMM	LAJM	LSM	MSM	SHLM	UMM
	DI	MBD	UA	2	AMMP	LAM	LUM	NEGR	TCM	UMMP
	DID	MD	UD	3	BDM	LAMP	LUR	PEM	TPCR	UR
	DIDP	MP	UH	4	DIDM	LATM	MAHM	PHAM	TR	WHAM
	L	NE	UJ	5	DIEM	LAUM	MAJM	PHEM	TRN	WHEM
	LA	NEC	UJP	6	DILM	LCR	MAM	PHGM	UAMM	WHGM
	LCHP	NECP	UTL	7	EDM	LDM	MAMP	PHLM	UDM	WHGR
	LD	P	UTLN	8	EGM	LEM	MAPM	PHM	UEM	WHLM
	LDC	PH	UTP	9	ELJM	LFØ	MATM	PHØM	UFW	WHM
	LDI	PHC	UW	10	ELM	LHR	MDM	PHPM	UHM	WHØM
	LJ	PHCP	WH	11	EM	LLF	MHR	PHTM	UHPR	WHTM
	LTM	PHØ	WHC	12	EMM	LMM	MLM	SHAM	UHR	WHUM
	LTU	SHD	WHCP	13	ETM	LMMP	MLR	SHDM	UJM	
	MA	SHDP	WHØ	14	LAHM	LR	MR		UM	

	thousands				units					

TIME										
−5.	16336.	7.806	377.31	1	.452	1.087	1.054	.344	1.060	.805
	16.474	.465	17.283	2	.449	.623	.712	.000	1.284	.802
	.464	4.849	17.275	3	1.190	.625	1.040	1.145	1.121	1.811
	.000	71.13	310.08	4	.939	.854	.931	1.549	1.966	1.542
	392.55	4.866	208.35	5	.886	.808	.296	1.000	2.248	1.000
	7.360	.462	.00	6	1.060	.878	.306	1.000	.936	1.000
	.000	.000	16.847	7	1.190	1.681	.307	.000	2.289	.000
	13.201	5729.4	5.497	8	1.000	1.073	1.300	.625	1.073	.625
	24.38	110.94	.000	9	.935	.815	.854	1.075	.557	.665
	379.15	3.142	210.06	10	.655	1.170	3.408	.948	1.529	1.352
	403.53	.000	335.65	11	.768	.029	1.069	1.300	.000	.854
	3.643	3.155	5.885	12	1.556	.466	1.262	.854	.811	.808
	11.349	9.054	.000	13	.805	.464	.181	1.378	.276	
	.655	.000	9.075	14	.830	.973	1.380	1.460	.045	
10.	18212.	8.555	397.02	1	.682	1.297	1.186	.456	1.000	.944
	16.247	.468	21.119	2	.507	.739	.729	.022	1.261	.866
	.460	4.251	12.317	3	1.093	.667	1.097	1.183	1.153	1.488
	.000	80.00	208.88	4	.944	.855	.966	1.276	1.959	1.596
	435.54	7.203	266.86	5	.944	.819	.371	1.172	2.127	1.043
	8.715	.831	.00	6	1.000	.826	.398	1.084	.972	1.053
	.000	.000	22.485	7	1.093	1.435	.349	.010	1.551	.007
	12.496	6189.4	10.758	8	1.172	1.092	1.300	.917	1.092	.917
	45.30	128.90	.000	9	.812	.769	.855	1.652	.654	1.126
	434.87	5.275	259.52	10	.793	1.186	2.657	.638	1.447	.949
	480.17	.000	367.17	11	.879	.026	1.034	1.300	.000	.855
	4.549	2.469	10.244	12	1.444	.631	1.267	.855	1.267	.819
	11.447	13.729	.000	13	.806	.522	.134	.786	.410	
	.839	10.444	6.966	14	.814	.907	1.287	.786	.048	
50.	20755.	11.534	515.66	1	.447	1.164	1.103	.361	1.158	.812
	23.512	.794	25.333	2	.478	.563	.717	−.009	1.278	.813
	.632	7.023	23.883	3	1.377	.587	1.056	1.055	1.046	1.693
	.000	99.77	190.63	4	.896	.852	.867	2.066	1.987	1.920
	544.43	6.613	304.59	5	.774	.811	.307	.931	2.420	.974
	9.591	.692	.00	6	1.158	.859	.295	.983	.981	.994
	.000	.000	24.836	7	1.377	1.827	.296	−.002	2.316	−.001
	19.895	7890.7	9.587	8	.931	1.027	1.300	.502	1.027	.502
	33.48	146.73	.000	9	.886	.840	.852	1.052	.592	.645
	540.39	3.976	305.33	10	.581	1.300	3.519	.964	1.339	1.379
	573.86	.000	418.83	11	.592	.028	1.133	1.300	.000	.852
	5.163	4.242	6.964	12	1.539	.469	1.267	.852	1.803	.811
	15.216	11.645	.000	13	.802	.474	.183	.479	.323	
	.885	9.532	11.548	14	.700	.949	1.366	.554	.048	

(d)

Figure B-13 (cont.)

B.4   Normal Population Densities

In the urban model, as a unit of factory space ages it is characterized by declining employment. The normal occupancy of a housing unit, on the other hand, increases with the age of the unit. How important are these population assumptions in the urban stagnation process?

Figure B-14 lists the population-density coefficients in the basic model and substitutes a new set of values which assume no change in employment and population densities connected with the age of structures.

	Symbol	Equation	Original	Fig. B-13
New-enterprise labor	NEL	132.1	20	15
Mature-business labor	MBL	132.2	15	15
Declining-industry labor	DIL	132.3	10	15
New-enterprise management	NEM	37.1	4	2
Mature-business management	MBM	37.2	2	2
Declining-industry management	DIM	37.3	1	2
Premium-housing population density	PHPD	61.1	3	6
Worker-housing population density	WHPD	48.1	6	6
Underemployed-housing population density	UHPD	6.1	12	6

Figure B-14   Changes in men per productive unit and in people per housing unit so that densities do not vary with age of structures.

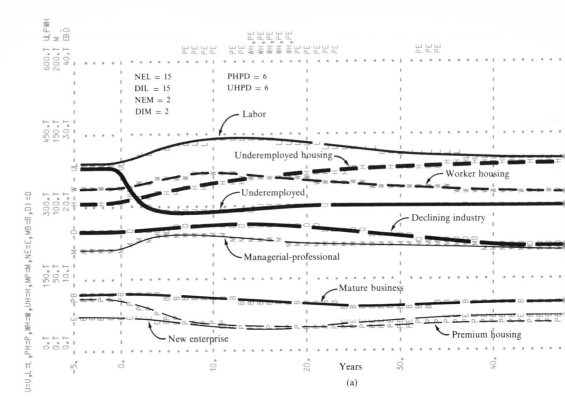

NEL = 15   PHPD = 6
DIL = 15   UHPD = 6
NEM = 2
DIM = 2

Labor

Underemployed housing

Worker housing

Underemployed

Declining industry

Managerial-professional

Mature business

New enterprise

Premium housing

Years

(a)

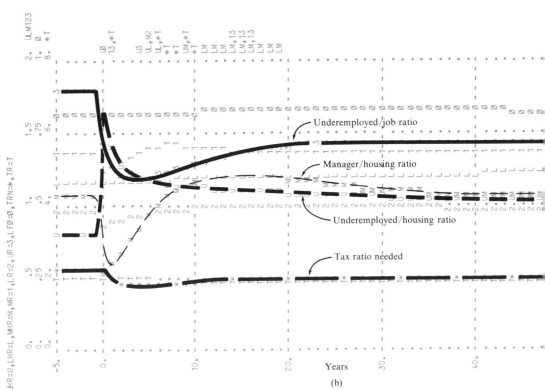

Underemployed/job ratio

Manager/housing ratio

Underemployed/housing ratio

Tax ratio needed

Years

(b)

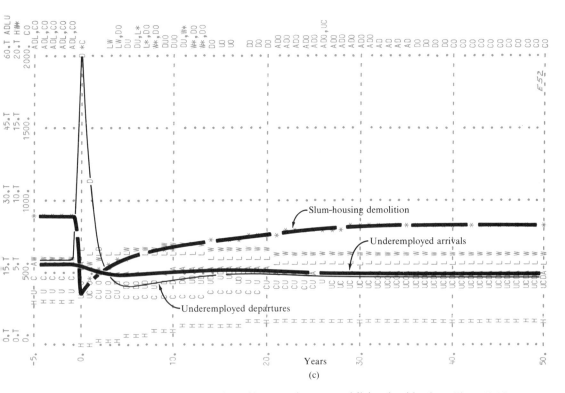

Figure B-15 New equilibrium caused by the uniform employment and living densities from Figure B-14.

In Figure B-15 the new values have been substituted at time = 0, with the urban area already in its condition of stagnant equilibrium. The new equilibrium reached after 20 or 30 years is little different from that at the start. Some changes do occur during the first two decades as new employment demands and new living preferences cause a readjustment in the system, but most of these reverse themselves. The employment and occupancy densities do not have a substantial influence on the equilibrium condition of the system. Figure B-15a shows that the housing units change to compensate for the new occupancy densities. Because fewer people live in each underemployed-housing unit, the amount of housing has risen in response to the greater housing need. Because more people live in each premium-housing unit, the number of units declines to create a new balance between housing and the managerial-professional population.

TIME	AV	MB	U		AMM	LAJM	LSM	MSM	SHLM	UMM
	DI	MBD	UA	2	AMMP	LAM	LUM	NEGR	TCM	UMMP
	DID	MD	UD	3	BDM	LAMP	LUR	PEM	TPCR	UR
	DIDP	MP	UH	4	DIDM	LATM	MAHM	PHAM	TR	WHAM
	L	NE	UJ	5	DIEM	LAUM	MAJM	PHEM	TRN	WHEM
	LA	NEC	UJP	6	DILM	LCR	MAM	PHGM	UAMM	WHGM
	LCHP	NECP	UTL	7	EDM	LDM	MAMP	PHGR	UDM	WHGR
	LD	P	UTLN	8	EGM	LEM	MAPM	PHLM	UEM	WHLM
	LDC	PH	UTP	9	ELJM	LFØ	MATM	PHM	UFW	WHM
	LDI	PHC	UW	10	ELM	LHR	MDM	PHØM	UHM	WHØM
	LJ	PHCP	WH	11	EM	LLF	MHR	PHPM	UHPR	WHTM
	LTM	PHØ	WHC	12	EMM	LMM	MLM	PHTM	UHR	WHUM
	LTU	SHD	WHCP	13	ETM	LMMP	MLR	SHAM	UJM	
	MA	SHDP	WHØ	14	LAHM	LR	MR	SHDM	UM	

	thousands				units					
-5.	16336.	7.806	377.31	1	.452	1.087	1.054	.344	1.060	.805
	16.474	.465	17.283	2	.449	.623	.712	.000	1.284	.802
	.464	4.849	17.275	3	1.190	.625	1.040	1.145	1.121	1.811
	.000	71.13	310.08	4	.939	.854	.931	1.549	1.966	1.542
	392.55	4.866	208.35	5	.886	.808	.296	1.000	2.248	1.000
	7.360	.462	.00	6	1.060	.878	.306	1.000	.936	1.000
	.000	.000	16.847	7	1.190	1.681	.307	.000	2.289	.000
	13.201	5729.4	5.497	8	1.000	1.073	1.300	.625	1.073	.625
	24.38	110.94	.000	9	.935	.815	.854	1.075	.557	.665
	379.15	3.142	210.06	10	.655	1.170	3.408	.948	1.529	1.352
	403.53	.000	335.65	11	.768	.029	1.069	1.300	.000	.854
	3.643	3.155	5.885	12	1.556	.466	1.262	.854	.811	.808
	11.349	9.054	.000	13	.805	.464	.181	1.378	.276	
	.655	.000	9.075	14	.830	.973	1.380	1.460	.045	
10.	14669.	7.248	290.96	1	.459	1.039	1.024	.309	1.098	.894
	17.315	.491	15.557	2	.428	.650	.850	-.019	1.100	.918
	.449	6.285	13.052	3	1.355	.683	1.500	1.054	1.045	1.299
	.000	79.62	345.10	4	.864	.861	.832	2.344	1.904	1.615
	436.30	3.687	224.01	5	.787	.900	.273	.845	1.922	.942
	8.936	.340	.00	6	1.098	.890	.254	.571	1.105	1.035
	.000	.000	18.969	7	1.355	1.620	.332	-.054	2.243	.004
	14.138	5343.5	6.378	8	.845	1.027	1.300	.578	1.027	.578
	17.87	56.81	.000	9	.890	.824	.861	.731	.710	.705
	423.76	1.110	206.68	10	.627	1.192	3.947	1.450	.702	1.302
	441.63	.000	365.98	11	.611	.030	1.168	1.300	.000	.861
	4.170	2.471	6.892	12	1.591	.402	1.265	.861	1.124	.900
	12.878	6.823	.000	13	.815	.478	.182	.901	.561	
	.793	.000	9.530	14	.808	.988	1.409	.989	.063	
50.	14399.	6.983	303.35	1	.443	1.078	1.049	.352	1.094	.849
	14.411	.411	15.267	2	.433	.626	.797	.004	1.170	.844
	.423	4.771	14.245	3	1.177	.625	1.324	1.031	1.026	1.431
	.000	71.62	388.03	4	.978	.867	.927	1.587	1.851	1.722
	401.66	4.677	211.92	5	.894	.865	.301	1.030	2.054	1.008
	7.529	.430	.00	6	1.094	.880	.315	.997	1.050	.987
	.000	.000	17.170	7	1.177	1.674	.310	-.000	2.348	-.002
	13.449	5194.9	5.493	8	1.030	1.016	1.300	.582	1.016	.582
	20.68	55.60	.000	9	.946	.824	.867	1.070	.671	.748
	391.06	1.571	203.42	10	.629	1.226	3.331	.951	.898	1.251
	411.74	.000	327.74	11	.782	.029	1.073	1.300	.000	.867
	3.584	1.587	6.471	12	1.548	.449	1.257	.867	1.042	.865
	11.657	8.203	.000	13	.823	.446	.178	.966	.455	
	.667	.000	8.202	14	.774	.976	1.374	1.057	.056	

(d)

Figure B-15 (cont.)

Note to the reader: In order to preserve the consistent placement of figures, this page has been left blank.

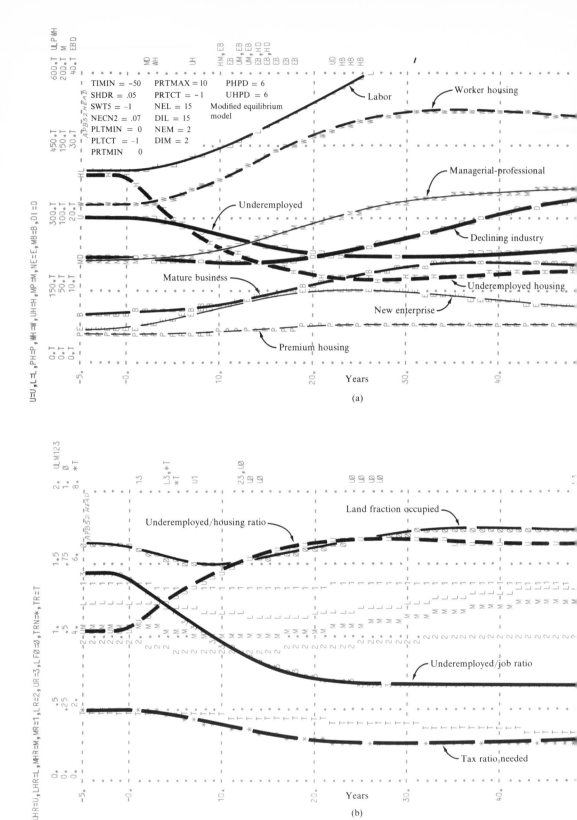

(a)

(b)

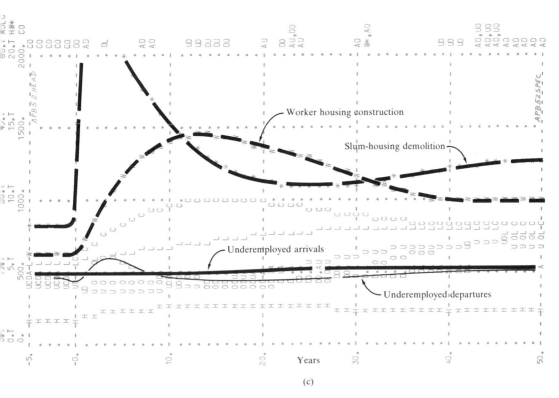

Figure B-16 Revival policies applied to the system in equilibrium and having uniform employment and living densities.

Figure B-13 showed that, even when a parameter change produces no change in the existing equilibrium, it can affect proposed policy changes. In Figure B-16 we test the influence of the revival policies of Figure 5-16 on the urban condition reached in Figure B-15. Under the new urban condition, where employment and living densities do not change with the aging of structures, do the revival policies produce changes similar to those produced before?

Figure B-16* shows changes caused by the revival policies that are much like those in Figure 5-16. In Figure B-16a labor and worker housing rise, the underemployed and underemployed housing decline, and all categories of industry rise. In Figure B-16b the underemployed/job ratio improves with the accompanying pressures arising from the underemployed/housing ratio. The tax ratio declines as in Figure 5-16b. In Figure B-16c the changes are similar to those in Figure 5-16c.

A comparison of Figures B-16 and 5-16 shows that the effectiveness of the revival policies is not influenced by the parameter changes for employment and population densities tabulated in Figure B-14.

*The method of obtaining this computer run is similar to that described for Figure B-9, using the modified model described in Section B.3.

TIME	AV	MB	U		AMM	LAJM	LSM	MSM	SHLM	UMM
	DI	MBD	UA	2	AMMP	LAM	LUM	NEGR	TCM	UMMP
	DID	MD	UD	3	BDM	LAMP	LUR	PEM	TPCR	UR
	DIDP	MP	UH	4	DIDM	LATM	MAHM	PHAM	TR	WHAM
	L	NE	UJ	5	DIEM	LAUM	MAJM	PHEM	TRN	WHEM
	LA	NEC	UJP	6	DILM	LCR	MAM	PHGM	UAMM	WHGM
	LCHP	NECP	UTL	7	EDM	LDM	MAMP	PHGR	UDM	WHGR
	LD	P	UTLN	8	EGM	LEM	MAPM	PHLM	UEM	WHLM
	LDC	PH	UTP	9	ELJM	LFØ	MATM	PHM	UFW	WHØM
	LDI	PHC	UW	10	ELM	LHR	MDM	PHØM	UHM	WHØM
	LJ	PHCP	WH	11	EM	LLF	MHR	PHPM	UHPR	WHTM
	LTM	PHØ	WHC	12	EMM	LMM	MLM	PHTM	UHR	WHUM
	LTU	SHD	WHCP	13	ETM	LMMP	MLR	SHAM	UJM	
	MA	SHDP	WHØ	14	LAHM	LR	MR	SHDM	UM	

	thousands				units					
-5.	14381.	6.802	302.91	1	.443	1.074	1.046	.351	1.098	.848
	14.549	.394	15.162	2	.430	.627	.798	.007	1.169	.841
	.434	4.769	14.221	3	1.159	.624	1.327	1.032	1.027	1.433
	.000	71.56	387.80	4	.993	.867	.929	1.572	1.854	1.709
	401.86	4.683	211.37	5	.905	.865	.301	1.053	2.054	1.013
	7.523	.440	.00	6	1.098	.882	.314	.996	1.050	.982
	.000	.000	17.062	7	1.159	1.672	.307	-.000	2.347	-.002
	13.441	5192.2	5.339	8	1.053	1.016	1.300	.577	1.016	.577
	20.83	55.66	.000	9	.954	.825	.867	1.073	.670	.736
	390.51	1.579	202.97	10	.626	1.222	3.332	.949	.900	1.264
	411.35	.000	328.98	11	.802	.029	1.071	1.300	.000	.867
	3.578	1.585	6.406	12	1.549	.448	1.256	.867	1.041	.865
	11.685	8.234	.000	13	.822	.445	.178	.967	.454	APB 52 HD
	.660	.000	8.319	14	.778	.977	1.374	1.062	.056	
10.	16680.	8.082	261.58	1	.394	1.310	1.194	.415	1.000	1.197
	13.832	.397	14.630	2	.414	.898	.912	.029	1.059	.969
	.429	4.273	14.030	3	.983	.700	1.705	1.200	1.167	.949
	.000	78.72	242.95	4	1.034	.872	1.000	.997	1.806	1.528
	445.99	7.892	275.71	5	1.034	.941	.344	1.229	1.552	1.057
	9.365	.963	.00	6	1.000	.822	.390	1.086	1.162	1.082
	.000	.000	20.401	7	.983	1.155	.346	.011	2.682	.010
	10.298	5162.2	8.742	8	1.229	1.100	1.300	1.043	1.100	1.043
	46.82	65.65	.000	9	.811	.751	.872	1.575	.805	1.497
	447.09	2.551	210.60	10	.847	1.165	2.714	.673	.252	.826
	493.91	.000	382.81	11	1.040	.026	.999	1.300	.000	.872
	4.324	1.326	14.137	12	1.485	.573	1.253	.872	1.436	.941
	11.649	15.313	.000	13	.830	.485	.177	.652	1.123	APB 52 SP EC
	.817	12.147	6.322	14	.835	.903	1.321	.652	.070	
50.	21296.	13.511	236.17	1	.300	1.037	1.023	.385	1.386	1.114
	22.840	.915	15.695	2	.339	.744	1.184	-.008	.816	1.171
	.748	8.237	16.399	3	1.355	.799	2.921	.893	.866	.667
	.000	118.98	194.46	4	1.091	.936	.764	2.884	1.347	2.045
	689.85	7.852	353.84	5	.787	1.184	.323	.933	1.137	.975
	16.542	.818	.00 '	6	1.386	.891	.301	1.001	1.297	1.001
	.000	.000	23.053	7	1.355	1.425	.302	.000	3.472	.000
	19.660	6623.4	2.732	8	.933	.920	1.300	.334	.920	.334
	34.92	80.25	.000	9	.984	.873	.936	1.094	.833	.738
	663.04	2.346	196.79	10	.480	1.352	3.461	.935	.152	1.262
	697.96	.000	510.16	11	.611	.030	1.236	1.300	.000	.936
	6.368	2.252	10.061	12	1.515	.441	1.245	.936	1.619	1.184
	20.375	12.700	.000	13	.914	.462	.172	.552	1.699	APB 52 SP EC
	1.079	9.723	12.881	14	.648	.988	1.346	.766	.099	

(d)

Figure B-16 (cont.)

B.5 Improvement in External Environment

The model of urban behavior developed in this book depicts an urban area as an island in an extended environment. People come from and go to that environment as the attractiveness of the area rises and falls relative to it. What effect do changes in the environment have on the urban area? Would a major change in the attractiveness of the environment substantially affect the conditions in a depressed city?

Figure B-17 shows the effect on the urban area if the external environment were suddenly to become more attractive. This is done by halving the under-employed arrivals normal UAN (equation line 1.1) and doubling the under-employed departures normal UDN (line 13.1). For any given set of conditions in the urban area, the result is to halve the rate of arrival of the underemployed and to double the rate of departure.

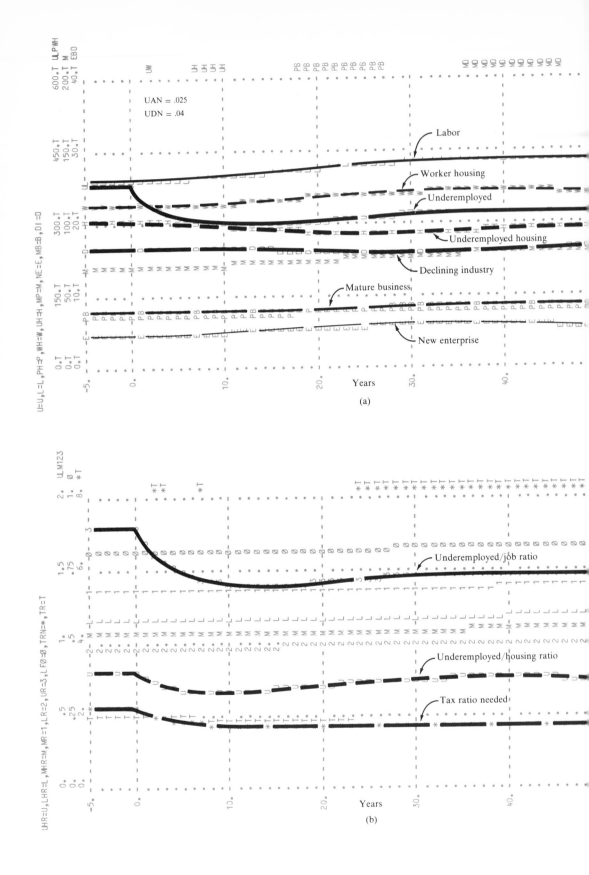

(a)

(b)

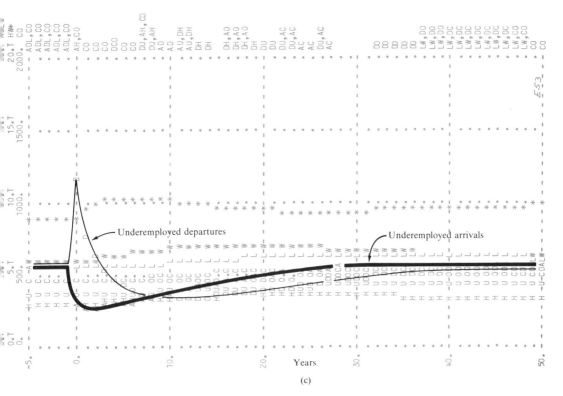

Figure B-17 Halved underemployed-arrival rate and doubled underemployed-departure rate.

Figure B-17 again shows the high degree of independence that complex systems can exhibit in the face of changed conditions. Figure B-17a shows some decline in underemployed and a slight rise in labor, with other system levels almost unchanged. Figure B-17b shows the most significant changes, even though they appear small. The underemployed/job ratio has fallen some, indicating greater job availability. The underemployed/housing ratio has declined too. The fact that these two variables have changed in the same direction is unusual.

In spite of the apparent small changes in Figure B-17, the attractiveness-for-migration multiplier AMM in Figure B-17d has risen from .452 to .850. The conditions within the urban area have improved to correspond to the improved external conditions. However, the new mix of attractiveness components is still not desirable. The area is still characterized by excess slum housing and a shortage of economic opportunity. It appears that improvement in the outside environment, even if it occurs, is not likely to solve the problems of the cities.

TIME	AV	MB	U		AMM	LAJM	LSM	MSM	SHLM	UMM
	DI	MBD	UA	2	AMMP	LAM	LUM	NEGR	TCM	UMMP
	DID	MD	UD	3	BDM	LAMP	LUR	PEM	TPCR	UR
	DIDP	MP	UH	4	DIDM	LATM	MAHM	PHAM	TR	WHAM
	L	NE	UJ	5	DIEM	LAUM	MAJM	PHEM	TRN	WHEM
	LA	NEC	WP	6	DILM	LCR	MAM	PHGM	UAMM	WHGM
	LCHP	NECP	UTL	7	EDM	LDM	MAMP	PHGR	UDM	WHGR
	LD	P	UTLN	8	EGM	LEM	MAPM	PHLM	UEM	WHLM
	LDC	PH	UTP	9	ELJM	LFØ	MATM	PHM	UFW	WHM
	LDI	PHC	UW	10	ELM	LHR	MDM	PHØM	UHM	WHØM
	LJ	PHCP	WH	11	EM	LLF	MHR	PHPM	UHPR	WHTM
	LTM	PHØ	WHC	12	EMM	LMM	MLM	PHTM	UHR	WHUM
	LTU	SHD	WHCP	13	ETM	LMMP	MLR	SHAM	WM	
	MA	SHDP	WHØ	14	LAHM	LR	MR	SHDM	UM	

thousands   units

TIME	AV	MB	U	#	AMM	LAJM	LSM	MSM	SHLM	UMM
-5.	16336.	7.806	377.31	1	.452	1.087	1.054	.344	1.060	.805
	16.474	.465	17.283	2	.449	.623	.712	.000	1.284	.802
	.464	4.849	17.275	3	1.190	.625	1.040	1.145	1.121	1.811
	.000	71.13	310.08	4	.939	.854	.931	1.549	1.966	1.542
	392.55	4.866	208.35	5	.886	.808	.296	1.000	2.248	1.000
	7.360	.462	.00	6	1.060	.878	.306	1.000	.936	1.000
	.000	.000	16.847	7	1.190	1.681	.307	.000	2.289	.000
	13.201	5729.4	5.497	8	1.000	1.073	1.300	.625	1.073	.625
	24.38	110.94	.000	9	.935	.815	.854	1.075	.557	.665
	379.15	3.142	210.06	10	.655	1.170	3.408	.948	1.529	1.352
	403.53	.000	335.65	11	.768	.029	1.069	1.300	.000	.854
	3.643	3.155	5.885	12	1.556	.466	1.262	.854	.811	.808
	11.349	9.054	.000	13	.805	.464	.181	1.378	.276	
	.655	.000	9.075	14	.830	.973	1.380	1.460	.045	
10.	16467.	7.816	296.77	1	1.167	1.073	1.046	.346	1.037	.952
	16.435	.450	11.152	2	.642	.673	.803	.002	1.163	.878
	.465	4.817	10.554	3	1.152	.641	1.343	1.268	1.223	1.416
	.000	71.66	295.79	4	.943	.861	.935	1.521	1.903	1.519
	398.51	4.984	209.55	5	.909	.869	.297	1.016	1.757	1.004
	7.666	.494	.00	6	1.037	.882	.311	1.007	1.058	1.013
	.000	.000	17.598	7	1.152	1.571	.308	.001	.889	.002
	12.522	5123.6	5.923	8	1.016	1.134	1.300	.653	1.134	.653
	26.61	112.14	.000	9	.937	.809	.861	1.137	.675	.755
	381.26	3.374	200.36	10	.672	1.162	3.361	.907	1.862	1.243
	407.87	.000	342.93	11	.810	.029	1.065	1.300	.000	.861
	3.798	3.052	6.844	12	1.554	.495	1.260	.861	.669	.869
	11.590	10.200	.000	13	.815	.476	.180	1.662	.467	
	.662	.000	8.527	14	.838	.977	1.378	1.724	.057	
50.	17614.	8.941	322.87	1	.850	1.022	1.013	.338	1.136	.855
	16.474	.533	16.599	2	.878	.635	.803	-.002	1.163	.867
	.497	5.374	15.933	3	1.192	.642	1.343	1.102	1.085	1.467
	.000	78.46	287.94	4	1.005	.883	.908	1.739	1.718	1.608
	433.56	5.578	220.01	5	.885	.869	.292	.987	1.788	.995
	8.347	.514	.00	6	1.136	.895	.305	1.000	1.062	1.001
	.000	.000	18.466	7	1.192	1.655	.307	-.000	1.234	.000
	14.349	5576.6	5.598	8	.987	1.051	1.300	.530	1.051	.530
	26.10	119.71	.000	9	.984	.834	.883	1.044	.660	.651
	410.40	3.355	213.01	10	.598	1.190	3.424	.969	1.705	1.371
	436.50	.000	364.33	11	.766	.030	1.092	1.300	.000	.883
	4.000	3.479	6.366	12	1.562	.449	1.262	.883	.748	.869
	12.890	9.844	.000	13	.844	.461	.181	1.505	.426	
	.722	.000	9.988	14	.810	.993	1.385	1.709	.058	

(d)

Figure B-17 (cont.)

B.6 Mechanization of Agriculture

One occasionally hears that mechanization of southern agriculture, which has forced the migration of the Negro to cities, is responsible for the plight of the American city. While such an external pressure can intensify urban difficulties, the earlier chapters of this book make clear that the basic causes of urban slums are internal. Another common source of blame for urban decay is low outward mobility, a result of rejection of Negroes by the more affluent urban and suburban sections.

Because the problems of agricultural mechanization and outward mobility from slum areas have become evident at about the same time, we are led to ask how the two would affect the model of an urban area. Mechanizing agriculture would create greater pressure on the underemployed in rural areas and, other conditions being equal, would cause a higher underemployed-arrival rate UA into the urban area. This effect can be created by increasing the underemployed arrivals normal UAN (equation line 1.1). Such a change would be in the opposite direction from that in the preceding section. Suppose we change UAN from .05 to .1, which doubles the inflow rate, all other things being equal.

At the same time the lack of outward mobility can be represented by reducing the underemployed departures normal UDN (equation line 13.1). By changing UDN from its original value of .02 to .01, the outward mobility is reduced to half, all other conditions being equal. But, of course, other conditions do not remain equal.

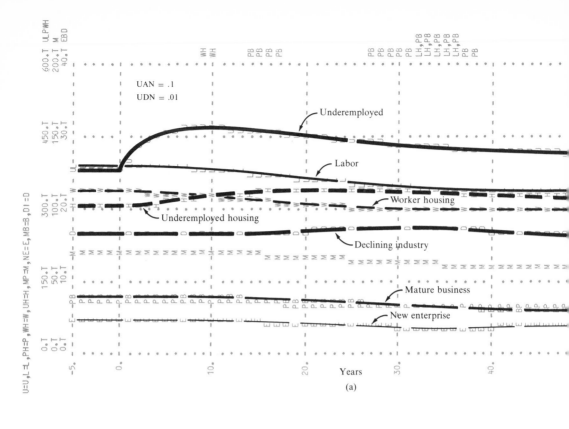

UAN = .1
UDN = .01

Underemployed

Labor

Worker housing

Underemployed housing

Declining industry

Mature business

New enterprise

Years

(a)

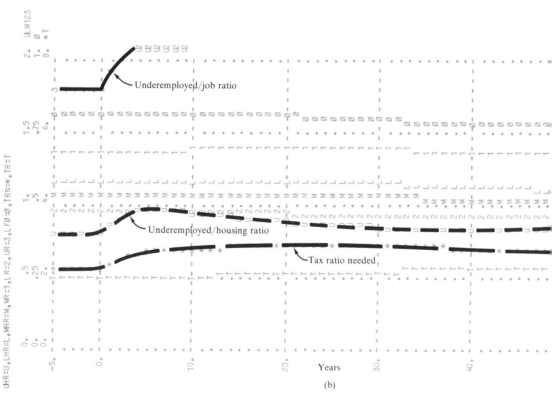

Underemployed/job ratio

Underemployed/housing ratio

Tax ratio needed

Years

(b)

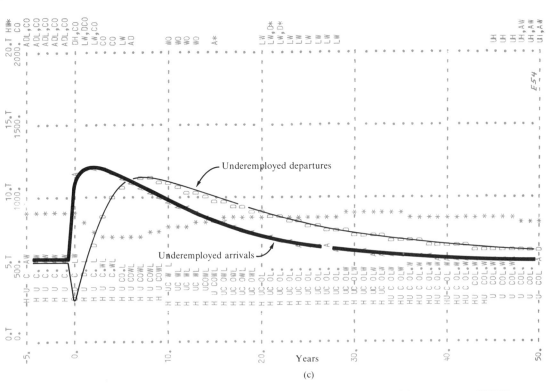

Figure B-18   Doubled underemployed arrival normal UAN and halved underemployed departure normal UDN.

The effects of doubling UAN and halving UDN appear in Figure B-18. Figure B-18*a* shows that the urban condition deteriorates, but not very much. The underemployed population rises and then falls again to near its original value. Figure B-18*b* shows an underemployed/housing ratio that rises and then declines. The largest change, and one that is detrimental, is the increase in the underemployed/job ratio, which rises from 1.81 to 2.16 (values from Figure B-18*d*).

Figure B-18 has 4 times the underemployed-arrival rate and $\frac{1}{4}$ the departure rate shown in Figure B-17. Although conditions at the 50-year points in Figures B-17*a* and B-18*a* do differ, the differences are much less than would probably have been expected.

TIME	AV	MB	U	#	AMM	LAJM	LSM	MSM	SHLM	UMM
	AV	MB	U	1	AMM	LAJM	LSM	MSM	SHLM	UMM
	DI	MBD	UA	2	AMMP	LAM	LUM	NEGR	TCM	UMMP
	DID	MD	UD	3	BDM	LAMP	LUR	PEM	TPCR	UR
	DIDP	MP	UH	4	DIDM	LATM	MAHM	PHAM	TR	WHAM
	L	NE	UJ	5	DIEM	LAUM	MAJM	PHEM	TRN	WHEM
	LA	NEC	UJP	6	DILM	LCR	MAM	PHGM	UAMM	WHGM
	LCHP	NECP	UTL	7	EDM	LDM	MAMP	PHGR	UDM	WHGR
	LD	P	UTLN	8	EGM	LEM	MAPM	PHLM	UEM	WHLM
	LDC	PH	UTP	9	ELJM	LFØ	MATM	PHM	UFW	WHM
	LDI	PHC	UW	10	ELM	LHR	MDM	PHØM	UHM	WHØM
	LJ	PHCP	WH	11	EM	LLF	MHR	PHPM	UHPR	WHTM
	LTM	PHØ	WHC	12	EMM	LMM	MLM	PHTM	UHR	WHUM
	LTU	SHD	WHCP	13	ETM	LMMP	MLR	SHAM	UJM	
	MA	SHDP	WHØ	14	LAHM	LR	MR	SHDM	UM	

	thousands				units					
-5.	16336.	7.806	377.31	1	.452	1.087	1.054	.344	1.060	.805
	16.474	.465	17.283	2	.449	.623	.712	.000	1.284	.802
	.464	4.849	17.275	3	1.190	.625	1.040	1.145	1.121	1.811
	.000	71.13	310.08	4	.939	.854	.931	1.549	1.966	1.542
	392.55	4.866	208.35	5	.886	.808	.296	1.000	2.248	1.000
	7.360	.462	.00	6	1.060	.878	.306	1.000	.936	1.000
	.000	.000	16.847	7	1.190	1.681	.307	.000	2.289	.000
	13.201	5729.4	5.497	8	1.000	1.073	1.300	.625	1.073	.625
	24.38	113.94	.000	9	.935	.815	.854	1.075	.557	.665
	379.15	3.142	210.06	10	.655	1.170	3.408	.948	1.529	1.352
	403.53	.000	335.65	11	.768	.029	1.069	1.300	.000	.854
	3.643	3.155	5.885	12	1.556	.466	1.262	.854	.811	.808
	11.349	9.054	.000	13	.805	.464	.181	1.378	.276	
	.655	.000	9.075	14	.830	.973	1.380	1.460	.045	
10.	16110.	7.755	466.09	1	.149	1.123	1.077	.339	1.084	.670
	16.562	.485	29.340	2	.346	.572	.609	-.004	1.409	.727
	.457	4.888	32.521	3	1.251	.603	.819	1.041	1.034	2.246
	.000	70.18	328.23	4	.920	.846	.927	1.585	2.045	1.548
	381.51	4.661	207.49	5	.849	.727	.293	.972	2.849	.989
	6.902	.414	.00	6	1.084	.869	.298	.989	.824	.982
	.000	.000	15.532	7	1.251	1.804	.305	-.001	6.977	-.002
	13.763	6368.7	4.758	8	.972	1.021	1.300	.595	1.021	.595
	21.56	108.99	.000	9	.923	.821	.846	.997	.458	.564
	375.16	2.833	213.53	10	.637	1.171	3.482	1.005	1.149	1.494
	396.73	.000	325.73	11	.705	.028	1.073	1.300	.000	.846
	3.464	3.285	4.794	12	1.561	.439	1.268	.846	.947	.746
	10.860	7.872	.000	13	.791	.454	.184	1.107	.151	*E 54*
	.642	.000	9.734	14	.829	.962	1.384	1.199	.035	
50.	14586.	6.194	413.91	1	.228	1.186	1.116	.351	1.000	.743
	16.258	.363	17.032	2	.227	.630	.606	.004	1.413	.728
	.437	4.075	18.646	3	1.173	.611	.812	1.197	1.164	2.168
	.000	61.03	324.29	4	.896	.825	.974	1.212	2.248	1.355
	336.16	3.939	190.88	5	.896	.725	.300	1.030	2.794	1.007
	6.158	.400	.00	6	1.000	.854	.314	1.002	.810	1.003
	.000	.000	14.195	7	1.173	1.664	.307	.000	4.505	.000
	11.190	5633.4	4.868	8	1.030	1.098	1.300	.849	1.098	.849
	22.61	99.09	.000	9	.860	.779	.825	1.138	.471	.713
	334.28	2.888	195.10	10	.764	1.111	3.339	.907	1.417	1.292
	356.88	.000	302.58	11	.786	.028	1.026	1.300	.000	.825
	3.138	2.696	5.524	12	1.549	.487	1.263	.825	.851	.744
	9.304	8.420	.000	13	.750	.467	.182	1.298	.166	*E 54*
	.563	.000	7.821	14	.889	.942	1.374	1.298	.034	

(d)

Figure B-18 (cont.)

Note to the reader: In order to preserve the consistent placement of figures, this page has been left blank.

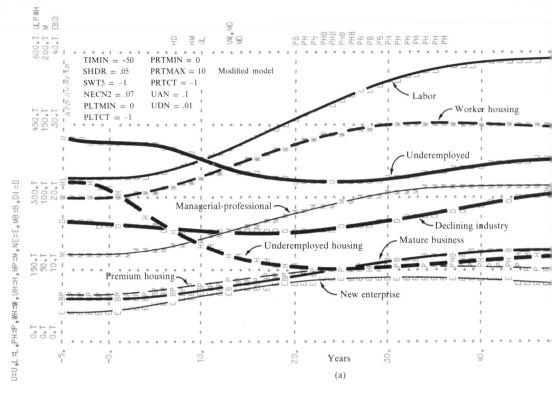

(a)

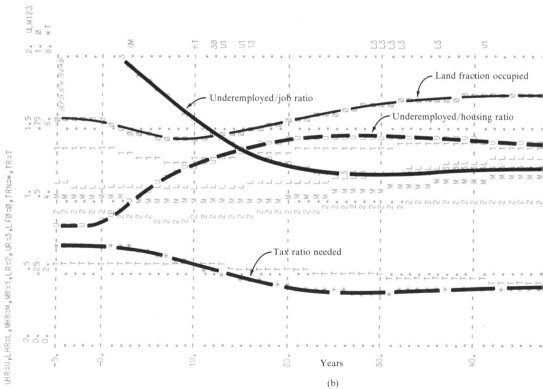

(b)

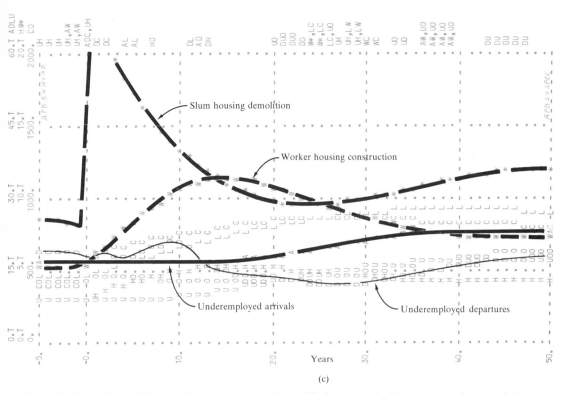

Figure B-19   Revival policies applied to the system in equilibrium with doubled underemployed arrival normal UAN and halved underemployed departure normal UDN.

Given the new equilibrium at the fiftieth year in Figure B-18 that results from increased inward pressure from the underemployed and reduced outward mobility, we can now re-examine the revival policies of Figure 5-16 to see if the policy for improvement would fail because of changed migration conditions. Figure B-19 starts from the final conditions in Figure B-18 and, at time = 0, the slum-demolition and new-enterprise-construction policies are started (as in Figure 5-16).*

In Figure B-19a the changes are similar to those in Figure 5-16a. The underemployed population declines and the labor population rises. Figure B-19c shows that the large changes in populations after the twelfth year occur even though the arrival rate of underemployed exceeds the departure rate. From Figure B-19d the underemployed to labor net UTLN rises from 4,700 to 10,200 per year as a measure of improved upward economic mobility.

Figure B-19b shows the desired changes with a falling underemployed/job ratio, a rising underemployed/housing ratio, and a falling tax ratio needed.

Figure B-19 shows that the doubling of UAN (representing a higher external pressure on the underemployed to move to the city) and a simultaneous halving of UDN (representing a reduced outward mobility) do not defeat the effectiveness of the revival policies.

*This uses the modified model described in Section B.3.

TIME	AV	MB	U		AMM	LAJM	LSM	MSM	SHLM	UMM
	AV	MB	U	1	AMM	LAJM	LSM	MSM	SHLM	UMM
	DI	MBD	UA	2	AMMP	LAM	LUM	NEGR	TCM	UMMP
	DID	MD	UD	3	BDM	LAMP	LUR	PEM	TPCR	UR
	DIDP	MP	UH	4	DIDM	LATM	MAHM	PHAM	TR	WHAM
	L	NE	UJ	5	DIEM	LAUM	MAJM	PHEM	TRN	WHEM
	LA	NEC	UJP	6	DILM	LCR	MAM	PHGM	UAMM	WHGM
	LCHP	NECP	UTL	7	EDM	LDM	MAMP	PHGR	UDM	WHGR
	LD	P	UTLN	8	EGM	LEM	MAPM	PHLM	UEM	WHLM
	LDC	PH	UTP	9	ELJM	LFØ	MATM	PHM	UFW	WHM
	LDI	PHC	UW	10	ELM	LHR	MDM	PHØM	UHM	WHØM
	LJ	PHCP	WH	11	EM	LLF	MHR	PHPM	UHPR	WHTM
	LTM	PHØ	WHC	12	EMM	LMM	MLM	PHTM	UHR	WHUM
	LTU	SHD	WHCP	13	ETM	LMMP	MLR	SHAM	UJM	
	MA	SHDP	WHØ	14	LAHM	LR	MR	SHDM	UM	

	thousands				units					
-5.	14515.	6.205	416.21	1	.225	1.187	1.117	.349	1.000	.736
	16.631	.369	17.106	2	.227	.625	.604	.001	1.415	.720
	.442	4.082	19.157	3	1.189	.604	.808	1.181	1.151	2.177
	.000	60.79	327.86	4	.887	.826	.969	1.248	2.240	1.381
	336.42	3.788	191.21	5	.887	.723	.300	1.008	2.824	1.002
	6.093	.390	.00	6	1.000	.853	.312	.993	.808	.997
	.000	.000	14.074	7	1.189	1.677	.303	-.001	4.603	-.000
	11.287	5652.1	4.743	8	1.008	1.090	1.300	.840	1.090	.840
	22.19	98.26	.000	9	.861	.780	.826	1.127	.470	.711
	335.14	2.835	195.60	10	.760	1.119	3.358	.914	1.430	1.295
	357.33	.000	300.62	11	.769	.028	1.031	1.300	.000	.826
	3.094	2.694	5.469	12	1.551	.481	1.261	.826	.846	.742
	9.305	8.573	.000	13	.752	.460	.181	1.307	.165	*APB 54 THE AD*
	.553	.000	7.785	14	.881	.941	1.376	1.307	.034	
10.	16476.	7.031	380.20	1	.192	1.367	1.229	.458	1.000	1.012
	15.185	.373	17.063	2	.225	.801	.699	.026	1.301	.827
	.439	3.700	20.879	3	1.061	.674	.998	1.355	1.296	1.560
	.000	70.28	203.75	4	.963	.827	1.003	.977	2.230	1.363
	379.35	6.361	243.77	5	.963	.799	.372	1.206	2.244	1.051
	7.669	.750	.00	6	1.000	.808	.401	1.094	.911	1.067
	.000	.000	19.864	7	1.061	1.320	.356	.012	5.492	.008
	10.015	5669.1	9.932	8	1.206	1.178	1.300	1.263	1.178	1.263
	44.00	117.97	.000	9	.745	.720	.827	1.750	.632	1.277
	384.53	5.004	240.32	10	.941	1.114	2.632	.597	.414	.894
	428.52	.000	340.66	11	.919	.025	.993	1.300	.000	.827
	4.116	2.114	10.549	12	1.442	.685	1.271	.827	1.244	.799
	9.639	13.467	.000	13	.754	.542	.185	.805	.376	*APB 54 EC*
	.750	10.187	6.093	14	.886	.885	1.285	.805	.043	
50.	22098.	12.837	379.81	1	.222	1.063	1.040	.355	1.285	.946
	20.981	.856	23.153	2	.240	.575	.863	-.004	1.091	.989
	.647	7.743	17.781	3	1.334	.632	1.544	1.107	1.089	1.240
	.000	107.78	180.40	4	1.027	.879	.828	2.378	1.749	1.975
	586.52	7.998	306.30	5	.800	.909	.304	.970	1.675	.989
	11.126	.806	.00	6	1.285	.884	.287	.996	1.172	.999
	.000	.000	27.352	7	1.334	1.796	.291	-.001	4.682	-.000
	21.069	7096.5	10.236	8	.970	1.054	1.300	.397	1.054	.397
	36.05	153.24	.000	9	.965	.861	.879	1.042	.728	.619
	562.32	4.237	276.50	10	.518	1.323	3.592	.970	.277	1.415
	598.37	.000	443.35	11	.629	.029	1.172	1.300	.000	.879
	5.917	4.459	7.278	12	1.545	.475	1.268	.879	1.404	.909
	17.131	12.159	.000	13	.839	.504	.184	.677	.616	*APB 54 SP EC*
	.942	9.020	12.543	14	.677	.980	1.370	.870	.071	

(d)

Figure B-19 (cont.)

C Definitions of Terms

Following are the definitions of terms used in this book. The letter group is the abbreviation used in the system model. The definition gives the meaning and the dimensions of measurement.

```
*         DEFINITIØNS FØR CITY GRØWTH, STAGNATIØN, AND REVIVAL MØDEL
AMF       ATTRACTIVENESS-FØR-MIGRATIØN FACTØR (DIMENSIØNLESS)
AMM       ATTRACTIVENESS-FØR-MIGRATIØN MULTIPLIER (DIMENSIØNLESS)
AMMP      ATTRACTIVENESS-FØR-MIGRATIØN MULTIPLIER PERCEIVED (DIMENSIØNLESS)
AMMPT     ATTRACTIVENESS-FØR-MIGRATIØN-MULTIPLIER PERCEPTIØN TIME (YEARS)
AREA      LAND AREA (ACRES)
AV        ASSESSED VALUE (THØUSAND DØLLARS)
BAV       BUSINESS ASSESSED VALUE (THØUSAND DØLLARS)
BDM       BUSINESS-DECLINE MULTIPLIER (DIMENSIØNLESS)
BDMT      BUSINESS-DECLINE-MULTIPLIER TABLE
DI        DECLINING INDUSTRY (PRØDUCTIVE UNITS)
DIAV      DECLINING-INDUSTRY ASSESSED VALUE (THØUSAND DØLLARS/PRØDUCTIVE UNIT)
DICF      DECLINING-INDUSTRY-CØNSTRUCTIØN FACTØR (DIMENSIØNLESS)
DID       DECLINING-INDUSTRY DEMØLITIØN (PRØDUCTIVE UNITS/YEAR)
DIDF      DECLINING-INDUSTRY-DEMØLITIØN FACTØR (DIMENSIØNLESS)
DIDM      DECLINING-INDUSTRY-DEMØLITIØN MULTIPLIER (DIMENSIØNLESS)
DIDN      DECLINING-INDUSTRY DEMØLITIØN NØRMAL (FRACTIØN/YEAR)
DIDP      DECLINING-INDUSTRY-DEMØLITIØN PRØGRAM (PRØDUCTIVE UNITS/YEAR)
DIDR      DECLINING-INDUSTRY-DEMØLITIØN RATE (FRACTIØN/YEAR)
DIEM      DECLINING-INDUSTRY ENTERPRISE MULTIPLIER (DIMENSIØNLESS)
DIEMT     DECLINING-INDUSTRY-ENTERPRISE-MULTIPLIER TABLE
DIL       DECLINING-INDUSTRY LABØR (MEN/PRØDUCTIVE UNIT)
DILM      DECLINING-INDUSTRY LAND MULTIPLIER (DIMENSIØNLESS)
DILMT     DECLINING-INDUSTRY-LAND-MULTIPLIER TABLE
DIM       DECLINING-INDUSTRY MANAGEMENT (MEN/PRØDUCTIVE UNIT)
EDM       ENTERPRISE-DECLINE MULTIPLIER (DIMENSIØNLESS)
EDMT      ENTERPRISE-DECLINE-MULTIPLIER TABLE
EF        ENTERPRISE FACTØR (DIMENSIØNLESS)
EGM       ENTERPRISE-GRØWTH MULTIPLIER (DIMENSIØNLESS)
EGMT      ENTERPRISE-GRØWTH-MULTIPLIER TABLE
ELJM      ENTERPRISE LABØR/JØB MULTIPLIER (DIMENSIØNLESS)
ELJMT     ENTERPRISE LABØR/JØB MULTIPLIER TABLE
ELM       ENTERPRISE LAND MULTIPLIER (DIMENSIØNLESS)
ELMT      ENTERPRISE-LAND-MULTIPLIER TABLE
EM        ENTERPRISE MULTIPLIER (DIMENSIØNLESS)
```

EMM	ENTERPRISE MANAGER/JØB MULTIPLIER (DIMENSIØNLESS)
EMMT	ENTERPRISE MANAGER/JØB MULTIPLIER TABLE
ETM	ENTERPRISE TAX MULTIPLIER (DIMENSIØNLESS)
ETMT	ENTERPRISE-TAX-MULTIPLIER TABLE
HAV	HØUSING ASSESSED VALUE (THØUSAND DØLLARS)
HUT	HØUSING UNITS TØTAL (HØUSING UNITS)
L	LABØR (MEN)
LA	LABØR ARRIVALS (MEN/YEAR)
LAF	LABØR-ARRIVAL FACTØR (DIMENSIØNLESS)
LAHM	LABØR-ARRIVAL HØUSING MULTIPLIER (DIMENSIØNLESS)
LAHMT	LABØR-ARRIVAL-HØUSING-MULTIPLIER TABLE
LAJM	LABØR-ARRIVAL JØB MULTIPLIER (DIMENSIØNLESS)
LAJMT	LABØR-ARRIVAL-JØB-MULTIPLIER TABLE
LAM	LABØR-ARRIVAL MULTIPLIER (DIMENSIØNLESS)
LAMP	LABØR-ARRIVAL MULTIPLIER PERCEIVED (DIMENSIØNLESS)
LAMPT	LABØR-ARRIVAL-MULTIPLIER PERCEPTIØN TIME (YEARS)
LAN	LABØR ARRIVALS NØRMAL (FRACTIØN/YEAR)
LATM	LABØR-ARRIVAL TAX MULTIPLIER (DIMENSIØNLESS)
LATMT	LABØR-ARRIVAL-TAX-MULTIPLIER TABLE
LAUM	LABØR-ARRIVAL UNDEREMPLØYED MULTIPLIER (DIMENSIØNLESS)
LAUMT	LABØR-ARRIVAL-UNDEREMPLØYED-MULTIPLIER TABLE
LB	LABØR BIRTHS (MEN/YEAR)
LBR	LABØR BIRTH RATE (FRACTIØN/YEAR)
LCHCD	LØW-CØST-HØUSING CØNSTRUCTIØN DESIRED (HØUSING UNITS/YEAR)
LCHCL	LØW-CØST-HØUSING-CØNSTRUCTIØN LABØR (MAN-YEARS/HØUSING UNIT)
LCHP	LØW-CØST-HØUSING PRØGRAM (HØUSING UNITS/YEAR)
LCHPC	LØW-CØST-HØUSING-PRØGRAM CØEFFICIENT (HØUSING UNITS/MAN/YEAR)
LCR	LABØR CØNSTRUCTIØN RATIØ (DIMENSIØNLESS)
LCRT	LABØR-CØNSTRUCTIØN-RATIØ TABLE
LD	LABØR DEPARTURES (MEN/YEAR)
LDC	LABØR DESIRED FØR CØNSTRUCTIØN (MEN)
LDI	LABØR DESIRED FØR INDUSTRY (MEN)
LDM	LABØR-DEPARTURE MULTIPLIER (DIMENSIØNLESS)
LDMT	LABØR-DEPARTURE-MULTIPLIER TABLE
LDN	LABØR DEPARTURES NØRMAL (FRACTIØN/YEAR)
LEM	LABØR EDUCATIØNAL MULTIPLIER (DIMENSIØNLESS)
LEMT	LABØR-EDUCATIØNAL-MULTIPLIER TABLE
LFØ	LAND FRACTIØN ØCCUPIED (DIMENSIØNLESS)
LFS	LABØR FAMILY SIZE (PEØPLE/MAN)
LHR	LABØR/HØUSING RATIØ (DIMENSIØNLESS)
LJ	LABØR JØBS (MEN)
LLF	LABØR-LAYØFF FRACTIØN (FRACTIØN/YEAR)
LLFT	LABØR-LAYØFF-FRACTIØN TABLE
LMF	LABØR-MØBILITY FACTØR (DIMENSIØNLESS)
LMM	LABØR-MØBILITY MULTIPLIER (DIMENSIØNLESS)
LMMP	LABØR-MØBILITY MULTIPLIER PERCEIVED (DIMENSIØNLESS)
LMMPT	LABØR-MØBILITY-MULTIPLIER PERCEPTIØN TIME (YEARS)
LMN	LABØR MØBILITY NØRMAL (FRACTIØN/YEAR)
LPH	LAND PER HØUSE (ACRES/HØUSING UNIT)
LPP	LAND PER PRØDUCTIØN UNIT (ACRES/PRØDUCTIØN UNIT)
LR	LABØR/JØB RATIØ (DIMENSIØNLESS)
LRP	LABØR/JØB RATIØ PERCEIVED (DIMENSIØNLESS)
LRPT	LABØR/JØB RATIØ PERCEPTIØN TIME (YEARS)
LSM	LABØR-SUPPLY MULTIPLIER (DIMENSIØNLESS)
LSMT	LABØR-SUPPLY-MULTIPLIER TABLE
LTM	LABØR TØ MANAGER (MEN/YEAR)
LTPG	LABØR-TRAINING PRØGRAM (MEN/YEAR)
LTR	LABØR-TRAINING RATE (FRACTIØN/YEAR)
LTU	LABØR TØ UNDEREMPLØYED (MEN/YEAR)
LUM	LABØR/UNDEREMPLØYED MULTIPLIER (DIMENSIØNLESS)

LUMT	LABØR/UNDEREMPLØYED MULTIPLIER TABLE
LUR	LABØR/UNDEREMPLØYED RATIØ (DIMENSIØNLESS)
MA	MANAGER ARRIVALS (MEN/YEAR)
MAF	MANAGER-ARRIVAL FACTØR (DIMENSIØNLESS)
MAHM	MANAGER-ARRIVAL HØUSING MULTIPLIER (DIMENSIØNLESS)
MAHMT	MANAGER-ARRIVAL-HØUSING-MULTIPLIER TABLE
MAJM	MANAGER-ARRIVAL JØB MULTIPLIER (DIMENSIØNLESS)
MAJMT	MANAGER-ARRIVAL-JØB-MULTIPLIER TABLE
MAM	MANAGER-ARRIVAL MULTIPLIER (DIMENSIØNLESS)
MAMP	MANAGER-ARRIVAL MULTIPLIER PERCEIVED (DIMENSIØNLESS)
MAMPT	MANAGER-ARRIVAL-MULTIPLIER PERCEPTIØN TIME (YEARS)
MAN	MANAGER ARRIVALS NØRMAL (FRACTIØN/YEAR)
MAPM	MANAGER-ARRIVAL PØPULATIØN MULTIPLIER (DIMENSIØNLESS)
MAPMT	MANAGER-ARRIVAL-PØPULATIØN-MULTIPLIER TABLE
MATM	MANAGER-ARRIVAL TAX MULTIPLIER (DIMENSIØNLESS)
MATMT	MANAGER-ARRIVAL-TAX-MULTIPLIER TABLE
MB	MATURE BUSINESS (PRØDUCTIVE UNITS)
MBAV	MATURE-BUSINESS ASSESSED VALUE (THØUSAND DØLLARS/PRØDUCTIVE UNIT)
MBCF	MATURE-BUSINESS-CØNSTRUCTIØN FACTØR (DIMENSIØNLESS)
MBD	MATURE-BUSINESS DECLINE (PRØDUCTIVE UNITS/YEAR)
MBDN	MATURE-BUSINESS DECLINE NØRMAL (FRACTIØN/YEAR)
MBL	MATURE-BUSINESS LABØR (MEN/PRØDUCTIVE UNIT)
MBM	MATURE-BUSINESS MANAGEMENT (MEN/PRØDUCTIVE UNIT)
MD	MANAGER DEPARTURES (MEN/YEAR)
MDM	MANAGER-DEPARTURE MULTIPLIER (DIMENSIØNLESS)
MDMT	MANAGER-DEPARTURE-MULTIPLIER TABLE
MDN	MANAGER DEPARTURES NØRMAL (FRACTIØN/YEAR)
MHR	MANAGER/HØUSING RATIØ (DIMENSIØNLESS)
MJ	MANAGER JØBS (MEN)
MLM	MANAGER/LABØR MULTIPLIER (DIMENSIØNLESS)
MLMT	MANAGER/LABØR MULTIPLIER TABLE
MLR	MANAGER/LABØR RATIØ (DIMENSIØNLESS)
MP	MANAGERIAL-PRØFESSIØNAL (MEN)
MPB	MANAGERIAL-PRØFESSIØNAL BIRTHS (MEN/YEAR)
MPBR	MANAGERIAL-PRØFESSIØNAL BIRTH RATE (FRACTIØN/YEAR)
MPFS	MANAGERIAL-PRØFESSIØNAL FAMILY SIZE (PEØPLE/MAN)
MPR	MANAGER/PØPULATIØN RATIØ (DIMENSIØNLESS)
MR	MANAGER/JØB RATIØ (DIMENSIØNLESS)
MSM	MANAGER-SUPPLY MULTIPLIER (DIMENSIØNLESS)
MSMT	MANAGER-SUPPLY-MULTIPLIER TABLE
NE	NEW ENTERPRISE (PRØDUCTIVE UNITS)
NEA	NEW-ENTERPRISE AVERAGE (PRØDUCTIVE UNITS)
NEAT	NEW-ENTERPRISE AVERAGING TIME (YEARS)
NEAV	NEW-ENTERPRISE ASSESSED VALUE (THØUSAND DØLLARS/PRØDUCTIVE UNIT)
NEC	NEW-ENTERPRISE CØNSTRUCTIØN (PRØDUCTIVE UNITS/YEAR)
NECD	NEW-ENTERPRISE CØNSTRUCTIØN DESIRED (PRØDUCTIVE UNITS/YEAR)
NECF	NEW-ENTERPRISE-CØNSTRUCTIØN FACTØR (DIMENSIØNLESS)
NECL	NEW-ENTERPRISE-CØNSTRUCTIØN LABØR (MAN-YEARS/PRØDUCTIVE UNIT)
NECN	NEW-ENTERPRISE CØNSTRUCTIØN NØRMAL (FRACTIØN/YEAR)
NECP	NEW-ENTERPRISE-CØNSTRUCTIØN PRØGRAM (PRØDUCTIVE UNITS/YEAR)
NECR	NEW-ENTERPRISE-CØNSTRUCTIØN RATE (FRACTIØN/YEAR)
NED	NEW-ENTERPRISE DECLINE (PRØDUCTIVE UNITS/YEAR)
NEDN	NEW-ENTERPRISE DECLINE NØRMAL (FRACTIØN/YEAR)
NEGR	NEW-ENTERPRISE GRØWTH RATE (FRACTIØN/YEAR)
NEGRI	NEW-ENTERPRISE GRØWTH RATE INITIAL (FRACTIØN/YEAR)
NEL	NEW-ENTERPRISE LABØR (MEN/PRØDUCTIVE UNIT)
NEM	NEW-ENTERPRISE MANAGEMENT (MEN/PRØDUCTIVE UNIT)
P	PØPULATIØN (MEN)
PEM	PUBLIC-EXPENDITURE MULTIPLIER (DIMENSIØNLESS)
PEMT	PUBLIC-EXPENDITURE-MULTIPLIER TABLE

PH	PREMIUM HØUSING (HØUSING UNITS)
PHA	PREMIUM-HØUSING AVERAGE (HØUSING UNITS)
PHAM	PREMIUM-HØUSING-ADEQUACY MULTIPLIER (DIMENSIØNLESS)
PHAMT	PREMIUM-HØUSING-ADEQUACY-MULTIPLIER TABLE
PHAT	PREMIUM-HØUSING AVERAGING TIME (YEARS)
PHAV	PREMIUM-HØUSING ASSESSED VALUE (THØUSAND DØLLARS/HØUSING UNIT)
PHC	PREMIUM-HØUSING CØNSTRUCTIØN (HØUSING UNITS/YEAR)
PHCD	PREMIUM-HØUSING CØNSTRUCTIØN DESIRED (HØUSING UNITS/YEAR)
PHCL	PREMIUM-HØUSING-CØNSTRUCTIØN LABØR (MAN-YEARS/HØUSING UNIT)
PHCN	PREMIUM-HØUSING CØNSTRUCTIØN NØRMAL (HØUSING UNITS/YEAR)
PHCP	PREMIUM-HØUSING-CØNSTRUCTIØN PRØGRAM (HØUSING UNITS/YEAR)
PHCR	PREMIUM-HØUSING-CØNSTRUCTIØN RATE (FRACTIØN/YEAR)
PHEM	PREMIUM-HØUSING ENTERPRISE MULTIPLER (DIMENSIØNLESS)
PHEMT	PREMIUM-HØUSING-ENTERPRISE-MULTIPLIER TABLE
PHF	PREMIUM-HØUSING FACTØR (DIMENSIØNLESS)
PHGM	PREMIUM-HØUSING-GRØWTH MULTIPLIER (DIMENSIØNLESS)
PHGMT	PREMIUM-HØUSING-GRØWTH-MULTIPLIER TABLE
PHGR	PREMIUM-HØUSING GRØWTH RATE (FRACTIØN/YEAR)
PHGRI	PREMIUM-HØUSING GRØWTH RATE INITIAL (FRACTIØN/YEAR)
PHLM	PREMIUM-HØUSING LAND MULTIPLIER (DIMENSIØNLESS)
PHLMT	PREMIUM-HØUSING-LAND-MULTIPLIER TABLE
PHM	PREMIUM-HØUSING MULTIPLIER (DIMENSIØNLESS)
PHØ	PREMIUM-HØUSING ØBSØLESCENCE (HØUSING UNITS/YEAR)
PHØM	PREMIUM-HØUSING-ØBSØLESCENCE MULTIPLIER (DIMENSIØNLESS)
PHØMT	PREMIUM-HØUSING-ØBSØLESCENCE-MULTIPLIER TABLE
PHØN	PREMIUM-HØUSING ØBSØLESCENCE NØRMAL (FRACTIØN/YEAR)
PHPD	PREMIUM-HØUSING PØPULATIØN DENSITY (PEØPLE/HØUSING UNIT)
PHPM	PREMIUM-HØUSING PØPULATIØN MULTIPLIER (DIMENSIØNLESS)
PHPMT	PREMIUM-HØUSING-PØPULATIØN-MULTIPLIER TABLE
PHTM	PREMIUM-HØUSING TAX MULTIPLIER (DIMENSIØNLESS)
PHTMT	PREMIUM-HØUSING-TAX-MULTIPLIER TABLE
PLTCT	PLØT-PERIØD CHANGE TIME (YEARS)
PLTMAX	PLØT PERIØD MAXIMUM (YEARS)
PLTMIN	PLØT PERIØD MINIMUM (YEARS)
PLTPER	PLØT PERIØD (YEARS)
PRTCT	PRINT-PERIØD CHANGE TIME (YEARS)
PRTMAX	PRINT PERIØD MAXIMUM (YEARS)
PRTMIN	PRINT PERIØD MINIMUM (YEARS)
PRTPER	PRINT PERIØD (YEARS)
PUT	PRØDUCTIVE UNITS TØTAL (PRØDUCTIVE UNITS)
SHAM	SLUM-HØUSING-ABANDØNED MULTIPLIER (DIMENSIØNLESS)
SHAMT	SLUM-HØUSING-ABANDØNED-MULTIPLIER TABLE
SHD	SLUM-HØUSING DEMØLITIØN (HØUSING UNITS/YEAR)
SHDF	SLUM-HØUSING-DEMØLITIØN FACTØR (DIMENSIØNLESS)
SHDM	SLUM-HØUSING-DEMØLITIØN MULTIPLIER (DIMENSIØNLESS)
SHDN	SLUM-HØUSING DEMØLITIØN NØRMAL (FRACTIØN/YEAR)
SHDP	SLUM-HØUSING-DEMØLITIØN PRØGRAM (HØUSING UNITS/YEAR)
SHDR	SLUM-HØUSING-DEMØLITIØN RATE (FRACTIØN/YEAR)
SHLM	SLUM-HØUSING LAND MULTIPLIER (DIMENSIØNLESS)
SHLMT	SLUM-HØUSING-LAND-MULTIPLIER TABLE
SWT1	SWITCH TIME 1 (YEARS)
SWT2	SWITCH TIME 2 (YEARS)
SWT3	SWITCH TIME 3 (YEARS)
SWT4	SWITCH TIME 4 (YEARS)
SWT5	SWITCH TIME 5 (YEARS)
SWT6	SWITCH TIME 6 (YEARS)
SWT7	SWITCH TIME 7 (YEARS)
SWT8	SWITCH TIME 8 (YEARS)
SWT9	SWITCH TIME 9 (YEARS)
SWT10	SWITCH TIME 10 (YEARS)

TAI	TAX ASSESSMENT INDICATED (DOLLARS/YEAR/THOUSAND DOLLARS)
TAN	TAX ASSESSMENT NORMAL (DOLLARS/YEAR/THOUSAND DOLLARS)
TC	TAX COLLECTIONS (DOLLARS/YEAR)
TCM	TAX-COLLECTION MULTIPLIER (DIMENSIONLESS)
TCMT	TAX-COLLECTION-MULTIPLIER TABLE
TLP	TAX PER LABOR PERSON (DOLLARS/PERSON/YEAR)
TMP	TAX PER MANAGEMENT PERSON (DOLLARS/PERSON/YEAR)
TN	TAXES NEEDED (DOLLARS/YEAR)
TPCN	TAX PER CAPITA NORMAL (DOLLARS/YEAR/PERSON)
TPCR	TAX PER CAPITA RATIO (DIMENSIONLESS)
TPCS	TAX PER CAPITA SUBSIDY (DOLLARS/PERSON/YEAR)
TPCSP	TAX-PER-CAPITA-SUBSIDY PROGRAM (DOLLARS/PERSON/YEAR)
TR	TAX RATIO (DIMENSIONLESS)
TRN	TAX RATIO NEEDED (DIMENSIONLESS)
TRNP	TAX RATIO NEEDED PERCEIVED (DIMENSIONLESS)
TRNPT	TAX-RATIO-NEEDED PERCEPTION TIME (YEARS)
TRT	TAX-RATIO TABLE
TUP	TAX PER UNDEREMPLOYED PERSON (DOLLARS/PERSON/YEAR)
U	UNDEREMPLOYED (MEN)
UA	UNDEREMPLOYED ARRIVALS (MEN/YEAR)
UAMM	UNDEREMPLOYED-ARRIVALS-MOBILITY MULTIPLIER (DIMENSIONLESS)
UAMMT	UNDEREMPLOYED-ARRIVALS-MOBILITY-MULTIPLIER TABLE
UAN	UNDEREMPLOYED ARRIVALS NORMAL (FRACTION/YEAR)
UB	UNDEREMPLOYED BIRTHS (MEN/YEAR)
UBR	UNDEREMPLOYED BIRTH RATE (FRACTION/YEAR)
UD	UNDEREMPLOYED DEPARTURES (MEN/YEAR)
UDM	UNDEREMPLOYED-DEPARTURE MULTIPLIER (DIMENSIONLESS)
UDMT	UNDEREMPLOYED-DEPARTURE-MULTIPLIER TABLE
UDN	UNDEREMPLOYED DEPARTURES NORMAL (FRACTION/YEAR)
UEM	UNDEREMPLOYED EDUCATIONAL MULTIPLIER (DIMENSIONLESS)
UEMT	UNDEREMPLOYED-EDUCATIONAL-MULTIPLIER TABLE
UFS	UNDEREMPLOYED FAMILY SIZE (PEOPLE/MAN)
UFW	UNDEREMPLOYED FRACTION WORKING (DIMENSIONLESS)
UFWT	UNDEREMPLOYED-FRACTION-WORKING TABLE
UH	UNDEREMPLOYED HOUSING (HOUSING UNITS)
UHAV	UNDEREMPLOYED-HOUSING ASSESSED VALUE (THOUSAND DOLLARS/HOUSING UNIT)
UHM	UNDEREMPLOYED/HOUSING MULTIPLIER (DIMENSIONLESS)
UHMT	UNDEREMPLOYED-HOUSING-MULTIPLIER TABLE
UHPD	UNDEREMPLOYED-HOUSING POPULATION DENSITY (PEOPLE/HOUSING UNIT)
UHPM	UNDEREMPLOYED-HOUSING-PROGRAM MULTIPLIER (DIMENSIONLESS)
UHPMT	UNDEREMPLOYED-HOUSING-PROGRAM-MULTIPLIER TABLE
UHPR	UNDEREMPLOYED-HOUSING-PROGRAM RATE (HOUSES/YEAR/MAN)
UHR	UNDEREMPLOYED/HOUSING RATIO (DIMENSIONLESS)
UJ	UNDEREMPLOYED JOBS (MEN)
UJM	UNDEREMPLOYED/JOB MULTIPLIER (DIMENSIONLESS)
UJMT	UNDEREMPLOYED/JOB MULTIPLIER TABLE
UJP	UNDEREMPLOYED-JOB PROGRAM (MEN)
UJPC	UNDEREMPLOYED-JOB-PROGRAM COEFFICIENT (DIMENSIONLESS)
ULJR	UNDEREMPLOYED/LABOR JOB RATIO (DIMENSIONLESS)
ULJRT	UNDEREMPLOYED/LABOR JOB-RATIO TABLE
UM	UNDEREMPLOYED MOBILITY (FRACTION/YEAR)
UMF	UNDEREMPLOYED-MOBILITY FACTOR (DIMENSIONLESS)
UMM	UNDEREMPLOYED-MOBILITY MULTIPLIER (DIMENSIONLESS)
UMMP	UNDEREMPLOYED-MOBILITY MULTIPLIER PERCEIVED (DIMENSIONLESS)
UMMPT	UNDEREMPLOYED-MOBILITY-MULTIPLIER PERCEPTION TIME (YEARS)
UMN	UNDEREMPLOYED MOBILITY NORMAL (FRACTION/YEAR)
UR	UNDEREMPLOYED/JOB RATIO (DIMENSIONLESS)
UTL	UNDEREMPLOYED TO LABOR (MEN/YEAR)
UTLN	UNDEREMPLOYED TO LABOR NET (MEN/YEAR)
UTLP	UNDEREMPLOYED TO LABOR PERCEIVED (DIMENSIONLESS)

```
UTLPT      UNDEREMPLØYED-TØ-LABØR PERCEPTIØN TIME (YEARS)
UTP        UNDEREMPLØYED-TRAINING PRØGRAM (MEN/YEAR)
UTR        UNDEREMPLØYED-TRAINING RATE (FRACTIØN/YEAR)
UW         UNDEREMPLØYED WØRKING (MEN)
WH         WØRKER HØUSING (HØUSING UNITS)
WHA        WØRKER-HØUSING AVERAGE (HØUSING UNITS)
WHAM       WØRKER-HØUSING-ADEQUACY MULTIPLIER (DIMENSIØNLESS)
WHAMT      WØRKER-HØUSING-ADEQUACY-MULTIPLIER TABLE
WHAT       WØRKER-HØUSING AVERAGING TIME (YEARS)
WHAV       WØRKER-HØUSING ASSESSED VALUE (THØUSAND DØLLARS/HØUSING UNIT)
WHC        WØRKER-HØUSING CØNSTRUCTIØN (HØUSING UNITS/YEAR)
WHCD       WØRKER-HØUSING CØNSTRUCTIØN DESIRED (HØUSING UNITS/YEAR)
WHCL       WØRKER-HØUSING-CØNSTRUCTIØN LABØR (MAN-YEARS/HØUSING UNIT)
WHCN       WØRKER-HØUSING CØNSTRUCTIØN NØRMAL (FRACTIØN/YEAR)
WHCP       WØRKER-HØUSING-CØNSTRUCTIØN PRØGRAM (HØUSING UNITS/YEAR)
WHCR       WØRKER-HØUSING-CØNSTRUCTIØN RATE (FRACTIØN/YEAR)
WHEM       WØRKER-HØUSING ENTERPRISE MULTIPLIER (DIMENSIØNLESS)
WHEMT      WØRKER-HØUSING-ENTERPRISE-MULTIPLIER TABLE
WHF        WØRKER-HØUSING FACTØR (DIMENSIØNLESS)
WHGM       WØRKER-HØUSING-GRØWTH MULTIPLIER (DIMENSIØNLESS)
WHGMT      WØRKER-HØUSING-GRØWTH-MULTIPLIER TABLE
WHGR       WØRKER-HØUSING GRØWTH RATE (FRACTIØN/YEAR)
WHGRI      WØRKER-HØUSING GRØWTH RATE INITIAL (FRACTIØN/YEAR)
WHLM       WØRKER-HØUSING LAND MULTIPLIER (DIMENSIØNLESS)
WHLMT      WØRKER-HØUSING-LAND-MULTIPLIER TABLE
WHM        WØRKER-HØUSING MULTIPLIER (DIMENSIØNLESS)
WHØ        WØRKER-HØUSING ØBSØLESCENCE (HØUSING UNITS/YEAR)
WHØM       WØRKER-HØUSING-ØBSØLESCENCE MULTIPLIER (DIMENSIØNLESS)
WHØMT      WØRKER-HØUSING-ØBSØLESCENCE-MULTIPLIER TABLE
WHØN       WØRKER-HØUSING ØBSØLESCENCE NØRMAL (FRACTIØN/YEAR)
WHPD       WØRKER-HØUSING PØPULATIØN DENSITY (PEØPLE/HØUSING UNIT)
WHTM       WØRKER-HØUSING TAX MULTIPLIER (DIMENSIØNLESS)
WHTMT      WØRKER-HØUSING-TAX-MULTIPLIER TABLE
WHUM       WØRKER-HØUSING UNDEREMPLØYED MULTIPLIER (DIMENSIØNLESS)
WHUMT      WØRKER-HØUSING-UNDEREMPLØYED-MULTIPLIER TABLE
```

D Analyzer Tabulation

The flow diagrams of the model in Appendix A indicate diagrammatically which variables are inputs to any particular equation. Also on the flow diagrams are indications of the destinations of each computed variable. These destinations are obtained from the following tabulation, which is an inversion of the model equations to tell where each variable is used. The reader is most likely to use this tabulation to identify the equation in which a variable or a constant is to be found. The first column gives alphabetically the letter symbol of the term and the second column gives the equation number corresponding to Appendixes A and E. The third column tells the type of term, whether a constant C, an auxiliary variable A, a level variable L, an initial value statement N, a rate variable R, a table of values T, or a supplementary equation S. The fourth column lists each variable, equation number, and equation type in which the quantity in the first column is used.

NAME	NØ.	T	USED IN EQUATIØNS FØR
AMF	3.1	C	AMM,3,A
AMM	3	A	AMMP,2,L/UDM,14,A
AMMP	2	L	UA,1,R
	2.1	N	
AMMPT	2.2	C	AMMP,2,L
AREA	69.3	C	LFØ,69,A
AV	128	A	TC,121,A/TAI,125,A
BAV	130	A	AV,128,A
BDM	115	A	MBD,114,R
BDMT	115.1	T	BDM,115,A
DI	116	L	MJ,37,A/PUT,71,A/NECD,102,A/DID,117,R
	116.1	N	BAV,130,A/LDI,132,A/DIDP,146,A
DIAV	130.3	C	BAV,130,A
DICF	102.3	C	NECD,102,A
DID	117	R	DI,116,L
DIDF	118.1	C	DIDM,118,A
DIDM	118	A	DID,117,R
DIDN	117.1	C	DID,117,R

```
DIDP     146     A   DID,117,R
DIDR     146.1   C   DIDP,146,A
DIEM     119     A   DIDM,118,A
DIEMT    119.1   T   DIEM,119,A
DIL      132.3   C   LDI,132,A
DILM     120     A   DIDM,118,A
DILMT    120.1   T   DILM,120,A
DIM      37.3    C   MJ,37,A
DT       151     C

EDM      112     A   NED,111,R
EDMT     112.1   T   EDM,112,A
EF       103.1   C   EM,103,A
EGM      108     A   EM,103,A
EGMT     108.1   T   EGM,108,A
ELJM     106     A   EM,103,A
ELJMT    106.1   T   ELJM,106,A
ELM      105     A   EM,103,A/NECP,145,A
ELMT     105.1   T   ELM,105,A
EM       103     A   NECD,102,A/EDM,112,A/BDM,115,A/DIEM,119,A
EMM      104     A   EM,103,A
EMMT     104.1   T   EMM,104,A
ETM      107     A   EM,103,A
ETMT     107.1   T   ETM,107,A
HAV      129     A   AV,128,A
HUT      70      A   LFØ,69,A/WHCP,143,A
L        29      L   UA,1,R/P,9,A/UR,26,A/LB,28,R
         29.1    N      LTU,30,R/LTM,32,R/MLR,39,A/LA,41,R
                        LHR,48,A/LD,49,R/MPR,58,A/TN,126,A
                        LR,134,A/LTPG,141,A
LA       41      R   L,29,L
LAF      43.1    C   LAM,43,A
LAHM     47      A   LAM,43,A
LAHMT    47.1    T   LAHM,47,A
LAJM     44      A   LAM,43,A
LAJMT    44.1    T   LAJM,44,A
LAM      43      A   LAMP,42,L/LDM,50,A
LAMP     42      L   LA,41,R
         42.1    N
LAMPT    42.2    C   LAMP,42,L
LAN      41.1    C   LA,41,R
LATM     46      A   LAM,43,A
LATMT    46.1    T   LATM,46,A
LAUM     45      A   LAM,43,A
LAUMT    45.1    T   LAUM,45,A
LB       28      R   L,29,L
LBR      28.1    C   LB,28,R
LCHCD    150     A   LDC,131,A/LCHP,149,R
LCHCL    131.4   C   LDC,131,A
LCHP     149     R   UHPR,12,A/UH,95,L
LCHPC    150.1   C   LCHCD,150,A
LCR      138     A   PHC,64,R/WHC,82,R/NEC,101,R/LCHP,149,R
LCRT     138.1   T   LCR,138,A
LD       49      R   L,29,L
LDC      131     A   LJ,133,A
LDI      132     A   LJ,133,A
LDM      50      A   LD,49,R
LDMT     50.1    T   LDM,50,A
LDN      49.1    C   LD,49,R
LEM      40      A   LMM,34,A
```

```
LEMT     40.1    T    LEM,40,A
LENGTH   151.1   C
LFØ      69       A    PHLM,68,A/WHLM,86,A/SHLM,99,A/ELM,105,A
                          DILM,120,A
LFS      9.2     C    P,9,A/LHR,48,A/TN,126,A
LHR      48       A    LAHM,47,A/WHAM,85,A
LJ       133     A    LR,134,A/UJ,136,A
LLF      31       A    LTU,30,R
LLFT     31.1    T    LLF,31,A
LMF      34.1    C    LMM,34,A
LMM      34       A    LMMP,33,L
LMMP     33       L    LTM,32,R
         33.1    N
LMMPT    33.2    C    LMMP,33,L
LMN      32.1    C    LTM,32,R
LPH      69.1    C    LFØ,69,A
LPP      69.2    C    LFØ,69,A
LR       134     A    LSM,24,A/LLF,31,A/LAJM,44,A/ULJR,135,A
                          LCR,138,A/LRP,139,L
LRP      139     L    ELJM,106,A
         139.1   N
LRPT     139.2   C    LRP,139,L
LSM      24       A    UMM,23,A
LSMT     24.1    T    LSM,24,A
LTM      32       R    L,29,L/MP,52,L
LTPG     141     A    LTM,32,R
LTR      141.1   C    LTPG,141,A
LTU      30       R    U,16,L/L,29,L/UTLN,154,S
LUM      25       A    UMM,23,A
LUMT     25.1    T    LUM,25,A
LUR      26       A    LUM,25,A/LAUM,45,A/WHUM,87,A/TCM,127,A
MA       53       R    MP,52,L
MAF      55.1    C    MAM,55,A
MAHM     60       A    MAM,55,A
MAHMT    60.1    T    MAHM,60,A
MAJM     56       A    MAM,55,A
MAJMT    56.1    T    MAJM,56,A
MAM      55       A    MAMP,54,L/MDM,63,A
MAMP     54       L    MA,53,R
         54.1    N
MAMPT    54.2    C    MAMP,54,L
MAN      53.1    C    MA,53,R
MAPM     57       A    MAM,55,A
MAPMT    57.1    T    MAPM,57,A
MATM     59       A    MAM,55,A
MATMT    59.1    T    MATM,59,A
MB       113     L    MJ,37,A/PUT,71,A/NECD,102,A/MBD,114,R
         113.1   N       BAV,130,A/LDI,132,A
MBAV     130.2   C    BAV,130,A
MBCF     102.2   C    NECD,102,A
MBD      114     R    MB,113,L/DI,116,L
MBDN     114.1   C    MBD,114,R
MBL      132.2   C    LDI,132,A
MBM      37.2    C    MJ,37,A
MD       62       R    MP,52,L
MDM      63       A    MD,62,R
MDMT     63.1    T    MDM,63,A
MDN      62.1    C    MD,62,R
MHR      61       A    MAHM,60,A/PHAM,67,A
MJ       37       A    MR,36,A
```

```
PHM      66      A   PHCD,65,A /PHØM,80,A
PHØ      79      R   PH,78,L /WH,81,L
PHØM     80      A   PHØ,79,R
PHØMT    80.1    T   PHØM,80,A
PHØN     79.1    C   PHØ,79,R
PHPD     61.1    C   MHR,61,A
PHPM     72      A   PHM,66,A
PHPMT    72.1    T   PHPM,72,A
PHTM     73      A   PHM,66,A
PHTMT    73.1    T   PHTM,73,A
PLTCT    152.3   C   PLTPER,152,A
PLTMAX   152.2   C   PLTPER,152,A
PLTMIN   152.1   C   PLTPER,152,A
PLTPER   152     A
PRTCT    153.3   C   PRTPER,153,A
PRTMAX   153.2   C   PRTPER,153,A
PRTMIN   153.1   C   PRTPER,153,A
PRTPER   153     A
PUT      71      A   LFØ,69,A /NECP,145,A
SHAM     98      A   SHDM,97,A
SHAMT    98.1    T   SHAM,98,A
SHD      96      R   UH,95,L
SHDF     97.1    C   SHDM,97,A
SHDM     97      A   SHD,96,R
SHDN     96.1    C   SHD,96,R
SHDP     144     A   SHD,96,R
SHDR     144.1   C   SHDP,144,A
SHLM     99      A   SHDM,97,A
SHLMT    99.1    T   SHLM,99,A
STD      156.6   R
SWT1     140.2   C   UTP,140,A
SWT10    150.2   C   LCHCD,150,A
SWT2     141.2   C   LTPG,141,A
SWT3     142.2   C   PHCP,142,A
SWT4     143.2   C   WHCP,143,A
SWT5     144.2   C   SHDP,144,A
SWT6     145.2   C   NECP,145,A
SWT7     146.2   C   DIDP,146,A
SWT8     147.2   C   TPCSP,147,A
SWT9     148.2   C   UJP,148,A
TAI      125     A   TRN,124,A
TAN      121.1   C   TC,121,A /TRN,124,A
TC       121     A   TPCR,8,A
TCM      127     A   TN,126,A
TCMT     127.1   T   TCM,127,A
TIME                 UTP,140,A /LTPG,141,A /PHCP,142,A /WHCP,143,A
                        SHDP,144,A /NECP,145,A /DIDP,146,A /TPCSP,147,A
                        UJP,148,A /LCHCD,150,A /PLTPER,152,A /PRTPER,153,A
TLP      126.2   C   TN,126,A
TMP      126.1   C   TN,126,A
TN       126     A   TAI,125,A
TPCN     8.1     C   TPCR,8,A
TPCR     8       A   PEM,7,A /UEM,27,A /LEM,40,A
TPCS     147.1   C   TPCSP,147,A
TPCSP    147     A   TPCR,8,A
TR       122     A   LATM,46,A /MATM,59,A /PHTM,73,A /WHTM,88,A
                        ETM,107,A /TC,121,A
TRN      124     A   TRNP,123,L /TRNP,123.1,N
TRNP     123     L   TR,122,A
         123.1   N
```

```
TRNPT    123.2    C    TRNP,123,L
TRT      122.1    T    TR,122,A
TUP      126.3    C    TN,126,A
U        16       L    UA,1,R/UHR,6,A/P,9,A/UHPR,12,A
         16.1     N       UD,13,R/UB,15,R/UW,18,A/UM,21,A
                          LUR,26,A/MPR,58,A/TN,126,A/UR,137,A
                          UTP,140,A/UJP,148,A/LCHCD,150,A
UA       1        R    U,16,L
UAMM     4        A    AMM,3,A
UAMMT    4.1      T    UAMM,4,A
UAN      1.1      C    UA,1,R
UB       15       R    U,16,L
UBR      15.1     C    UB,15,R
UD       13       R    U,16,L
UDM      14       A    UD,13,R
UDMT     14.1     T    UDM,14,A
UDN      13.1     C    UD,13,R
UEM      27       A    UMM,23,A
UEMT     27.1     T    UEM,27,A
UFS      9.3      C    UHR,6,A/P,9,A/TN,126,A
UFW      19       A    UW,18,A
UFWT     19.1     T    UFW,19,A
UH       95       L    UHR,6,A/HUT,70,A/SHD,96,R/HAV,129,A
         95.1     N       SHDP,144,A
UHAV     129.3    C    HAV,129,A
UHM      5        A    AMM,3,A
UHMT     5.1      T    UHM,5,A
UHPD     6.1      C    UHR,6,A
UHPM     11       A    AMM,3,A
UHPMT    11.1     T    UHPM,11,A
UHPR     12       A    UHPM,11,A
UHR      6        A    UHM,5,A/SHAM,98,A
UJ       136      A    UR,137,A
UJM      10       A    AMM,3,A
UJMT     10.1     T    UJM,10,A
UJP      148      A    UJ,136,A
UJPC     148.1    C    UJP,148,A
ULJR     135      A    UJ,136,A
ULJRT    135.1    T    ULJR,135,A
UM       21       A    UAMM,4,A
UMF      23.1     C    UMM,23,A
UMM      23       A    UMMP,22,L
UMMP     22       L    UTL,17,R
         22.1     N
UMMPT    22.2     C    UMMP,22,L
UMN      17.1     C    UTL,17,R
UR       137      A    UJM,10,A/UFW,19,A
UTL      17       R    U,16,L/UTLP,20,L/L,29,L/UTLN,154,S
UTLN     154      S
UTLP     20       L    UM,21,A
         20.1     N
UTLPT    20.2     C    UTLP,20,L
UTP      140      A    UTL,17,R
UTR      140.1    C    UTP,140,A
UW       18       A    UTL,17,R
WH       81       L    LHR,48,A/HUT,70,A/WHCD,83,A/WHGR,91,A
         81.1     N       WHA,92,L/WHA,92.1,N/WHØ,93,R/HAV,129,A
WHA      92       L    WHGR,91,A
         92.1     N
WHAM     85       A    WHM,84,A
```

```
WHAMT    85.1    T    WHAM,85,A
WHAT     92.2    C    WHGR,91,A/WHA,92,L/WHA,92.1,N
WHAV     129.2   C    HAV,129,A
WHC      82      R    WH,81,L
WHCD     83      A    WHC,82,R/LDC,131,A
WHCL     131.2   C    LDC,131,A
WHCN     83.1    C    WHCD,83,A
WHCP     143     A    WHCD,83,A
WHCR     143.1   C    WHCP,143,A
WHEM     89      A    WHM,84,A
WHEMT    89.1    T    WHEM,89,A
WHF      84.1    C    WHM,84,A
WHGM     90      A    WHM,84,A
WHGMT    90.1    T    WHGM,90,A
WHGR     91      A    WHGM,90,A
WHGRI    92.3    C    WHA,92.1,N
WHLM     86      A    WHM,84,A/WHCP,143,A/LCHCD,150,A
WHLMT    86.1    T    WHLM,86,A
WHM      84      A    WHCD,83,A/WHØM,94,A
WHØ      93      R    WH,81,L/UH,95,L
WHØM     94      A    WHØ,93,R
WHØMT    94.1    T    WHØM,94,A
WHØN     93.1    C    WHØ,93,R
WHPD     48.1    C    LHR,48,A
WHTM     88      A    WHM,84,A
WHTMT    88.1    T    WHTM,88,A
WHUM     87      A    WHM,84,A
WHUMT    87.1    T    WHUM,87,A
```

E Model Equations

Following are the model equations used for the urban area life cycle simulations in this book. A description of each equation is found in Appendix A.

The model used for the simulations that start with the urban area in equilibrium stagnation are the same as the following except for the changes in initial conditions which are given in Appendix A, Section A.14.

```
0.1    *      CITY GRØWTH
0.2    NØTE
0.3    NØTE   **********UNDEREMPLØYED SECTØR
1      R      UA.KL=(U.K+L.K)(UAN)(AMMP.K)
1.1    C      UAN=.05
2      L      AMMP.K=AMMP.J+(DT/AMMPT)(AMM.J-AMMP.J)
2.1    N      AMMP=1
2.2    C      AMMPT=20
3      A      AMM.K=(UAMM.K)(UHM.K)(PEM.K)(UJM.K)(UHPM.K)(AMF)
3.1    C      AMF=1
4      A      UAMM.K=TABLE(UAMMT,UM.K,0,.15,.025)
4.1    T      UAMMT=.3/.7/1/1.2/1.3/1.4/1.5
5      A      UHM.K=TABHL(UHMT,UHR.K,0,2,.25)
5.1    T      UHMT=2.5/2.4/2.2/1.7/1/.4/.2/.1/.05
6      A      UHR.K=(U.K*UFS)/(UH.K*UHPD)
6.1    C      UHPD=12
7      A      PEM.K=TABHL(PEMT,TPCR.K,0,3,.5)
7.1    T      PEMT=.2/.6/1/1.6/2.4/3.2/4
8      A      TPCR.K=((TC.K/P.K)+TPCSP.K)/TPCN
8.1    C      TPCN=250
9      A      P.K=(MP.K)(MPFS)+(L.K)(LFS)+(U.K)(UFS)
9.1    C      MPFS=5
9.2    C      LFS=6
9.3    C      UFS=8
10     A      UJM.K=TABHL(UJMT,UR.K,0,3,.25)
10.1   T      UJMT=2/2/1.9/1.6/1/.6/.4/.3/.2/.15/.1/.05/.02
11     A      UHPM.K=TABHL(UHPMT,UHPR.K,0,.05,.01)
11.1   T      UHPMT=1/1.2/1.5/1.9/2.4/3
12     A      UHPR.K=LCHP.JK/U.K
13     R      UD.KL=(UDN)(U.K)(UDM.K)
```

```
13.1    C    UDN=.02
14      A    UDM.K=TABHL(UDMT,1.44*LØGN(AMM.K),-3,3,1)
14.1    T    UDMT=8/4/2/1/.5/.25/.125
15      R    UB.KL=(U.K)(UBR)
15.1    C    UBR=.015
16      L    U.K=U.J+(DT)(UA.JK+UB.JK+LTU.JK-UD.JK-UTL.JK)
16.1    N    U=1200
16.4    NØTE
16.5    NØTE ********** LABØR SECTØR
17      R    UTL.KL=(UMN)(UW.K)(UMMP.K)+UTP.K
17.1    C    UMN=.1
18      A    UW.K=(U.K)(UFW.K)
19      A    UFW.K=TABHL(UFWT,UR.K,0,4,1)
19.1    T    UFWT=.9/.8/.5/.33/.25
20      L    UTLP.K=UTLP.J+(DT/UTLPT)(UTL.JK-UTLP.J)
20.1    N    UTLP=75
20.2    C    UTLPT=10
21      A    UM.K=UTLP.K/U.K
22      L    UMMP.K=UMMP.J+(DT/UMMPT)(UMM.J-UMMP.J)
22.1    N    UMMP=1
22.2    C    UMMPT=10
23      A    UMM.K=(LSM.K)(LUM.K)(UEM.K)(UMF)
23.1    C    UMF=1
24      A    LSM.K=TABHL(LSMT,LR.K,0,2,.5)
24.1    T    LSMT=2.4/2/1/.4/.2
25      A    LUM.K=TABHL(LUMT,LUR.K,0,5,1)
25.1    T    LUMT=.2/.7/1/1.2/1.3/1.4
26      A    LUR.K=L.K/U.K
27      A    UEM.K=TABHL(UEMT,TPCR.K,0,3,.5)
27.1    T    UEMT=.2/.7/1/1.3/1.5/1.6/1.7
28      R    LB.KL=(L.K)(LBR)
28.1    C    LBR=.01
29      L    L.K=L.J+(DT)(UTL.JK+LB.JK-LTM.JK+LA.JK-LD.JK-LTU.JK)
29.1    N    L=14000
30      R    LTU.KL=(L.K)(LLF.K)
31      A    LLF.K=TABLE(LLFT,LR.K,0,2,.5)
31.1    T    LLFT=0/.01/.03/.1/.3
32      R    LTM.KL=(LMN)(L.K)(LMMP.K)+LTPG.K
32.1    C    LMN=.02
33      L    LMMP.K=LMMP.J+(DT/LMMPT)(LMM.J-LMMP.J)
33.1    N    LMMP=1
33.2    C    LMMPT=15
34      A    LMM.K=(MSM.K)(MLM.K)(LEM.K)(LMF)
34.1    C    LMF=1
35      A    MSM.K=TABHL(MSMT,MR.K,0,2,.25)
35.1    T    MSMT=2.3/2.2/2/1.6/1/.5/.2/.1/.05
36      A    MR.K=MP.K/MJ.K
37      A    MJ.K=(NE.K)(NEM)+(MB.K)(MBM)+(DI.K)(DIM)
37.1    C    NEM=4
37.2    C    MBM=2
37.3    C    DIM=1
38      A    MLM.K=TABHL(MLMT,MLR.K,0,.2,.05)
38.1    T    MLMT=.2/.7/1/1.2/1.3
39      A    MLR.K=MP.K/L.K
40      A    LEM.K=TABHL(LEMT,TPCR.K,0,3,.5)
40.1    T    LEMT=.2/.7/1/1.3/1.5/1.6/1.7
41      R    LA.KL=(LAN)(L.K)(LAMP.K)
41.1    C    LAN=.03
42      L    LAMP.K=LAMP.J+(DT/LAMPT)(LAM.J-LAMP.J)
42.1    N    LAMP=1
```

```
42.2    C       LAMPT=15
43      A       LAM.K=(LAJM.K)(LAUM.K)(LATM.K)(LAHM.K)(LAF)
43.1    C       LAF=1
44      A       LAJM.K=TABLE(LAJMT,LR.K,0,2,.25)
44.1    T       LAJMT=2.6/2.6/2.4/1.8/1/.4/.2/.1/.05
45      A       LAUM.K=TABHL(LAUMT,LUR.K,0,5,1)
45.1    T       LAUMT=.4/.8/1/1.2/1.3/1.3
46      A       LATM.K=TABLE(LATMT,1.44*LØGN(TR.K),-2,4,2)
46.1    T       LATMT=1.2/1/.7/.3
47      A       LAHM.K=TABLE(LAHMT,LHR.K,0,3,.5)
47.1    T       LAHMT=1.3/1.2/1/.5/.2/.1/.05
48      A       LHR.K=(L.K*LFS)/(WH.K*WHPD)
48.1    C       WHPD=6
49      R       LD.KL=(LDN)(L.K)(LDM.K)
49.1    C       LDN=.02
50      A       LDM.K=TABHL(LDMT,1.44*LØGN(LAM.K),-3,3,1)
50.1    T       LDMT=8/4/2/1/.5/.25/.125
50.4    NØTE
50.5    NØTE    **********MANAGERIAL-PRØFESSIØNAL SECTØR
51      R       MPB.KL=(MP.K)(MPBR)
51.1    C       MPBR=.0075
52      L       MP.K=MP.J+(DT)(LTM.JK+MPB.JK+MA.JK-MD.JK)
52.1    N       MP=3900
53      R       MA.KL=(MAN)(MP.K)(MAMP.K)
53.1    C       MAN=.03
54      L       MAMP.K=MAMP.J+(DT/MAMPT)(MAM.J-MAMP.J)
54.1    N       MAMP=1
54.2    C       MAMPT=10
55      A       MAM.K=(MAJM.K)(MAPM.K)(MATM.K)(MAHM.K)(MAF)
55.1    C       MAF=1
56      A       MAJM.K=TABLE(MAJMT,MR.K,0,2,.25)
56.1    T       MAJMT=2.7/2.6/2.4/2/1/.4/.2/.1/.05
57      A       MAPM.K=TABHL(MAPMT,MPR.K,0,.1,.02)
57.1    T       MAPMT=.3/.7/1/1.2/1.3/1.3
58      A       MPR.K=MP.K/(L.K+U.K)
59      A       MATM.K=TABLE(MATMT,1.44*LØGN(TR.K),-2,4,2)
59.1    T       MATMT=1.4/1/.7/.3
60      A       MAHM.K=TABLE(MAHMT,MHR.K,0,3,.5)
60.1    T       MAHMT=1.3/1.2/1/.5/.2/.1/.05
61      A       MHR.K=(MP.K*MPFS)/(PH.K*PHPD)
61.1    C       PHPD=3
62      R       MD.KL=(MDN)(MP.K)(MDM.K)
62.1    C       MDN=.02
63      A       MDM.K=TABHL(MDMT,1.44*LØGN(MAM.K),-3,3,1)
63.1    T       MDMT=8/4/2/1/.5/.25/.125
63.4    NØTE
63.5    NØTE    **********PREMIUM HØUSING SECTØR
64      R       PHC.KL=(PHCD.K)(LCR.K)
65      A       PHCD.K=(PHCN)(PH.K)(PHM.K)+PHCP.K
65.1    C       PHCN=.03
66      A       PHM.K=(PHAM.K)(PHLM.K)(PHPM.K)(PHTM.K)(PHEM.K)(PHGM.K)(PHF)
66.1    C       PHF=1
67      A       PHAM.K=TABLE(PHAMT,MHR.K,0,2,.25)
67.1    T       PHAMT=0/.001/.01/.2/1/3/4.6/5.6/6
68      A       PHLM.K=TABHL(PHLMT,LFØ.K,0,1,.1)
68.1    T       PHLMT=.4/.9/1.3/1.6/1.8/1.9/1.8/1.4/.7/.2/0
69      A       LFØ.K=(HUT.K*LPH+PUT.K*LPP)/AREA
69.1    C       LPH=.1
69.2    C       LPP=.2
69.3    C       AREA=100000
```

```
70      A       HUT.K =PH.K+WH.K+ UH .K
71      A       PUT.K =NE.K+MB.K+DI .K
72      A       PHPM.K =TABHL(PHPMT,MPR.K,0,.1,.02)
72.1    T       PHPMT=.3/.7/1/1.2/1.3/1.3
73      A       PHTM.K =TABHL(PHTMT,1.44*LØGN(TR.K),-2,4,2)
73.1    T       PHTMT=1.2/1/.7/.3
74      A       PHEM.K =TABHL(PHEMT,NEGR.K,-.1,.15,.05)
74.1    T       PHEMT=.2/.6/1/1.4/1.8/2.2
75      A       PHGM.K =TABHL(PHGMT,PHGR.K,-.1,.15,.05)
75.1    T       PHGMT=.2/.6/1/1.4/1.8/2.2
76      A       PHGR .K =(PH.K -PHA.K) /(PH.K* PHAT)
77      L       PHA.K=PHA.J+(DT/PHAT)(PH.J-PHA.J)
77.1    N       PHA=PH-(PHGRI)(PHAT)(PH)
77.2    C       PHAT=10
77.3    C       PHGRI =.03
78      L       PH.K=PH.J+(DT)(PHC.JK-PHØ.JK)
78.1    N       PH=5000
79      R       PHØ.KL=(PHØN)(PH.K)(PHØM.K)
79.1    C       PHØN=.03
80      A       PHØM.K =TABHL(PHØMT,1.44*LØGN(PHM.K),-3,3,1)
80.1    T       PHØMT=2.8/2.6/2/1/.5/.3/.2
80.4    NØTE
80.5    NØTE    **********WØRKER HØUSING SECTØR
81      L       WH.K=WH.J+(DT)(PHØ.JK+WHC.JK -WHØ.JK)
81.1    N       WH=21000
82      R       WHC.KL=(WHCD.K)(LCR.K)
83      A       WHCD.K =(WHCN (WH.K)(WHM.K)+WHCP.K
83.1    C       WHCN=.03
84      A       WHM.K =(WHAM.K)(WHLM.K)(WHUM.K)(WHTM.K)(WHEM.K)(WHGM.K)(WHF)
84.1    C       WHF=1
85      A       WHAM.K =TABHL(WHAMT,LHR.K,0,2,.25)
85.1    T       WHAMT=0/.05/.1/.3/1/1.8/2.4/2.8/3
86      A       WHLM.K =TABHL(WHLMT,LFØ.K,0,1,.1)
86.1    T       WHLMT=.4/.9/1.3/1.6/1.8/1.9/1.8/1.4/.7/.2/0
87      A       WHUM.K =TABHL(WHUMT,LUR.K,0,5,1)
87.1    T       WHUMT=.5/.8/1/1.2/1.3/1.3
88      A       WHTM.K =TABHL(WHTMT,1.44*LØGN(TR.K),-2,4,2)
88.1    T       WHTMT=1.2/1/.7/.3
89      A       WHEM.K =TABHL(WHEMT,NEGR.K,-.2,.3,.1)
89.1    T       WHEMT=.3/.7/1/1.2/1.3/1.4
90      A       WHGM.K =TABHL(WHGMT,WHGR.K,-.1,.15,.05)
90.1    T       WHGMT=.2/.6/1/1.4/1.8/2.2
91      A       WHGR .K =(WH.K -WHA.K) /(WH.K* WHAT)
92      L       WHA.K=WHA.J+(DT/WHAT)(WH.J -WHA.J)
92.1    N       WHA=WH-(WHGRI)(WHAT)(WH)
92.2    C       WHAT=10
92.3    C       WHGRI =.03
93      R       WHØ.KL=(WHØN)(WH.K)(WHØM.K)
93.1    C       WHØN=.02
94      A       WHØM.K =TABHL(WHØMT,1.44*LØGN(WHM.K),-3,3,1)
94.1    T       WHØMT=2.2/2/1.6/1/.7/.5/.4
94.4    NØTE
94.5    NØTE    **********UNDEREMPLØYED HØUSING SECTØR
95      L       UH.K=UH.J+(DT)(WHØ.JK-SHD.JK+LCHP.JK)
95.1    N       UH=1100
96      R       SHD.KL=(SHDN)(UH.K)(SHDM.K)+SHDP.K
96.1    C       SHDN=.02
97      A       SHDM.K =(SHAM.K)(SHLM.K)(SHDF)
97.1    C       SHDF=1
98      A       SHAM.K =TABLE(SHAMT,UHR.K,0,2,.5)
```

```
98.1    T     SHAMT=3.6/2/1/.6/.4
99      A     SHLM.K=TABHL(SHLMT,LFØ.K,.8,1,.05)
99.1    T     SHLMT=1/1.2/1.6/2.2/6
99.4    NØTE
99.5    NØTE  **********NEW ENTERPRISE SECTØR
100     L     NE.K=NE.J+(DT)(NEC.JK-NED.JK)
100.1   N     NE=200
101     R     NEC.KL=(NECD.K)(LCR.K)
102     A     NECD.K=(NECN)(NECF*NE.K+MBCF*MB.K+DICF*DI.K)(EM.K)+NECP.K
102.1   C     NECF=1
102.2   C     MBCF=.5
102.3   C     DICF=.3
102.4   C     NECN=.05
103     A     EM.K=(EMM.K)(ELM.K)(ELJM.K)(ETM.K)(EGM.K)(EF)
103.1   C     EF=1
104     A     EMM.K=TABHL(EMMT,MR.K,0,2,.25)
104.1   T     EMMT=.1/.15/.3/.5/1/1.4/1.7/1.9/2
105     A     ELM.K=TABHL(ELMT,LFØ.K,0,1,.1)
105.1   T     ELMT=1/1.15/1.3/1.4/1.45/1.4/1.3/1/.7/.4/0
106     A     ELJM.K=TABHL(ELJMT,LRP.K,0,2,.25)
106.1   T     ELJMT=0/.05/.15/.4/1/1.5/1.7/1.8/1.8
107     A     ETM.K=TABHL(ETMT,1.44*LØGN(TR.K),-2,4,1)
107.1   T     ETMT=1.3/1.2/1/.8/.5/.25/.1
108     A     EGM.K=TABHL(EGMT,NEGR.K,-.1,.15,.05)
108.1   T     EGMT=.2/.6/1/1.4/1.8/2.2
109     A     NEGR.K=(NE.K-NEA.K)/(NE.K*NEAT)
110     L     NEA.K=NEA.J+(DT/NEAT)(NE.J-NEA.J)
110.1   N     NEA=NE-(NEGRI)(NEAT)(NE)
110.2   C     NEAT=10
110.3   C     NEGRI=.03
110.6   NØTE
110.7   NØTE  **********MATURE BUSINESS SECTØR
111     R     NED.KL=(NEDN)(NE.K)(EDM.K)
111.1   C     NEDN=.08
112     A     EDM.K=TABHL(EDMT,1.44*LØGN(EM.K),-3,3,1)
112.1   T     EDMT=2/1.8/1.5/1/.7/.5/.5
113     L     MB.K=MB.J+(DT)(NED.JK-MBD.JK)
113.1   N     MB=1000
114     R     MBD.KL=(MBDN)(MB.K)(BDM.K)
114.1   C     MBDN=.05
115     A     BDM.K=TABHL(BDMT,1.44*LØGN(EM.K),-3,3,1)
115.1   T     BDMT=2/1.8/1.5/1/.7/.5/.4
115.4   NØTE
115.5   NØTE  **********DECLINING INDUSTRY SECTØR
116     L     DI.K=DI.J+(DT)(MBD.JK-DID.JK)
116.1   N     DI=100
117     R     DID.KL=(DIDN)(DI.K)(DIDM.K)+DIDP.K
117.1   C     DIDN=.03
118     A     DIDM.K=(DIEM.K)(DILM.K)(DIDF)
118.1   C     DIDF=1
119     A     DIEM.K=TABLE(DIEMT,1.44*LØGN(EM.K),-3,3,1)
119.1   T     DIEMT=.4/.5/.7/1/1.6/2.4/4
120     A     DILM.K=TABHL(DILMT,LFØ.K,.8,1,.05)
120.1   T     DILMT=1/1.2/1.6/2.2/6
120.4   NØTE
120.5   NØTE  **********TAX SECTØR
121     A     TC.K=(AV.K)(TAN)(TR.K)
121.1   C     TAN=50
122     A     TR.K=TABHL(TRT,1.44*LØGN(TRNP.K),-2,4,1)
122.1   T     TRT=.3/.5/1/1.8/2.8/3.6/4
```

123	L	TRNP.K=TRNP.J+(DT/TRNPT)(TRN.J-TRNP.J)
123.1	N	TRNP=TRN
123.2	C	TRNPT=30
124	A	TRN.K=TAI.K/TAN
125	A	TAI.K=TN.K/AV.K
126	A	TN.K=(TMP*MPFS*MP.K+TLP*LFS*L.K+TUP*UFS*U.K)(TCM.K)
126.1	C	TMP=150
126.2	C	TLP=200
126.3	C	TUP=300
127	A	TCM.K=TABHL(TCMT,LUR.K,0,3,.5)
127.1	T	TCMT=2/1.6/1.3/1.1/1/.9/.8
128	A	AV.K=(HAV.K+BAV.K)
129	A	HAV.K=PHAV*PH.K+WHAV*WH.K+UHAV*UH.K
129.1	C	PHAV=30
129.2	C	WHAV=15
129.3	C	UHAV=5
130	A	BAV.K=NEAV*NE.K+MBAV*MB.K+DIAV*DI.K
130.1	C	NEAV=500
130.2	C	MBAV=300
130.3	C	DIAV=100
130.6	NØTE	
130.7	NØTE	**********JØB SECTØR
131	A	LDC.K=PHCD.K*PHCL+WHCD.K*WHCL+NECD.K*NECL+LCHCD.K*LCHCL
131.1	C	PHCL=2
131.2	C	WHCL=1
131.3	C	NECL=20
131.4	C	LCHCL=.6
132	A	LDI.K=NE.K*NEL+MB.K*MBL+DI.K*DIL
132.1	C	NEL=20
132.2	C	MBL=15
132.3	C	DIL=10
133	A	LJ.K=LDC.K+LDI.K
134	A	LR.K=L.K/LJ.K
135	A	ULJR.K=TABHL(ULJRT,LR.K,0,2,.5)
135.1	T	ULJRT=1.15/.8/.5/.25/.1
136	A	UJ.K=LJ.K*ULJR.K+UJP.K
137	A	UR.K=U.K/UJ.K
138	A	LCR.K=TABHL(LCRT,LR.K,0,2,.5)
138.1	T	LCRT=0/.5/.9/1.1/1.15
139	L	LRP.K=LRP.J+(DT/LRPT)(LR.J-LRP.J)
139.1	N	LRP=1
139.2	C	LRPT=5
139.5	NØTE	
139.6	NØTE	**********CITY DEVELØPMENT PRØGRAMS
140	A	UTP.K=UTR*U.K*CLIP(0,1,SWT1,TIME.K)
140.1	C	UTR=0
140.2	C	SWT1=0
141	A	LTPG.K=LTR*L.K*CLIP(0,1,SWT2,TIME.K)
141.1	C	LTR=0
141.2	C	SWT2=0
142	A	PHCP.K=PHCR*PH.K*PHLM.K*CLIP(0,1,SWT3,TIME.K)
142.1	C	PHCR=0 NØTE LAND MULTIPLIER TERM
142.2	C	SWT3=0
143	A	WHCP.K=WHCR*HUT.K*WHLM.K*CLIP(0,1,SWT4,TIME.K)
143.1	C	WHCR=0 NØTE LAND MULTIPLIER TERM
143.2	C	SWT4=0
144	A	SHDP.K=SHDR*UH.K*CLIP(0,1,SWT5,TIME.K)
144.1	C	SHDR=0
144.2	C	SWT5=0
145	A	NECP.K=NECR*PUT.K*ELM.K*CLIP(0,1,SWT6,TIME.K)

```
145.1   C      NECR=0              NØTE LAND MULTIPLIER TERM
145.2   C      SWT6=0
146     A      DIDP.K=DIDR*DI.K*CLIP(0,1,SWT7,TIME.K)
146.1   C      DIDR=0
146.2   C      SWT7=0
147     A      TPCSP.K=TPCS*CLIP(0,1,SWT8,TIME.K)
147.1   C      TPCS=0
147.2   C      SWT8=0
148     A      UJP.K=UJPC*U.K*CLIP(0,1,SWT9,TIME.K)
148.1   C      UJPC=0
148.2   C      SWT9=0
149     R      LCHP.KL=(LCHCD.K)(LCR.K)
150     A      LCHCD.K=LCHPC*U.K*WHLM.K*CLIP(0,1,SWT10,TIME.K)
150.1   C      LCHPC=0
150.2   C      SWT10=0
150.5   NØTE
150.6   NØTE   CØNTRØL CARDS
150.7   NØTE
151     C      DT=1
151.1   C      LENGTH=250
152     A      PLTPER.K=CLIP(PLTMIN,PLTMAX,PLTCT,TIME.K)
152.1   C      PLTMIN=5
152.2   C      PLTMAX=5
152.3   C      PLTCT=500
153     A      PRTPER.K=CLIP(PRTMIN,PRTMAX,PRTCT,TIME.K)
153.1   C      PRTMIN=50
153.2   C      PRTMAX=100
153.3   C      PRTCT=160
154     S      UTLN.K=UTL.JK-LTU.JK
154.3   PLØT   U=U,L=L,PH=P,WH=W,UH=H(0,600E3)/MP=M(0,200E3)/NE=E,MB=B,DI=D(0,40E
154.3   X      3)
154.4   PLØT   UHR=U,LHR=L,MHR=M,MR=1,LR=2,UR=3(0,2)/LFØ=Ø(0,1)/TRN=*,TR=T(0,8)
154.5   PLØT   UA=A,UD=D,UTL=L,LTU=U(0,60E3)/PHC=H,WHC=W,SHD=*(0,20E3)/NEC=C,DID=
154.5   X      0(0,2E3)
154.6   PRINT  1)(3.0)AV
154.7   PRINT  1)(3.3)DI,DID,DIDP,L(3.2)
154.8   PRINT  1)(3.3)LA,LCHP,LD,LDC(3.2),LDI(3.2),LJ(3.2)
154.9   PRINT  1)(3.3)LTM,LTU,MA
155     PRINT  2)(3.3)MB,MBD,MD,MP(3.2),NE(3.3),NEC(3.3),NECP(3.3),P(3.1),PH(3.2)
155.1   PRINT  2)(3.3)PHC,PHCP,PHØ,SHD,SHDP
155.2   PRINT  3)U(3.2),UA(3.3),UD(3.3),UH(3.2),UJ(3.2),UJP(3.2),UTL(3.3)
155.3   PRINT  3)UTLN(3.3),UTP(3.3),UW(3.2),WH(3.2),WHC(3.3),WHCP(3.3),WHØ(3.3)
155.4   PRINT  4)(0.3)AMM,AMMP,BDM,DIDM,DIEM,DILM,EDM,EGM
155.5   PRINT  4)(0.3)ELJM,ELM,EM,EMM,ETM,LAHM
155.6   PRINT  5)(0.3)LAJM,LAM,LAMP,LATM,LAUM,LCR,LDM,LEM,LFØ
155.7   PRINT  5)(0.3)LHR,LLF,LMM,LMMP,LR
155.8   PRINT  6)(0.3)LSM,LUM,LUR,MAHM,MAJM,MAM,MAMP
155.9   PRINT  6)(0.3)MAPM,MATM,MDM,MHR,MLM,MLR,MR
156     PRINT  7)(0.3)MSM,NEGR,PEM,PHAM,PHEM,PHGM,PHGR
156.1   PRINT  7)(0.3)PHLM,PHM,PHØM,PHPM,PHTM,SHAM,SHDM
156.2   PRINT  8)(0.3)SHLM,TCM,TPCR,TR,TRN,UAMM,UDM
156.3   PRINT  8)(0.3)UEM,UFW,UHM,UHPR,UHR,UJM,UM
156.4   PRINT  9)(0.3)UMM,UMMP,UR,WHAM
156.5   PRINT  9)(0.3)WHEM,WHGM,WHGR,WHLM,WHM,WHØM,WHTM,WHUM
156.6   RUN    STD.
```

References

1. Forrester, Jay W. *Industrial Dynamics,* The M.I.T. Press, Cambridge, Massachusetts, 1961.

2. Forrester, Jay W. "Market Growth as Influenced by Capital Investment," *Industrial Management Review,* Volume 9, Number 2, Winter 1968, pp. 83–105.

3. Lewin, Kurt. *Field Theory in Social Science,* Harper and Brothers, New York, 1951.

4. Forrester, Jay W. "Industrial Dynamics: After the First Decade," *Management Science,* Volume XIV, Number 7, March 1968, pp. 398–415.

5. Forrester, Jay W. "Industrial Dynamics—A Response to Ansoff and Slevin," *Management Science,* Volume XIV, Number 9, May 1968, pp. 601–618.

6. Forrester, Jay W. *Principles of Systems,* Preliminary Edition, privately printed, available from the author, Room 516, 238 Main Street, Cambridge, Massachusetts 02142.

Index